PROPORTIONALITY OF CRIMINAL OFFENCES AND PENALTIES IN EU LAW

This book analyses the theorisation and application of proportionality of criminal offences and penalties in EU law, shedding light on its hybrid nature.

In the EU legal order, proportionality amounts to a general principle playing a crucial role in limiting the exercise of EU powers, assessing domestic measures' compatibility with internal market freedoms, and adjudicating fundamental rights. The EU concept of proportionality has a precise theorisation, but the principle assumes a distinct physiognomy in EU criminal law. Indeed, proportionality has a different meaning in criminal law, linked to theories of punishment. Not only do the two understandings of proportionality coexist in EU criminal law, but they are also intertwined. However, their uneasy relationship remains to be explored.

To understand this unique interaction, the book deepens the applications of the hybrid principle of proportionality of criminal offences and penalties in the EU legislative practice on the harmonisation of substantive criminal law and ECJ case-law on the review of domestic criminal measures. This analysis gives fresh insights into the relationship between the EU and criminal law concepts of proportionality.

Volume 23 in the series Hart Studies in European Criminal Law

Hart Studies in European Criminal Law

Series Editors: Professor Valsamis Mitsilegas, Queen Mary University of London; Professor Katalin Ligeti, University of Luxembourg; Professor Anne Weyembergh, Brussels Free University

Since the Lisbon Treaty, European criminal law has become an increasingly important field of research and debate. Working with the European Criminal Law Academic Network (ECLAN), the series will publish works of the highest intellectual rigour and cutting edge scholarship which will be required reading for all European criminal lawyers.

The series is happy to consider both edited and single authored titles. The series defines 'European' and 'criminal law' in the broadest sense so books on the European criminal law, justice and policy will be considered. The series also welcomes books which offer different methodological approaches.

Volume 1: *EU Criminal Law after Lisbon: Rights, Trust and the Transformation of Justice in Europe*
Valsamis Mitsilegas

Volume 2: *Challenges in the Field of Economic and Financial Crime in Europe and the US*
Edited by Vanessa Franssen and Katalin Ligeti

Volume 3: *Chasing Criminal Money: Challenges and Perspectives On Asset Recovery in the EU*
Edited by Katalin Ligeti and Michele Simonato

Volume 4: *Limits to EU Powers: A Case Study of EU Regulatory Criminal Law*
Jacob Öberg

Volume 5: *The Needed Balances in EU Criminal Law: Past, Present and Future*
Edited by Chloé Brière and Anne Weyembergh

Volume 6: *Redefining Organised Crime: A Challenge for the European Union?*
Edited by Stefania Carnevale, Serena Forlati and Orsetta Giolo

Volume 7: *White Collar Crime: A Comparative Perspective*
Edited by Katalin Ligeti and Stanislaw Tosza

Volume 8: *Criminal Liability of Managers in Europe: Punishing Excessive Risk*
Stanisław Tosza

Volume 9: *The European Union and Deprivation of Liberty: A Legislative and Judicial Analysis from the Perspective of the Individual*
Leandro Mancano

Volume 10: *The Legitimacy of EU Criminal Law*
Irene Wieczorek

Volume 11: *The Fight Against Impunity in EU Law*
Edited by Luisa Marin and Stefano Montaldo

Volume 12: *Controlling Immigration Through Criminal Law: European and Comparative Perspectives on 'Crimmigration'*
Edited by Gian Luigi Gatta, Valsamis Mitsilegas, and Stefano Zirulia

Volume 13: *The Principle of Mutual Trust in EU Criminal Law*
Auke Willems

Volume 14: *Surveillance and Privacy in the Digital Age: European, Transatlantic and Global Perspectives*
Edited by Valsamis Mitsilegas and Niovi Vavoula

Volume 15: *The External Dimension of the EU's Policy against Trafficking in Human Beings*
Chloé Brière

Volume 16: *Criminal and Quasi-criminal Enforcement Mechanisms in Europe: Origins, Concepts, Future*
Edited by Vanessa Franssen and Christopher Harding

Volume 17: *Data protection, Migration and Border Control: The GDPR, the Law Enforcement Directive and Beyond*
Teresa Quintel

Volume 18: *Corporations and the Privilege against Self-Incrimination*
Stijn Lamberigts

Volume 19: *EU Enforcement Authorities: Punitive Law Enforcement in a Composite Legal Order*
Edited by Michiel Luchtman, Katalin Ligeti and John Vervaele

Volume 20: *Admissibility of Evidence in EU Cross-Border Criminal Proceedings: Electronic Evidence, Efficiency and Fair Trial Rights*
Edited by Lorena Bachmaier Winter and Farsam Salimi

Volume 21: *Proportionality of Criminal Penalties in EU Law*
Edited by Stefano Montaldo, Valsamis Mitsilegas and Lorenzo Grossio

Volume 22: *Stronger Victims' Rights in EU Law?: Assessment and Prospects*
Edited by Julia Burchett and Anne Weyembergh

Volume 23: *Proportionality of Criminal Offences and Penalties in EU Law: A Hybrid Principle*
Lorenzo Grossio

Volume 11: *The Fight Against Impunity in EU Law*
Edited by Luisa Marin and Stefano Montaldo

Volume 12: *Controlling Immigration Through Criminal Law: European and Comparative Perspectives on 'Crimmigration'*
Edited by Gian Luigi Gatta, Valsamis Mitsilegas, and Stefano Zirulia

Volume 13: *The Principle of Mutual Trust in EU Criminal Law*
Auke Willems

Volume 14: *Surveillance and Privacy in the Digital Age: European, Transatlantic and Global Perspectives*
Edited by Valsamis Mitsilegas and Niovi Vavoula

Volume 15: *The External Dimension of the EU's Policy against Trafficking in Human Beings*
Chloé Brière

Volume 16: *Criminal and Quasi-criminal Enforcement Mechanisms in Europe: Origins, Concepts, Future*
Edited by Vanessa Franssen and Christopher Harding

Volume 17: *Data protection, Migration and Border Control: The GDPR, the Law Enforcement Directive and Beyond*
Teresa Quintel

Volume 18: *Corporations and the Privilege against Self-Incrimination*
Stijn Lamberigts

Volume 19: *EU Enforcement Authorities: Punitive Law Enforcement in a Composite Legal Order*
Edited by Michiel Luchtman, Katalin Ligeti and John Vervaele

Volume 20: *Admissibility of Evidence in EU Cross-Border Criminal Proceedings: Electronic Evidence, Efficiency and Fair Trial Rights*
Edited by Lorena Bachmaier Winter and Farsam Salimi

Volume 21: *Proportionality of Criminal Penalties in EU Law*
Edited by Stefano Montaldo, Valsamis Mitsilegas and Lorenzo Grossio

Volume 22: *Stronger Victims' Rights in EU Law?: Assessment and Prospects*
Edited by Julia Burchett and Anne Weyembergh

Volume 23: *Proportionality of Criminal Offences and Penalties in EU Law: A Hybrid Principle*
Lorenzo Grossio

Proportionality of Criminal Offences and Penalties in EU Law

A Hybrid Principle

Lorenzo Grossio

•HART•

OXFORD • LONDON • NEW YORK • NEW DELHI • SYDNEY

HART PUBLISHING

Bloomsbury Publishing Plc

Kemp House, Chawley Park, Cumnor Hill, Oxford, OX2 9PH, UK

1385 Broadway, New York, NY 10018, USA

Bloomsbury Publishing Ireland Limited, 29 Earlsfort Terrace, Dublin 2, D02 AY28, Ireland

HART PUBLISHING, the Hart/Stag logo, BLOOMSBURY and the Diana logo are trademarks of Bloomsbury Publishing Plc

First published in Great Britain 2025

A catalogue record for this book is available from the British Library.

A catalogue record for this book is available from the Library of Congress.

Library of Congress Control Number: 2025933512

ISBN: HB: 978-1-50998-474-9
ePDF: 978-1-50998-476-3
ePub: 978-1-50998-475-6

Typeset by Compuscript Ltd, Shannon

For product safety related questions contact productsafety@bloomsbury.com

To find out more about our authors and books visit www.hartpublishing.co.uk. Here you will find extracts, author information, details of forthcoming events and the option to sign up for our newsletters.

To the constellation of guiding stars
enlightening my journey

FOREWORD

The book addresses a central and multi-faceted principle of EU law, the principle of proportionality, by focusing on proportionality of criminal offences and penalties in EU law. Throughout the book, the multi-faceted character of proportionality is highlighted. From the outset, the author positions proportionality as a multidimensional general principle of EU law and highlights a number of key dimensions of proportionality: proportionality as a limit to the exercise of EU powers; proportionality as a legitimacy condition for obstacles to internal market freedoms; and proportionality in the context of fundamental rights protection, including both proportionality in fundamental rights adjudication under Article 52(1) of the Charter and proportionality as a fundamental right under Article 49(3) of the Charter.

The book complements this rigorous analysis of proportionality as a general principle of EU law with an analysis of the position of proportionality in the field of EU criminal law. A key finding underpinning the analysis concerns the hybridity of proportionality of criminal offences and penalties, positioned between EU law (including the Charter of Fundamental Rights) and criminal law. The book offers two comprehensive chapters in this context, a chapter on proportionality of offences and penalties in EU substantive criminal law (highlighting the multiplicity of legal sources and the distinction between prospective and retrospective proportionality) and a chapter on proportionality of domestic criminal offences and penalties in the light of EU law (analysing the evolution of ECJ case-law from *Greek Maize* to *NE* and extending the analysis to the principle of proportionality in the field of mutual recognition). The author highlights the Court's nuanced approach to the assessment of proportionality of criminal offences and the shifting balance between prospective and retrospective proportionality in the Court's review of domestic criminal penalties. In the conclusion, the author calls for a reconstruction of the proportionality of criminal offences and penalties in EU law. He reiterates the hybridity of the principle and its concurrent differentiation from, but also osmosis with, proportionality as a general principle of EU law and notes that hybridity also brings a theoretical diversity in relation to the study of proportionality in EU law.

Through elegant and sophisticated legal analysis, Lorenzo Grossio has produced an outstanding book which will become a reference point in the field of EU criminal law, but also in the field of EU law more broadly. The book offers rigorous and highly original analysis, which will remain relevant both in terms of scholarship and in terms of policy and law reform. The current litigation before the Court of Justice in the case of *Kinsa* provides a case in point in terms of the relevance of the volume, which will provide constant food for thought on the content and evolution of the contested legal principle of proportionality and its application.

Valsamis Mitsilegas
Liverpool, 14 November 2024

ACKNOWLEDGEMENTS

This book marks the end of an intense journey that began in November 2020, during the tragic COVID-19 pandemic. Looking back on the last four years, I can affirm without hesitation that I have been extremely fortunate. Indeed, while any journey needs a polar star to indicate the right direction, I had the opportunity to rely upon a true constellation of guiding stars. The many people I met while pursuing my research decisively enriched my doctoral and postdoctoral experiences, thus profoundly impacting my academic and personal growth. For this reason, I would like to dedicate this book to them.

Throughout my academic journey, I have relied on and learned daily from an incredible team of academics from the University of Turin – known as the *Stanza 19* group – who have supported me every day. For this reason, I will be forever grateful to my scientific supervisor, Professor Stefano Montaldo, as well as Professor Francesco Costamagna, Professor Alberto Miglio, Professor Michele Vellano, and all the other members of *Stanza 19*.

The second acknowledgment goes to my PhD supervisors, Professor Antonello Tancredi (University of Milano-Bicocca) and Professor Mehdi Mezaguer (Université Côte d'Azur), for patiently guiding me through each research step.

In the same vein, I would like to thank the members of my PhD Defense Committee – Professor Jean-Christophe Martin (Université Côte d'Azur), Professor Nicole Lazzerini (University of Florence), Professor Chloé Brière (Université Libre de Bruxelles), and Professor Guillemine Taupiac-Nouvel (Université de Pau et des Pays de l'Adour) – for their valuable comments, which were crucial for finalising this book.

Moreover, I would like to especially thank Professor Valsamis Mitsilegas (University of Liverpool) for his inspiring remarks and for writing the foreword to this book.

Some crucial experiences have enriched my research in the last four years, thus deeply marking my scholarly approach to EU law. First, an internship at the Court of Justice allowed me to expand my knowledge of the EU's architecture of judicial remedies. Therefore, I am particularly grateful to Professor Ornella Porchia (University of Turin), President of the Tenth Section of the General Court of the European Union. Working in her Cabinet has been a true honour and an unforgettable experience.

Second, I had the opportunity to spend two immensely enriching research stays at the Université Libre de Bruxelles and Université Côte d'Azur. Therefore, a special thank you goes, once again, to Professor Chloé Brière, together with

Professor Anne Weyembergh, Professor Chiara Armeni, Professor Paul Dermine, Dr Julia Burchett and all the members of the Centre for European Law of the Université Libre de Bruxelles. For the same reason, I would like to thank Professor Anne Millet-Devalle and, once again, Professor Jean-Christophe Martin for welcoming me to the Université Côte d'Azur and sharing their impressions and remarks on my work.

Finally, I would like to take this opportunity to express my collective and warm thanks to all the other scholars I have met in the last four years, whose remarks have deeply inspired my research.

Even with this vast constellation of guiding stars, a lonely journey can lead to a rocky road. Fortunately, I had the chance to share my path with wonderful fellow travellers from the Universities of Turin and Milano-Bicocca to whom I am particularly grateful.

On a more personal note, please allow me to conclude by thanking Marta, my amazing partner in life (and research), as well as my family and friends for their crucial support throughout this unforgettable journey.

Lorenzo Grossio
Turin, 30 November 2024

TABLE OF CONTENTS

LIST OF ABBREVIATIONS

AFSJ	Area of Freedom, Security and Justice
BVerfGE	Constitutional Court of the Federal Republic of Germany
CFSP	Common Foreign and Security Policy
CISA	Convention Implementing the Schengen Agreement
CoE	Council of Europe
EAW	European Arrest Warrant
EC	European Community
ECJ	Court of Justice of the European Union
ECHR	European Convention on Human Rights
ECSC	European Coal and Steel Community
ECtHR	European Court of Human Rights
EEC	European Economic Community
EU	European Union
TEU	Treaty on the European Union
TFEU	Treaty on the Functioning of the European Union

TABLE OF CASES

Judgments, Opinions and Orders of the Court of Justice of the European Union

Opinions of Advocates General at the Court of Justice of the European Union

Judgments and Decisions of the European Court of Human Rights

TABLE OF LEGISLATION

European Union Primary Law

European Union Secondary Law

Other Acts of EU Institutions, Bodies and Agencies

Council of Europe

Legal sources

Other Documents

International Law

Domestic Legislation

France

Germany

Italy

United Kingdom

Introduction

I. Proportionality in EU Criminal Law: Two Different Understandings

The title of this book may raise eyebrows. How can a principle qualify as 'hybrid' in the EU legal order? From a conceptual viewpoint, that term presupposes a relationship between heterogeneous sources, giving rise to a compound element.[1] That is the case of the proportionality of criminal offences and penalties in EU law. This study demonstrates that the principle's hybrid nature results from the peculiar intersection between theoretical paradigms derived from the EU legal order and substantive criminal law.

The emergence of a criminal law dimension within the EU legal order is a well-established consequence of the European integration process, and it has been subject to in-depth scholarly analysis.[2] Criminal law has traditionally been regarded as the 'secret garden' of states' sovereignty,[3] a legal domain tendentially unfettered from international and supranational obligations. However, the progressive deepening of the European integration process has brought a paradigm shift. In the current scenario, Member States' domestic criminal systems are systematically confronted

[1] Oxford English Dictionary, sv 'hybrid (adj.), sense 2.a', July 2023, https://doi.org/10.1093/OED/1053365483.

[2] Among many, see: V Mitsilegas, *EU Criminal Law*, 2nd edn (Oxford, Hart Publishing, 2022); J Öberg, *The Normative Foundations for EU Criminal Justice: Powers, Limits and Justifications* (Oxford, Hart Publishing, 2024); S Montaldo, *I limiti della cooperazione in materia penale nell'Unione europea* (Napoli, Editoriale Scientifica, 2015); E Pistoia, *Cooperazione penale nei rapporti fra diritto dell'Unione europea e diritto statale* (Napoli, Edizioni Scientifiche Italiane, 2008); S Miettinen, *Criminal Law and Policy in the European Union* (London, Routledge, 2013); V Mitsilegas and P Caeiro, 'European Criminal Law' in P Caeiro, S Gless and V Mitsilegas (eds), *Elgar Encyclopedia of Crime and Criminal Justice* (Cheltenham, Elgar, 2024); V Mitsilegas, 'The Transformation of Criminal Law in the Area of Freedom, Security and Justice' (2007) 26 *Yearbook of European Law* 1; V Manes and M Caianiello, *Introduzione al diritto penale europeo* (Torino, Giappichelli, 2020); R Sicurella, *Diritto penale e competenze dell'Unione europea: Linee guida di un sistema integrato di tutela dei beni giuridici sovrannazionali e dei beni giuridici di interesse comune* (Milano, Giuffrè, 2005); D Flore, *Droit pénal européen: les enjeux d'une justice pénale européenne*, 3rd edn (Bruxelles, Bruylant, 2009); G Tesauro, 'Diritto comunitario, Corte di giustizia e diritto penale' in G Grasso and R Sicurella (eds), *Per un rilancio del progetto europeo. Esigenze di tutela degli interessi comunitari e nuove strategie di integrazione penale* (Milano, Giuffrè, 2008); M Fletcher, 'EU Criminal Justice: Beyond Lisbon' in C Eckes and T Konstadinides (eds), *Crime Within the Area of Freedom, Security and Justice: A European Public Order* (Cambridge, Cambridge University Press, 2011); G Grasso, 'Introduzione: diritto penale e integrazione europea' in G Grasso and R Sicurella (eds), *Lezioni di diritto penale europeo* (Milano, Giuffrè, 2007); G Taupiac-Nouvel, 'L'espace pénal européen : heurts et malheurs d'une identité singulière' (2018) 617 *Revue de l'Union européenne* 206; C Harding, 'Exploring the Intersection Between European Law and National Criminal Law' (2000) 25 *EL Rev* 374.

[3] This expression has been advanced in Montaldo (n 2) 26.

with legal obligations deriving from EU law. Substantive criminal law is not an exception. In fact, the exercise of the domestic *ius puniendi* either fosters the effective implementation of EU law or constrains the exercise of individual rights secured by the Treaties. Moreover, criminal law in the AFSJ context also amounts to a key tool for ensuring 'a high level of security' as mandated by Article 67(3) TFEU. To attain this objective, Article 83 TFEU confers on the Union a specific legislative competence for the approximation of offences and penalties.[4]

Against this broader background, the book focuses on a specific facet of the interaction between EU law and substantive criminal law: the theorisation and application of the principle of proportionality of criminal offences and penalties. This principle entails unique features: in EU criminal law, proportionality lies at the crossroads between different normative levels – the EU legal order and domestic criminal systems – and distinct legal sciences.

On the one hand, the principle entails multiple declinations in EU law. Firstly, proportionality underpins the clash between domestic criminal measures and the enjoyment of fundamental rights under the Charter, as well as internal market freedoms secured by the Treaties. Secondly, proportionality constitutes a burden to Member States enacting criminal offences and penalties to ensure the effectiveness of EU law. Finally, proportionality limits the exercise of EU legislative powers, including harmonising Member States' offences and penalties under Article 83 TFEU.

On the other hand, proportionality also implies a peculiar intersection between distinct legal disciplines. Indeed, the principle assumes a different meaning depending on each area of law.[5] In the EU legal order, proportionality amounts to a general principle underpinning the whole system established by the Treaties. Proportionality is also a well-established principle of criminal law, but its understanding differs profoundly. As a result, the proportionality of criminal offences and penalties in EU law entails an intersection between two distinct theorisations of the principle: on the one hand, the EU concept of proportionality (A); on the other hand, the criminal law one (B).

A. The Conceptualisation of Proportionality in EU Law

In the EU legal order, proportionality is a general principle underpinning the whole EU construction.[6] Therefore, proportionality sits above secondary law in

[4] Art 83 of the Consolidated Version of the Treaty on the Functioning of the European Union [2016] OJ C202/47. Following a widely shared approach in scholarship (in the EU criminal law domain, in particular, see A Weyembergh, *L'harmonisation des législations : condition de l'espace pénal européen et révélateur de ses tensions* (Bruxelles, Editions de l'Université de Bruxelles, 2004) 34–35), the terms 'harmonisation' and 'approximation' shall be construed as synonyms for the purposes of the present work.

[5] Among many, see: S Cognetti, *Principio di proporzionalità. Profili di teoria generale e di analisi sistematica* (Torino, Giappichelli, 2011) 12; S Montaldo, 'EU Sanctioning Power and the Principle of Proportionality' in S Montaldo, F Costamagna and A Miglio (eds), *EU Law Enforcement. The Evolution of Sanctioning Powers* (Torino-Oxon, Giappichelli-Routledge, 2021) 136.

[6] Among many, see: T Tridimas, *The General Principles of EU Law*, 2nd edn (Oxford, Oxford University Press, 2007) 137–138; K Lenaerts, 'Proportionality as a Matrix Principle Promoting the

the hierarchy of EU legal sources. As such, it constitutes not only an interpretive and integrative tool for EU law as a whole but also a ground for reviewing acts of EU institutions, bodies and agencies.[7] As a general principle, proportionality has multiple declinations that could not be exhausted in this brief introductory section. Its evolution, theorisation, and application are framed in better detail in Chapter 1. At the same time, some distinctive features shall be anticipated here to define the EU concept of proportionality and distinguish it from the criminal law one.

As underlined in the literature,[8] proportionality results from extensive elaboration in the ECJ case-law. In the absence of explicit references to that principle in the ECSC and EEC Treaties, the Court of Justice built upon the Member States' common constitutional traditions to frame the EU concept of proportionality.[9] Indeed, that principle is well-routed in the Member States' domestic legal orders, embodying a precise understanding of their constitutional tradition. It postulates a legal relationship aimed at ensuring just proportion

Effectiveness of EU Law and the Legitimacy of EU Action – Keynote Speech' in *Continuity and Change – How the Challenges of Today Prepare the Ground for Tomorrow. ECB Legal Conference 2021* (Frankfurt, European Central Bank, 2022) 27; MC Ciciriello, *Il principio di proporzionalità nel diritto comunitario* (Napoli, Editoriale Scientifica, 1999) 161–162; G de Búrca, 'The Principle of Proportionality and Its Application in EC Law' (1993) 13 *Yearbook of European Law* 105, 105; P Craig, *EU Administrative Law*, 2nd edn (Oxford, Oxford University Press, 2012) 591. On the conceptualisation of and role played by general principles in the EU legal order, among many, see: K Lenaerts and JA Gutierrez-Fons, 'The Constitutional Allocation of Powers and General Principles of EU Law' (2010) 47 *CML Rev* 1629; C Amalfitano, *General Principles of EU Law and the Protection of Fundamental Rights* (Cheltenham, Edward Elgar Publishing, 2018); P Craig, 'General Principles of Law: Treaty, Historical and Normative Foundations' in KS Ziegler, PJ Neuvonen and V Moreno-Lax (eds), *Research Handbook on General Principles in EU Law: Constructing Legal Orders in Europe* (Cheltenham, Edward Elgar Publishing, 2022); G Tesauro, 'Il ruolo della Corte di giustizia nell'elaborazione dei princìpi generali dell'ordinamento europeo e dei diritti fondamentali' in *La Costituzione europea. Annuario 1999. Atti del XIV Convegno Annuale (Perugia, 7-8-9 ottobre 1999)* (Padova, CEDAM, 2000); A Tizzano, *Qualche riflessione sul contributo della Corte di giustizia allo sviluppo del sistema comunitario* (2009) 1 *Il Diritto dell'Unione Europea* 141; M Condinanzi, 'Diritti, principi e principi generali nell'ordinamento giuridico dell'Unione europea' in L D'Andrea, G Moschella, A Ruggeri and A Saitta (eds), *La Carta dei diritti dell'Unione Europea e le altre Carte (ascendenze culturali e mutue implicazioni)* (Torino, Giappichelli, 2016); A Adinolfi, 'I princìpi generali della giurisprudenza comunitaria e la loro influenza sugli ordinamenti degli Stati membri' (1994) *Rivista italiana di diritto pubblico comunitario* 521.

[7] For an account of the functions carried out by the general principles of EU law, see: Tridimas (n 6) 29–34; Adinolfi (n 6) 528-533; G Vitale, *Principi generali e diritto derivato. Contributo allo studio del sistema delle fonti dell'Unione europea* (Torino, Giappichelli, 2013) 22–27; C Amalfitano and M Condinanzi, *Unione europea: fonti, adattamento e rapporti tra ordinamenti* (Torino, Giappichelli, 2015) 31. In this respect, Tesauro underlined that the central role played by the principle of proportionality in the ECJ scrutiny stems from the inherent peculiarities of the EU legal order, as they imply an evaluation of the coherence of EU measures with respect to the objectives set out by the Treaties (G Tesauro, *La ragionevolezza nella giurisprudenza comunitaria* (Napoli, Editoriale Scientifica, 2012) 43).

[8] Among many, see: Tesauro (n 6) 301–302; Ciciriello (n 6) 157 *et seq*; R Palladino, *Il principio di proporzionalità nel diritto dell'Unione europea* (Bari, Cacucci Editore, 2024) 1–2; G Scaccia, 'Il principio di proporzionalità' in S Mangiameli (eds), *L'ordinamento europeo: l'esercizio delle competenze* (Milano, Giuffrè, 2006) 235; F Bestagno, U Draetta and A Santini, *Elementi di Diritto dell'Unione europea. Profili istituzionali*, 8th edn (Milano, Giuffrè, 2024) 65.

[9] On the distinction between general principles common to any legal system and those typical of the EU legal order, among many, see G Strozzi and R Mastroianni, *Diritto dell'Unione europea. Parte istituzionale*, 9th edn (Torino, Giappichelli, 2023) 233.

between competing interests.[10] Proportion is contextual since it struggles to provide reasonable balancing[11] by considering all the circumstances of a case. On that basis, proportionality requires that public power exercise be grounded on an accommodation of conflicting interests justified on objective and logical grounds. Thus construed, proportionality amounts to a corollary of the rule of law underlying European democratic systems,[12] as it conveys the idea that individuals shall be protected against excessive or arbitrary exercise of public prerogatives.[13]

Theoretically, the EU conceptualisation of proportionality is inherently entrenched in the principle theory derived from the twentieth century's philosophical reaction to positivism.[14] As underlined by Alexy, '[p]rinciple theory implies the principle of proportionality and the principle of proportionality implies principle theory'.[15] There is no room here for delving into this rich scholarly debate. It suffices to recall the well-known distinction between legal principles and rules, a dichotomy most influentially captured by Dworkin[16] and Alexy.[17]

[10] Scholarship traces the early origins of this finding back to Aristotle's *Ethica Nicomachea*, where the ancient philosopher expressed the need to enforce the ideal of justice by seeking a correct relationship between public powers and citizens (among many, see: E Engle, 'The History of the General Principle of Proportionality: An Overview' (2012) 10 *Dartmouth Law Journal* 1, 4; S Van Drooghenbroeck, *La proportionnalité dans le droit de la Convention européenne des droits de l'homme : Prendre l'idée simple au sérieux* (Bruxelles, Presses de l'Université Saint-Louis, 2001) 18). The rather vague Aristotelian idea of proportionality has been further developed by Cicero – who defined the concept of proportionality in the *De Republica* as *the recta ratio naturae congruens*, consisting in the idea of just proportion – and, in the context of States' use of force, by Aquinas (Engle 5). On the axiological nature of proportionality, among many, see M Feix, 'Subsidiarité, proportionnalité et construction européenne' (2011) 267 *Revue d'éthique et de théologie morale* 59; Ciciriello (n 6) 162.

[11] As argued in literature, the concept of reasonableness is inherently linked to the principle of proportionality, as it underpins balancing between opposing interests (on this point, see P De Pasquale and A Circolo, *Il criterio della ragionevolezza nella più recente giurisprudenza della Corte di giustizia* (2024) 2 *Il Diritto dell'Unione europea* 277, 325–326). Balancing consists of setting contrasts between opposing interests by creating new rules settling the clash between conflicting interests. This activity requires considering the position of the subjects involved and the need to treat their position equally or in a differentiated way, depending on the circumstances, to reach a fair assessment (in this regard, see: Cognetti (n 5) 44). In this perspective, proportionality represents a clear departure from the syllogistic legal reasoning (A Morrone, *Il bilanciamento nello stato costituzionale: teorie e prassi delle tecniche di giudizio nei conflitti tra diritti e interessi costituzionali* (Torino, Giappichelli, 2014) 9).

[12] In this line of reasoning, Tridimas considers proportionality among the 'general principles for the protection of the individual deriving from the rule of law' (T Tridimas, 'The General Principles of EU Law and the Europeanisation of National Laws' (2020) 13 *Review of European Administrative Law* 5).

[13] Palladino (n 8) 8.

[14] The beginning of the scholarly reaction to pure positivism is traditionally attributed to Dworkin's response to Hart's 'The Concept of Law'. The dichotomy between Hart and Dworkin dominated the subsequent debate on the theory of law: in this regard, see JM Steiner, 'Judicial Discretion and the Concept of Law' (1976) 35 *The Cambridge Law Journal* 135.

[15] R Alexy, 'On the Structure of Legal Principles' (2000) 13 *Ratio Juris* 294, 297.

[16] R Dworkin, 'The Model of Rules' (1967) 35 *The University of Chicago Law Review* 14.

[17] In particular, see R Alexy, *A Theory of Constitutional Rights* (Oxford, Oxford University Press, 2002).

Legal provisions qualifying as rules consist of commands to do something or abstain from pursuing a given behaviour.[18] In this light, compliance with rules constitutes an 'all-or-nothing' standard:[19] either the addressees comply with the prescribed behaviour, or they do not. Differently from rules, principles command 'that something be realized to the highest degree that is actually and legally possible'.[20] Thus construed, principles are optimisation requirements:[21] they indicate a result that can be realised to a different extent,[22] depending upon factual circumstances and countervailing principles.[23] Proportionality fits into this category of legal sources: it sets forth an objective that can be realised to a variable degree of intensity. More specifically, it features a conflict principle aimed at regulating the clash between legal provisions themselves qualifying as Alexynian principles (namely, legal commands that can be realised to a different extent). In this light, proportionality seeks to establish the conditions under which the realisation of one interest takes precedence over conflicting ones.

This understanding of proportionality – well routed in the Member States' legal orders – constitutes the theoretical soil on which the EU concept of proportionality is grounded. It results from a longstanding evolution pre-dating the beginning of the European integration process. In particular, the eighteenth- to nineteenth-century Prussian administrative law is unanimously recognised as the birthplace of the contemporary principle of proportionality. In this context, the reflections of Carl Gottlieb Svarez played a leading role. While involved in the elaboration of the 1794 Prussian civil code, Svarez was the leading supporter of the idea of limiting public power's interference with individual liberties to what was necessary in view to protect the freedoms and security of others.[24] This contention had been transposed in Article 10 II 17 of the Civil Code, which read 'the office of the police is to take the necessary measures for the maintenance of public peace, security, and order'. Following this development, proportionality emerged in the jurisprudence of administrative courts as the instrument for reviewing law enforcement authorities' actions. From that perspective, the latter's duties shall be exercised rationally to minimise interferences with the individuals' legal sphere. This paradigm entails

[18] Dworkin (n 16). Recognising a rule as 'legal' constitutes – according to Hart – the unavoidable step for qualifying it as part of the law. Therefore, any legal system features a fundamental rule – the 'rule of recognition' – allowing to distinguish legal rules from those pertaining to morals or ethics (HLA Hart, *The Concept of Law* (Oxford, Clarendon Press, 1961) 98; G Lamond, 'Legal Sources, the Rule of Recognition, and Customary Law' (2014) 59 *The American Journal of Jurisprudence* 25).

[19] R Dworkin, *Taking Rights Seriously* (Cambridge, Harvard University Press, 1977) 24.

[20] Alexy, 'On the Structure of Legal Principles' (n 15) 295.

[21] Alexy, *A Theory of Constitutional Rights* (n 17) 47–48.

[22] Dworkin, *Taking Rights Seriously* (n 19) 26.

[23] Alexy, 'On the Structure of Legal Principles' (n 15) 295.

[24] Among many: A Stone Sweet and J Mathews, 'Proportionality Balancing and Global Constitutionalism' (2008) 47 *Columbia Journal of Transnational Law* 72, 101; A Guilmain, 'Sur les traces du principe de proportionnalité: une esquisse généalogique' (2016) 61 *McGill Law Journal* 87, 108.

a ground-breaking corollary: individual freedom is consecrated as a natural right pre-existing public power.[25] In this line, proportionality expressed the idea that individuals shall be protected against the excessive exercise of public powers,[26] a cornerstone of the European constitutional tradition.

The evolution of liberal states to contemporary social constitutional democracies did not affect the leading role of proportionality as a key component of the rule of law. German constitutional law provided the principle with fertile soil for its progressive refinement. Against the rise of constitutional rights under the 1949 Basic Law, proportionality emerged as the essential tool for fundamental rights adjudication.[27] In particular, the principle became the main instrument employed by the BVerfGE to review the State's limitations to the enjoyment of fundamental rights.[28] Thanks to the BVerfGE case-law, proportionality evolved into an operative test capable of ensuring just proportion between conflicting interests.

In particular, proportionality requires public authority measures to be suitable, necessary and proportionate *stricto sensu* to the collective interest pursued. Firstly, the concept of suitability entails that the measure under scrutiny can attain the aim in question. Secondly, necessity demands that the measure involves the least sacrifice for individual rights. Finally, under proportionality *stricto sensu*, suitable and necessary measures shall also ensure appropriate balancing between the conflicting interests at stake.[29] The suitability, necessity and proportionality *stricto sensu* requirements are the conditions under which the realisation of a collective interest may take precedence over conflicting rights.

This test found fertile ground in various national legal orders across Europe and beyond,[30] as well as in the ECJ case-law, thus giving rise to the EU principle

[25] N Courakis and V Polyzoidou, 'The Principle of Proportionality: Tracing Its Historical Evolution' in E Billis, N Knust and JP Rui (eds), *Proportionality in Crime Control and Criminal Justice* (Oxford, Hart Publishing, 2021) 102.

[26] Among many, see A Barak, *Proportionality: Constitutional Rights and Their Limitations* (Cambridge, Cambridge University Press, 2012) 4, 64; DU Galetta, 'Il principio di proporzionalità fra diritto nazionale e diritto europeo (e con uno sguardo anche al di là dei confini dell'Unione europea)' (2019) 6 *Rivista italiana di diritto pubblico comunitario* 903, 909.

[27] See, in particular, the works by H Krüger, R Krauss and P Lerche. In particular, Krauss and Leche's studies were pivotal for the elaboration of the threefold proportionality test as applied by the BVerfGE. While the term 'proportionality *stricto sensu*' (namely, the third step of the test) has been coined by Krauss, Leche advanced a precise distinction between proportionality *stricto sensu* and the necessity (or least restrictive measure) test (Stone Sweet and Mathews (n 24) 104–105).

[28] The first ruling citing proportionality concerned the constitutionality of an election law of North Rhine Westphalia (BVerfGE 3, 383 (1954)). However, the first complete explanation of the BVerfGE proportionality test can be found in the well-renowned *Apotheken-Urteil* case (BVerfGE 7, 377 (1958)), where the German Federal Constitutional Court applied that principle in relation to freedom of expression under Art 12 of the Basic Law. In this regard, see: D Grimm, 'Proportionality in Canadian and German Constitutional Jurisprudence' (2015) 57 *The University of Toronto Law Journal* 383, 385.

[29] In this regard, among many, see Barak (n 26) 335–346.

[30] The emergence of a proportionality assessment in the Canadian Supreme Court's case-law on the Canadian Charter of Rights and Freedoms constitutes a proficient example in this regard. For a comparative analysis of the employment of the principle of proportionality in German and Canadian constitutional adjudication, see Grimm (n 28). For further assessment of the proportionality's influence on fundamental rights adjudication beyond Europe, see N Petersen, *Proportionality and Judicial Activism: Fundamental Rights Adjudication in Canada, Germany and South Africa* (Cambridge, Cambridge University Press, 2017).

of proportionality. This process, together with the relevant ECJ case-law, is deepened in Chapter 1: for the sake of an introduction, it is now time to frame the key features of the distinct criminal law concept of proportionality.

B. Proportionality of Offences and Penalties in the Criminal Law Discourse

Proportionality has a completely different meaning in criminal law. As previously outlined, the EU principle of proportionality has evolved in administrative law and then reworked at the supranational level. In the area of criminal law, proportionality postulates a purely domestic concept distinctive of this legal domain. It conveys the idea that individuals shall be protected against the excessive exercise of States' *ius puniendi*. The latter consists of the public power to impose sanctions by enacting criminal law provisions, the conviction of individuals by courts and, subsequently, the execution of the penalty.[31] In all these phases, proportionality is understood as a legal relationship between the criminal conduct and the corresponding punishment. More specifically, the criminal law principle of proportionality demands that the severity of punishment fits the seriousness of the wrongdoing.[32]

Notwithstanding its inherently domestic nature, the criminal law concept of proportionality enjoys key relevance in EU criminal law. Chapter 2 will deepen the theorisation and place of this understanding of the principle to conceptualise its intersection with EU law. For the sake of an introduction, two considerations shall be advanced here.

Firstly, the concept of proportionality in criminal law is twofold. Its traditional understanding is inherently *retrospective*: it implies a backwards-looking account of the appropriateness of the sanction imposed to the committed offence.[33] The latter shall be distinguished from the concept of *prospective* proportionality which, similarly to the EU principle previously analysed, postulates a forward-looking account of the effects of the punishment to reach the penological desired aim.[34]

Secondly, retrospective proportionality is inextricably entrenched with retributive theories of punishment derived from the deontological philosophical tradition. Deontological theories construe criminal sanctions as the inevitable retribution for

[31] A Harel, 'Punishment and the State', *Encyclopedia of Criminology and Criminal Justice* (Oxford, Oxford University Press, 2014) 4185.

[32] J Ryberg and T Søbirk Petersen, 'Proportionality', *Encyclopedia of Criminology and Criminal Justice* (Oxford, Oxford University Press, 2014) 4063.

[33] RA Duff, 'Proportionality and the Criminal Law: Proportionality of What to What?' in E Billis, N Knust and JP Rui (eds), *Proportionality in Crime Control and Criminal Justice* (Oxford, Hart Publishing, 2021) 29; A Martufi, 'Proportionality of Sanctions Under EU Law: Insights from Penal Theory' in L Grossio, S Montaldo and V Mitsilegas (eds), *Proportionality of Criminal Penalties in EU Law* (Oxford, Hart Publishing, 2025) 42–43.

[34] Duff (n 33) 34; Nils Jareborg, 'Criminalization as Last Resort (Ultima Ratio)' (2005) 2 *Ohio State Journal of Criminal Law* 521, 529.

the committed wrongdoing.[35] In this perspective, retribution implies per se a relationship of commensurability between the sanction and the offence.[36] However, proportionality in criminal law is not limited to retributivism. While retributivist theories assign a central role to proportionality, any theory of punishment shall address the principle under analysis.[37] That is the case of consequentialist theories, which frame criminal sanctions as an instrument for preventative purposes.[38] As Chapter 2 further discusses,[39] this finding entails a key role also for prospective proportionality as a complementary assessment to the retrospective scheme.

II. Developing an EU Law Perspective on Proportionality of Criminal Offences and Penalties: The Aim of the Book

The EU and criminal law theorisations of the principle differ widely. However, when dealing with criminal offences and penalties under EU law, proportionality inevitably bumps into its criminal law concept. Both dimensions are relevant for theorising the principle of proportionality of criminal offences and penalties, which manifests a peculiar intersection between the EU and criminal law concepts.

This complex relationship between distinct theoretical dimensions elicits a systematic approach. Legal scholarship, however, has provided limited contribution thus far. Until recently, the topic has been mainly assessed from a purely criminal law viewpoint.[40] A different angle of perspective is necessary to tackle the peculiar features of that principle in the EU legal order. This profile is currently raising momentum in the EU law scholarship, especially since the ECJ in *Bezirkshauptmannschaft Hartberg-Fürstenfeld (Effet direct)* recognised that the proportionality of criminal penalties has direct effect.[41] This remarkable

[35] Among many, see: A von Hirsch, 'Proportionality in the Philosophy of Punishment' (1992) 16 *Crime and Justice* 55, 79.

[36] On the relationship between retributivism and proportionality in criminal law, see Section III(B)(ii) of Chapter 2.

[37] von Hirsch, 'Proportionality in the Philosophy of Punishment' (n 35) 56.

[38] M Matravers, 'Penal Philosophy and Sentencing Theories', *Encyclopedia of Criminology and Criminal Justice* (Oxford, Oxford University Press, 2014) 3490.

[39] See Section III(B)(i) of Chapter 2.

[40] In this regard, among many, see Duff (n 33); von Hirsch, 'Proportionality in the Philosophy of Punishment' (n 35); A von Hirsch, 'Proportionality in the Philosophy of Punishment: From "Why Punish" to "How Much"' (1991) 25 *Israel Law Review* 549; A von Hirsch and A Ashworth, *Proportionate Sentencing: Exploring the Principle* (Oxford, Oxford University Press, 2005); A Ashworth, *Principles of Criminal Law* (Oxford, Oxford University Press, 1999); D van Zyl Smit and A Ashworth, 'Disproportionate Sentences as Human Rights Violations' (2004) 67 *Modern Law Review* 541; A Duff and SP Green, *Philosophical Foundations of Criminal Law* (Oxford, Oxford University Press, 2011); F Viganò, *La proporzionalità della pena: profili di diritto penale e costituzionale* (Torino, Giappichelli, 2021).

[41] Case C-205/20 *Bezirkshauptmannschaft Hartberg-Fürstenfeld (Effet direct)* ECLI:EU:C:2022:168.

development has sparked an emerging debate on the scope and implications of the principle in the EU legal order.[42] However, the scholarly analysis has concentrated on the proportionality of sanctions without touching upon the proportionality constraints to the EU and Member States' criminalisation choices. It thus appears that an EU law perspective on the principle of proportionality of criminal offences and penalties, capable of reconciling its EU and criminal law dimensions, is yet to be explored in full.

This book aims to fill this gap by systematically examining the proportionality of criminal offences and penalties in EU law. The study investigates the conceptualisation and application of the principle, thereby disclosing how the interaction between the EU and criminal law concepts of proportionality results in an original theoretical understanding. In EU criminal law, the EU principle of proportionality is hybridised because of its inevitable intersection with the criminal law dimension of proportionality. On those grounds, the book argues that the principle of proportionality of criminal offences and penalties is hybrid, as it combines within the EU legal order the distinctive features of the EU and criminal law understandings of proportionality.

III. The Concepts of Offences and Penalties in EU Criminal Law: The Scope of the Book

The scope of the proportionality of criminal offences and penalties – and, consequently, the extent of this book's analysis – depends upon the boundaries of criminal law within the EU legal order. Member States typically employ a formalistic approach: any provision or penalty qualified as 'criminal' falls under the scope of that domain. On those grounds, criminal law is generally understood as the set of provisions and principles governing the establishment of criminal offences and penalties, tackling violations of those provisions and imposing sanctions.[43] This definition does not provide any substantive criterion for distinguishing criminal law from different sanctioning schemes: offences and penalties are criminal insofar as they are qualified as such by the legislator.

The formalistic approach faces noteworthy shortcomings under EU law. Firstly, a question of uniformity emerges. At the domestic level, the boundaries of criminal law may differ from one legal order to another so that substantially analogous

[42] In particular, see S Montaldo, 'Handle with Care! The Direct Effect of the Requirement of Proportionality of Sanctions and the Remedy of Disapplication: *NE v. Bezirkshauptmannschaft Hartberg-Fürstenfeld*' (2023) 60 *CML Rev* 863; M Lanotte, 'La proporzionalità della sanzione: un principio ritrovato? Note a margine della sentenza *NE*' in *Quaderni AISDUE – Serie Speciale: Atti del Convegno 'Ambiente, digitale, economia: l'Unione europea verso il 2030'* (Napoli, Editoriale Scientifica, 2023); as well as the wide-ranging contributions published in L Grossio, S Montaldo and V Mitsilegas (eds), *Proportionality of Criminal Penalties in EU Law* (Oxford, Hart Publishing, 2025).

[43] Among many, see A Barletta, *La legalità penale tra diritto dell'Unione europea e Costituzione* (Napoli, Jovene, 2011) 12.

sanctioning frameworks may qualify as criminal or non-criminal. Secondly, States may avoid the application of a set of fundamental criminal law guarantees afforded by EU law – with particular emphasis on legality, non-retroactivity and *ne bis in idem* – by merely labelling the relevant sanctioning scheme as non-criminal.

This issue also emerged within the ECHR legal system, thus leading the Strasbourg Court to develop a substantive concept of 'criminal'. In the well-known *Engel and Others v The Netherlands* judgment, the ECtHR outlined three criteria for a penalty to be labelled as criminal under the Convention.[44] First of all, regard must be had to the qualification given by the domestic legislature. If the penalty under scrutiny has been labelled as criminal, that suffices to consider it as such under the ECHR. However, this evaluation only constitutes the starting point for the ECtHR assessment.[45] Subsidiarily, regard must be had to the very nature of the offence to verify whether it secures a public interest usually warranting criminal law protection.[46] Finally, the severity of the penalty constitutes the last element to be considered. Should the sanction feature an afflictive nature comparable to criminal penalties, the measure shall be considered criminal under the ECHR. The three criteria are alternative: realising one requirement is sufficient for qualifying the relevant sanction as criminal.[47]

The ECJ later adopted these criteria to frame the area of criminal law within the EU legal order.[48] Therefore, the scope of the present analysis shall include all offences and penalties falling under the substantive definition of 'criminal law' resulting from the *Engel* criteria as interpreted by the ECJ.

Building upon this premise, the concepts of 'offences' and 'penalties' shall now be defined. The two terms may be construed either in *in abstracto* or *in concreto*.[49] In the first dimension, 'offence' describes an abstract behaviour whose commission entails imposing criminal penalties.[50] Traditionally, criminal offences are established to sanction behaviours committed by natural persons. Still, the legislative

[44] *Engel and Others v The Netherlands* Series A No 22 (1974).

[45] *ibid*, para 83.

[46] *ibid*.

[47] However, this finding does not exclude the possibility of cumulatively assessing the three criteria in cases where a separate evaluation does not allow to reach a clear conclusion on the criminal or non-criminal nature of the offence (among many, see *Sergey Zolotukhin v Russia* App No 14939/03 (ECtHR, 10 February 2009), para 53; *A and B v Norway* App Nos 24130/11 and 29758/11 (ECtHR, 15 November 2016), para 105; *Jussila v Finland* ECHR 2006–XIV, paras 30–31; *Mihalace v Romania* App No 54012/10 (ECtHR, 8 July 2019), para 54). When assessing the three criteria separately, the Strasbourg Court's approach is quite variegated, as it relies mainly on either the second or the third criterion depending upon the type of sanctions under scrutiny. On this point, see M Delmas-Marty and C Teitgen-Colly, *Punir sans juger? De la répression administrative au droit administratif pénal* (Paris, Economica, 1992) 166–167.

[48] Case C-489/10 *Bonda* ECLI:EU:C:2012:319, paras 37–44. Even before that ruling, the *Engel* criteria have been recalled in several Opinions of Advocates General. On this point, in literature, see M Kettunen, *Legitimizing European Criminal Law*, vol 2 (Cham, Springer, 2020) 68.

[49] Among many, see M Gallo, *Appunti di diritto penale. Vol II: Il reato. Parte I: La fattispecie oggettiva* (Torino, Giappichelli, 2007) 3.

[50] T Padovani, *Diritto penale*, 12th edn (Milano, Giuffrè, 2019) 97.

practice has evolved towards widening the scope of individuals subject to criminal law provisions. Indeed, several Member States nowadays set forth criminal sanctioning schemes to punish wrongdoings attributable to legal persons.[51] Conversely, the same term *in concreto* postulates an individual conduct – committed by either natural or legal persons – sanctioned by criminal penalties because it corresponds to the abstract behaviour enshrined in the offence *in abstracto*.[52] These definitions frame offences objectively; still, this book does not overlook that offences also entail a mental element concerning the offenders' state of mind and culpability.[53] This aspect will be marginal to the analysis. Rather than describing the concept of offence, the mental element pertains to the theory of criminal responsibility, as it concerns the characteristics of given offenders and their criminal behaviours.[54] Therefore, while the mental element of the offence would be key from a criminal law viewpoint, a purely objective definition is more appropriate from an EU law perspective to draw the boundaries of the research subject.

The concept of 'penalties', on its part, refers to a category of punitive sanctions[55] provided for and applied in the criminal law field as a consequence of an offence. The categorisation of penalties varies from one criminal system to another; however, a distinction is traditionally drawn between custodial penalties – consisting of the offender's deprivation of liberty[56] – and financial ones – entailing the payment of a criminal law fine.[57] Similarly to offences, also the term 'penalties' shall be construed either *in abstracto* or *in concreto*. On the one hand, penalties *in abstracto* mean the sanctions attached to the offences defined in criminal law provisions. These may feature either fixed penalties or penalty scales ranging between a minimum and a maximum. On the other hand, penalties *in concreto* are the criminal sanctions as applied by trial courts by grading their type and amount in the light of the specific circumstances of each case.

Finally, it shall be underlined that these definitions concern offences and penalties as established and applied in domestic criminal systems, which must be distinguished from *harmonised* offences and penalties. For the purposes of the present book, the latter shall be construed as the harmonising provisions on the definition of offences and penalties adopted by the EU legislature under Article 83 TFEU.[58]

[51] For a wide-ranging comparative study on Member States' practice on the criminalisation of legal entities' wrongdoings, see the various contributions published in A Fiorella (ed), *Liability 'Ex Crimine' of Legal Entities in Member States*, vol 1 (Napoli, Jovene, 2012).

[52] Gallo (n 49) 5.

[53] Among many, see: J Herring, *Criminal Law* (Basingstoke, Palgrave Macmillan, 2005) 50.

[54] Among many, see R Merle and A Vitu, *Traité de droit criminel. Problèmes généraux de la science criminelle. Droit pénal général* (Paris, Editions Cujas, 1984) 472.

[55] Padovani (n 50) 363.

[56] Merle and Vitu (n 54) 857.

[57] *ibid*, 916.

[58] As noted in the literature, the EU harmonising competence enshrined in Article 83 TFEU only covers substantive criminal law in the formal sense, namely, those offences and penalties expressly labelled as criminal in the domestic legal orders. On this point, see J Öberg, 'The Definition of Criminal Sanctions in the EU' (2014) 3 *European Criminal Law Review* 273, 276.

IV. The Multiple Facets of Proportionality: Two Dichotomies

Before delving into the analysis, an additional layer of complexity shall be added. Indeed, further considerations are required to frame the distinct manifestations of proportionality covered by this book. The EU and criminal law concepts of the principle postulate both positive and negative assessments (A) to be carried out either *in abstracto* or *in concreto* (B).

A. Positive and Negative Proportionality

The positive and negative dimensions reflect the two stages of the proportionality dynamic. In the first stage, the principle is addressed to the legislature. In this context, a *positive* assessment is required: public authorities identify conflicting interests and weigh them to establish an abstract rule settling the conflict. This assessment is inherent to both the EU legislature's activity when adopting harmonising provisions on substantive criminal law and domestic legislators. The positive nature of this balancing also extends to the proportionality of criminal penalties: the EU and domestic legislatures shall carry out a positive appreciation of conflicting interests at stake to define legal provisions on penalties.

In the second stage of the proportionality dynamic, the principle is addressed to judicial authorities for reviewing the legislative choices. Under the separation of powers characterising constitutional democracies, as well as the EU legal order,[59] in principle the judiciary cannot replace the legislative balancing when reviewing their decisions.[60] However, proportionality requires courts to assess whether legislative provisions fall under the scope of an abstract category of 'proportionate' arrangements. That means that judicial authorities conduct a *negative* proportionality assessment: they investigate whether the measure constitutes a disproportionate accommodation of conflicting interests. Such an evaluation requires defining a standard of review, which may be stricter or looser depending on the circumstances.

The negative proportionality review of harmonising provisions on offences and penalties falls under the exclusive jurisdiction of the ECJ pursuant to Article 263 TFEU. Conversely, judicial review of domestic offences and penalties falls primarily

[59] As influentially argued in K Lenaerts, 'Some Reflections on the Separation of Powers in the European Communities' (1991) 28 *CML Rev* 11.

[60] As argued in constitutional law literature, legal provisions set a limit to the negative proportionality review. Indeed, balancing leads to 'declaring' a conflict rule underpinning a given provision, but it could not subvert the 'prior balancing' between opposing interests defined by the legislature as inherent in the provision itself (among many, see: G Scaccia, *Gli 'strumenti' della ragionevolezza nel giudizio costituzionale* (Milano, Giuffrè, 2000) 381).

under the competencies of domestic courts. Still, they may seek the guidance of the ECJ through the preliminary reference procedure under Article 267 TFEU when evaluating their compatibility vis-à-vis EU law, and particularly with the principle of proportionality of offences and penalties.

B. Proportionality *in Abstracto* and *in Concreto*

The formula 'proportionality *in abstracto*' covers two distinct assessments. On the one hand, it includes the legislature's positive proportionality appreciation for establishing abstract criminal law provisions. On the other hand, the same formula also materialises the negative proportionality assessment carried out by courts in the review of abstract criminal law provisions vis-à-vis EU law.

Symmetrically, proportionality *in concreto* consists of two different assessments. On one side, the formula covers the positive proportionality evaluation that trial courts carry out when applying offences and penalties in concrete cases. On the other side, proportionality *in concreto* refers to the negative proportionality review of the compatibility of a given conviction with EU law.

V. The Methodology

The book advances an analytical dogmatic study aimed at reconstructing the theorisation and application of the principle of proportionality of criminal offences and penalties in the EU legal order. The legal argumentation technique follows from the peculiar features of the research aim, which demands a general conclusion on the theorisation and application of the principle. To that aim, an inductive method appears appropriate: an analysis of the specific declinations of the principle will pave the way for a general conclusion in this regard. However, this analysis shall be grounded on a prior conceptual appraisal of the principle of proportionality of criminal offences and penalties. This preliminary theorisation follows from analysing the interaction between the EU and criminal law concepts of proportionality. That preliminary conceptualisation is conducted through a deductive assessment.

Therefore, the book follows a synthesis of the deductive and inductive methods. The deductive analysis of the interaction between the EU and criminal law proportionality in their multiple dimensions allows to theoretically frame the proportionality of criminal offences and penalties. This conceptualisation provides a preliminary hypothesis to be verified by inductively looking at the relevant legislative and judicial practice. In this regard, each specific declination of the principle is assessed to frame how the principle is applied in practice, thus tackling the intersection between the EU and criminal law understandings of proportionality.

VI. The Structure of the Book

Following these introductory considerations, everything is set for delving into the analysis. The latter is structured as follows. **Chapter 1** provides for a systematisation of the multiple dimensions of the principle of proportionality in the EU legal order. Building upon this assessment, **Chapter 2** frames from a theoretical viewpoint the intersection between the EU and criminal law dimensions of proportionality. This analysis offers a preliminary conceptualisation of the principle of proportionality of criminal offences and penalties, consisting of a general model capable of capturing its peculiar features. By so doing, the chapter advances the book's central argument: construing the principle of proportionality of criminal offences and penalties as a hybrid principle resulting from the intersection between EU and criminal law theoretical paradigms.

The subsequent chapters focus on the relevant legislative and judicial practice to assess whether it corroborates the principle's hybrid nature. The analysis is organised upon a vertical structure, based on a downward shift of the focus from the EU to the domestic substantive criminal law.

On that basis, **Chapter 3** focuses on EU harmonised offences and penalties to assess how the EU legislature applies positive proportionality *in abstracto*. In particular, the scope of the analysis extends to the *travaux préparatoires* of each act of secondary law harmonising offences and penalties currently in force or pending before the Parliament and Council. Then, the same chapter discusses the ECJ standard for the proportionality review of harmonised offences and penalties. Finally, **Chapter 4** delves into the ECJ proportionality review of domestic criminal offences and penalties. In this domain, the chapter separately considers criminal measures enacted to secure the effectiveness of EU law and those clashing with the enjoyment of individual rights and freedoms protected by the Treaties.

Finally, **Chapter 5** concludes the analysis by reconstructing the principle of proportionality of criminal offences and penalties. Building upon the findings from previous chapters, the concluding remarks validate the book's central argument: the proportionality of criminal offences and penalties amounts to a hybrid principle, combining the EU and criminal law understandings of proportionality in an original compound paradigm.

1

Proportionality in EU Law: A Multidimensional General Principle

I. Introduction

After briefly recalling the evolution of proportionality in the EU legal order (II), this chapter assesses its theorisation and functions as a general principle. In particular, the analysis sheds light on the multiple dimensions of proportionality (III), covering the exercise of EU powers, the scrutiny of Member States' interferences in the enjoyment of rights and freedoms protected by EU law, and fundamental rights adjudication. Against this multifaceted framework, the chapter defines a general theorisation of the EU concept of proportionality, framed as a common theoretical paradigm underpinning each dimension of that principle under EU law (IV).

II. The Emergence of Proportionality in the EU Legal Order

The concept and evolution of proportionality in EU law are inherently linked to the peculiar nature of the European Union. In *Van Gend en Loos*, the Court of Justice affirmed that the Treaties established not simply a legal framework under international law but a new legal order.[1] The emergence of the then European Communities – now the European Union – as an autonomous legal order implies including individuals among its subjects. Indeed, the EU legal order 'not only imposes obligations on individuals but is also intended to confer upon them rights which become part of their legal heritage'.[2]

This legal construction presented the EU architecture with several unprecedented challenges. Firstly, a fully-fledged legal order requires effective coordination between

[1] Case 26/62 *Van Gend en Loos v Administratie der Belastingen* ECLI:EU:C:1963:1, p 12.

[2] *ibid.* As recently argued in literature, conferring rights on individuals constitutes one of the key rationales behind Member States limiting their sovereign powers under the Treaties (F Munari, 'I valori dell'Unione europea: una visione prospettica' in B Cortese (ed), *Il diritto dell'Unione europea nei rapporti tra ordinamenti: tra collaborazione, integrazione e identità* (2024) 1 *Rivista Quaderni AISDUE* 77, 79–80). On the implications of *Van Gend en Loos* for the position of individuals under

supranational regulatory powers and those retained by domestic authorities.[3] This issue is particularly sensitive in shared competencies, as Member States have only partially conferred their sovereign powers to the supranational legislator. Secondly, the protection of the legal sphere of individuals from arbitrary intrusions by supranational or domestic public powers emerged as a pressing issue. In particular, the progressive rise of fundamental rights protection within the Community required the accommodation of public interests vis-à-vis individual rights. Against these challenges, proportionality as derived from the Prussian administrative law and then encapsulated in the Member States' constitutional systems – with particular emphasis on the German one – represented a flexible criterion providing a holistic answer.

The emergence of proportionality in the EU legal order is mainly the result of an evolution in the ECJ case-law, since neither the 1951 ECSC Treaty nor the 1957 EEC Treaty enshrined any explicit reference to that principle. The starting point is represented by the 1956 judgment of the ECSC Court in case *Fédération charbonnière de Belgique v High Authority*.[4] In that case, which concerned the ECSC equalisation policy in the context of fixing coal prices, the Court for the first time established a necessity test as a ground for reviewing decisions of the High Authority. Following that ruling, the ECJ subsequent case-law developed proportionality paradigms from interpreting several provisions of the Treaties, with particular emphasis on those prohibiting restrictions to the enjoyment of EEC individual rights and freedoms.[5] As a result, the principle of proportionality became a true protagonist of the ECJ jurisprudence. As Emiliou reported, the Court relied

EU law, among many, see: JHH Weiler, 'Van Gend En Loos: The Individual as Subject and Object and the Dilemma of European Legitimacy' (2014) 1 *International Journal of Constitutional Law* 94. At the same time, the existence of duties upon individuals under EU law is particularly controversial. Indeed, at the current stage of evolution of the EU legal order, no obligation upon individuals may be traced within the EU legal order. This aspect poses critical issues, in particular, for the legal construction of EU citizenship (among many, see: B Nascimbene and F Rossi dal Pozzo, *Diritti di cittadinanza e libertà di circolazione nell'Unione europea* (Padova, CEDAM, 2012) 64; M Condinanzi, B Nascimbene and A Lang, *Cittadinanza dell'Unione e libera circolazione delle persone* (Milano, Giuffrè, 2006) 22; R Davis, 'Citizenship of the Union … Rights for All?' (2002) 27 *EL Rev* 121). Being citizenship traditionally construed as comprising both rights conferred on individuals and obligations imposed on them because of their membership to the community, the absence of duties upon EU citizens may be interpreted as a weakness of the EU citizenship concept. Against this background, some authors advocated for theorising EU-derived obligations from the *abus de droit* concept: while citizens enjoy rights conferred by the EU legal order, the inherent obligation not to abuse from the latter may be seen as a substitute for individual obligations (N Reich, 'Union Citizenship-Metaphor or Source of Rights?' (2001) 7 *European Law Journal* 4).

[3] The interaction between the EU and domestic legal orders also involves other general principles, with particular emphasis on loyal cooperation. On that topic, among extensive literature, see O Porchia, *Principi dell'ordinamento europeo. La cooperazione pluridirezionale* (Bologna, Zanichelli, 2008).

[4] Case 8/55 *Fédération charbonnière de Belgique v High Authority* ECLI:EU:C:1956:11, p 306.

[5] The jurisprudential origins of the principle of proportionality in EU law reflects the development of the very same principle within national public law, thereby amounting to a 'judge-made doctrine of public law' (N Emiliou, *The Principle of Proportionality in European Law: A Comparative Study* (London, Kluwer Law International, 1996) 16. On the role of the ECJ in developing general principles, among many, see P Craig, 'General Principles of Law: Treaty, Historical and Normative Foundations' in KS Ziegler, PJ Neuvonen and V Moreno-Lax (eds), *Research Handbook on General Principles in EU Law: Constructing Legal Orders in Europe* (Cheltenham, Edward Elgar Publishing, 2022); C Amalfitano,

upon that principle in its reasoning more than 500 times just until 1994.[6] Indeed, as Advocate General Jacobs contended in *Commission v Greece*, 'there are few areas of Community law, if any at all, where the principle of proportionality is not relevant'.[7]

The underlying reasons for the proportionality's success story in EU law stem from the broad consensus gained by this principle in Member States' public law. As the very flagship of the European legal tradition based on the rule of law,[8] proportionality found fertile soil in various national legal orders across Europe. Following this cross-fertilisation process, all EU Member States nowadays entrench the principle of proportionality in the substantive ideal of justice.[9] Proportionality thus became the expression of a precise understanding of democracy deeply rooted in contemporary Europe.[10] This axiological feature permeated the principle of proportionality at the supranational level as well. Indeed, the Court early recognised in *Mannesman* that proportionality constitutes a manifestation of the value of justice underpinning the action of the Community.[11]

III. Proportionality as a General Principle of EU Law: Assessing its Multiple Dimensions

Following this evolutive path, proportionality has been consecrated as a general principle underpinning the whole EU construction.[12] Proportionality enjoys three distinct dimensions in the EU legal order, which are now reflected in the Treaties.

General Principles of EU Law and the Protection of Fundamental Rights (Cheltenham, Edward Elgar Publishing, 2018) 28 *et seq*; A Tizzano, *Qualche riflessione sul contributo della Corte di giustizia allo sviluppo del sistema comunitario* (2009) 1 *Il Diritto dell'Unione Europea* 141; G Tesauro, 'Il ruolo della Corte di giustizia nell'elaborazione dei principi generali dell'ordinamento europeo e dei diritti fondamentali' in *La Costituzione europea. Annuario 1999. Atti del XIV Convegno Annuale (Perugia, 7-8-9 ottobre 1999)* (Padova, CEDAM, 2000); A Adinolfi, 'I princìpi generali della giurisprudenza comunitaria e la loro influenza sugli ordinamenti degli Stati membri' (1994) *Rivista italiana di diritto pubblico comunitario* 521, 534 *et seq*.; G Strozzi and R Mastroianni, *Diritto dell'Unione europea. Parte istitizionale*, 9th edn (Torino, Giappichelli, 2023) 230–233.

[6] Emiliou (n 5) 134.

[7] Case C-120/94 *Commission v Greece*, Opinion of AG Jacobs, ECLI:EU:C:1995:109, para 70.

[8] In this respect, see Section I(A) of the Introduction to this book. Proportionality also enjoys key relevance in public international law: for an in-depth analysis, see E Cannizzaro, *Il principio della proporzionalità nell'ordinamento internazionale* (Milano, Giuffrè, 2000).

[9] Among many, see: M Newton, *Proportionality in International Law* (Oxford, Oxford University Press, 2014) 40; Emiliou (n 5) 39, 88.

[10] MC Ciciriello, *Il principio di proporzionalità nell'ordinamento comunitario* (Napoli, Editoriale Scientifica, 1999) 132.

[11] Case 19/61 *Mannesmann AG v High Authority* ECLI:EU:C:1962:31, p 371.

[12] As early affirmed by the ECJ in Case 11/70 *Internationale Handelsgesellschaft mbH v Einfuhr- und Vorratsstelle für Getreide und Futtermittel* ECLI:EU:C:1970:114, paras 4 and 16 of the Grounds of judgment. Indeed, in that case, the Court grounded fundamental rights protection and the related proportionality review in the realm of general principles (Craig (n 5) 35). General principles thus emerged as a structural component of the EU legal order as a 'community based on the rule of law' (Case 294/83 *Les Verts v Parliament* ECLI:EU:C:1986:166, para 23). On this point, see T Tridimas, *The General Principles of EU Law*, 2nd edn (Oxford, Oxford University Press, 2007) 4–5, 19; Craig (n 5) 38;

First, it shapes the exercise of EU powers (A). Second, the principle amounts to a ground for reviewing EU and domestic measures affecting the enjoyment of internal market freedoms (B). Third, proportionality plays a crucial role in fundamental rights adjudication under the Charter (C).

A. Proportionality as a Limit to the Exercise of EU Powers

With the principles of conferral and subsidiarity, proportionality enshrined in Article 5(4) TEU represents a keystone of the EU competencies' architecture. The distinction between conferral – according to which the EU powers are limited to the competencies conferred by the Member States in the Treaties[13] – and proportionality is almost self-evident. Conversely, the dividing line between the latter and subsidiarity deserves greater attention. While subsidiarity aims to identify who between the Union and the Member States is best placed to intervene in shared competencies,[14] proportionality relates to the intensity of obligations ensuing from EU law provisions.[15] To protect Member States' sovereign powers from the unduly exercise of supranational competencies,[16] the Union's action shall be limited to the measure sufficient to attain the objective pursued.

M Maresca, 'Il ruolo dei «principi» nel progetto di Trattato costituzionale e il diritto alla mobilità' in M Maresca (ed), *Valori e principi nella Costituzione europea. Il diritto alla mobilità* (Bologna, Il Mulino, 2004) 105–106.

[13] Art 5(2) of the Consolidated Version of the Treaty on the European Union [2016] OJ C202/13. On the principle of conferral under EU law, among many, see: P De Pasquale, 'Art 5 TUE' in A Tizzano (ed), *Trattati dell'Unione europea* (Milano, Giuffrè, 2014) 47–49; G Tusseau, 'Theoretical Deflation: The EU Order of Competences and Power-Conferring Norms Theory' in L Azoulai (ed), *The Question of Competence in the European Union* (Oxford, Oxford University Press, 2014) 55.

[14] For further analysis of the principle of subsidiarity in the system of EU competencies, see: F Ippolito, *Fondamento, attuazione e controllo del principio di sussidiarietà nel diritto della comunità e dell'Unione europea* (Milano, Giuffrè, 2007); A Biondi, 'Subsidiarity in the Courtroom' in A Biondi, P Eeckhout and S Ripley (eds), *EU Law after Lisbon* (Oxford, Oxford University Press, 2012); T Konstadinides, *Division of Powers in European Union Law: The Delimitation of Internal Competence Between the EU and the Member States* (Alphen aan den Rijn, Kluwer Law International, 2009); C Timmermans, 'The Competence Divide of the Lisbon Treaty Six Years After' in S Garben and I Govaere (eds), *The Division of Competences between the EU and the Member States: Reflections on the Past, the Present and the Future* (Oxford, Hart Publishing, 2017); O Porchia, 'La sussidiarietà attraverso il riordino delle competenze? Il trattato di riforma e la ripartizione delle competenze' (2010) 5 *Studi sull'integrazione europea* 631; C Favilli, 'Il principio di sussidiarietà nel diritto dell'Unione europea' (2011) 231 *Archivio giuridico Filippo Serafini* 257; P De Pasquale, 'Sharing Is Caring: I primi trent'anni del principio di sussidiarietà nell'Unione europea' (2021) *Il Diritto dell'Unione europea* 429.

[15] R Adam and A Tizzano, *Manuale di Diritto dell'Unione europea*, 4th edn (Torino, Giappichelli, 2024) 496–497; Strozzi and Mastroianni (n 5) 93; R Geiger, 'Article 5 TEU' in R Geiger, D-E Khan and M Kotzur (eds), *European Union Treaties: A Commentary* (Munchen, Beck, 2015) 40. Other authors distinguish proportionality and subsidiarity on a timescale ground: while subsidiarity operates ex ante to identify who between the EU and the Member States is entitled to act in a given domain, proportionality applies ex post, as a guiding criteria for exercising legislative competence (F Pocar and MC Baruffi, *Commentario breve ai Trattati dell'Unione europea* (Padova, CEDAM, 2014) 30; Ciciriello (n 10) 170).

[16] U Villani, *Valori comuni e rilevanza delle identità nazionali e locali nel processo d'integrazione europea* (Napoli, Editoriale Scientifica, 2011) 94.

By providing that 'the content and form of Union action shall not exceed what is necessary to achieve the objectives of the Treaties', Article 5(4) TEU lays down some important – yet inexhaustive – clarifications in this domain. This provision emphasises the necessity requirement: an EU measure is not proportionate if less restrictive means would be equally effective for attaining the objective pursued. At the same time, necessity does not represent the only criterion for reviewing the exercise of EU competencies. As the ECJ case-law clarifies, the suitability requirement shall integrate Article 5(4) TEU: no measure can be deemed proportionate if not adequate *per se* for attaining the aim pursued.[17] The suitability requirement thus represents a precondition for the necessity assessment. When a given measure is unsuitable, there is no room for considering whether a less restrictive measure would have been available. Therefore, the proportionality test to be applied under the EU competencies system is more articulated than the wording of Article 5(4) TEU. More specifically, proportionality in the exercise of EU competencies 'requires that measures implemented through Community law provisions be appropriate for attaining the legitimate objectives pursued by the legislation at issue and must not go beyond what is necessary to achieve them'.[18] Moreover, the case-law sometimes shows reliance also on the proportionality *stricto sensu* assessment, consisting of balancing between the importance attached to the aim pursued and the countervailing interests involved.[19] As underlined in the literature, this evaluation in the context of limits to EU powers usually consists of a cost-benefit analysis, meaning that the measure under scrutiny shall not entail excessive negative consequences compared to its benefits.[20]

The application of proportionality in the exercise of EU competencies shall be governed by Protocol No 2,[21] which has the same legal value as the Treaties. The said Protocol introduces two features of particular importance for the principle's enforcement. Firstly, Article 5 compels the Commission to state reasons regarding any legislative proposal's compliance with the principles of proportionality and subsidiarity, particularly by considering its impact on existing legislation. Secondly, Article 8 confirms that the ECJ is entitled to scrutinise EU secondary

[17] Among extensive case-law, see: Joined Cases C-453/03, C-11/04, C-12/04 and C-194/04 *ABNA and Others* ECLI:EU:C:2005:741, para 68; Case C-434/02 *Arnold André* ECLI:EU:C:2004:800, para 45; Case C-151/17 *Swedish Match* ECLI:EU:C:2018:938, para 35; Case C-304/16 *American Express* ECLI:EU:C:2018:66, para 85.

[18] Case C-58/08 *Vodafone and Others* ECLI:EU:C:2010:321, para 51.

[19] Among many, see: Case C-508/13 *Estonia* v *Parliament and Council* ECLI:EU:C:2015:403, para 39; Joined Cases C-643/15 and C-647/15 *Slovakia v Council* ECLI:EU:C:2017:631, para 290; Case C-358/14 *Poland* v *Parliament and Council* ECLI:EU:C:2016:323, para 78; Case C-128/17 *Poland v Parliament and Council* ECLI:EU:C:2019:194, para 94.

[20] On this point, see: R Palladino, *Il principio di proporzionalità nel diritto dell'Unione europea* (Bari, Cacucci Editore, 2024) 30; S Barbou des Places, 'Revisiting Proportionality in Internal Market Law: Looking at the Unnamed Actors in the CJEU's Reasoning' in U Linderfalk and E Gill-Pedro, *Revisiting Proportionality in International and European Law: Interests and Interest-Holders* (Leiden-Boston, Brill Nijhoff, 2021) 14.

[21] Protocol (No 2) on the Application of the Principles of Subsidiarity and Proportionality [2016] OJ C202/206.

law's compliance with the mentioned principles. That provision reaffirms that proportionality represents not only a criterion driving ex ante the EU institutions' positive assessment but also a standard for ex post negatively reviewing the exercise of Union powers.[22]

B. Proportionality as a Legitimacy Condition for Obstacles to Internal Market Freedoms

Primary law provisions on internal market freedoms (Articles 36, 45(3), 52(1) and 65(1)–(3) TFEU) define the conditions under which Member States can restrict their enjoyment. Compared to Article 5(4) TEU, they do not expressly recall the principle of proportionality. Indeed, Article 36 TFEU provides a limited range of grounds for derogating from the prohibition of quantitative restrictions on imports and exports and measures with equivalent effects. Articles 45(3) and 52(1) TFEU, on their part, allow national authorities to derogate on grounds of public policy, public security or public health, respectively, from free movement for workers,[23] freedom of establishment and, based on Article 62 TFEU,[24] freedom of providing services. Under Article 65(1)(b) TFEU, the same grounds allow Member States to derogate from Treaty provisions on the free movement of capital.

These grounds typically apply to distinctly applicable measures, namely national provisions introducing direct or indirect discriminations between imported and non-imported goods, as well as between national and other Member States' establishments or providers of services.[25] Direct discriminations cannot, in principle, be justified on the grounds mentioned above,[26] but justifications may

[22] The ECJ scrutiny on the legality of EU acts may be triggered by EU institutions, Member States' governments as well as by natural or legal persons by filing a direct action under the conditions set up by Art 263 TFEU, or by domestic jurisdictions by means of preliminary references under Art 267 TFEU. Further on this topic, among many, see: K Lenaerts, K Gutman and JT Nowak, *EU Procedural Law*, 3rd edn (Oxford, Oxford University Press, 2024) 275 *et seq*.

[23] While the Treaties do not include a specific clause on limitations to free movement of persons other than workers, grounds allowing derogations from this freedom have been included in Art 27 of Directive 2004/38/EC of the European Parliament and of the Council of 29 April 2004 on the Right of Citizens of the Union and Their Family Members to Move and Reside Freely Within the Territory of the Member States Amending Regulation (EEC) No 1612/68 and Repealing Directives 64/221/EEC, 68/360/EEC, 72/194/EEC, 73/148/EEC, 75/34/EEC, 75/35/EEC, 90/364/EEC, 90/365/EEC and 93/96/EEC [2004] OJ L 158/77. This provision states that 'Member States may restrict the freedom of movement and residence of Union citizens and their family members, irrespective of nationality, on grounds of public policy, public security or public health. These grounds shall not be invoked to serve economic ends'. For a deeper analysis, see P Syrpis, 'EU Secondary Legislation and Its Impact on Derogations from Free Movement' in P Koutrakos, NN Shuibhne and P Syrpis (eds), *Exceptions from EU Free Movement Law: Derogation, Justification and Proportionality* (Oxford, Hart Publishing, 2016).

[24] According to the cited provision, Art 52 TFEU applies by way of reference to free provision of services under Art 56 TFEU.

[25] Among many, see: L Daniele, *Diritto del mercato unico europeo e dello spazio di libertà, sicurezza e giustizia*, 3rd edn (Milano, Giuffrè, 2016) 36–37.

[26] This notwithstanding, the ECJ has sometimes admitted a theoretical possibility to justify direct discriminations on grounds of a legitimate aim pursued in the general interest. See, in particular, Case C-322/13 *Grauel Rüffer* ECLI:EU:C:2014:189, para 23.

be attached to indirect discriminations introduced by distinctly applicable measures. At the same time, the ECJ has clarified that internal market law prohibits not only disguised discrimination but also any national measure that, although applying indistinctly, amounts to an obstacle to the enjoyment of EU free movement rights.[27] These obstacles may be justified only to fulfil an 'overriding reason in the general interest'.[28]

Against this background, the ECJ consistently held that any derogation from EU internal market freedoms must rely on legitimate grounds and comply with the principle of proportionality.[29] In this respect, the Luxembourg Court has shaped a holistic proportionality test to scrutinise measures derogating from internal market freedoms, whose requirements have been codified in *Gebhard*. In particular, any measure posing an obstacle to the enjoyment of EU internal market freedoms shall i) be applied in a non-discriminatory manner; ii) be justified by imperative requirements in the general interest; iii) be suitable for attaining the objective pursued; and iv) not go beyond what is necessary to attain the same aim.[30] The assessment defined in *Gebhard* enjoys remarkable similarities to the threefold proportionality test derived from the tradition of German administrative law.[31] In later rulings, the ECJ mainly focused on the last two prongs of the test, namely the suitability and necessity of the measure for attaining the aim pursued. In fact, according to the most recent case-law, 'the provision of national law must be appropriate for securing the attainment of the objective pursued and must not go beyond what is necessary in order to attain it'.[32] However, the ECJ also constantly recalls that 'the disadvantages caused must not be disproportionate to the aims pursued',[33] thus paving the way for a proportionality *stricto sensu* assessment.[34]

[27] Daniele (n 25) 38; S Amadeo, 'Art 36' in A Tizzano (ed), *Trattati dell'Unione europea*, 2nd edn (Milano, Giuffrè, 2014) 597–598.

[28] This notion has been firstly framed in the famous *Cassis de Dijon* case, where the ECJ affirmed that an indistinctly applicable regulation on alcoholic products amounting to a restriction to imports under free movement of goods may be justified on grounds of the need to satisfy 'mandatory requirements' (Case 120/78 *Rewe v Bundesmonopolverwaltung für Branntwein* ECLI:EU:C:1979:42). As a result of the evolution of the case-law, the Court currently refers to 'mandatory requirements' as 'imperative requirements' or 'overriding reasons in the general interest' (C Barnard, *The Substantive Law of the EU: The Four Freedoms*, 2nd edn (Oxford, Oxford University Press, 2007) 115).

[29] Among many: Case C-488/20 *Delfarma* ECLI:EU:C:2021:956, para 38; Case C-602/19 *Kohlpharma* ECLI:EU:C:2020:804, para 41; Case C-333/08 *Commission v France* ECLI:EU:C:2010:44, para 90. On criminal measures specifically, see J Öberg, 'Conceptualising Proportionality and Criminal Sanctions in EU Law: Three Different Visions' in L Grossio, S Montaldo and V Mitsilegas (eds), *Proportionality of Criminal Penalties in EU Law* (Oxford, Hart Publishing, 2025) 10–11.

[30] Case C-55/94 *Gebhard v Consiglio dell'Ordine degli Avvocati e Procuratori di Milano* ECLI:EU:C:1995:411, para 37. For an analysis of the *Gebhard* formula's relevance in criminal matters, see: S Miettinen, *Criminal Law and Policy in the European Union* (London, Routledge, 2013) 125 *et seq.*

[31] On the threefold proportionality test derived from German administrative law, see Section I(A) of the Introduction to this book.

[32] Among many, see: Case C-663/18 *B S and C A [Commercialisation du cannabidiol (CBD)]* ECLI:EU:C:2020:938, para 83; Case C-591/17 *Austria v Germany* ECLI:EU:C:2019:504, para 122.

[33] Case C-126/15 *Commission v Portugal* ECLI:EU:C:2017:504, para 64. In the same vein, see: Case C-727/17 *ECO-WIND Construction* ECLI:EU:C:2020:393, para 81.

[34] As recently underlined by scholarship, this assessment is, in principle, demanded to domestic courts in the context of preliminary reference procedures, while the ECJ embraces balancing under

C. The Fundamental Rights Dimension of Proportionality

Following the profound influence exercised by the ECHR (i), proportionality has emerged as the key criterion for fundamental rights adjudication under the Charter (ii). The latter instrument gives distinct significance to proportionality in substantive criminal law. Indeed, Article 49(3) of the Charter enshrines retrospective proportionality of penalties within the catalogues of fundamental rights secured by EU law. Given its peculiar theoretical features, that provision deserves separate consideration (iii).

i. The ECHR's Influence: The Equivalence Clause Enshrined in Article 52(3) of the Charter and the Dichotomy between Absolute and Conditional Rights

The origins of fundamental rights adjudication under EU law goes back to the 1969 ECJ judgment in *Stauder*, recognising for the first time that human rights are part of the EEC legal order as general principles.[35] The subsequent ruling in *Nold* enshrined international human rights obligations binding for the Member States as a source of inspiration for framing fundamental rights as general principles of EU law.[36] In that context, the ECHR entails a profound influence, as it enjoys 'special significance' for fundamental rights protection in EU law.[37]

Following the Treaty of Lisbon's entry into force, the Charter enjoys the same legal status as the Treaties, thus representing the formal source of fundamental rights protection in the EU legal order.[38] According to Article 6(2) TEU, the system

proportionality *stricto sensu* when scrutinising domestic measures vis-à-vis internal market freedoms in infringement proceedings (Palladino (n 20) 113).

[35] Case 29/69 *Stauder v Stadt Ulm* ECLI:EU:C:1969:57, para 7 of the Grounds of judgment. The ruling grounded fundamental rights on Member States' common constitutional traditions: being individual rights protected in each domestic legal system, the same rights shall be afforded legal protection in the EC one, thus emerging as general principles.

[36] Case 4/73 *Nold KG v Commission* ECLI:EU:C:1974:51, para 13.

[37] Opinion 2/13 *Adhésion de l'Union à la CEDH* ECLI:EU:C:2014:2454, para 37, which reiterates judgments in Case C-260/89 *ERT* ECLI:EU:C:1991:254, para 41 and Case C-402/05 P and C-415/05 P *Kadi and Al Barakaat International Foundation v Council and Commission* ECLI:EU:C:2008:461, para 283; Case C-222/84 *Johnston v Chief Constable of the Royal Ulster Constabulary* ECLI:EU:C:1986:206, para 18.

[38] Charter of Fundamental Rights of the European Union [2016] OJ C202/389. For a legal analysis of the implications of equating the Charter to the Treaties in the hierarchy of sources of the EU legal order, see: S Iglesias Sánchez, 'The Court and the Charter: The impact of the entry into force of the Lisbon Treaty on the ECJ's approach to fundamental rights' (2012) 49 *CML Rev* 1565; D Sarmiento, 'Who's Afraid of the Charter? The Court of Justice, National Courts and the New Framework of Fundamental Rights Protection in Europe' (2013) 50 *CML Rev* 267; G Di Federico, 'Fundamental Rights in the EU: Legal Pluralism and Multi-Level Protection After the Lisbon Treaty' in G Di Federico (ed), *The EU Charter of Fundamental Rights: From Declaration to Binding Instrument* (Dordrecht, Springer, 2011); L Daniele, 'Carta dei diritti fondamentali dell'Unione europea e Trattato di Lisbona' in G Venturini and S Bariatti (eds), *Diritti individuali e giustizia internazionale – Individual Rights and International Justice – droits individuels et justice international. Liber Fausto Pocar* (Milano, Giuffrè, 2009). Still, this development does not deprive the ECJ of its role in refining the content and

of fundamental rights adjudication should be completed by the EU accession to the ECHR.[39] Following the failed attempt in 2014,[40] a new accession treaty has been recently negotiated, and a provisional agreement has been reached in 2023.[41] Should the latter be concluded, the ECHR would become a formal source of obligations for the Union in fundamental rights protection.

Pending the Union's accession, the ECHR and Strasbourg Court's case-law still influence fundamental rights adjudication under EU law. On the one hand, Article 6(3) TEU affirms that the rights enshrined in the ECHR must be regarded as general principles of the EU legal order, not differently from those deriving from Member States' common constitutional traditions. As outlined in literature, this provision shall be construed as a tool for securing individual rights other than those codified in the Charter.[42]

On the other hand, the Charter establishes a legal connection between the rights secured therein and those enshrined in the Convention. Indeed, Article 52(3) of the Charter provides an equivalence clause: Charter provisions shall be interpreted in line with the ECHR insofar as corresponding to a right secured therein, without prejudice for the possibility of recognising a higher level of protection. Provided that most rights enshrined in the Charter are analogous to ECHR provisions, the latter exercises a key influence on their scope and the conditions under which they may be lawfully limited.[43] Therefore, glancing at the machinery for fundamental rights adjudication under the Convention system is pivotal to contextualising the key features of proportionality under the Charter.

Within the ECHR system, proportionality constitutes the tool for ensuring a 'fair balance' between public and individual interests, thus resulting in a ground

level of protection afforded by fundamental rights under EU law, by interpreting both Charter provisions and general principles derived from common constitutional traditions and the ECHR (on this point, see B Nascimbene and I Anrò, 'La tutela dei diritti fondamentali nella giurisprudenza della Corte di giustizia: nuove sfide, nuove prospettive' (2017) 27 *Rivista italiana di diritto pubblico comunitario* 323, 330).

[39] On this topic, see M Parodi, *L'adesione dell'Unione europea alla CEDU: dinamiche sostanziali e prospettive formali* (Napoli, Edizioni Scientifiche Italiane, 2020); Amalfitano (n 5) 35 *et seq.*

[40] Opinion 2/13 *Adhésion de l'Union à la CEDH* ECLI:EU:C:2014:2454. Among wide scholarly debate, see I Anrò, *L'adesione dell'Unione europea alla CEDU. L'evoluzione dei sistemi di tutela dei diritti fondamentali in Europa* (Milano, Giuffrè, 2015) 273 *et seq*; B De Witte and Š Imamović, 'Opinion 2/13 on Accession to the ECHR: Defending the EU Legal Order against a Foreign Human Rights Court' (2015) 5 *EL Rev* 683; E Perillo, 'Adhésion à la Convention européenne des droits de l'homme, deux ans plus tard' (2016) 10 *Journal de droit européen* 377; B Pirker and S Reitemeyer, 'Between Discursive and Exclusive Autonomy – Opinion 2/13, the Protection of Fundamental Rights and the Autonomy of EU Law' in *Cambridge Yearbook of European Legal Studies* (Cambridge, Cambridge University Press, 2015).

[41] For a comprehensive analyisis of the draft accession instruments, see N Bergamaschi, 'Prime considerazioni sul nuovo tentativo di adesione dell'Unione alla CEDU e sui suoi principali ostacoli' (2024) 1 *Rivista Quaderni AISDUE* 1.

[42] N Lazzerini, *La Carta dei diritti fondamentali dell'Unione europea. I limiti di applicazione* (Milano, Franco Angeli, 2018) 60, 74.

[43] *ibid*, 67. The close link between the Charter and the ECHR is reflected in the ECJ case-law, which manifests a growing emphasis on the Strasbourg Court's jurisprudence: on this point, see LS Rossi, 'I rapporti fra la Carta dei diritti fondamentali e la CEDU nella giurisprudenza delle rispettive Corti' in *Annali AISDUE* (Napoli, Editoriale Scientifica, 2020) 43–44.

for reviewing the legality of Contracting Parties' limitations to the enjoyment of fundamental rights.[44] The operation of proportionality under the ECHR implies that the enjoyment of fundamental rights can be lawfully limited subject to some conditions. This finding is a crucial feature of the European understanding of human rights as opposed to the Anglo-American tradition. The latter presupposes that 'rights are absolute but for the exceptional circumstances in which they may be limited'. Conversely, under the European legal tradition, 'rights are limited but for the exceptional circumstances in which they are absolute'.[45] Following the first perspective, limiting rights is an interpretive activity, as their enjoyment cannot be affected by acts of public authorities. Therefore, any conflict between the public powers and human rights shall be settled by delimiting their sphere of protection in the concrete case. Conversely, the continental legal tradition – of which the ECHR represents a prominent example – is characterised by a different understanding. In principle, the sphere of protection afforded by fundamental rights does not represent an impenetrable fortress for public authorities. Limitations to the enjoyment of fundamental rights may be lawfully enacted, provided some imperative requirements are met.

The Convention does not enshrine a general clause defining under which circumstances the enjoyment of rights may be legitimately restricted. Conditions for legitimacy are included in each provision establishing a 'relative' or 'conditional' right. These are, in particular, the right to respect for private and family life,[46] freedom of thought, conscience and religion,[47] freedom of expression,[48] freedom of assembly and association,[49] the right to property,[50] freedom of movement[51] and individual rights against the expulsion of aliens.[52] While each ground for limitations entails some peculiarities, all of them have been interpreted by the Strasbourg Court as postulating proportionality scrutiny.[53]

[44] In this regard, see: A Mowbray, 'A Study of the Principle of Fair Balance in the Jurisprudence of the European Court of Human Rights' (2010) 10 *Human Rights Law Review* 289.

[45] J Greene, 'Rights As Trumps ?' (2018) 1 *Harvard Law Review* 28, 30.

[46] Art 8 ECHR.

[47] Art 9 ECHR.

[48] Art 10 ECHR.

[49] Art 11 ECHR.

[50] Art 1 of Protocol No 1 to the European Convention for the Protection of Human Rights and Fundamental Freedoms (Paris, 20 March 1952) [1952] CETS No 9.

[51] Art 2(3)–(4) of Protocol No 4 to the European Convention for the Protection of Human Rights and Fundamental Freedoms Securing Certain Rights and Freedoms Other Than Those Already Included in the Convention and in the First Protocol Thereto (Strasbourg, 16 September 1963) [1963] CETS No 46.

[52] Art 1(2) of Protocol No 7 to the European Convention for the Protection of Human Rights and Fundamental Freedoms (Strasbourg, 22 November 1984) [1984] CETS No 117.

[53] Among many, see S Van Drooghenbroeck, *La proportionnalité dans le droit de la Convention européenne des droits de l'homme : prendre l'idée simple au sérieux* (Bruxelles, Presses de l'Université Saint-Louis, 2001) 79, 81–82; J Christoffersen, *Fair Balance: Proportionality, Subsidiarity and Primarity in the European Convention on Human Rights* (Leiden, Brill-Nijhoff, 2009) 76–77. In particular, since the well-renowned *Handyside* ruling, the ECtHR has consistently held that the enjoyment of conditional rights may be limited to meet 'a pressing social need', meaning 'amongst other things, that every "formality", "condition", "restriction" or "penalty" imposed in this sphere must be proportionate to the legitimate aim pursued' (*Handyside v The United Kingdom* (1972) Series A No 24, para 49).

At the same time, the ECtHR acknowledges that some rights are absolute. This is the case of several ECHR provisions – such as the ones enshrining the prohibition of torture and inhuman or degrading treatments or punishments,[54] as well as the prohibition of forced labour and slavery,[55] the right to no punishment without law[56] and the prohibition of collective expulsion of aliens.[57] Whether the enjoyment of an individual right could be lawfully limited represents the dividing line between absolute and conditional rights. In principle, absolute rights do not leave room for holding any interference legitimate on a proportionality basis. Their adjudication consists of an interpretive operation similar to the Anglo-American tradition, thereby delimiting the scope of application of the right under scrutiny. Still, the latter is defined on a case-by-case basis,[58] thus leaving room for the Strasbourg Court to exercise a balancing assessment – defined in literature as '*proportionnalité-interprétation*'[59] – between the interests at stake.

Thanks to the equivalence clause provided by Article 52(3) of the Charter, the dichotomy between absolute and conditional rights also characterises EU law. Differently from the Convention, the Charter enshrines in Article 52(1) a general clause defining under which conditions the enjoyment of rights may be lawfully limited. In principle, that clause may apply to all provisions of the Charter. However, by taking inspiration from the ECtHR case-law, even the pre-Lisbon case-law had recognised that certain fundamental rights are absolute. That is the case, for instance, of the *Schmidberger* ruling, where an *obiter dictum* held that the prohibition of torture and inhuman or degrading treatments or punishments also enshrined in Article 3 ECHR does not admit any restriction.[60] In the post-Lisbon era, that stance is crystallised by the operation of Article 52(3) of the Charter: EU fundamental rights corresponding to those regarded as absolute under the Convention admit no restriction even under the Charter. *Aranyosi and Căldăraru* is a prominent example in this regard.[61] In that case, the referring court sought to ascertain whether the execution of a European arrest warrant pursuant

[54] Art 3 ECHR. The absolute nature of that provision clearly emerges also from the *travaux préparatoires* of ECHR, which states that 'torture cannot be permitted by any purpose of whatsoever, neither by extracting evidence for saving life nor even for the safety of the State' (see: Council of Europe, *Collected Edition of the 'Travaux Préparatoires' of the European Convention on Human Rights*, Vol. 1: Preparatory Commission of the Council of Europe, Committee of Ministers, Consultative Assembly, 11 May – 8 September 1949 (The Hague, Martinus Nijhoff, 1998) 254).

[55] Art 4 ECHR.

[56] Art 7 ECHR.

[57] Art 4 of Protocol No 4 to the European Convention for the Protection of Human Rights and Fundamental Freedoms Securing Certain Rights and Freedoms Other Than Those Already Included in the Convention and in the First Protocol Thereto (Strasbourg, 16 September 1963) [1963] CETS No 46.

[58] Among many, see Christoffersen (n 53) 83.

[59] Van Drooghenbroeck (n 53) 118–120.

[60] Case C-112/00 *Schmidberger* ECLI:EU:C:2003:333, paras 79–80. The Court relied on that consideration to distinguish between absolute rights and those invoked in that case, namely, freedom of assembly and freedom of expression, which can be lawfully limited subject to certain conditions. In literature, see A Tancredi, 'L'emersione dei diritti fondamentali "assoluti" nella giurisprudenza comunitaria' (2006) 89 *Rivista di Diritto internazionale* 644.

[61] Joined Cases C-404/15 e C-659/15 PPU *Aranyosi and Căldăraru* ECLI:EU:C:2016:198.

to Framework Decision 2002/584/JHA may be refused in case detention conditions in the requesting Member States are so serious as to expose the surrender to inhuman or degrading treatment in violation of Article 4 of the Charter.[62] To uphold the absolute nature of Article 4 of the Charter, the Court not only recalled the *obiter dictum* in *Schmidberger* but also added that this finding 'is confirmed by Article 3 ECHR, to which Article 4 of the Charter corresponds'.[63]

ii. Proportionality in Fundamental Rights Adjudication under Article 52(1) of the Charter

The influence of the ECHR also extends to the test for reviewing limitations to the enjoyment of conditional rights.[64] In the pre-Lisbon era, the ECJ proportionality assessment for fundamental rights adjudication has not always been consistent. In some cases, the Luxembourg Court applied the ECtHR proportionality technique based on the threefold suitability, necessity and proportionality *stricto sensu* test. On other occasions, the Court took a different path and limited its scrutiny to domestic arrangements affecting the very essence of the right in question.[65] Several ECJ judgments witness a merger between these two approaches. As an example, in *Hauer* the Luxembourg Court deemed it

> necessary to examine whether the restrictions introduced by the provisions in dispute in fact correspond to objectives of general interest pursued by the Community or whether, with regard to the aim pursued, they constitute a disproportionate and intolerable interference with the rights of the owner, impinging upon the very substance of the right.[66]

This formula became a refrain in the ECJ case-law, thus anticipating the structure of the general clause later enshrined in the Charter.[67] Article 52(1) sought to codify

[62] Among the wide scholarly analysis of the ruling, see S Montaldo, 'On a Collision Course! Mutual Recognition, Mutual Trust and the Protection of Fundamental Rights in the Recent Case-Law of the Court of Justice' (2016) 1 *European Papers* 965; G Anagnostaras, 'Mutual Confidence Is Not Blind Trust! Fundamental Rights Protection and the Execution of the European Arrest Warrant: Aranyosi and Căldăraru' (2016) 53 *CML Rev* 1675; S Gáspár-Szilágyi, 'Joined Cases Aranyosi and Căldăraru: Converging Human Rights Standards, Mutual Trust and a New Ground for Postponing a European Arrest Warrant' (2016) 24 *European Journal of Crime, Criminal Law and Criminal Justice* 197; A Lazowski, 'The Sky Is Not the Limit: Mutual Trust and Mutual Recognition Après Aranyosi and Căldăraru' (2018) 14 *Croatian Yearbook of European Law and Policy* 2; N Lazzerini, 'Gli obblighi in materia di protezione dei diritti fondamentali come limite all'esecuzione del mandato di arresto europeo: la sentenza Aranyosi e Căldăraru' (2016) 10 *Diritti umani e diritto internazionale* 445.

[63] Joined Cases C-404/15 e C-659/15 PPU *Aranyosi and Căldăraru* ECLI:EU:C:2016:198, para 86.

[64] In this regard, see: S Peers and S Prechal, 'Article 52 – Scope and Interpretation of Rights and Principles' in S Peers, T Hervey, J Kenner and A Ward (eds), *The EU Charter of Fundamental Rights: A Commentary*, 2nd edn (Oxford, Hart Publishing, 2021) 1617, 1619.

[65] Among extensive case-law, see: Case 4/73 *Nold KG v Commission* ECLI:EU:C:1974:51, para 14. For a discussion over the definition of the boundaries of the 'essence of the right', see Section IV(A)(iii) below in this chapter.

[66] Case 44/79 *Hauer v Land Rheinland-Pfalz* ECLI:EU:C:1979:290, para 23.

[67] In literature, among many, see: P Manzini, 'La portata dei diritti garantiti dalla Carta dell'Unione europea: problemi interpretativi posti dall'art. 52' in LS Rossi (ed), *Carta dei diritti fondamentali e Costituzione dell'Unione europea* (Milano, Giuffrè, 2002) 129. Some authors also underlined that

the proportionality test applicable to any EU or national measure interfering with the enjoyment of Charter rights. According to the wording of Article 52(1), such measures shall (i) be provided for by law; (ii) be genuinely suitable to attain a general interest recognised by the Treaties or to protect the rights and freedoms of other; (iii) be necessary in this respect; and (iv) respect the essence of the right.[68]

As far as the (i) criterion is concerned, the ECJ has scarcely made application of the 'provided by law' paradigm in its case-law.[69] In fact, the reasoning of the Luxembourg Court appears to be mainly centred on the limits of EU and domestic authorities' discretion vis-à-vis fundamental rights rather than the formal requirements of the act under scrutiny.[70] However, the ECJ took inspiration from the corresponding ECtHR case-law in that regard. The Strasbourg Court has established a qualitative assessment of the source posing a limitation to fundamental rights. This approach entails a substantive rather than formal evaluation.[71] To meet the 'provided for by law' requirement, the measure shall be sufficiently clear and accessible to allow individuals concerned to foresee in which circumstances it will apply. Building upon the ECtHR findings, the ECJ affirmed that 'the legal basis which permits the interference with those rights must itself define the scope of the limitation on the exercise of the right concerned'.[72]

The (ii) suitability requirement entails that the measure is adequate for attaining a legitimate general interest under the Treaties. This test is twofold: firstly, the justifying aim shall be 'recognised by the Union'; secondly, the measure must genuinely meet that objective. By so doing, Article 52(1) designs a broad

the Charter provision follows in essence the ECtHR approach as defined by the Strasbourg Court's case-law. Among many, see: AW Heringa and L Verhey, 'The EU Charter: Text and Structure' (2001) 8 *Maastricht Journal of European and Comparative Law* 11.

[68] In literature, see: D Triantafyllou, 'The European Charter of Fundamental Rights and the "Rule of Law": Restricting Fundamental Rights by Reference' (2002) 39 *CML Rev* 53; F Ferraro and N Lazzerini, 'Art. 52 – Portata e interpretazione dei diritti e dei principi' in R Mastroianni, O Pollicino, S Allegrezza, F Pappalardo and O Razzolini (eds), *Carta dei diritti fondamentali dell'Unione europea* (Milano, Giuffrè, 2017). Notwithstanding the absence of express references to proportionality *stricto sensu*, Van Drooghenbroeck and Rizcallah underly that the definition of proportionality enshrined in Art 52(1) of the Charter stems from the threefold proportionality test (S Van Drooghenbroeck and C Rizcallah, 'Article 52-1. Limitations aux droits garantis' in F Picod, C Rizcallah and S Van Drooghenbroeck (eds), *Charte de droits fondamentaux de l'Union européenne: Commentire article par article* (Bruxelles, Bruylant, 2023) 1371).

[69] Peers and Prechal (n 64) 1625.

[70] P Mori, 'La "qualità" della legge e la clausola generale di limitazione dell'art. 52, par. 1, della Carta dei diritti fondamentali dell'UE', in *Scritti in onore di Giuseppe Tesauro* (Napoli, Editoriale Scientifica, 2014) 507. For some references in the ECtHR case-law, see *Sunday Times v The United Kingdom* (1979) Series A No 30, para 49; *Halford v The United Kingdom* ECHR 1997 – III, para 49; *Centro Europa 7 S.r.l. and Di Stefano v Italy* App No 38433/09 (ECtHR, 7 June 2012), para 140; *Delfi AS v Estonia* App No 64569/09 (ECtHR, 10 October 2013), para 120; *Afgan Mammadov v Azerbaijan* App No 43327/14 (ECtHR, 14 November 2024), para 58.

[71] Mori (n 70) 507; F Sudre, L Milano, B Pastre-Belda and A Schahmaneche, *Droit européen et international des droits de l'homme*, 16th edn (Paris, Presses Universitaires de France, 2023) 205–206. With respect to EU acts, the ECJ recognised that even a Commission Implementing Regulation must be regarded as 'provided for by law' pursuant to Article 52(1) of the Charter (in particular, see Joined Cases C-92/09 and C-93/09 *Volker und Markus Schecke and Eifert* ECLI:EU:C:2010:662, para 66).

[72] Case C-311/18 *Facebook Ireland and Schrems* ECLI:EU:C:2020:559, para 175. On the same point, see also Case C-401/19 *Poland v Parliament and Council* ECLI:EU:C:2022:297, para 64.

category of legitimate aims, including EU and domestic objectives, provided that they are 'recognised' by the Treaties as legitimate.[73] In addition to legitimate aims, Article 52(1) of the Charter allows the EU and the Member States to limit the enjoyment of a given right to protect other rights and freedoms. This provision outlines a 'conflict of rights' scenario: protecting a given right to the fullest extent would entail a curtailment of a different one.[74] In that context, it is interesting to note that the express reference to 'freedoms' entails the inclusion of the four EU internal market freedoms within the legitimate grounds justifying a restriction to the enjoyment of an individual right.[75]

The (iii) necessity requirement postulates an assessment based on the 'least restrictive means' test. The contested measure is legitimate only if no less restrictive alternative for the enjoyment of Charter rights would be available. Finally, Article 52(1) compels EU and national authorities to (iv) respect the essence of the right. This requirement, derived from the pre-Lisbon review of limitations to fundamental rights, enjoys renewed relevance under the Charter. The 'essence of the right' emerges as the ultimate boundary for any limitation to be lawful. Even if the 'provided for by law', suitability and necessity requirements were fulfilled, an EU or domestic measure, in any case, could never affect the very essence of the right in question.[76] As the analysis of judicial practice will show,[77] defining the boundaries of the inviolable core of fundamental rights represents a critical issue that the ECJ has only recently started delving into under the edge of Article 52(1) of the Charter.

iii. Proportionality of Criminal Sanctions: The Uneasy Nature of Article 49(3) of the Charter

Proportionality has a further declination under the Charter, but specific to the substantive criminal law domain. Indeed, Article 49(3) therein encapsulates the retrospective declination of that principle, as derived from the criminal law

[73] For a systematisation of the various interests recognised as legitimate under Art 52(1) of the Charter by the ECJ see, among many: K Lenaerts, 'Exploring the Limits of the EU Charter of Fundamental Rights' (2012) 8 *European Constitutional Law Review* 375, 391–392; R Cisotta, 'Brevi note sulla giurisprudenza sull'art. 52, par. 1 della Carta dei diritti fondamentali dell'UE in materia di limitazioni ai diritti fondamentali … con uno sguardo in avanti' (2021) 14 *Osservatorio sulle fonti* 19, 48–51.

[74] Pocar and Baruffi (n 15) 1793.

[75] Peers and Prechal (n 64) 1629. The same authors point out, however, that securing EU fundamental freedoms may also fall within the scope of 'objectives of general interest recognised by the Union'. In fact, this aim uncontestably represents an EU objective recognised by the Treaties.

[76] In this light, the obligation to respect the essence of fundamental rights has been defined as the 'limitation to the limitations' to the enjoyment of Charter rights (Ferraro and Lazzerini (n 68) 1065). Within the scholarly debate on the 'essence of the right' concept, see: K Lenaerts, 'Limits on Limitations: The Essence of Fundamental Rights in the EU' (2019) 20 *German Law Journal* 779; M Brkan, 'The Concept of Essence of Fundamental Rights in the EU Legal Order: Peeling the Onion to Its Core' (2018) 20 *European Constitutional Law Review* 332; F de Cecco, 'The Trouble with Trumps: On How (and Why) Not To Define the Core of Fundamental Rights' (2023) 60 *CML Rev* 1551.

[77] See Section IV(A)(iii) below in this chapter.

understanding of proportionality.[78] In particular, that provision postulates a relationship of commensurability between criminal sanctions and the seriousness of respective offences.

The codification of retrospective proportionality of criminal penalties in the Charter is a consequence of its unanimous recognition in domestic criminal systems. In fact, Article 49(3) of the Charter reflects a principle rooted in the Member States' common constitutional traditions.[79] However, that provision does not provide insights into how the proportionality of criminal penalties shall be applied in concrete cases. Against this background, how to construe Article 49(3) of the Charter represents one of the main streams of analysis in the subsequent chapters of this work.

To that aim, some preliminary considerations may be briefly anticipated here. Similarly to the proportionality clauses previously analysed, Article 49(3) of the Charter serves a twofold purpose. It constitutes a requirement governing the actions of the EU and domestic criminal legislators and a ground for reviewing the latter. Concerning the material scope of that provision, both EU and national criminal measures falling under the scope of EU law must comply with Article 49(3).[80] As the EU is nowadays empowered to adopt minimum rules for the definition of offences and penalties under Article 83 TFEU, harmonising criminal penalties is subject to the proportionality requirement under Article 49(3) of the Charter. Moreover, domestic criminal sanctions may be subject to review based on this provision if they fall under the scope of application of the Charter pursuant to Article 51(1) therein. From a horizontal perspective, both substantive criminal law provisions and criminal sanctions imposed in concrete cases fall under the scope of the provision at stake.

Article 49(3) has a different nature and deserves separate consideration than the other dimensions of proportionality under EU law. Indeed, it purports to

[78] On the concept and implications of retrospective proportionality in the criminal law discourse, see Section III(B)(ii) of Chapter 2. As outlined in literature, this provision manifests a retributivist rationale. Among many, see M Fichera, 'EU Fundamental Rights and the European Arrest Warrant' in S Douglas-Scott and N Hatzis (eds), *Research Handbook on EU Law and Human Rights*, 2nd edn (Cheltenham, Edward Elgar Publishing, 2019) 428.

[79] JB Banach-Gutierrez and C Harding, 'Fundamental Rights in European Criminal Justice: An Axiological Perspective' (2012) 20 *European Journal of Crime, Criminal Law and Criminal Justice* 239, 259. In the same line of reasoning, Śliwiński contends that proportionality of criminal penalties 'forms part of the common legacy of the Western World' (E Śliwiński, 'Principle of Proportionality as a Threat to Criminal-Law-Related Fundamental Rights' (2023) 14 *New Journal of European Criminal Law* 327, 327.

[80] V Mitsilegas and E Billis, 'Article 49 – Principles of Legality and Proportionality of Criminal Offences and Penalties' in S Peers, T Hervey, J Kenner and A Ward (eds), *The EU Charter of Fundamental Rights: A Commentary*, 2nd edn (Oxford, Hart Publishing, 2021)1498–1499. This finding follows from the scope of application of the Charter as defined by Art 51(1) therein. The present study does not delve into a systematic analysis of the Charter's scope of application in the criminal law field, as a similar assessment would fall outside of the scope of the research question. For a comprehensive study of the scope of application of the Charter, among many, see Lazzerini (n 42).

identify which penalties could represent a legitimate punitive response to a given offence, thus obliging the former to be proportionate to the latter. In that respect, Article 49(3) does not shape a relationship of commensurability between penalties and the attainment of a legitimate aim. The proportionality bond which it designed is inherently backwards-looking, as the legitimacy of penalties is measured against the seriousness of the committed offence.

It follows that Article 49(3) departs from the EU conceptualisation of proportionality, which it shall be kept separate from. Article 49(3) of the Charter is the codification in the EU legal order of the criminal law retrospective understanding of proportionality.

IV. Multiple Dimensions, One Common Proportionality Matrix in EU Law

The three dimensions of the EU concept of proportionality have distinct features, but they all adhere to a unifying theoretical understanding. This finding emerges from assessing the structure (A), object (B), and terms (C) of the proportionality relationship.

A. The Threefold Structure of Proportionality as Fine-grained by the ECJ Case-law

Except for Article 49(3) of the Charter, the three dimensions of proportionality under EU law are built upon a common matrix: the threefold test derived from German legal tradition. However, the Luxembourg Court has reworked it by enhancing some peculiarities in assessing the suitability (i), necessity (ii) and proportionality *stricto sensu* (iii) requirements.

i. The Suitability of a Measure to Fulfil a Legitimate Aim

An EU or domestic measure is suitable only if adequate for attaining a legitimate aim. The concept of suitability is functional: it requires establishing a rational link between the measure and the aim justifying the interference.[81]

The definition of 'legitimate' objectives requires closer attention. On the one hand, the objectives that the EU legislator can pursue in exercising its competencies are predefined by the Treaties. Similarly, EU primary law provisions on internal market freedoms list several legitimate aims justifying limitations to their

[81] A Barak, *Proportionality: Constitutional Rights and Their Limitations* (Cambridge, Cambridge University Press, 2012) 303.

enjoyment.[82] However, the ECJ widened that category, as indistinctly applicable measures can be justified by 'overriding reasons in the general interest'. The boundaries of this ground cannot be defined a priori and are contextual by nature. The Luxembourg Court ascertains whether the objective of the measure at stake may be qualified as 'overriding' vis-à-vis the protection of individual interests in the light of the circumstances of each case.[83] To provide an example, in *Viking*[84] and *Laval* the ECJ held that a restriction to the right of free movement aimed at securing the workers' right to take collective action may be justified by an overriding reason in the general interest.[85]

On the other hand, when the principle of proportionality is invoked for fundamental rights adjudication under the Charter, the perimeter of the 'legitimate aim' paradigm is even broader. Unlike ECHR provisions establishing conditional rights,[86] Article 52(1) of the Charter does not provide a list of lawful grounds for justification. Any measure interfering with the enjoyment of a Charter right may be justified insofar as suitable for attaining a 'general interest recognised by the Union or the need to protect the rights and freedoms of others'. The ECJ has usually maintained quite a liberal approach towards identifying potential legitimate aims under Article 52(1) of the Charter. Indeed, the Court has construed this category as not limited to the purposes expressly referred to in the Treaties' provisions.[87] As a result, some authors have warned that the range of grounds capable of justifying restrictions to the enjoyment of fundamental rights may be limitless.[88]

Suitability, however, does not represent the decisive step of the proportionality test.[89] It frames an overinclusive category of arrangements entailing different degrees of interference with the protected interest or right.[90] Thus, the core of the test lies in the necessity and proportionality *stricto sensu* assessments.[91]

[82] See Section III(B) above in this chapter.

[83] In literature, see: W Sauter, 'Proportionality in EU Law: A Balancing Act?' (2013) 15 *Cambridge Yearbook of European Legal Studies* 439, 463.

[84] Case C-438/05 *International Transport Workers' Federation and Finnish Seamen's Union v Viking Line ABP and OÜ Viking Line Eesti* ECLI:EU:C:2007:772, para 77, 84.

[85] Case C-341/05 *Laval un Partneri* ECLI:EU:C:2007:809, para 93.

[86] The ECHR defines a priori a list of grounds whose attainment may justify a limitation to the enjoyment of an individual right. Therefore, the perimeter of 'legitimate aims' depends on the specific limiting clause on which the proportionality test is based upon, since each of them provides for a slightly different number of grounds. Against this background, it must be verified whether the aim of a specific measure falls under the scope of one of the listed general aims. This is a hermeneutic operation, as it requires, firstly, to assess the scope of the legitimate aim codified in the ECHR and, subsequently, to verify whether the measure's aim may fall thereunder.

[87] Among many, see Peers and Prechal (n 64) 1630–1633.

[88] *ibid*, 1629.

[89] Among many: Emiliou (n 5) 191.

[90] Barak (n 81) 335.

[91] *ibid*, 337. As the author points out, this view seems to be shared also outside the European context, with particular reference to the case-law of the Israeli Supreme Court and the Canadian Supreme Court's one. In this regard, see: PW Hogg and AA Bushell, 'The Charter Dialogue between Courts and Legislatures (Or Perhaps the Charter of Rights Isn't Such a Bad Thing after All)' (1997) 35 *Osgoode Hall Law Journal* 187.

ii. The Necessity Requirement: A Dividing Line between EU and Domestic Measures

A suitable measure may entail an excessive sacrifice for countervailing interests. This profile calls into question the necessity criterion, according to which proportionate measures shall also represent the least restrictive means for attaining the aim pursued.[92] Together with proportionality *stricto sensu*, the necessity requirement represents the very heart of the proportionality test, since it allows to parameterise the measure to the sacrifice for individual interests it entails.[93]

That requirement plays a fundamental role in the ECJ scrutiny. By relying on the necessity assessment,[94] the ECJ leaves limited room for balancing under proportionality *stricto sensu*. On that basis, the proportionality test is sometimes exhausted by a functional assessment embodied by the necessity criterion. Still, the standard of review differs widely depending on the domestic or EU nature of the act subject to review. The Court's scrutiny is stringent for domestic measures interfering with the enjoyment of rights and freedoms secured by EU law. In this stream of case-law, a given arrangement qualifies as necessary only if it constitutes the least restrictive means to attain the legitimate aim pursued.[95] This stance has noteworthy consequences for the extent of Member States' discretion, which is remarkably reduced. Among several suitable arrangements, national authorities may only opt for that one entailing the least sacrifice for the individual's legal sphere.[96]

Conversely, the ECJ scrutiny of EU acts is usually characterised by a looser approach. The Court typically holds that 'in the exercise of the powers conferred on it the Community legislature must be allowed a *broad discretion* in areas in which its action involves political, economic and social choices and in which it is called

[92] As pointed out by Emiliou, the term 'necessity' shall not be construed according to its common meaning, namely, the need to pursue the aim at stake. In fact, public authorities are tendentially free to decide whether to pursue the legitimate aim at stake, thus deeming the measure under analysis as 'necessary' (Emiliou (n 5) 30).

[93] Notwithstanding the tendency to establish a conceptual coincidence between proportionality and necessity, the latter step is not capable itself to exhaust the proportionality control from a theoretical viewpoint. While the necessity test is based on the existence of potential factual alternatives, Alexy points out that proportionality *stricto sensu* takes into consideration whether legal alternatives may be available for striking a correct balance in the concrete case (S Cognetti, *Principio di proporzionalità. profili di teoria generale e di analisi sistematica* (Torino, Giappichelli, 2011) 224–225). Therefore, it may be held that the necessity test represents a partial manifestation of the proportionality principle (Ciciriello (n 10) 132).

[94] Tridimas (n 12) 139, 209.

[95] To provide some recent examples in case-law, see: Case C-452/20 *Agenzia delle dogane e dei monopoli and Ministero dell'Economia e delle Finanze* ECLI:EU:C:2022:111, paras 37–38; Case C-501/14 *EL-EM-2001* ECLI:EU:C:2016:777, para 39; Case C-394/20 *Finanzamt V (Successions – Abattement partiel et déduction des parts réservataires)* ECLI:EU:C:2021:1044, para 36; Case C-555/19 *Fussl Modestraße Mayr* ECLI:EU:C:2021:89, para 56; Case C-454/19 *ZW* ECLI:EU:C:2020:947, para 44.

[96] In this regard, see Sauter (n 83) 447–448. A Stone Sweet and J Mathews, 'Proportionality, Balancing and Global Constitutionalism' (2008) 47 *Columbia Journal of Transnational Law* 72, 75.

upon to undertake complex assessments and evaluations' (emphasis added).[97] The broad discretion paradigm confers on the EU a margin of manoeuvre justified, in the Court's view, by the complexity of the 'assessments and evaluations' exercised by the legislature. As outlined in literature, the ECJ has relied upon the 'broad discretion' paradigm in several policy fields, such as agriculture, fishery, transport, social, environmental policy and health protection.[98] What is more, this approach has been extended not only to acts adopted by the Parliament and the Council, but also to acts of other institutions, such as the European Central Bank (ECB). *Weiss* and *Gauweiler* are remarkable examples in this regard. In those cases, the Court enhanced the ECB's margin of discretion to justify its quantitative easing policy against pleas of disproportion.[99]

The 'broad discretion' paradigm decisively affects the Court's interpretation of the necessity requirement, resulting in a less severe criterion than the 'least restrictive means' test. Given the wide margin of appreciation the EU legislature enjoys, the ECJ adopts a self-restraint approach. When applying proportionality as a standard for judicial review of EU acts,

> the criterion to be applied is not whether a measure adopted in such an area was the only or the best possible measure, since its legality can be affected only if the measure is manifestly inappropriate having regard to the objectives which the competent institution(s) seek to pursue.[100]

The difference between this standard of review and the 'least restrictive means' test applied to domestic measures is straightforward. The 'manifestly inappropriate'

[97] Case C-58/08 *Vodafone and Others* ECLI:EU:C:2010:321, para 52. For similar affirmations in case-law, see: Case C-189/01 *Jippes and Others* ECLI:EU:C:2001:420, paras 82–83; Case C-491/01 *British American Tobacco (Investments) and Imperial Tobacco* ECLI:EU:C:2002:741, para 123; Joined Cases C-154/04 and C-155/04 *Alliance for Natural Health and Others* ECLI:EU:C:2005:449, para 52; Case C-558/07 *S.P.C.M. and Others* ECLI:EU:C:2009:430, para 42. In literature, see Adam and Tizzano (n 15) 497–498.

[98] *Ex multis*, see: TI Harbo, 'The Function of the Proportionality Principle in EU Law' (2010) 16 *European Law Journal* 158.

[99] Case C-493/17 *Weiss and Others* ECLI:EU:C:2018:1000, para 24; Case C-62/14 *Gauweiler and Others* ECLI:EU:C:2015:400, paras 68–69). For an analysis of the *Weiss – Gauweiler* saga between the ECJ and the German *Bundesvefassungsgericht*, among extensive scholarship, see: N De Boer and J Van't Klooster, 'The ECB, the Courts and the Issue of Democratic Legitimacy after Weiss' (2020) 57 *CML Rev* 1689.

[100] Case C-482/17 *Czech Republic v Parliament and Council*, Opinion of AG Sharpston, ECLI:EU:C:2019:321, para 84. In the same vein, see Case C-5/16 *Poland v Parliament and Council* ECLI:EU:C:2018:483, para 150; Case C-151/17 *Swedish Match* ECLI:EU:C:2018:938, para 36; Case C-380/03 *Germany v Parliament and Council* ECLI:EU:C:2006:772, para 145; Case C-84/94 *United Kingdom v Council* ECLI:EU:C:1996:431, para 58; Case C-233/94 *Germany v Parliament and Council* ECLI:EU:C:1997:231, para 56; Case C-157/96 *The Queen v Ministry of Agriculture, Fisheries and Food and Commissioners of Customs & Excise, ex parte National Farmers' Union and Others* ECLI:EU:C:1998:191, para 61. In literature, among many, see: Harbo (n 98) 158; M Jarvis, 'The Proportionality Test: Constructive Dialogue between the English and Scottish Courts' in P Koutrakos, NN Shuibhne and P Syrpis (eds), *Exceptions from EU Free Movement Law: Derogation, Justification and Proportionality* (Oxford, Hart Publishing, 2016) 267–268; G Tesauro, *Manuale di Diritto dell'Unione europea*, 4th edn (P De Pasquale and F Ferraro eds, Napoli, Editoriale Scientifica, 2023) 75.

standard designs a broader scope for the EU institutions to reconcile the legal interests at stake and, consequently, a higher scrutiny threshold.[101]

Against that dichotomy of standards between EU and domestic acts, since *Volker und Markus Schecke*[102] the ECJ case-law on data protection manifested an exception for the proportionality review of EU acts interfering with fundamental rights. *Digital Rights Ireland and Others* is an illustrative example in that respect.[103] This case concerned a preliminary reference on the validity of Directive 2006/24/EC on data retention.[104] Since this piece of secondary law required providers of electronic communications services and networks to retain a wide range of data for law enforcement purposes, the ECJ held that the Directive entails 'a particularly serious interference'[105] with the right to privacy under Article 7 of the Charter. In this context, no broad discretion may be left to the EU legislature to accommodate the need to fight against crime and the right to privacy. Therefore, 'review of that discretion should be strict'.[106] On that basis, the ECJ did not limit its scrutiny to 'manifestly inappropriate' arrangements; conversely, it verified whether Directive 2006/24/EC was 'strictly necessary'[107] for attaining the aim pursued.

This stance from the Court, further confirmed by subsequent rulings,[108] has inaugurated a renewed approach towards the proportionality review of acts of EU institutions. While the latter generally enjoy broad discretion in accommodating conflicting interests, those acts that severely interfere with fundamental

[101] As argued in the literature, the dichotomy between the 'manifestly inappropriate' and 'least restrictive means' standards follows from the different nature of interests at stake in the proportionality analysis. When reviewing EU acts, the clash between individual interests underlying the plea and public interests pursued by the Union's institutions warrants due consideration of the latter's margin of discretion. Therefore, a 'manifestly inappropriate' test applies in those circumstances. Conversely, the review of domestic acts *vis-à-vis* EU law entails a contrast between national and supranational public interests. Given the former's primacy, the Court carries out a strict necessity assessment (T Tridimas, 'Proportionality in Community Law: Searching for the Appropriate Standard of Scrutiny' in E Ellis (ed), *The Principle of Proportionality in the Laws of Europe* (Oxford, Hart Publishing, 1999) 66).

[102] Joined Cases C-92/09 and C-93/09 *Volker und Markus Schecke and Eifert* ECLI:EU:C:2010:662. On this point, in literature, see Peers and Prechal (n 64) 1635.

[103] Joined Cases C-293/12 and C-594/12 *Digital Rights Ireland and Others* ECLI:EU:C:2014:238. For an analysis of the judgment, see: A Arena, 'La Corte di giustizia sulla conservazione dei dati: quali conseguenze per le misure nazionali di recepimento? Note dall'Europa' (2014) 3 *Quaderni Costituzionali* 722; A Christofi, 'La jurisprudence de la Cour et du Tribunal de l'Union européenne. Chronique des arrêts. Arrêt « Digital Rights Ireland »' (2014) *Revue du droit de l'Union européenne* 399.

[104] Directive 2006/24/EC of the European Parliament and of the Council of 15 March 2006 on the Retention of Data Generated or Processed in Connection with the Provision of Publicly Available Electronic Communications Services or of Public Communications Networks and Amending Directive 2002/58/EC [2006] OJ L 105/54.

[105] Joined Cases C-293/12 and C-594/12 *Digital Rights Ireland and Others* ECLI:EU:C:2014:238, para 39.

[106] *ibid*, para 48.

[107] *ibid*, para 56.

[108] In particular, see: Case C-401/19 *Poland v Parliament and Council* ECLI:EU:C:2022:297, para 67; Case C-817/19 *Ligue des droits humains* ECLI:EU:C:2022:491, paras 115–117; Joined Cases C-37/20 and C-601/20 *Luxembourg Business Registers* ECLI:EU:C:2022:912, paras 64–65.

rights – particularly the rights to privacy and the protection of personal data – warrant a necessity assessment based on the 'least restrictive means' standard of review.[109]

iii. Proportionality Stricto Sensu *under EU Law and its Relationship with the 'Essence of the Right' Paradigm*

Proportionality *stricto sensu* represents the last step of the threefold proportionality test. Differently from the functional nature of the suitability and necessity assessments, proportionality *stricto sensu* is a balancing exercise.[110] Provided a measure constitutes a suitable and necessary means to attain the desired aim, that arrangement may be held proportionate only if it strikes a correct balance between the opposing interests. The role played by proportionality *stricto sensu* in EU law is particularly challenging. As shown in previous sections, the ECJ case-law witnesses an evolution in this regard, consisting of the progressive emergence of a proportionality test comparable to the German one, thus including reliance also on proportionality *stricto sensu*. As a result, this assessment is now enshrined in the judicial review of the exercise of EU powers, Member States' restrictions to the enjoyment of internal market freedoms, and limitations to the enjoyment of fundamental rights.

However, the ECJ case-law previously manifested a reticent approach to proportionality *stricto sensu*. Tridimas contended that this assessment was generally absent from the Court of Justice's case-law since its scrutiny is mainly based on suitability and necessity assessments.[111] At the same time, Emiliou proposed a conceptual equivalence between proportionality *stricto sensu* and the 'essence of the right' concept.[112] According to the author, assessing whether a given arrangement impairs 'the very substance of the right'[113] consists of a balancing exercise that is not substantially different from proportionality *stricto sensu*. In fact, if the measure under scrutiny infringes the core of a right, it cannot be deemed to strike a correct balance between competing interests, even if it represents a suitable and necessary measure to attain a legitimate purpose. Hence, according to Emiliou, the 'essence of the right' paradigm should be conceived as the transposition of proportionality *stricto sensu* in the EU legal order.

[109] On this point, in literature, see E Bjorge and J Zglinski, 'The Principle of Proportionality in EU Law and Its Domestic Application: *ni tout à fait le même, ni tout à fait un autre*' in KS Ziegler, PJ Neuvonen and V Moreno-Lax (eds), *Research Handbook on General Principles in EU Law: Constructing Legal Orders in Europe* (Cheltenham, Edward Elgar Publishing, 2022) 199–200.

[110] TI Harbo, *The Function of Proportionality Analysis in European Law* (Leiden-Boston, Brill Nijhoff, 2015) 22.

[111] Tridimas (n 12) 139.

[112] Emiliou (n 5) 191–193.

[113] Among many: Case C-238/20 *'Sātiņi-S' SIA* ECLI:EU:C:2022:57, para 35; Case C-393/19 *Okrazhna prokuratura – Haskovo and Apelativna prokuratura – Plovdiv* ECLI:EU:C:2021:8, para 53; Case C-686/18 *Adusbef and Others* ECLI:EU:C:2020:567, para 85.

This claim elicits further considerations on the relationship between proportionality *stricto sensu* and the essence of the right concept. Before the entry into force of the Charter, the ECJ usually deemed interferences with the enjoyment of individual rights incompatible with EU law only if they breached the very essence of that right. The traditional understanding of the 'essence of the right' paradigm established quite a high threshold for holding an individual right to be violated: only measures touching the right's core may be deemed unlawful. It may thus appear that the 'essence of the right' paradigm in the ECJ case-law stems from a different rationale compared to the one underpinning proportionality *stricto sensu*.

Conversely, the argument advanced by Emiliou suggests that the 'essence of the right' concept has evolved in the ECJ case-law from a stand-alone test to the final step of a proportionality test comprising suitability and necessity evaluations. From this perspective, its significance would change completely, and it could effectively bear some similarities to proportionality *stricto sensu*. The latter implies a regression in the legal reasoning: although suitable and necessary for attaining a legitimate aim, the measure under scrutiny still entails an excessive sacrifice for the interests secured by EU law.[114] This feature may fit well even with respect to the 'essence of the right' paradigm: although suitable and necessary to attain a legitimate aim, the measure is not proportionate since it infringes on the right's very essence.

Moreover, the ECJ case-law shows that defining the essence of the right's scope requires a contextual approach by considering (and weighting) all conflicting interests. In particular, the ECJ in *Wachauf* held that fundamental rights under EC law should be seen in relationship with their social function, an aspect which plays a pivotal role in defining their essence.[115] Consequently, the standard of review – namely, the boundaries of the essence of the right – shall reflect the nature of the right itself and the interests underpinning the case at stake.[116] On these grounds, postulating proximity between proportionality *stricto sensu* and the 'essence of the right' test may be theoretically convincing.

Judicial practice, however, discloses a different reality. The ECJ does not employ the 'essence of the right' test as the final step of proportionality scrutiny. The *Schrems* judgment is particularly instructive in this regard, as it constitutes the first case where the Court relied on a violation of the essence of the right to strike down an act of EU institutions.[117] In *Schrems*, the Court held that an act of EU institutions permitting generalised access to electronic communications

[114] Cognetti (n 93) 239–240.

[115] Case 5/88 *Wachauf* ECLI:EU:C:1989:321, para 18.

[116] Emiliou (n 5) 172.

[117] Case C-362/14 *Schrems* ECLI:EU:C:2015:650. That case concerned, in particular, the Commission Decision of 26 July 2000 Pursuant to Directive 95/46/EC of the European Parliament and of the Council on the Adequacy of the Protection Provided by the Safe Harbour Privacy Principles and Related Frequently Asked Questions Issued by the US Department of Commerce [2000] OJ L 215/7.

by public authorities is contrary to the essence of the right to respect for private life secured by Article 7 of the Charter.[118] Following the same reasoning, the Court held that any legislative arrangement not providing individuals with legal remedies for having access to their personal data or for obtaining their rectification or erasure does not respect the essence of the right to effective judicial protection under Article 47 of the Charter.[119] However, the ECJ did not consider the 'essence of the right' to be the final step of an overall proportionality assessment. Conversely, the Court construed the 'essence of the right' paradigm as a preliminary step before conducting the suitability and necessity tests. If a measure infringes the right's core, there is no need to apply proportionality;[120] if it does not represent a violation of the essence of the right, the Court continues its scrutiny by undergoing proportionality review. This approach is even more evident in *Digital Rights Ireland and Others*.[121] The ECJ assessed the validity of Directive 2006/24/EC on proportionality basis only after establishing that such a piece of legislation did not represent an infringement of the essence of the rights to privacy and data protection.[122]

A further element discloses a clear dividing line between proportionality *stricto sensu* and the 'essence of the right' paradigm. Indeed, the most recent case-law on fundamental rights adjudication referred to proportionality *stricto sensu* as a distinct assessment. To provide an explicative example, in *Luxembourg Business Registers* the Court held that 'an objective of general interest may not be pursued without having regard to the fact that it must be reconciled with the fundamental rights affected by the measure, by properly balancing the objective of general interest against the rights at issue, in order to ensure that the disadvantages caused by that measure are not disproportionate to the aims pursued'.[123] This approach to proportionality *stricto sensu* has primarily emerged in cases concerning serious interferences with fundamental rights, with particular emphasis on Articles 7 and 8 of the Charter.[124] This is not surprising: fundamental rights adjudication represents the perfect context for establishing a hierarchy between the objectives pursued by public authorities and weighing their importance against the seriousness of the

[118] Case C-362/14 *Schrems* ECLI:EU:C:2015:650, para 94.

[119] *ibid*, para 95. For a deeper account of the technique employed by the ECJ to identify the right's essence in this stream of case-law, see: Brkan (n 76).

[120] See: Lenaerts (n 76) 782; Ferraro and Lazzerini (n 68) 1065.

[121] Joined Cases C-293/12 and C-594/12 *Digital Rights Ireland and Others* ECLI:EU:C:2014:238.

[122] *ibid*, paras 39–40. In the same line of reasoning, see: Case C-470/21 *La Quadrature du Net and Others (and lutte contre la contrefaçon)* ECLI:EU:C:2024:370, para 70; Joined Cases C-511/18, C-512/18 and C-520/18 *La Quadrature du Net and Others* ECLI:EU:C:2020:791, para 121; Case C-401/19 *Poland v Parliament and Council* ECLI:EU:C:2022:297, para 80; Case C-203/15 *Tele2 Sverige* ECLI:EU:C:2016:970, para 101; Case C-258/14 *Florescu and Others* ECLI:EU:C:2017:448, para 55; Case C-190/16 *Fries* ECLI:EU:C:2017:513, para 38; Case C-650/13 *Delvigne* ECLI:EU:C:2015:648, para 48.

[123] Joined Cases C-37/20 and C-601/20 *Luxembourg Business Registers* ECLI:EU:C:2022:912, para 64.

[124] In this regard, see: Case C-140/20 *Commissioner of An Garda Síochána and Others* ECLI:EU:C:2022:258, paras 93–94; Case C-204/21 *Commission v Poland (Indépendance et vie privée des juges)* ECLI:EU:C:2023:442, paras 358–359.

interference with individual rights that they entail under proportionality *stricto sensu*.[125] Thus construed, the proportionality *stricto sensu* assessment carried out by the Luxembourg Court is highly contextual, as weighing is much dependent upon the circumstances of each case. However, this operation has allowed the Court to establish some criteria applicable to specific domains. For instance, in most recent cases concerning data retention the ECJ has reiterated that

> only action to combat serious crime and measures to prevent serious threats to public security are capable of justifying serious interference with the fundamental rights enshrined in Articles 7 and 8 of the Charter [...]. Accordingly, only non-serious interference with those fundamental rights may be justified by the objective of preventing, investigating, detecting and prosecuting criminal offences in general.[126]

Moreover, recent scholarship suggested that the weighting exercise between the importance of pursuing public interests and countervailing rights provides the ECJ with room for relying on findings developed by ECtHR.[127]

It follows that proportionality *stricto sensu* and the 'essence of the right' paradigm are two distinct techniques which pursue different functions under the ECJ proportionality reasoning. On the one hand, the 'essence of the rights' requirement is a precondition for a proportionality assessment of public authorities' measures vis-à-vis individual rights secured by the Charter. On the other hand, proportionality *stricto sensu* amounts to the third limb of the proportionality assessment that, while long neglected in the ECJ case-law, is currently gaining centrality.

B. Proportionality of What to What? A Matrix Principle and the Need for a Contextual Approach

As the previous section disclosed, the judicial application of the suitability, necessity, and proportionality *stricto sensu* requirements entails some differences, depending on each declination of the principle in the EU legal order and the circumstances of case. However, the ECJ review hinges on a holistic understanding of proportionality. In all its three dimensions under EU law – as a limit to the exercise of EU powers, as well as to measures interfering with internal market freedoms and with fundamental rights secured by the Charter – the principle establishes a legal relationship between conflicting interests to accommodate their respective realisation on objective and logical grounds, materialised by the threefold test just

[125] Case C-140/20 *Commissioner of An Garda Síochána and Others* ECLI:EU:C:2022:258, para 56.

[126] Case C-511/18 *La Quadrature du Net and Others* ECLI:EU:C:2020:791, para 140, as further recalled by Case C-140/20 *Commissioner of An Garda Síochána and Others* ECLI:EU:C:2022:258, para 59; Case C-162/22 *Lietuvos Respublikos generalinė prokuratūra* ECLI:EU:C:2023:631, para 37.

[127] Palladino (n 20) 203.

analysed. That accommodation is axiologically orientated: in line with the traditional understanding of proportionality, balancing between conflicting interests is intrinsically linked to the ideal of justice.[128]

Thus, the EU general principle of proportionality amounts to a common theoretical paradigm – or, to use the words of the ECJ President, Koen Lenaerts, a 'matrix'[129] – characterising each of its dimensions. Notwithstanding physiological discrepancies in its application, the threefold suitability, necessity, and proportionality *stricto sensu* test gives expression to a holistic principle ensuring just accommodation between opposing interests in the context of EU competencies, internal market freedoms and fundamental rights adjudication.

The different categories of conflicting interests remain to be assessed. However, the multifaceted nature of the EU principle of proportionality prevents us from advancing a general categorisation in this chapter. In fact, the principle may accommodate multiple categories of legal interests depending upon its declination in EU law. These are, respectively, the review of the exercise of EU competencies, of national derogation from internal market freedoms and fundamental rights under the Charter.[130]

Against this background, a contextual approach is required. Since this book is dedicated to the principle of proportionality of criminal offences and penalties, only the substantive criminal law context shall be considered here. However, this finding is insufficient for defining which categories of interests are at stake under the proportionality of criminal offences and penalties. Indeed, all the dimensions of the EU principle of proportionality are relevant to the substantive criminal law field. On the one hand, the enactment of offences and penalties at the domestic level may clash with the enjoyment of either EU internal market freedoms or fundamental rights under the Charter. On the other hand, the harmonisation of substantive criminal law is subject to the proportionality principle regulating the exercise of the Union competencies under Article 5(4) TEU. On top of these considerations, Article 49(3) of the Charter – which codifies the retrospective dimension of criminal law proportionality – applies not only to harmonising provisions on penalties but also to domestic criminal sanctions falling under the Charter's scope of application.

In this complex framework, defining in an all-encompassing way *what shall be proportionate to what* is impossible. This aspect will be clarified in the following chapter by appraising the intersection between the EU conceptualisation of proportionality and the criminal law dimension of the principle.

[128] Among many: Cognetti (n 93) 16–17; Ciciriello (n 10) 132; Newton (n 9) 40.

[129] K Lenaerts, 'Proportionality as a Matrix Principle Promoting the Effectiveness of EU Law and the Legitimacy of EU Action – Keynote Speech' in *Continuity and Change – How the Challenges of Today Prepare the Ground for Tomorrow. ECB Legal Conference 2021* (Frankfurt, European Central Bank, 2022) 41.

[130] See Section III above.

V. Concluding Remarks

This chapter explored the multifaceted nature of the principle of proportionality under EU law. The principle enjoys three distinct dimensions since it limits the exercise of EU powers and the legitimacy of public authorities' interferences with the exercise of both internal market freedoms and fundamental rights secured by the Charter. However, the three dimensions disclose a common matrix, materialised by the threefold suitability, necessity and proportionality *stricto sensu* test. Indeed, this assessment materialises a proportionality relationship between opposing interests, aimed at ensuring just proportion between their degree of realisation.

Notwithstanding this holistic paradigm, the multidimensional nature of the EU principle implies that several categories of individual interests may be balanced and accommodated depending on the specific circumstances of each domain. Therefore, the next chapter will narrow the analysis by assessing which conflicting interests arise when the EU principle of proportionality permeates the criminal law domain. This analysis will clarify the reach of Article 49(3) of the Charter in EU law and, most importantly, conceptualise the principle of proportionality of criminal offences and penalties by assessing the uneasy intersection between the EU and criminal law understandings of proportionality.

2

Proportionality of Criminal Offences and Penalties as a Hybrid Principle of EU Law

I. Introduction

As anticipated in the Introduction,[1] proportionality plays a key role in EU criminal law. On the one hand, it shapes EU harmonising provisions on offences and penalties. On the other hand, it settles the interaction between domestic criminalisation and the EU legal order, particularly when offences and penalties implement EU law or clash with internal market freedoms and fundamental rights secured by the Charter. Still, proportionality in criminal law has a different understanding than the EU principle of proportionality. How can the latter be reconciled with the principle's criminal law conceptualisation, which resonates in Article 49(3) of the Charter?

Having identified its normative foundations in EU law (II), the chapter digs into the conceptualisation and structure of the proportionality of criminal offences and penalties. In particular, a double-layered theorisation is advanced to theorise its hybrid nature (III). When applied to offences and penalties, the EU and criminal law concepts of proportionality are inherently intertwined. Therefore, the analysis will show that the interaction between the EU and criminal law dimensions of proportionality gives rise to a peculiar theoretical construct. The threefold understanding of EU proportionality is hybridised by the criminal law one, thereby giving rise to a compound principle. Building upon this theorisation, the specific prongs of the principle are then analysed (IV). Finally, the chapter highlights that a similar hybrid construction emerges also under the ECHR legal system, thus explaining how a glance at the Strasbourg Court's case-law would be beneficial for assessing the principle's application under EU law (V).

[1] See Section I of the Introduction to this book.

II. The Multiple Normative Foundations of the Proportionality of Criminal Offences and Penalties

By affirming that 'the severity of penalties must not be disproportionate to the criminal offence', Article 49(3) of the Charter is the only primary law provision dealing explicitly with proportionality in substantive criminal law. On that premise, one may contend that Article 49(3) of the Charter constitutes the only normative source for the principle of proportionality of criminal offences and penalties in EU law.

However, two considerations show that this is not the case. In fact, Article 49(3) of the Charter only applies to criminal penalties.[2] Instead, the scope of the principle under analysis is broader, as proportionality in substantive criminal law also involves limiting criminalisation choices. In that respect, criminal offences and penalties shall be framed through the three proportionality lenses outlined in the previous chapter. Firstly, at the supranational level, harmonising substantive criminal law pursuant to Article 83 TFEU is subject to proportionality constraints under Article 5(4) TEU. Since criminalisation interferes with the enjoyment of fundamental rights, the EU action in this domain shall also be proportionate under Article 52(1) of the Charter.[3] Secondly, at the domestic level, the exercise of *ius puniendi* may be warranted to secure the effectiveness of EU law. Thirdly, domestic criminalisation could clash with EU internal market freedoms and fundamental rights of the Charter.[4] In both circumstances, the principle of proportionality defines the legitimacy of national criminalisation and enforcement vis-à-vis EU law.

In other words, Article 5(4) TEU, primary law provisions on limitations to the enjoyment of internal market freedoms and Article 52(1) of the Charter – which recall the general principle of proportionality – are all relevant for scrutinising the legitimacy of EU and domestic criminalisation choices and respective penalties. Therefore, Article 49(3) of the Charter is not the only legal basis for the proportionality of criminal offences and penalties in EU law. As anticipated in Chapter 1, Article 49(3) codifies a retrospective assessment deeply embedded in the elaboration of proportionality in criminal law. As such, its understanding radically differs from the EU general principle of proportionality.[5] Therefore, Article 49(3) of the Charter entails an interaction between the EU and criminal law concepts of proportionality. That intersection gives rise to a peculiar theoretical construct that shall now be framed.

[2] Among many, see V Mitsilegas and E Billis, 'Article 49 – Principles of Legality and Proportionality of Criminal Offences and Penalties' in S Peers, T Hervey, J Kenner and A Ward (eds), *The EU Charter of Fundamental Rights:A Commentary*, 2nd edn (Oxford, Hart Publishing, 2021); R Palladino, *Il principio di proporzionalità nel diritto dell'Unione europea* (Bari, Cacucci Editore, 2024) 146.

[3] For an analysis of relevant EU legislative practice, see Chapter 3.

[4] On this point, see the case-law analysed in Chapter 4.

[5] See Section III(C)(iii) of Chapter 1.

III. A Double-layered Theorisation

The theorisation of the proportionality of criminal offences and penalties relies on the threefold test characterising the general principle of proportionality, which also applies to substantive criminal law measures (A). However, this scheme is insufficient to frame the principle under analysis. Indeed, the necessity and proportionality *stricto sensu* of criminal offences and penalties are inevitably assessed by reference to traditional criminal law proportionality paradigms (B). This approach implies a hybrid understanding, which may be resumed in a double-layered assessment.

A. Applying the Threefold Proportionality Test to Criminal Offences and Penalties: The Principle's Primary Scheme

The threefold test characterising the EU principle of proportionality entails a legal relationship between conflicting interests to ensure just proportion between their respective fulfilment. This test is an open-ended paradigm, potentially applicable to weigh any conflicting interests. Therefore, the EU concept of proportionality shall now be analysed in the substantive criminal law domain specifically. To conceptualise the proportionality of criminal offences and penalties, the key interrogative is: *what shall be proportionate to what?*

Setting the scene for an answer to this question requires a twofold assessment. It is necessary to separately consider which interests are accommodated by the principle (i) and, consequently, how the threefold test shall be framed to ensure this balance (ii).

i. The Opposing Interests Underlying Proportionality of Offences and Penalties in EU Criminal Law

As previously recalled, the EU principle of proportionality has a threefold significance in substantive criminal law. It first represents the criterion for assessing the legitimacy of any limitation that criminal measures pose to the enjoyment of fundamental rights secured by the Charter and internal market freedoms. Second, when domestic criminalisation is warranted to implement EU law or secure its effectiveness, the principle of proportionality represents the essential criterion for accommodating collective interests in crime control and the protection of individuals' legal sphere. This is the case, in particular, of secondary law providing for the establishment of 'effective, proportionate and dissuasive' penalties, including criminal ones, for any violation of provisions therein enshrined.[6] Third, EU

[6] For a deeper analysis, see Section II(A) of Chapter 4.

criminalisation through harmonising provisions calls into question the proportionate exercise of EU powers and the compatibility of those provisions with fundamental rights.

Each of these declinations of proportionality entails accommodating conflicting legal interests. The first envisages a contrast between the domestic *ius puniendi* and the protection of rights and freedoms granted by EU law. Conversely, in the second dimension, criminalisation at the domestic level stems from a supranational interest which needs to be accommodated with the protection of individual rights and freedoms.

Finally, the proportionate exercise of EU harmonisation powers has a twofold dimension. From one point of view, it requires accommodating the Union's interest to harmonise criminal law provisions vis-à-vis Member States' interest to withhold their domestic *ius puniendi.*[7] From another viewpoint, harmonising offences and penalties imposes a constraint not only on Member States' interests but also on individual ones. By setting common rules on 'the definition of criminal offences and sanctions',[8] the EU legislature compels the Member States to criminalise certain conducts and to sanction them through a given type and level of penalties. This implies the existence of an EU interest in criminalisation, which shall be accommodated vis-à-vis the protection of individuals from excessive penalisation.[9] Consequently, proportionality here entails a dual dimension: an institutional one concerning the allocation of competencies in substantive criminal law, and an individual one dealing with the protection of natural and legal persons.

Therefore, the principle of proportionality of criminal offences and penalties postulates three different clashes between opposing interests. Indeed, the protection of rights and freedoms is accommodated vis-à-vis either domestic or EU public interests in domestic criminalisation and EU interests in supranational criminalisation.

[7] For the theorisation of proportionality in the exercise of EU competencies, see Section III(A) of Chapter 1.

[8] Art 83(1) TFEU.

[9] Any piece of secondary law adopted under Art 83 TFEU establishes a positive obligation to criminalise upon Member States, which are compelled to adhere to the definition of the crime provided for in a given directive (A Klip, *European Criminal Law: An Integrative Approach*, 4th edn (Cambridge, Intersentia, 2021) 229). Thus, EU criminalisation entails accommodating supranational interests in criminalisation vis-à-vis protecting individuals' rights and freedoms. This is one of the reasons why a relevant body of scholarship has recently started to elaborate a set of principles capable of driving the exercise of the supranational *ius puniendi*. In this regard, see: N Peršak, 'EU Criminal Law and Its Legitimation: In Search for a Substantive Principle of Criminalisation' (2018) 26 *European Journal of Crime, Criminal Law and Criminal Justice* 20; JW Ouwerkerk, 'Evidence-Based Criminalisation in EU Law: Evidence of What Exactly?' in JW Ouwerkerk, J Altena, J Öberg and S Miettinen (eds), *The Future of EU Criminal Justice Policy and Practice: Legal and Criminological Perspectives* (Leiden, Brill | Nijhoff, 2019); SS Buisman, 'The Future of EU Substantive Criminal Law: Towards a Uniform Set of Criminalisation Principles at the EU Level' (2022) 30 *European Journal of Crime, Criminal Law and Criminal Justice* 161.

ii. A Hybrid EU and Criminal Law Principle

The threefold test characterising the EU principle of proportionality is finalistic: a given arrangement shall be adequate, necessary and proportionate *stricto sensu* to fulfil a legitimate interest. This conceptualisation is easily transposable to the substantive criminal law domain: the scope of offences and the type and amount of related penalties shall be adequate, necessary and proportionate *stricto sensu* to attaining a legal interest justifying criminalisation. The latter may be a domestic public interest in criminalisation, a supranational public interest in domestic criminalisation to ensure the effectiveness of EU law or the EU's interest in supranational criminalisation.

However, the threefold test derived from the EU principle only represents the first theoretical layer – the primary scheme – of the proportionality of criminal offences and penalties. Because of offences and penalties' peculiar nature, this assessment cannot exhaust the theorisation of the principle under analysis. Indeed, the intrusiveness of substantive criminal law provisions in the individuals' sphere depends on penological considerations. The exercise of *ius puniendi* is instrumental in pursuing various penological purposes, such as general prevention, special prevention and retribution.[10] Therefore, a reference to the functions of criminal justice is essential to understand *how* and *to what extent* a legitimate interest may be proportionately pursued through criminal law. This assessment exceeds the scope of the primary scheme by large and therefore calls into play the criminal law dimension of proportionality.

Some brief examples may help to explain this contention. To establish harmonised penalty levels, the 2012 Commission's Impact Assessment attached to the Proposal for a Directive on the Fight Against Fraud to the Union's Financial Interests took deterrence as a benchmark for assessing their proportionality. To evaluate the suitability and necessity of punishment, it shall be acknowledged whether the severity of harmonised sanctions is such as to achieve 'foreseeable and sufficiently significant, though not excessive, consequences'.[11] The ECJ case-law witnesses an analogous interaction between EU and criminal law concepts, such as deterrence and retrospective proportionality between the severity of the sanction and the seriousness of the wrongdoing.[12] When secondary law provisions require Member States to adopt 'effective, proportionate and dissuasive penalties', the ECJ usually complements the threefold test with criminal law proportionality paradigms. As clarified in *K. M. (Sanctions infligées au capitaine de navire)*, offences and penalties shall be 'commensurate with the seriousness of the breaches

[10] For a general appraisal of the different rationales underpinning substantive criminal law, see: A Duff and SP Green, *Philosophical Foundations of Criminal Law* (Oxford University Press 2011); D Husak, *The Philosophy of Criminal Law: Selected Essays* (Oxford, Oxford University Press, 2010).

[11] Commission Staff Working Paper – Impact Assessment Accompanying the Proposal for a Directive of the European Parliament and of the Council on the Fight Against Fraud to the Union's Financial Interests by Means of Criminal Law (Part I), SWD (2012) 195 final, 14.

[12] For further analysis on this profile, see Chapter 4.

for which they are imposed, in particular by ensuring a genuinely dissuasive effect, while respecting the general principle of proportionality'.[13] The same approach applies to domestic criminal measures clashing with the enjoyment of internal market freedoms or fundamental rights. The Court in *ECOTEX Bulgaria* stated that penalties shall be adequate and necessary to pursue a legitimate aim and then recalled that '[i]n this context, the severity of penalties must be commensurate with the seriousness of the infringements [...], in particular by ensuring a genuinely dissuasive effect, while respecting the general principle of proportionality'.[14]

These examples provide solid evidence of a departure from a purely EU understanding of proportionality, as the latter is hybridised by criminal law proportionality paradigms. When dealing with offences and penalties, the EU concept of proportionality inevitably bumps into the principle's criminal law dimension. The latter amounts to a complementary perspective to the threefold test, thus giving rise to a second theoretical layer of the proportionality of offences and penalties. Consequently, in the EU legal order, the principle of proportionality of criminal offences and penalties has a hybrid nature, since it combines the distinctive features of the EU and criminal law understandings of proportionality.

B. At the Intersection between the EU and Criminal Law Understandings of Proportionality: Two Secondary Schemes

Against this premise, the theorisation of the hybrid principle of proportionality of criminal offences and penalties requires digging into its second theoretical layer. The latter derives from the criminal law dimension of proportionality, whose understanding is inherently linked to the theories of punishment, with particular emphasis on consequentialism and deontology.[15] Consequentialist theories enhance the prospective deterrent effects of punishment.[16] In this line, criminal sanctions are seen from a utilitarian viewpoint, as they constitute a tool to attain a given penological aim. Conversely, deontological theories revolve around moral and individualistic considerations. They entail a retrospective account, whereby penalties represent the inherent retribution for past wrongdoings.[17]

[13] Case C-77/20 *K. M. (Sanctions infligées au capitaine de navire)* ECLI:EU:C:2021:112, para 38.

[14] Case C-544/19 *ECOTEX Bulgaria* ECLI:EU:C:2021:803, para 100.

[15] A doctrinal confrontation defined by Feinberg as 'the classic debate' of criminal law scholarship: see J Feinberg, 'The Classic Debate' in J Feinberg and H Gross (eds), *The Philosophy of Law* (Belmont, Wadsworth Publishing, 1991).

[16] Among many, see: A von Hirsch, 'Proportionality in the Philosophy of Punishment' (1992) *Crime and Justice* 55, 57.

[17] *ibid.* Both categories are well-routed in the philosophical tradition characterising the contemporary understanding of criminal justice (see, in particular, J Rawls, *A Theory of Justice* (Harvard, Harvard University Press, 1971) 22). It has been contended in literature that the origins of the utilitarian and deontological theories may be both traced back to the works of Beccaria (see, in particular, C Beccaria, *Edizione nazionale delle opere di Cesare Beccaria. 1: Dei delitti e delle pene* (L Firpo and G Francioni eds, Milano, Mediobanca, 1984)). In fact, his theory of criminal justice is based upon both the recognition

Consequentialism and deontology in the philosophy of punishment imply different features for proportionality,[18] thus giving rise to two distinct secondary assessments for the proportionality of criminal offences and penalties.[19] These are the prospective (i) and retrospective (ii) schemes. As shown below, the two proportionality paradigms shall be seen as complementary within the principle under analysis (iii).

i. Prospective Proportionality vis-à-vis the Attainment of a Non-Retributive Penological Aim

Bentham's theorisation of the principle of utility constitutes the backdrop of the consequentialist approach to criminal punishment. Because 'the general object which all laws have, or ought to have, in common, is to augment the total happiness of the community',[20] criminal repression must be oriented to attain this goal. In Bentham's view, criminal punishment is evil since 'it brings harm or dissatisfaction to those punished'.[21] Thus, recourse to criminal law is justified only if it generates a beneficial effect in crime prevention capable of counterbalancing the evil of punishment.[22] More specifically, 'if it ought to all be admitted, [criminal punishment] ought only to be admitted in as far as it promises to exclude a greater evil',[23] in particular by discouraging individuals from committing crimes.

The utilitarian legal tradition is thus inherently prospective: it frames sanctions as tools for attaining penological goals[24] presupposing a non-retributive

of rights upon individuals and the need to maximise the societal wealth in a utilitarian perspective. In this regard, see: DAJ Richards, 'Rights, Utility, and Crime' (1981) 3 *Crime and Justice* 247, 250.

[18] von Hirsch, 'Proportionality in the Philosophy of Punishment' (n 16) 56.

[19] RA Duff, 'Proportionality and the Criminal Law: Proportionality of What to What?' in E Billis, N Knust and JP Rui (eds), *Proportionality in Crime Control and Criminal Justice* (Oxford, Hart Publishing, 2021) 29.

[20] J Bentham, 'An Introduction to the Principles of Morals and Legislation', in A Bailey (ed), *The Broadview Anthology of Social and Political Thought: From Machiavelli to Nietzsche* (Peterborough, Broadview Press, 2020) 472.

[21] von Hirsch, 'Proportionality in the Philosophy of Punishment' (n 16) 58. Reading the concept of 'evil' from a fundamental rights point of view, Tulkens puts forward that 'it is not difficult to translate his statements into 'infringements of human rights' by seeing any criminalization of an act as an infringement of whatever right or freedom it restricts' (F Tulkens, 'The Paradoxical Relationship between Criminal Law and Human Rights' (2011) 9 *Journal of International Criminal Justice* 577, 581–582).

[22] von Hirsch, 'Proportionality in the Philosophy of Punishment' (n 16) 58.

[23] J Bentham, 'An Introduction to the Principles of Morals and Legislation', in Bailey (n 20). This understanding of the principle of utility is at the basis of Bentham's critique of capital punishment; for a discussion on this topic, see HA Bedau, 'Bentham's Utilitarian Critique of the Death Penalty' (1983) 74 *Journal of Criminal Law and Criminology* 1033.

[24] As outlined by Dolcini, contemporary scholarship and practice fall short from putting forward a holistic definition of which prospective goals shall be taken into consideration and how they should be pursued (E Dolcini, 'La commisurazione della pena tra teoria e prassi' (1991) *Rivista italiana di diritto e procedura penale* 55, 56–57).

function of the criminal punishment.[25] This construction is traditionally matched with negative general prevention. Based on the principle of utility developed by Bentham, criminal sanctions are conceived as functional to deter other individuals from offending.[26]

Moreover, general prevention may also be positively conceptualised. Rather than deterring individuals from committing an offence, penalties are understood as instruments to enhance spontaneous respect for the law.[27] The sanction imposed on a given offender would result in 'reinforcing citizens' inhibitions against predatory behaviours'.[28] Shaping general prevention in positive terms entails a shift from the social fear generated by the imposition of criminal sanctions to its perceived legitimacy.[29] In fact, positive general prevention implies a link between the sanction and the moral judgments and values inherent in the society, thereby postulating censure as an inherent component of criminal punishments.[30]

The utilitarian model also fits special prevention goals, which entail criminal penalties as tools to prevent convicted individuals from reoffending.[31] Offenders' social rehabilitation is well-established in contemporary European countries.[32] It results from a key paradigm shift during the last century when criminal justice systems started addressing offenders' drivers of crime.[33] Criminal penalties thus

[25] In this perspective, Frase conceives the terms 'utilitarian' and 'non-retributive' as interchangeable (RS Frase, 'Excessive Prison Sentences, Punishment Goals, and the Eighth Amendment: Proportionality Relative to What' (2005) 89 *Minnesota Law Review* 571, 592).

[26] More extensively on this topic, see: V Militello, *Prevenzione generale e commisurazione della pena* (Milano, Giuffrè, 1982); M Romano and F Stella, *Teoria e prassi della prevenzione generale dei reati* (Bologna, Il Mulino, 1980).

[27] CF Grosso, M Pelissero, D Petrini and P Pisa, *Manuale di Diritto penale. Parte generale*, 2nd edn (Milano, Giuffrè, 2017) 594–595.

[28] von Hirsch, 'Proportionality in the Philosophy of Punishment' (n 16) 68.

[29] K Nuotio, 'A Legitimacy-Based Approach to EU Criminal Law: Maybe We Are Getting There, after All' (2020) 11 *New Journal of European Criminal Law* 20, 29.

[30] In this regard, see: S Bonini, *La funzione simbolica nel diritto penale del bene giuridico* (Napoli, Editoriale Scientifica, 2018) 190–191, fn 8.

[31] Among many, see: A Pagliaro, 'Empirical Verification of the Effects of General Prevention and Incapacitation' (2003) 4 *European Journal of Crime, Criminal Law and Criminal Justice* 398, 400.

[32] Among extensive literature, see: PH van Kempen and W Young, 'Obligations et Moyens de Prévention de La Récidive : Introduction, Contexte et Conclusions' in PH van Kempen and Warren Young (eds), *Prevention of Reoffending: The Value of Rehabilitation and the Management of High Risk Offenders – Prévention de la récidive: valeur de la réhabilitation et gestion des délinquants à haut risque* (Cambridge, Intersentia, 2014); J Pradel, 'La réhabilitation des détenus – Introduction générale' in PH van Kempen and W Young (eds), *Prevention of Reoffending: The Value of Rehabilitation and the Management of High Risk Offenders – Prévention de la récidive: valeur de la réhabilitation et gestion des délinquants à haut risque* (Cambridge, Intersentia, 2014); M Jendly and N Delgrande, 'La valeur de la réhabilitation d'un point de vue criminologique' in PH van Kempen and W Young (eds), *Prevention of Reoffending: The Value of Rehabilitation and the Management of High Risk Offenders – Prévention de la récidive: valeur de la réhabilitation et gestion des délinquants à haut risque* (Cambridge, Intersentia, 2014).

[33] S Montaldo, 'Offenders' Rehabilitation: Towards a New Paradigm for EU Criminal Law?' (2018) 8 *European Criminal Review* 222, 222–223; J Alix, 'Chapitre premier. Une liaison dangereuse. Dangerosité et droit pénal en France' in G Giudicelli-Delage and C Lazerges (eds), *La dangerosité saisie par le droit pénal* (Paris, Presses Universitaires de France, 2011) 56.

acquire a new educational function and become a tool to rebuild offenders' moral inhibitions to enhance their reintegration into society.

It follows that general and special prevention are the non-retributive penological purposes underpinning the consequentialist theorisation of criminal justice. These aims are the parameters against which offences and penalties are assessed under prospective proportionality. Pursuing general or special prevention is instrumental to attain the public interest through criminalisation. In this respect, verifying the proportionality of offences' scope and penalties' type and level vis-à-vis the policy interest pursued requires assessing whether the same offences and penalties are adequate, necessary and proportionate *stricto sensu* to the prospective attainment of general or special prevention goals. Therefore, prospective proportionality in EU law is not only functionally linked but also theoretically similar to the threefold test: it implies an analogous finalistic assessment, although with respect to a penological goal rather than the policy aim driving criminalisation.

Theorising this assessment is not particularly problematic from the viewpoint of special prevention. This goal may be achieved only insofar as the criminal punishment is tailored to the resocialisation needs of the individual offender.[34] It follows that recourse to criminalisation and the given type and level of penalty shall be adequate, necessary and proportionate *stricto sensu* to the attainment of the offender's rehabilitation.

Conversely, general prevention's positive and negative aspects shall be separately considered. As previously recalled, the positive general prevention theory is built upon the premise that individuals perceive proportionate sentences as fairer.[35] Citizens would be more willing to respect rules whose enforcement is secured by proportionate penalties rather than those whose violations are disproportionately sanctioned. Therefore, under the positive general prevention theory, offences and penalties shall be proportionate to the seriousness of the crime at stake.[36] Interestingly, this conclusion entails a retrospective assessment rather than a prospective one. The retrospective proportionality scheme will be analysed below in Section (ii).

Negative general prevention, on its part, requires a prospective account. In the criminal law discourse, dissuasiveness is typically seen as a constraint to proportionality, as it may justify departures from this principle on crime control grounds.[37]

[34] Among many, see R Vienne, 'De l'individualisation de la peine à la personnalisation de la mesure. À propos du soixante-quinzième anniversaire de la parution de l'ouvrage de Saleilles (1898–1973)' in *Aspects nouveaux de la pensée juridique. Recueil d'études en hommage à Marc Ancel*, vol 2 (Paris, Pedone, 1975).

[35] Von Hirsch considers this assumption as one of the main weaknesses of the positive general prevention theory. In fact, the premise that individuals perceive proportionate penalties as fairer, thus reinforcing their moral inhibitions with respect to the relevant proscribed actions or omissions, may not be empirically demonstrated (A von Hirsch, *Censure and Sanctions* (Oxford, Clarendon Press, 1993) 133). That criticism is widely shared in contemporary criminal law literature: among many, see A Duff and A von Hirsch, 'Responsibility, Retribution and the 'Voluntary': A Response to Williams' (1997) 1 *Cambridge Law Journal* 103, 112.

[36] von Hirsch, 'Proportionality in the Philosophy of Punishment' (n 16) 68.

[37] *ibid*, 56.

At the same time, this finding does not imply that negative general prevention is incompatible with the principle of proportionality. Indeed, the former can be framed as a penological aim for the prospective proportionality review. From that viewpoint, deterrence does not constitute a trump to proportionality: achieving a sufficiently dissuasive effect represents the specific goal to which the proportionality threshold should be parameterised. In this light, the criminal law response to any wrongdoing shall not exceed what is necessary to attain a genuinely dissuasive effect.[38] Any form of criminalisation which exceeds such a threshold – although generating a greater deterrent effect – does not comply with that requirement.

Following these considerations, the prospective secondary scheme of the principle should be framed as a suitability, necessity and proportionality *stricto sensu* assessment of offences' scope and penalties' type and level vis-à-vis attaining a genuinely dissuasive effect (negative general prevention) or offenders' social rehabilitation (special prevention).

ii. Retrospective Proportionality vis-à-vis the Seriousness of the Wrongdoing

Utilitarianism is contested by deontological theories, which establish the theoretical justification of criminal punishment on moral concerns. Deontology in criminal law may be traced back to Kant's metaphysics of morals, affirming that individuals shall always be regarded as a value, not a means for attaining societal benefits.[39] This aspect distinguishes Kant's perspective from Bentham's: people are moral beings and shall thus be treated according to their nature.[40]

Unlike utilitarianism, Kant's deontological theory is inherently retrospective and retributivist. It conceives criminal punishment as just retribution for past wrongdoing in the light of the offender's desert,[41] namely, what the offender deserves in light of the specific circumstances of the case.[42] This understanding also features Hegel's theory of punishment, although it does not refer to a moral dimension. By conceptualising the offence as an infringement of freedom, Hegel

[38] Among many, see Case C-255/14 *Chmielewski* ECLI:EU:C:2015:475, para 23; Case C-544/19 *ECOTEX Bulgaria* ECLI:EU:C:2021:803, para 100.

[39] I Kant, *Groundwork for the Metaphysics of Morals* (New Haven, Yale University Press, 2018) 45, as recalled in von Hirsch, 'Proportionality in the Philosophy of Punishment' (n 16) 59.

[40] DE Scheid, 'Kant's Retributivism' (1983) 2 *Ethics* 262, 274.

[41] On this concept, see F Feldman and B Skow, 'Desert' in *The Stanford Encyclopedia of Philosophy* (Stanford, Stanford University, 2020).

[42] The retributivist rationale has sometimes been construed in terms of 'societal revenge' for the wrongdoing rather than on the basis of a desert model (on that dichotomy in the US discourse on the capital punishment's legitimacy, see: JO Finckenauer, 'Public Support for the Death Penalty: Retribution as Just Deserts or Retribution as Revenge?' (1988) 5 *Justice Quarterly* 81. However, scholars have underlined that the 'just desert' model represents the predominant conceptualisation of retributivism in the contemporary legal discourse on the philosophy of punishment (in this regard, see: T Sommers, 'The Three Rs: Retribution, Revenge, and Reparation' (2016) 44 *Philosophia* 327, 328.

conceives the punishment as a means to restore this value.[43] This contention justifies the imposition of criminal penalties in a retributivist perspective: any punishment shall be seen 'as a necessary complement to the crime, not as some external and coercive deterrent'.[44]

From this viewpoint, criminal punishment may be conceptualised as expressing public disapproval of the offender's conduct.[45] As underlined by Feinberg,[46] since punishment is a means to express reprobation towards the offender, 'what justice requires is that the condemnatory aspect of the punishment suits the crime, that the crime be of a kind that is truly worthy of reprobation'.[47] Similarly, Duff deems censure essential for a punishment which 'respects and addresses the criminal as a rational moral agent'.[48] From that viewpoint, censure may be regarded as the distinctive characteristic of criminal penalties compared to different categories of sanctions.[49] Criminal law would inherently require the manifestation of public disapproval; as a result, no criminal sanction would be legitimate if not deserved by the offender.[50]

The deontological perspective has various implications for a theory of proportionality of criminal offences and penalties. Indeed, proportionality plays an essential role within the retributivist model. While prospective proportionality is functional and forward-looking, retributivism implies a backwards-looking proportionality assessment between past wrongdoing and criminal punishment.[51] It follows that the retrospective secondary scheme of the principle entails that the material scope of criminal offences and the type and amount of the relevant penalties shall be proportionate to the seriousness of the wrongdoing.

This definition, however, deserves further analysis. First, the expression 'seriousness of the wrongdoing' may convey the idea that only the objective circumstances of the conduct – namely, the offender's action or omission in its phenomenal objectivity – qualify as the term of reference for the proportionality assessment. Still, the retributivist legal scholarship suggests a different understanding. The concept of 'just desert' does not encompass only the specificities of the conduct but, more in general, the offender's blameworthiness, described as a

[43] MA Pauley, 'The Jurisprudence of Crime and Punishment from Plato to Hegel' (1994) 39 *American Journal of Jurisprudence* 97, 140–141.

[44] P Franco, *Hegel's Philosophy of Freedom* (New Haven, Yale University Press, 1999) 64.

[45] Indeed, censure represents the common element of any retributive theory: on this point, see F Viganò, *La proporzionalità della pena: profili di diritto penale e costituzionale* (Torino, Giappichelli, 2021) 136.

[46] J Feinberg, 'The Expressive Function of Punishment' (1965) 49 *The Monist* 397.

[47] *ibid*, 423.

[48] RA Duff, *Trials and Punishments* (Cambridge, Cambridge University Press, 1986).

[49] Viganò (n 45) 154–155.

[50] That is the perspective advanced, within the Italian criminal law discourse, by Padovani: T Padovani, 'Teoria della colpevolezza e scopi della pena' (1987) *Rivista italiana di diritto e procedura penale* 798.

[51] More extensively on this topic, see: JA Corlett, 'Making More Sense of Retributivism: Desert as Responsibility and Proportionality' (2003) 78 *Philosophy* 279.

'combination of harmful or wrongful conduct and culpability for that conduct'.[52] Therefore, the personal characteristics of the offender shall also form part of the assessment of the 'just desert' as the penalty deserved may vary in the light of the individual moral character.

Secondly, the concept of 'proportionate' within a retrospective-retributivist scheme cannot be based on the threefold test. This theoretical scheme is in essence functional and finalistic[53] and, therefore, inapplicable to retrospective proportionality. Conversely, the concept of 'proportionate' shall be construed here as postulating a relationship of commensurability between the scope of the criminalised conduct and the severity of the penalty on one hand and the seriousness of the wrongdoing on the other. This issue will be further deepened later in this chapter while analysing the specific prongs of the principle.[54]

iii. Prospective and Retrospective Proportionality as Complementary Secondary Schemes of the Principle

Prospective and retrospective proportionality are distinct perspectives grounding two different secondary schemes. However, the complex and multifaceted reality of contemporary criminal justice systems may be hardly confined to a purely utilitarian or retributivist understanding. The two approaches coexist, combining retributivism, general prevention, and special prevention.[55] It is commonly agreed that criminal sanctions are inherently multifunctional,[56] as they fulfil retributivist, deterrence, positive general prevention and social rehabilitation purposes at the same time.

The criminal law scholarly discourse fully recognises this finding. Since the second half of the last century, the criminal law discourse has seen the emergence of legal models establishing a connection between the consequentialist and deontological traditions.[57] Hart's theory, in particular, revolves around a dichotomy between the 'general justifying aim' of criminal sanctions, namely the ultimate reasons for establishing criminal justice systems, and the 'distribution' criteria of criminal punishment in concrete cases.[58] According to Hart, these two aspects shall be considered separately. While a prospective-utilitarian crime prevention

[52] N Lacey and H Pickard, 'The Chimera of Proportionality: Institutionalising Limits on Punishment in Contemporary Social and Political Systems' (2015) 78 *Modern Law Review* 216, 216; KM Carlsmith, JM Darley and PH Robinson, 'Why Do We Punish? Deterrence and Just Deserts as Motives for Punishment' (2002) 83 *Journal of Personality and Social Psychology* 284, 286.

[53] See Section IV(A) of Chapter 1.

[54] See Section IV below in this chapter.

[55] Among many, see: Nuotio (n 29) 27; Viganò (n 45) 159.

[56] Among many, see P-J Delage, 'Prolégomènes. Fragments archéologiques de la défense sociale' in G Giudicelli-Delage and C Lazerges (eds), *La dangerosité saisie par le droit pénal* (Paris, Presses Universitaires de France, 2011) 29–30.

[57] von Hirsch, 'Proportionality in the Philosophy of Punishment' (n 16) 89–93.

[58] HLA Hart, 'Prolegomenon to the Principles of Punishment' in HLA Hart (ed), *Punishment and Responsibility: Essays in the Philosophy of Law*, 2nd edn (Oxford, Oxford University Press, 2008).

goal constitutes the general justification of criminal justice, the 'distribution' of sanctions in concrete cases is subject to retrospective deontological constraints.[59] A utilitarian rationale may thus coexist with sentencing rules based upon the deontological need to tailor criminal sanctions to the specific features of the wrongdoing and of the offender.[60]

Other theories try to reconcile utilitarianism and retributivism. These are the 'negative retributivist' and 'limiting retributivist' theories. According to the first, retrospective proportionality may only establish an upper severity threshold for the penalty, which public authorities shall not overstep. Below this limit, the degree of intensity of criminal repression should be determined based on a consequentialist approach grounded on prospective proportionality.[61] Conversely, 'limiting retributivism' entails a range of 'deserved' criminal measures within an upper and lower threshold.[62] Within this range, and similarly to negative retributivism, consequentialist considerations define the exact amount of punishment.[63]

Ascertaining which of these theories prevails in the criminal justice systems would vastly exceed the scope of the EU law perspective developed in this book. It suffices to underline that a clear-cut choice between retrospective retributivism and prospective utilitarianism cannot be made at a theoretical level. Prospective and retrospective proportionality coexist in the criminal law discourse. Consequently, theorising the proportionality of criminal offences and penalties requires considering both secondary schemes as part of the principle's conceptual structure.

IV. The Structure of the Principle: Assessing the Different Prongs of Proportionality of Criminal Offences and Penalties

Having framed its hybrid nature, the various prongs composing the proportionality of criminal offences and penalties shall now be analysed. Indeed, the principle

[59] von Hirsch, 'Proportionality in the Philosophy of Punishment' (n 16) 62.

[60] This theoretical perspective is based upon a non-absolutist conception of moral constraints, as opposed to the Kantian absolutist understanding of deontology (among many, see: L Alexander and M Moore, 'Deontological Ethics', in *The Stanford Encyclopedia of Philosophy* (Stanford, Stanford University, 2021)).

[61] Among many, see: J Ryberg, 'Retributivism and the Proportionality Dilemma' (2021) 34 *Ratio* 158, 159.

[62] *ibid.*

[63] Among many: J Bronsther, 'The Limits of Retributivism' (2021) 24 *New Criminal Law Review* 301, 302. Both negative and limiting retributivism shall be seen as antagonistic to the so-called 'positive retributivism'. The latter is based upon an absolutist conception of deontology, as it considers the upper and lower retrospective thresholds as actually coincident, thus ruling out any possibility of defining criminal punishment on consequentialist grounds. Under a positive retributivist approach, there may be only one deserved sanction with respect to the seriousness of the wrongdoing, and that criminal measure shall be defined on the basis of a retrospective proportionality assessment. In this regard, see S Dimock, 'Retributivism and Trust' (1997) 16 *Law and Philosophy* 37, 41.

covers the whole criminal law enforcement spectrum. On the one hand, it shapes the legislative definition of crimes *in abstracto* and the judicial review of their legitimacy vis-à-vis EU law. On the other hand, the proportionality of criminal offences and penalties shapes the application of substantive criminal law provisions *in concreto* by domestic criminal courts, including judicial scrutiny on its compatibility with EU law. Both declinations should be separately considered with respect to the proportionality of offences (A) and penalties (B).

A. Proportionality of Criminal Offences

i. In Abstracto: *From the Definition of the Proscribed Action or Omission to its Criminalisation*

On the one hand, the proportionality of offences *in abstracto* consists of accommodating conflicting interests by domestic legislators when defining substantive criminal law provisions and by the EU legislature when drafting harmonising provisions on the definition of offences. On the other hand, the same paradigm applies to domestic and Union courts respectively in assessing the legitimacy of those provisions.

Establishing criminal offences encompasses two consequential features: defining the offence's conduct and qualifying its commission as criminal.[64] The first aspect entails the legislature describing an abstract behaviour regarded as prohibited or compulsory upon a range of individuals. These subjects may comprise the entire community of individuals within the jurisdiction of a given legal order or categories of individuals identified by qualitative characteristics. The range of individuals falling under the scope of a given offence includes natural persons and, whenever the domestic legal order so provides, even legal entities.[65] The ensuing legal obligation may consist of either the negative duty to abstain from a given conduct or the positive requirement to comply with an abstract behaviour. As a result, offences aim to penalise actions or omissions, depending on the case.[66]

Legislators typically enjoy considerable discretion in criminal law, but proportionality is crucial in limiting the exercise of *ius puniendi*. Criminalisation restricts individual freedom of choice and, therefore, requires an objective justification for that interference.[67] This is inherent in contemporary European constitutional

[64] N Recchia, *Il principio di proporzionalità nel diritto penale. Scelte di criminalizzazione e ingerenza nei diritti fondamentali* (Torino, Giappichelli, 2020) 123–125.

[65] On the emergence of criminal liability schemes for legal entities, see Section III of the Introduction to this book.

[66] For a conceptualisation of criminalised omissions, see: K Ambos, 'Omissions' in K Ambos, A Duff, J Roberts, T Weigend and A Heinze (eds), *Core Concepts in Criminal Law and Criminal Justice* (Cambridge University Press 2019); J Pradel, *Droit pénal comparé*, 4th edn (Paris, Dalloz, 2016) 75–81.

[67] On that ground, Recchia contends that proportionality constitutes a legal machinery underpinned by an 'argumentative' conception of the law, thus requiring any legislative choice to be adequately justified in the light of logical and explicit arguments (Recchia (n 64) 248).

legal orders[68] and is further confirmed by the emergence of rights and freedoms at the EU level. Whenever a duty deriving from an offence amounts to a restriction upon the enjoyment of a right or freedom secured by EU law, proportionality regulates this clash.

Then, establishing an offence entails a political choice by the legislature to resort to criminal law to punish the relevant action or omission. This is a separate legal profile from defining the conduct.[69] Criminal law is not the only sanctioning framework available to states for tackling wrongdoings. Once the scope of the illegality has been defined, legislatures may qualify their commission as administrative or criminal offences. This option depends on the intensity of states' response to a given wrongdoing. Criminal law is traditionally regarded as 'the most intrusive means available to the state'.[70] Then, the option for criminalisation may be subject to review to assess whether it is justified in the light of a legitimate interest. The EU and domestic legislatures enjoy considerable discretion in this respect,[71] subject to the constraints deriving from the principle of proportionality of offences *in abstracto*.

It follows that the proportionality of offences *in abstracto* applies to two distinct legislative assessments: the definition of the relevant conduct and its criminalisation. Whenever an offence is subject to judicial review *in abstracto*, courts may either censure the conduct's scope, its criminalisation or even both. In the case of harmonising provisions of substantive criminal law, that assessment is carried out by the ECJ in the context of actions for annulment[72] or preliminary references on the validity of those EU provisions.[73] Conversely, the scrutiny of domestic criminal measures vis-à-vis EU law is primarily under the responsibility of national courts, which may nonetheless seek guidance from the ECJ via preliminary references.

In all these cases, the proportionality of offences entails that the intensity of the legal obligation derived from the offence shall be adequate, necessary and proportionate *stricto sensu* to attain the pertinent public interest.[74] Then, the principle's

[68] M Cohen-Eliya and I Porat, *Proportionality and Constitutional Culture* (Cambridge, Cambridge University Press, 2013) 132.

[69] In this regard, see the theorisation proposed by Recchia (n 64) 123–125.

[70] Among many: S Melander, 'Effectiveness in EU Criminal Law and Its Effects on the General Part of Criminal Law' (2014) 5 *New Journal of European Criminal Law* 274, 274; Peršak (n 9) 35, fn 50.

[71] For what concerns EU criminalisation, Art 83 TFEU confers on the EU legislature the power to harmonise criminal offences only. Therefore, when legislating on the basis of this provision, the Parliament and Council are not entitled to compel Member States to qualify a given action or omission as an administrative rather than criminal offence. The only option available under Art 83 TFEU is between criminalising a given conduct or not, while administrative penalties may be required by EU harmonising provisions adopted on other legal bases. These forms of harmonisation shall be clearly distinguished from EU direct sanctioning powers, which are usually qualified as inherently administrative. For an exhaustive assessment of the EU direct sanctioning competence, see the wide-ranging contributions published in S Montaldo, F Costamagna and A Miglio (eds), *EU Law Enforcement: The Evolution of Sanctioning Powers* (Torino-Oxon, Giappichelli-Routledge, 2021).

[72] Art 263 TFEU.

[73] Art 267 TFEU.

[74] For a categorisation of the mentioned legal interests, see Section III(A)(i) of this chapter.

hybrid nature requires resorting to prospective and retrospective proportionality. Both schemes may be framed in a twofold way, depending on whether the proportionality assessment concerns the scope of the criminalised conduct or its criminalisation as such. On the one hand, prospective proportionality demands that the scope of the offence not amount to an excessive deterrent against the public. On the other hand, the same secondary scheme requires legislatures and courts to assess whether recourse to criminal law would be necessary to pursue general or special prevention.

The same duplicity of assessments applies to the retrospective scheme. From one point of view, it requires that including a given action or omission in the criminal offence's conduct fits its inherent seriousness. From the other viewpoint, retrospective proportionality entails the legislature and the judiciary assessing whether criminal law constitutes a proportionate option in the light of the seriousness of the relevant action or omission.

In the latter evaluation, the dividing line between positive and negative proportionality is not clear-cut, at least from a theoretical viewpoint. The positive-negative dichotomy presupposes that several different arrangements meeting the proportionality requirement are available to legislators when positively weighing conflicting interests.[75] However, the second prong of the proportionality of offences *in abstracto* revolves around a binary option – to criminalise or not the relevant action or omission – and only one between them may be regarded as proportionate. The binary nature of the policy option under analysis may vastly reduce the practical difference between positive and negative proportionality. However, a distinction between them still appears to be justified from a theoretical point of view, as it reflects the different tasks assigned to legislative and judicial authorities.[76]

ii. In Concreto: *The Clash between Domestic Criminal Law Enforcement and EU Law*

Can criminal courts assess the proportionality of offences *in concreto*? The answer is not self-evident. European contemporary constitutional systems are deeply rooted in the separation of powers, which traditionally assigns the role of 'bouche de la loi' to the judiciary.[77] In that perspective, trial judges may appear to be prevented from exercising a proportionality assessment over criminalisation

[75] See Section IV(A)(i) above in this chapter.

[76] On this point, see *ibid.*

[77] An expression which, as commonly known, has been put forward by Montesquieu within his theorisation of public powers. In this regard, among many, see: KM Schönfeld, 'Rex, Lex et Judex: Montesquieu and La Bouche de la Loi Revisited' (2008) 4 *European Constitutional Law Review* 274; M Pifferi, *L'individualizzazione della pena: difesa sociale e crisi della legalità penale tra Otto e Novecento* (Milano, Giuffrè, 2013) 198.

choices in *concreto*. Once the legislature has qualified a proscribed action or omission as a criminal offence, trial judges may not be entitled to question that policy choice in concrete cases by exercising a new proportionality assessment. Such a possibility is available only to constitutional or supreme courts entitled to review criminal law provisions, but this is an *in abstracto* scrutiny.

At the same time, excluding any room for proportionality of penalties *in concreto* does not correspond to the role assigned to judicial systems within the EU legal order. Indeed, the Treaties have established a judicial framework of which national courts are an integral part.[78] In cooperation with the ECJ, they are called upon to ensure the effective implementation of Union law at the domestic level.[79] In this context, should the application of substantive criminal law provisions in concrete cases unduly clash with directly enforceable provisions of EU law, the principle of primacy entails that the domestic offences and penalties shall be set aside. This aspect is particularly evident in the interaction between domestic criminal law provisions and internal market freedoms. As Chapter 1 disclosed, any restriction to the latter is legitimate only if proportionate to attaining a legitimate aim.[80] EU primary law provisions securing internal market freedoms are endowed with direct effect, thus requiring domestic jurisdictions to set aside any incompatible domestic provision.[81]

Consequently, trial judges may exercise a proportionality assessment *in concreto* where the imposition of criminal penalties limits the enjoyment of directly enforceable rights and freedoms secured by EU law. Indeed, a disproportionate restriction may stem either from the *incompatibility of the offence as such* with individual freedoms or from the *incompatibility of the offence's application to a given individual for its specific conduct*. While the former constitutes anything but a particular feature of proportionality *in abstracto*, the second aspect amounts to an *in concreto* assessment. In the latter case, the trial court would assess whether criminal prosecution, irrespective of the type or amount of the penalty eventually imposed, would amount to a disproportionate restriction on enjoying the freedoms secured by EU law. To that aim, the domestic courts may seek the ECJ guidance through a preliminary reference pursuant to Article 267 TFEU, thus entrusting the Luxembourg Court to review the conditions under which punishment would be proportionate in circumstances such as those in the main proceedings.

[78] Among many, see K Lenaerts, K Gutman and JT Nowak, *EU Procedural Law*, 2nd edn (Oxford, Oxford University Press, 2023) 13; G Tesauro, 'Art 19 TUE' in A Tizzano (ed), *Trattati dell'Unione europea*, 2nd edn (Milano, Giuffrè, 2014) 201.

[79] Among extensive case-law, see Opinion 2/13 *Adhésion de l'Union à la CEDH* ECLI:EU:C:2014:2454, para 175.

[80] See Section III(B) of Chapter 1.

[81] Among many, see P Craig and G de Búrca, *EU Law: Text, Cases and Materials*, 7th edn (Oxford, Oxford University Press, 2020) 223–225.

B. Proportionality of Criminal Penalties

i. In Abstracto: *The Definition of Sanctions' Type and Scale*

Once a given action or omission has been qualified as a criminal offence, establishing the type and amount of the relevant penalty constitutes the last stage of the criminalisation process. Again, this choice raises proportionality issues, to be assessed through the lenses of the proportionality of criminal penalties. This principle covers two distinct assessments: firstly, the selection of the type of criminal sanction and, secondly, the definition of its amount.

The choice among different types of criminal penalties is not reduced to a mere binary option between custodial and financial sanctions, as the range of alternatives is broader. Firstly, European criminal justice systems usually offer the possibility of offences to be punished through a combination of custodial and financial penalties. Secondly, several alternative sanctions, such as probation measures,[82] are now recurring in legislative and judicial practice. Therefore, this varied context makes selecting the type of criminal penalties attached to each offence complex.

According to contemporary criminal law practice, defining the sanctions' amount *in abstracto* typically involves establishing a penalty scale, ranging from a minimum to a maximum.[83] In that regard, the structure of the primary scheme is intuitive: the type and amount (ie the scale) of the penalty attached to a given offence shall be adequate, necessary and proportionate *stricto sensu* to attaining a supranational or domestic interest justifying criminalisation.[84]

This assessment is complemented by the two secondary evaluations based upon, respectively, a prospective-utilitarian or retrospective-retributivist rationale. Under prospective proportionality, once the relevant action or omission has been defined, the degree of severity necessary to deter offenders from perpetrating that crime shall be assessed. This evaluation presupposes a negative general prevention rationale. The penalty shall be adequate, necessary and proportionate *stricto sensu* to attain a sufficiently dissuasive effect, a minimum severity threshold capable of preventing other individuals from committing the crime. Similar considerations apply to special prevention: the type and amount of the penalty

[82] Probation measures may fulfil a range of different criminological purposes in contemporary criminal justice systems. In this regard, see the categorisation put forward by I Durnescu, 'An Exploration of the Purposes and Outcomes of Probation in European Jurisdictions' (2008) 55 *Probation Journal* 273.

[83] There are cases where the legislature establishes a fixed penalty for a given offence. However, this practice has been deemed tendentially illegitimate in some EU Member States countries because it restrains the possibility for criminal judges to adjust the penalty imposed *in concreto* to the specificities of the committed crime and the offender's characteristics. That is the case, for instance, of the Italian criminal justice system. According to the Constitutional Court, fixed penalties may be exceptionally held legitimate only insofar as they appear to be 'reasonably proportionate to the entire range of wrongdoings potentially falling under the scope of the offence in question' (Italian Constitutional Court, Judgment of 14 April 1980, No 50).

[84] For a categorisation of these aims, see Section III(A)(i) above in this chapter.

shall be adequate, necessary, and proportionate *stricto sensu* to maximise the chances of resocialisation of the offender.

The retrospective scheme, according to which the type and amount of the penalty shall be proportionate to the seriousness of the wrongdoing, deserves further attention. As anticipated,[85] proportionality in a retributivist perspective cannot be defined by reference to the threefold test, which entails a finalistic assessment. Well-established criminal law scholarship describes retributivist proportionality of penalties as a twofold technique. Building on the assumption that 'persons convicted of crimes of comparable seriousness should receive punishments of comparable severity [and] persons convicted of crimes of differing gravity punishments correspondingly graded in their onerousness',[86] ordinal proportionality entails a comparison between different offences and penalties within the same criminal justice system. More specifically, the legislature or the court shall range crimes and penalties on two parallel scales. Each scale shall be internally ordered: crimes from the least to the most serious; penalties from the least to the most onerous. The extremes of the two scales – namely, the least onerous penalty attached to the least serious crime and the most serious crime paired with the most onerous sanction – represent the 'anchoring points' for the comparison required by ordinal proportionality.[87] The type and amount of the penalty for a given offence are thus defined through a comparison with the regime of the least or most serious crimes set forth by the criminal justice system. Therefore, retrospective proportionality would be violated if, based on the purported comparative analysis, the relative gravity of the penalty does not correspond to the relative seriousness of the offence.[88]

Ordinal proportionality faces several shortcomings. Ranging crimes on the grounds of their seriousness is not always reliable because of the variety of elements potentially characterising the conduct.[89] Moreover, any assessment

[85] See III(B)(ii) above in this chapter.

[86] von Hirsch, 'Proportionality in the Philosophy of Punishment' (n 16) 76. On the same point, see also: A von Hirsch and A Ashworth, *Proportionate Sentencing: Exploring the Principle* (Oxford, Oxford University Press, 2005) 139.

[87] Von Hirsch further explains that ordinal proportionality postulates a relative consideration over the intensity of censure, expressed by the severity of the punishment which a given offence deserves. In fact, the author conceives the level of censure inherent in the sanction as a human convention, which shall be determined on the basis of a comparative approach (von Hirsch, 'Proportionality in the Philosophy of Punishment' (n 16) 77).

[88] Viganò (n 45) 160. In that perspective, ordinal proportionality may amount to a means to assess the internal coherence of a given criminal justice system, thus requiring any difference in treatment between offenders to be rationally and objectively justified. On that point, see: D Pulitanò, 'Sulla pena. Fra teoria, principi e politica' (2016) *Rivista italiana di diritto e procedura penale* 641, 650.

[89] In that respect, Viganò put forward some examples to show the difficulties inherent in the purported comparison. Considering a single type of offence, such as robbery, Viganò highlights that assessing the comparative seriousness between a 1000 euros robbery committed by threatening violence, and a 10 euros robbery committed through violence is not so intuitive. Moreover, as the same scholar underlines, similar hurdles emerge by comparing different types of crimes. For instance, while robbery is typically regarded as a more serious crime if compared to theft, whether a robbery committed without

based on ordinal proportionality depends on the anchoring points. Therefore, ordinal proportionality is unfit to disclose whether a given type and amount of penalty is per se disproportionate to the seriousness of the wrongdoing. This issue is tackled by a complementary concept called 'cardinal proportionality'. Rather than comparing crimes and penalties, cardinal proportionality postulates a direct legal relationship between a given action or omission and the respective criminal sanction. It seeks to establish a threshold above which the sanction attached to a given offence cannot be regarded as per se appropriate.[90]

However, the substance of this 'appropriateness' relationship is particularly elusive. Offences and penalties constitute two ontologically different entities between which a relationship of commensurability can hardly be established.[91] Consequently, other criteria are needed. Firstly, because any criminal sanction temporarily restricts the offender's enjoyment of certain fundamental rights,[92] one may compare the intensity of such a deprivation vis-à-vis the seriousness of the wrongdoing.[93] Secondly, the intensity of the censure inherent in a given criminal punishment[94] may be confronted with the seriousness of the relevant conduct.[95] These alternatives, however, are not entirely satisfactory.[96] Given the theoretical impossibility of establishing a precise methodology to assess crimes and penalties under the edge of cardinal proportionality, this criterion 'is not only considerably less precise than ordinal; it is also more dependent on one's other moral assumptions'.[97]

the employment of weapons is still more severe than residential burglary is more controversial. In this regard, see Viganò (n 45) 64–65.

[90] According to Von Hirsch, cardinal proportionality does not define which exact penalty shall be regarded as appropriate to a given wrongdoing, since the criterion under analysis 'places only broad constraints on how much the penalty scale can be escalated or deflated' (A von Hirsch, 'Proportionality in the Philosophy of Punishment: From "Why Punish" to "How Much"' (1991) 25 *Israel Law Review* 549, 576.

[91] In that regard, Donini denies the possibility to establish a retrospective-retributive legal relationship on sound scientific premises (M Donini, 'Per una concezione post-riparatoria della pena. Contro la pena come raddoppio del male' (2013) *Rivista italiana di diritto e procedura penale* 1162, 1175.

[92] Among many, see: von Hirsch, 'Proportionality in the Philosophy of Punishment: From "Why Punish" to "How Much"' (n 90) 574.

[93] Viganò (n 45) 169.

[94] On that topic, see Section III(B)(ii) above in this chapter.

[95] von Hirsch, 'Proportionality in the Philosophy of Punishment: From "Why Punish" to "How Much"' (n 90) 574.

[96] Viganò contends that resorting to an assessment of the intensity of the limitation of offenders' individual rights may help in better defining the seriousness of the wrongdoing. At the same time, the same scholar admits that the two cited elements are inherently heterogenous. As a result, such a relationship of proportionality may not be strictly and precisely defined in 'Cartesian terms', while its boundaries are inherently more blurred (Viganò (n 45) 169–170).

[97] von Hirsch, 'Proportionality in the Philosophy of Punishment: From 'Why Punish' to 'How Much"' (n 90) 574. In this regard, see also the contention put forward by Lacey and Pickard, according to which it 'is not a naturally existing relationship, but a product of political and social construction, cultural meaning-making and institution-building' (Lacey and Pickard (n 52) 221).

The evident difficulty of translating cardinal proportionality into a solid methodology affects its effective employment in legislative activity.[98] As recently suggested by Viganò, cardinal proportionality should be better construed as a negative standard of review that courts may rely upon.[99] In this way, it would allow the judiciary to assess whether the intensity of the individual rights' limitation inherent in a given type and amount of criminal sanction would be disproportionate vis-à-vis the seriousness of the abstract wrongdoing. Still, in light of the irreducible theoretical ambiguity surrounding the concept of cardinal proportionality, only manifestly disproportionate penalties may be struck down on that basis.[100]

ii. In Concreto: *The Individualisation of Sanctions*

Building upon the penalty's type and scale defined *in abstracto*, trial courts must establish which sanction shall be imposed *in concreto*. This assessment entails the exercise of certain discretion. Defining the penalty *in concreto* may requires choosing between different types of sanctions. Moreover, trial courts shall determine, within a sanctioning range, the exact amount of penalty to be imposed. This form of judicial discretion is meant to secure the individualisation of the criminal penalty to the circumstances of a case.

Domestic criminal systems typically enshrine various methods to limit judicial discretion. In that regard, two distinct legal techniques may be considered. The legislature may dictate criteria that trial judges shall apply when adjudicating concrete criminal allegations. This is, for instance, the method employed within the Italian legal order, as Article 133 of the Criminal Code enumerates criteria to that end.[101] A similar approach may be traced within the French criminal justice system. Indeed, French Criminal Code enshrines an entire section – titled '*modes de personnalisation des peines*' – on the issue under analysis.[102] Also the German legal order is characterised by a comparable regulatory approach.[103] Conversely, common law systems like the UK have developed sentencing guidelines. These rules purport to define a clear methodological (or even mathematical) approach guiding the judges' tasks and are usually drafted by ad hoc committees supervised by the Government.

[98] Viganò (n 45) 169. For an even more radical criticism of cardinal proportionality's potential of establishing a relationship of commensurability between crimes and penalties, see A Ashworth, 'Prisons, Proportionality and Recent Penal History' (2017) 80 *Modern Law Review* 473, 482.

[99] Viganò (n 45) 169.

[100] *ibid*, 170.

[101] More specifically, said provision requires trial judges to consider both the seriousness of the wrongdoing as such – taking into account, in particular, the offence's nature and duration, the damage caused, as well as the mental element – and the offender's personal characteristics. In this regard, see: G Marinucci, E Dolcini and GL Gatta, *Manuale di Diritto penale. Parte generale*, 10th edn (Milano, Giuffrè, 2021) 764 *et seq*.

[102] Within French scholarship on the topic, see the numerous contributions published in R Ottenhof (ed), *L'individualisation de la peine : de Saleilles à aujourd'hui* (Ramonville Saint-Agne, Érès, 2001).

[103] In this regard, see §46 of the German Criminal Code.

The methodology followed by sentencing guidelines may be briefly summarised as follows. Firstly, a 'starting point' for the sanction within the penalty scale of the relevant offence is identified, thus representing the crime's 'standard disvalue'. Then, the trial judge may increase or diminish that standard penalty based on some characteristics of the wrongdoing suggesting greater or lower seriousness.[104]

The proportionality of penalties *in concreto* is primarily directed to domestic criminal courts. However, also the ECJ is entitled to exercise that proportionality review. Indeed, preliminary references may concern the compatibility with EU law of penalties such as the ones imposed at the domestic level. While a preliminary ruling ascertaining the disproportionate nature of criminal law provisions belongs to the *in abstracto* dimension of the principle,[105] a censure involving only the type or amount of the penalty imposed in a specific case represents a manifestation of proportionality of penalties *in concreto*.

The primary scheme of the proportionality of penalties *in concreto* may be framed as follows: the type and amount of the penalty imposed for the committed wrongdoing shall be adequate, necessary and proportionate *stricto sensu* to attaining a legitimate interest justifying criminalisation.[106] This assessment is again highly influenced by further criteria stemming from the secondary schemes. According to prospective proportionality, the type and amount of the penalty imposed *in concreto* shall be adequate, necessary and proportionate *stricto sensu* to attaining a genuinely dissuasive effect or the resocialisation of the offender. The retrospective secondary scheme shall be construed by reference to ordinal and cardinal proportionality concepts. Therefore, considerations related to these paradigms in the previous section apply *mutatis mutandis*. While ordinal proportionality postulates positive and negative standards, cardinal proportionality only implies a negative assessment to be employed for judicial review.

V. The Hybrid Principle between the Law of the EU and ECHR: The Relevance of a Combined Analysis for the Purposes of this Book

The threefold test characterises the principle of proportionality not only in EU law but also in the ECHR legal system.[107] Similarly to fundamental rights adjudication under the Charter, criminal offences and penalties may either implement or pose a burden to individual rights secured by the Convention. The suitability, necessity

[104] Viganò (n 45) 163–164. For an analysis of the UK sentencing guidelines, see A Ashworth and JV Roberts (eds), *Sentencing Guidelines: Exploring the English Model* (Oxford, Oxford University Press, 2013).

[105] See Section IV(B)(i) above in this chapter.

[106] As consistently recalled within the present chapter, these goals shall fall under the scope of the general categories identified in Section III(A)(i) above in this chapter.

[107] As anticipated in Section III(C)(i) of Chapter 1.

and proportionality *stricto sensu* test allows us to assess whether such a measure complies with obligations stemming from the ECHR.

Interestingly, reviewing criminal offences and penalties under the ECHR entails a hybridisation of proportionality by criminal law schemes as in the EU legal order. Similarly to the ECJ, the Strasbourg Court constantly relies on prospective and retrospective proportionality to assess whether punishment is necessary and proportionate *stricto sensu* to attaining a legitimate purpose. A few examples may illustrate this approach. Facing a criminal conviction for incitement of hatred and hostility, in *Incal v Turkey* the Strasbourg Court held this measure disproportionate as there was no evidence that the individual was in any way responsible for acts of terrorism in Turkey.[108] More specifically, the harmfulness of the conduct – spreading a leaflet criticising measures adopted by local authorities – was not as serious as to warrant criminal prosecution under terrorism-related offences. Regarding the proportionality of criminal penalties, the ECtHR has repeatedly affirmed that custodial sanctions in cases involving freedom of expression are legitimate only in exceptional circumstances, 'notably where other fundamental rights have been seriously impaired'.[109] In this line of reasoning, the Strasbourg Court confines the imposition of custodial measures only to cases involving particularly harmful wrongdoings, such as causing a severe prejudice to other human rights. Based on a complementary prospective assessment, the same penalties shall not result in a 'chilling effect' – namely, an excessive deterrent – on exercising freedom of expression.[110] For instance, in *Cumpănă and Mazăre*, the ECtHR recognised that custodial sentences entail an evident chilling effect on exercising journalistic freedom of expression, 'a factor which goes to the proportionality, and thus the justification, of the sanctions imposed'.[111]

The principle's hybrid nature under both EU law and the ECHR paves the way for considering the Strasbourg Court's practice in this analysis. This book specifically focuses on the principle in EU law, but examining the ECHR adds significant value for two main reasons.

On the one hand, the EU legal order and the ECHR are distinct legal systems but strictly interrelated because of Articles 6 TEU and 52(3) of the Charter. As Chapter 1 showed, the equivalence clause enshrined in the latter provision entailed noteworthy influence from the European Convention in the proportionality review

[108] *Incal v Turkey* ECHR 1998–IV, para 58.

[109] *Mariapori v Finland* App No 37751/07 (ECtHR, 6 July 2011), para 67; *Balaskas v Greece* App No 73087/17 (ECtHR, 5 November 2020), para 61; *Matalas v Greece* App No 1864/18 (ECtHR, 25 March 2021), para 59.

[110] Among many, see *Perinçek v Switzerland* App No 27510/08 (ECtHR, 15 October 2015), paras 127 and 129; *Öztürk v Turkey* ECHR 1999–VI, para 70; *Atamanchuk v Russia* App No 4493/11 (ECtHR, 11 February 2020), para 66; *Kyprianou v Cyprus* ECHR 2005–XIII, para 181; *Kudeshkina v Russia* App No 29492/05 (ECtHR, 26 February 2009), para 99.

[111] *Cumpănă and Mazăre v Romania* ECHR 2004–XI, para 114. For a scholarly analysis, see: Viganò (n 45) 94-96; M Oetheimer and A Cardone, 'Art. 10' in S Bartole, P De Sena and V Zagrebelsky (eds), *Commentario breve alla Convenzione europea dei diritti dell'uomo* (Padova, CEDAM, 2012) 409.

of measures interfering with Charter rights.[112] It thus appears that proportionality in EU law cannot be analysed without considering the ECHR dimension of the principle.[113] What is more, the prospect of the EU's accession to the Convention warrants consideration of the ECHR dimension not only for fundamental rights adjudication under the Charter but also for the whole spectrum of the proportionality of criminal offences and penalties in the EU legal order. Indeed, should a new accession agreement be finally concluded, a potential inconsistency of the EU legislative approach in substantive criminal law to proportionality standards developed by the Strasbourg Court may result in a violation of the Convention attributable to the Union.[114]

[112] See Section III(C)(i) of Chapter 1. In literature, among many, see N Lazzerini, *La Carta dei diritti fondamentali dell'Unione europea. I limiti di applicazione* (Milano, Franco Angeli, 2018) 65 *et seq*.

[113] This point is even more emphasised by the ECJ case-law following Opinion 2/13. Notwithstanding the autonomy of the EU legal order resulted in a burden to the EU 'formally' acceding the ECHR, intense judicial dialogue between the Luxembourg and Strasbourg courts gave rise to comparable levels of protection of fundamental rights, a phenomenon defined in literature as the 'substantive' EU accession to the Convention (in particular, see M Parodi, *L'adesione dell'Unione Europea alla CEDU: dinamiche sostanziali e prospettive formali* (Napoli, Edizioni Scientifiche Italiane, 2020) 322).

[114] As argued in literature, the primary implications of the EU acceding to the ECHR consists of establishing an external judicial review mechanism on the Union's institution's adherence to fundamental rights protection (among extensive scholarship, see C Amalfitano, *General Principles of EU Law and the Protection of Fundamental Rights* (Cheltenham, Edward Elgar Publishing, 2018) 36; P Ivaldi and CE Tuo, 'Diritti fondamentali e diritto internazionale privato dell'Unione europea nella prospettiva dell'adesione alla CEDU' (2012) 53 *Rivista di diritto internazionale private e processuale* 7, 22). Still, as the ECJ clarified in said Opinion, such an external review would be incompatible with the autonomy of EU law if it encompassed actions and omissions to which the Court of Justice's jurisdiction is excluded or limited (Opinion 2/13 *Adhésion de l'Union à la CEDH* ECLI:EU:C:2014:2454, para 256). Indeed, the principle of autonomy is one of the fundamental features characterising EU law as a 'new legal order of international law for the benefit of which the states have limited their sovereign rights' (Case 26/62 *Van Gend en Loos v Administratie der Belastingen* ECLI:EU:C:1963:1, p 12). In particular, the autonomous nature of EU law entails a dividing line between EU law, Member States' legal orders and international law. This finding has various implications that cannot be exhausted in this footnote. It suffices to recall here two key aspects. First, as a consequence of the principle of autonomy, only EU law can provide for conditions for the legitimacy of Union actions and omissions (R Barents, *The Autonomy of Community Law* (The Hague, Kluwer Law International, 2004) 262). Second, to preserve the distinct and autonomous nature of the EU legal order, 'the Treaties have established a judicial system intended to ensure consistency and uniformity in the interpretation of EU law' (Opinion 2/13 *Adhésion de l'Union à la CEDH* ECLI:EU:C:2014:2454, para 174). On the implications of the principle of autonomy for the EU accession to the ECHR, among extensive literature, see: B Pirker and S Reitemeyer, 'Between Discursive and Exclusive Autonomy – Opinion 2/13, the Protection of Fundamental Rights and the Autonomy of EU Law' in *Cambridge Yearbook of European Legal Studies* (Cambridge, Cambridge University Press, 2015); I Anrò, *L'adesione dell'Unione europea alla CEDU. L'evoluzione dei sistemi di tutela dei diritti fondamentali in Europa* (Milano, Giuffrè, 2015) 282 *et seq*; S Vezzani, 'L'autonomia dell'ordinamento giuridico dell'Unione Europea. Riflessioni all'indomani del Parere 2/13 della Corte di giustizia' (2016) 1 *Rivista di diritto internazionale* 68. For an analysis of the multiple implications of the principle of autonomy of EU law, among many, see: L Lionello, *L'autonomia dell'ordinamento giuridico dell'Unione europea. Significato, portata e resistenze alla sua applicazione* (Torino, Giappichelli, 2024); C Eckes, 'The Autonomy of the EU Legal Order' (2020) 4 *Europe and the World* 1; V Moreno-Lax and KS Ziegler, 'Autonomy of the EU Legal Order a General Principle? On the Risks of Normative Functionalism and Selective Constitutionalisation' in KS Ziegler, PJ Neuvonen and V Moreno-Lax (eds), *Research Handbook on General Principles in EU Law* (Cheltenham, Elgar, 2022).

On the other hand, the profound differences between the two legal systems are themselves an added value for the present analysis. The Convention constitutes a treaty-based human rights instrument governed by international law. Conversely, EU law postulates a legal order derived from progressive integration between the Member States.[115] Given their different nature, a comparison between the relevant ECJ and ECtHR case-law provides the opportunity to explore whether the EU and ECtHR institutional characteristics and the two courts' different tasks influence the principle's application. The book's following chapters will explore how the schemes composing the proportionality of criminal offences and penalties are employed in practice, aiming to assess their mutual relationship in EU law and, ultimately, to verify the principle's hybrid nature. In that regard, a glance at the ECtHR practice will provide insights into the reasons underpinning the ECJ approach in this regard.

VI. Concluding Remarks

This chapter has shown that the EU concept of proportionality is insufficient to accommodate public and individual interests underlying criminal law repression. A reference to the criminal law prospective and retrospective understandings of proportionality is pivotal to assess in which manner criminal offences and penalties are necessary and proportionate *stricto sensu* to attain a public interest justifying criminalisation. In that light, the question of whether criminalisation is characterised by a consequentialist or deontological rationale – thus fulfilling, respectively, a preventive or retributive goal – profoundly influences the definition of the principle of proportionality of criminal offences and penalties under EU law.

Therefore, the principle of proportionality of criminal offences and penalties should be framed as inherently hybrid, as it combines two dimensions of proportionality. This peculiar intersection between EU and criminal law gives rise to a double-layered theorisation composed of primary and secondary schemes. The primary scheme involves translating the threefold test underlying the EU concept of proportionality to the substantive criminal law domain. In this light, the offence's scope and the penalty's type and amount shall be suitable, necessary, and proportionate *stricto sensu* to attaining a legitimate aim justifying criminalisation. This assessment requires penological considerations, which imply recourse to secondary proportionality evaluations derived from the criminal law discourse. These are the prospective and retrospective schemes.

The double-layered theorisation sought to systematise the coexistence of and interaction between EU and criminal law proportionality within the principle under analysis. This theoretical model addresses the primary goal of this chapter:

[115] Among extensive literature, see R Adam and A Tizzano, *Manuale di Diritto dell'Unione europea*, 4th edn (Torino, Giappichelli, 2024) 10.

to advance a preliminary conceptual appraisal of the principle of proportionality of criminal offences and penalties.

However, not only shall this preliminary conceptualisation be confirmed by analysing the relevant practice, but it is also insufficient to frame the principle in the EU legal order exhaustively. A purely theoretical approach falls short of disclosing the complex relationships between the primary and secondary schemes. The double-layered model may be applied differently in the EU legislative and judicial practice. In particular, the necessity and proportionality *stricto sensu* of a given offence or penalty may be assessed by relying either on prospective or retrospective considerations or a combination of these schemes. Moreover, proportionality may give rise to different standards for judicial review, as shown in Chapter 1 above.[116]

Therefore, further analysis is required. The book will now embrace a different perspective to analyse the principle's application. The double-layered model theorised so far constitutes the research hypothesis to be verified and refined in the light of the relevant legislative and judicial practice. Only a systematic analysis of the latter may disclose the mutual relationships between prospective and retrospective proportionality and the intensity of the proportionality review of offences and penalties under EU law.

[116] See Section IV(A)(ii) of Chapter 1.

3

Proportionality of Offences and Penalties in EU Substantive Criminal Law

I. Introduction

This chapter assesses the application of proportionality of offences and penalties at the EU level, thereby focusing on the harmonisation of substantive criminal law by the Union's legislature. In this domain, the principle features an *in abstracto* assessment shaping the legislative definition of harmonised offences and penalties and their review by the ECJ.

Having identified which legal interests drive EU criminalisation (II), the chapter reconstructs the proportionality of (harmonised) offences (III) and penalties (IV) from EU legislative practice. This assessment shows how the principle's primary and secondary schemes are applied in EU substantive criminal law and their reciprocal interaction. Then, the chapter discusses the potential approach of the ECJ in reviewing provisions harmonising offences and penalties (V).

II. The Objectives of EU Substantive Criminal Law: From a Functional Rationale to the Slow Emergence of a Constitutional Value-based Dimension

As disclosed in Chapter 2, proportionality of offences and penalties seeks to accommodate, inter alia, the EU's interests in criminalisation against individual rights and freedoms. The former deserves closer attention as it results from a remarkable evolution in the EU legal order. Indeed, the Treaty of Rome did not confer any express competence to the EEC in criminal law. At the same time, the progressive deepening of the European integration process unveiled the need to enhance the effectiveness of EEC – then EC and now EU – action in non-criminal domains by adopting substantive criminal law provisions.[1] In fact, criminalisation has played a

[1] V Mitsilegas, *EU Criminal Law after Lisbon. Rights, Trust and the Transformation of Justice in Europe* (Oxford, Hart Publishing, 2016) 54.

crucial role in the gradual establishment of the internal market by securing the effective enjoyment of EU fundamental freedoms.[2] Therefore, a link between internal market regulation – or, from a broader point of view, the former First Pillar – and substantive criminal law has progressively emerged.[3] This relationship is of a functional nature. Indeed, criminal law is warranted to ensure that behaviours potentially hindering the exercise of internal market freedoms are criminalised in all Member States. From this perspective, EU criminalisation contributes to the functioning of the internal market itself.

The Treaty of Maastricht established a specific competence upon the Union to harmonise domestic criminal provisions within the Third Pillar.[4] Still, the functional relationship between criminalisation and internal market law remained the guiding star of the Commission's policy approach to criminal law.[5] Indeed, the Commission framed the adoption of harmonising provisions on substantive criminal law as a tool for the effectiveness of EU policies under the First Pillar.[6] From that perspective, the Commission proposed several directives incorporating provisions for harmonising domestic offences and penalties. The Council strongly opposed this approach, thus adopting these proposals as Framework Decisions based on the Third Pillar.[7]

[2] The fight against money-laundering represents a far-reaching example in this regard. That form of crime has been perceived by the Commission as a threat to the financial stability of the Community as a whole, thus requiring to consider these behaviours as criminal offences (Proposal for a Council Directive on Prevention of the Financial System for the Purpose of Money Laundering, COM(1990) 106 final; in that regard, see: V Mitsilegas, *Money Laundering Counter-measures in the European Union: A New Paradigm of Security Governance versus Fundamental Legal Principles* (The Hague, Kluwer Law International, 2003) 89. The finally adopted directive (Council Directive 91/308/EEC on Prevention of the Use of the Financial System for the Purpose of Money Laundering [1991] OJ L166/77) did not include specific provisions compelling Member States to adopt criminal sanctions. However, the very fact that the Commission proposed criminal law harmonisation by relying on the EC internal market legal basis shows that the absence of explicit conferral of powers by the Treaties had not been perceived as a bar for EC action in the criminal domain (Mitsilegas, *EU Criminal Law after Lisbon. Rights, Trust and the Transformation of Justice in Europe* (n 1) 54).

[3] That relationship is not, however, uncontroversial in literature. See, in this regard, the criticism raised by Herlin-Karnell with respect to the possibility to employ post-Lisbon Art 114 TFEU as a legal basis for substantive criminal law harmonisation, in E Herlin-Karnell, *The Constitutional Dimension of European Criminal Law* (Oxford, Hart Publishing, 2012) 106–109.

[4] While the harmonisation of domestic provisions was not expressly included within the list of 'question of common interest' under Art K 1 of the Maastricht Treaty, that legal basis allowed the adoption of a number of instruments approximating Member States' criminal law provisions, such as the 1995 Convention on the Protection of EU Financial Interests (Convention drawn up on the basis of Art K.3 of the Treaty on European Union, on the Protection of the European Communities' Financial Interests [1995] OJ C316/49). Five years after Maastricht, the Treaty of Amsterdam clarified the extent of EU powers within the Third Pillar by including an explicit reference to the harmonisation of domestic provisions. In that regard, see: A Weyembergh, *L'harmonisation des législations : condition de l'espace pénal européen et révélateur de ses tensions* (Bruxelles, Editions de l'Université de Bruxelles, 2004) 49–50.

[5] Mitsilegas, *EU Criminal Law after Lisbon. Rights, Trust and the Transformation of Justice in Europe* (n 1) 55.

[6] I Wieczorek, *The Legitimacy of EU Criminal Law* (Oxford, Hart Publishing, 2020) 126.

[7] For a categorisation of EU secondary law acts falling under the scope of the former Third Pillar, see E Pistoia, *Cooperazione penale nei rapporti fra diritto dell'Unione europea e diritto statale* (Napoli, Edizioni Scientifiche Italiane, 2008) 41–53.

Against these diverging approaches, the ECJ upheld the Commission's position in the well-known 2005 Environmental Crimes Case.[8] Faced with an action for the annulment of Framework Decision 2003/80/JHA on the Protection of the Environment by Means of Criminal Law[9] – an act initially proposed by the Commission in the form of a First Pillar directive – the Court held that EU law does not prevent

> the Community legislature, when the application of effective, proportionate and dissuasive criminal penalties by the competent national authorities is an essential measure for combating serious environmental offences, from taking measures which relate to the criminal law of the Member States which it considers necessary in order to ensure that the rules which it lays down on environmental protection are fully effective.[10]

This finding, partially confirmed by the 2007 ruling in the Ship-Source Pollution Case,[11] consecrates the functional rationale of EU harmonisation of offences and penalties: the EU legislature can resort to criminalisation to ensure the effectiveness of EU law.

From the same functional perspective, calls for harmonising offences and penalties have also emerged to facilitate judicial cooperation in criminal matters. Indeed, the harmonisation of domestic criminal provisions has traditionally been justified by the need to allow for the fulfilment of dual criminality.[12] Since judicial cooperation was, in most cases, conditional upon criminalising the relevant behaviour in the Member States involved, approximating offences could ease meeting the dual criminality requirement.

Since the adoption of the Treaty of Maastricht, new far-reaching judicial cooperation instruments based on the principles of mutual recognition and mutual trust have been adopted.[13] Mutual recognition implies overcoming some traditional bars to cooperation, such as dual criminality.[14] Therefore, that

[8] Case C-176/03 *Commission v Council* ECLI:EU:C:2005:542.

[9] Council Framework Decision 2003/80/JHA on the Protection of the Environment through Criminal Law [2003] OJ L29/55.

[10] Case C-176/03 *Commission v Council* ECLI:EU:C:2005:542, para 48.

[11] Case C-440/05 *Commission v Council* ECLI:EU:C:2007:625, para 66. This ruling partially tempered the ECJ findings in the 2005 Environmental Crimes Case. The Court clarified that the First Pillar's legal bases allow the EC legislature to lay down minimum rules only on the definition of crimes, and not of penalties. EC directives, therefore, could only provide that Member States shall lay down 'effective, proportionate and dissuasive' penalties with respect to offences defined therein. Minimum rules on the definition of penalties may be provided by means of Framework Decisions adopted under the Third Pillar (*ibid*, para 70).

[12] Weyembergh, *L'harmonisation des législations : condition de l'espace pénal européen et révélateur de ses tensions* (n 4) 138.

[13] The European Arrest Warrant (Council Framework Decision 2002/584/JHA on the European Arrest Warrant and the Surrender Procedures between Member States [2002] OJ L190/1) constitutes the most notable example in this regard, as it represents the first judicial cooperation instrument implementing the principle of mutual recognition in the criminal law field. For an analysis of the role and implications of proportionality in the EAW framework, see Section VI of Chapter 4.

[14] Among extensive literature, see: G Taupiac-Nouvel, *Le principe de reconnaissance mutuelle des décisions répressives dans l'Union européenne. Contribution à l'étude d'un modèle de libre circulation des décisions de justice* (Clermont-Ferrand, Institut Universitaire Varenne, 2011) 238; C Janssens,

requirement enjoys a narrower scope in the current judicial cooperation landscape. This finding raises doubts about the feasibility of invoking the need to enhance judicial cooperation to justify the harmonisation of offences and penalties. Two distinct positions have emerged in the literature. From one point of view, it has been argued that the constant expansion of mutual recognition may prevent the adoption of EU criminalisation instruments based on the pretended need to facilitate judicial cooperation.[15] From an opposite perspective, it has been highlighted that the abolition of dual criminality in EU judicial cooperation is only partial. Therefore, harmonisation of offences and penalties may still be required in some cases to meet this requirement.[16] Moreover, establishing mutual trust as the precondition for mutual recognition reinforces the need to harmonise Member States' offences and penalties even more. Indeed, the approximation of domestic substantive criminal law upholds mutual trust, particularly by fostering substantive trust[17] between Member States on their respective legal orders.[18]

Notwithstanding divergent positions in literature, Öberg[19] recently observed that easing judicial cooperation still emerges as an objective of EU criminalisation in the *travaux préparatoires* of relevant Directives and Framework Decisions.[20] Moreover, the European Parliament in 2012 expressed the view that 'harmonisation measures should be proposed primarily to support the application of the principle of mutual recognition in practice, rather than merely expanding the scope of harmonised EU criminal law'.[21] It follows that enhancing

The Principle of Mutual Recognition in EU Law (Oxford, Oxford University Press, 2013) 170; JW Ouwerkerk, *Quid pro Quo? A Comparative Law Perspective on the Mutual Recognition of Judicial Decisions in Criminal Matters* (Cambridge, Intersentia, 2011) 47; A Damato, 'La cooperazione giudiziaria in materia penale' in G Tesauro, *Manuale di Diritto dell'Unione europea*, vol 2 (P De Pasquale and F Ferraro eds, Napoli, Editoriale Scientifica, 2021) 342, 344.

[15] JW Ouwerkerk, 'The Potential of Mutual Recognition as a Limit to the Exercise of EU Criminalisation Powers' (2017) 7 *European Criminal Law Review* 5.

[16] Weyembergh, *L'harmonisation des législations : condition de l'espace pénal européen et révélateur de ses tensions* (n 4) 144.

[17] On the need of continuous strengthening of substantive trust between Member States for upholding mutual trust, see: R Sicurella, 'Fostering a European Criminal Law Culture: In Trust We Trust' (2018) 9 *New Journal of European Criminal Law* 308.

[18] A Weyembergh, 'Le rapprochement des incriminations et des sanctions penales' (2006) 77 *Revue internationale de droit penal* 185, 190.

[19] J Öberg, *The Normative Foundations for EU Criminal Justice: Powers, Limits and Justifications* (Oxford, Hart Publishing, 2024) 87.

[20] See, for instance, the Proposal for a Directive of the European Parliament and of the Council on Countering Money Laundering by Criminal Law, COM(2016) 826 final, 9; Commission Staff Working Document – Impact Assessment accompanying the Proposal for a Directive of the European Parliament and of the Council on the Protection of the Euro and Other Currencies Against Counterfeiting by Criminal Law, and Replacing Framework Decision 2000/383/JHA, SWD(2013) 19 final Part 1/2, 15; Proposal for a Council Framework Decision on Combating Racism and Xenophobia, COM(2001) 664 final, 7.

[21] European Parliament Resolution of 22 May 2012 on an EU Approach to Criminal Law (2010/2310(INI)) [2013] OJ C264E/7, para 7 of the operative part.

judicial cooperation still represents one of the functional objectives driving EU criminalisation.

An additional objective for EU criminalisation can be identified. The Treaty of Amsterdam expressed the Union's aim to 'provide citizens with a high level of safety [...] by preventing and combating crime'.[22] This scope for the EU intervention, functional to 'offer enhanced security to [...] citizens but also to defend the Union's interests',[23] reflects the perceived need for common action between Member States to tackle global security threats.[24] From this viewpoint, the establishment of the AFSJ clarified and broadened the EU competence on substantive criminal law by introducing a new rationale for supranational criminalisation, defined by Mitsilegas as 'securitised criminalisation'.[25]

It follows that two main objectives have driven the development of EU substantive criminal law in the pre-Lisbon era: on the one hand, the effectiveness of EU policies and judicial cooperation (functional criminalisation); on the other hand, the enhancement of a high level of security within the Union (securitised criminalisation). The Treaty of Lisbon crystallised these two rationales in Article 83 TFEU,[26] the current legal basis for adopting directives harmonising offences and penalties. According to that provision, the EU action in the substantive criminal law field may be warranted either to tackle some 'areas of particularly serious crime with a cross-border dimension resulting from the nature or impact of such offences or from a special need to combat them on a common basis',[27] or to 'ensure the effective implementation of a Union policy in an area which has been subject to harmonisation measures'.[28]

Against this background, a third and distinct rationale has emerged. Indeed, some of the most recent initiatives in the substantive criminal law field have been

[22] *ibid.*

[23] Action Plan of the Council and the Commission on How Best to Implement the Provisions of the Treaty of Amsterdam on an Area of Freedom, Security and Justice – Text Adopted by the Justice and Home Affairs Council of 3 December 1998 [1999] OJ C19/1, para 11.

[24] V Mitsilegas, *EU Criminal Law*, 2nd edn (Oxford, Hart Publishing, 2022) 115. In this respect, Peršak (N Peršak, 'Principles of EU Criminalisation and Their Varied Normative Strength: Harm and Effectiveness' (2022) 27 *European Law Journal* 463, 475) and Öberg (Öberg (n 19) 67) framed the enumeration of areas of serious crime in Article 83(1) TFEU as an expression of the harm principle as a normative justification for the Union's action in substantive criminal law.

[25] Mitsilegas, *EU Criminal Law after Lisbon. Rights, Trust and the Transformation of Justice in Europe* (n 1) 54. In that regard, Monar has recently suggested that even securitised criminalisation can be theorised as a functional rationale. It is instrumental to offering citizens a high level of security, by tackling either some forms of severe crime or conducts 'endangering of the security of certain common goods and interests' (J Monar, 'Reflections on the Place of Criminal Law in the European Construction' (2021) 27 *European Law Journal* 356, 359). The author thus proposes a broad concept of 'functional', 'in the sense of not pursuing a distinct European integration objective regarding criminal law as such but [...] to address specific cross-border crime challenges which at least partly have been generated or enhanced by the progress of EU integration in other fields' (*ibid*).

[26] Mitsilegas, *EU Criminal Law after Lisbon. Rights, Trust and the Transformation of Justice in Europe* (n 1) 57.

[27] Art 83(1) TFEU.

[28] Art 83(2) TFEU.

grounded on the need to protect and uphold the Union values.[29] Monar recently labelled this feature as the 'constitutional dimension' of EU criminal law.[30]

Elements of a constitutional dimension in EU substantive criminal law may be identified even in the pre-Lisbon era.[31] In that regard, it is notable that Article 29 TEU, as amended by the Treaty of Amsterdam, included 'preventing and combating racism and xenophobia' as one of the objectives to ensure a high safety level within the AFSJ.[32] That provision discloses a value-based rationale: as clarified by the Commission Proposal for a Framework Decision on this topic,

> racism and xenophobia are direct violations of the principles of freedom, democracy, respect for human rights and fundamental freedoms and the rule of law, principles upon which the European Union is founded and which are common to the Member States.[33]

The same wording has been included in the finally adopted Framework Decision, thus disclosing the value-based pattern underpinning that piece of secondary law.[34]

The reforms brought by the Treaty of Lisbon seem to have fostered a value-driven dimension in EU criminalisation.[35] In fact, the emphasis put by the Treaties on the Union's founding values and fundamental rights entails noteworthy consequences for the criminal law sphere. The protection and promotion of EU values enshrined in Article 2 TEU has become an objective whose pursuance potentially requires EU criminalisation. There is already some evidence of that development.

[29] From a broader perspective, EU harmonisation can be framed as a value-based operation rather than a neutral end goal, and this feature also holds with respect to the approximation of domestic criminal systems (Wieczorek (n 6) 85).

[30] Monar (n 25) 361–362. Di Stasi has advanced a similar perspective, suggesting that the Union's action against cross-border crime is teleologically driven by promoting and upholding the common values enshrined in Article 2 TEU (A Di Stasi, 'Introduzione – Spazio europeo, rivisitate priorità dell'UE e garanzia dei valori comuni. La cooperazione giudiziaria in materia penale per la repressione dei cross-border crimes' in A Oriolo, AR Castaldo, A Di Stasi and M Nino (eds), *Criminalità transnazionale e Unione europea* (Napoli, Editoriale Scientifica, 2024) 216–217).

[31] The development of a constitutional perspective on the EU legal order has long preceded the Treaty of Lisbon. Indeed, the ECJ early defined the EEC as a 'community based on the rule of law' (Case 294/83 *Les Verts v Parliament* ECLI:EU:C:1986:166, para 23), as well as on a set of 'constitutional principles' (Joined Cases C-402/05 P and C-415/05 P *Kadi and Al Barakaat International Foundation v Council and Commission* ECLI:EU:C:2008:461, para 285).

[32] On the harmonisation of Member States' criminal systems to combat racism and xenophobia see, among many, V Mitsilegas, 'The Third Wave of Third Pillar Law: Which Direction for EU Criminal Justice?' (2009) 34 *European Law Review* 523; P Lobba, 'Punishing Denialism beyond Holocaust Denial: EU Framework Decision 2008/913/JHA and Other Expansive Trends' (2014) 5 *New Journal of European Criminal Law* 58.

[33] Proposal for a Council Framework Decision on Combating Racism and Xenophobia, COM(2001) 664 final, 2.

[34] Council Framework Decision 2008/913/JHA of 28 November 2008 on Combating Certain Forms and Expressions of Racism and Xenophobia by Means of Criminal Law [2008] OJ L328/55, recital 1.

[35] A deeper discussion on the EU constitutional dimension would exceed the scope of the present work. Among extensive literature on the topic, see the wide-ranging contributions published in A Von Bogdandy and J Bast (eds), *Principles of European Constitutional Law* (Oxford – Munchen, Hart Publishing – Beck, 2009).

In particular, the 2021 Commission Proposal for Expanding the List of Areas of Crime under Article 83(1) TFEU to Hate Crime and Hate Speech clarifies that 'only a common initiative at EU level can effectively protect the common values enshrined in Article 2 of the TEU'.[36]

It follows that the EU's interest in criminalisation consists of three distinct objectives. The harmonisation of offences and penalties may be warranted either by the need to ensure the effectiveness of EU policies and judicial cooperation (functional criminalisation), to address common security threats (securitised criminalisation) or to uphold EU fundamental values (constitutional dimension of EU criminalisation).

III. Assessing the EU Legislative Approach: Proportionality in the Definition of Harmonised Criminal Offences

All three rationales drive the exercise of EU powers in substantive criminal law, thus requiring the EU legislature to balance them against individual rights and freedoms on proportionality grounds.[37] This section focuses on the proportionality assessment for the legislative definition of harmonised offences. The scope of this analysis extends to the *travaux préparatoires* of each act of secondary law harmonising offences and penalties currently in force, including Commission Proposals and Impact Assessment Reports.[38] Building upon this *corpus*, the section explores the specific declinations of the principle in the legislative practice (A) and the application of its schemes (B).

A. Two Competing Declinations of the Principle in the Legislative Practice

The proportionality of harmonised offences may be framed as a competence issue under Article 5(4) TEU (i) or as a fundamental rights one, thereby requiring an assessment based on Article 52(1) of the Charter (ii). The EU legislature relies on both proportionality declinations but to a different extent.

[36] Communication from the Commission to the European Parliament and the Council – A More Inclusive and Protective Europe: Extending the List of EU Crimes to Hate Speech and Hate Crime, COM(2021) 777 final, 18.

[37] On the impact of EU harmonised offences and penalties on the rights, freedom and dignity of individuals, see Wieczorek (n 6) 56.

[38] As outlined in literature, these categories of acts fall under the scope of the 'primary preparatory works' of EU secondary law. On this point, see S Lattanzi, *I 'travaux préparatoires' del diritto dell'Unione europea: tassonomia, ruolo e funzioni* (Padova, CEDAM, 2022) 96.

i. From Proportionality of the Content of Union Action to Proportionality of Union Criminalisation: The Nuanced Influence of Article 5(4) TEU

Like any piece of EU secondary law, the adoption of harmonising provisions in the substantive criminal law field stems from a conferral of powers by Member States to the Union. The exercise of this legislative competence, enshrined in Article 83 TFEU, is subject to the principles of subsidiarity and proportionality under Article 5 TEU.[39] Therefore, proportionality in the definition of harmonised offences may first emerge as a limit to exercising EU normative powers as such. Since 'the content and form of Union action shall not exceed what is necessary to achieve the objectives of the Treaties', Article 5(4) TEU postulates a limit to the intensity of the EU action in substantive criminal law.[40]

This limit is potentially twofold. In the first place, Article 5(4) provides for an accommodation between, on the one hand, the EU objectives pursued through approximation of offences and, on the other hand, Member States' interest in retaining legislative powers in substantive criminal law. This balancing operation forms part of the institutional dimension of proportionality previously introduced.[41] In the second place, Article 5(4) TEU may also shape EU criminalisation choices under Article 83 TFEU. When defining 'minimum rules concerning the definition of criminal offences',[42] the 'Union action' referred to in Article 5(4) TEU consists of criminalising a range of conducts. Article 83 TFEU empowers the Union to establish minimum rules only, which do not qualify as an exercise of *ius puniendi* in the proper sense. However, it establishes obligations to criminalise at the EU level, which bind the Member States' exercise of domestic *ius puniendi*.[43] It follows that the concept of 'criminalisation' – namely, the direct or indirect qualification of a given conduct as a criminal offence – is appropriate to define the 'content' of the Union action under Article 83 TFEU.[44]

[39] See the distinction between subsidiarity and proportionality in Section III(A) of Chapter 1.

[40] Further on Art 5(4) TEU, see Section III(A) of Chapter 1.

[41] On the dichotomy between the institutional and individualistic dimensions of the principle of proportionality of criminal offences and penalties, see Section III(A)(i) of Chapter 2.

[42] Art 83(1) TFEU.

[43] In this regard, Wieczorek underlines that 'regardless of the debate on minimum rules as minimum or maximum criminalisation, it remains the case that directives harmonising definition of crimes often include very precise definitions of crimes. Member States are bound to implement such policy choices in several instances and almost verbatim in national legal systems' (Wieczorek (n 6) 51).

[44] That finding seems confirmed by well-established literature, since most authors refer to the concept of EU criminalisation while analysing the harmonisation of offences and penalties by the EU legislature. In particular, a number of authors have recently contended the need to develop a set of criminalisation principles for the EU action in the substantive criminal law field. In that regard, see Peršak (n 24); SS Buisman, 'The Future of EU Substantive Criminal Law: Towards a Uniform Set of Criminalisation Principles at the EU Level' (2022) 30 *European Journal of Crime, Criminal Law and Criminal Justice* 161; N Peršak, 'EU Criminal Law and Its Legitimation: In Search for a Substantive Principle of Criminalisation' (2018) 26 *European Journal of Crime, Criminal Law and Criminal Justice* 20; L Micheletto, 'Towards an Integrated (and Possibly Pan-European?) Prima Facie Legitimacy Test: Merging the Rechtsgut Theory, the Offensività Principle, and the Harm Principle' (2021) 29 *European Journal of Crime, Criminal Law and Criminal Justice* 241.

Therefore, in the substantive criminal law domain, Article 5(4) TEU entails that the form and content of EU criminalisation shall not exceed what is necessary to achieve the objectives of the Treaties. These objectives include ensuring the effectiveness of EU policies (functional criminalisation), tackling threats to the Union's internal security (securitised criminalisation), and promoting and upholding EU common values (constitutional dimension of EU criminalisation).

Looking at the practice, this proportionality scheme emerges from the 2012 European Parliament Resolution 'On an EU Approach to Criminal Law'.[45] The Resolution highlights the potentialities of Article 5(4) TEU for limiting criminalisation under Article 83 TFEU. After expressly recalling that 'the principles of subsidiarity and proportionality, *as mentioned in Article 5 TEU*, are [...] particularly relevant in the case of legislative proposals governing criminal law (emphasis added)',[46] the Parliament encouraged 'the Commission to continue to include in its impact assessments the necessity and proportionality test'.[47] Under this test,

> the necessity of new substantive criminal law provisions must be demonstrated by the necessary factual evidence, making it clear that:
>
> — the criminal provisions focus on conduct causing significant pecuniary or non-pecuniary damage to society, individuals or a group of individuals;
> — there are no other, less intrusive measures available for addressing such conduct.[48]

These two criteria are insightful. Indeed, they suggest that Article 5(4) TEU requires assessing not only the intensity of harmonisation as such but also the compelling need to criminalise a given conduct. In this perspective, the proportionality scheme based upon Article 5(4) TEU may well accommodate the clash between EU interests in criminalisation and the protection of the individual legal sphere.

Notwithstanding this affirmation, legislative practice discloses ambivalent trends. Article 5(4) TEU is always a protagonist of the Commission's Explanatory Memoranda and Impact Assessments accompanying legislative proposals on substantive criminal law. However, the same provision usually falls short of establishing a thorough assessment of the implications of harmonised offences. Some examples from the practice may explain the overwhelming trend. The 2010 Proposal for a Directive on Attacks against Information Systems merely affirms that the Directive 'confines itself to the minimum required in order to achieve [the objectives pursued] and does not go beyond what is necessary for that purpose, taking into account the accuracy of criminal legislation'.[49] In the

[45] European Parliament Resolution of 22 May 2012 on an EU Approach to Criminal Law (2010/2310(INI)) [2013] OJ C264E/7.

[46] *ibid*, recital D.

[47] *ibid*, para 8 of the operative part.

[48] *ibid*, para 3 of the operative part.

[49] Proposal for a Directive of the European Parliament and of the Council on Attacks Against Information Systems and Repealing Council Framework Decision 2005/222/JHA, COM(2010) 517 final, 8.

same vein, in the 2017 Proposal for a Directive on Fraud and Counterfeiting of Non-cash Means of Payment, the Commission only highlights that 'the proposed new Directive is limited to what is necessary and proportionate to implement international standards and adapt existing legislation on offences in this area to new threats'.[50] These findings appear as a simple rubber-stamp by the Commission on compliance with Article 5(4) TEU, failing to state any reason justifying this claim.

Sometimes, the proportionality assessment has even been reduced to a mere cost-benefit evaluation. In this perspective, the Commission contended in the 2007 Proposal for a Directive on the Protection of the Environment by Means of Criminal Law that

> the implementation of the Directive entails no significant financial and administrative burden as the criminal law and judicial structures already exist in Member States. Some additional burden for the Member States could result from a potential increase in prosecutions and criminal proceedings, but at the same time, the deterrent effect of higher sanctions should lead to a decrease of offences committed and thus reduce the number of criminal proceedings in the long run.[51]

This example clarifies the significantly reduced role of Article 5(4) TEU for the principle of proportionality of criminal offences. The Commission and the EU legislature seem not eager to expand their scrutiny of the intensity of Union action to assess the extent of Union criminalisation as such.

Against this trend, the 2022 Proposal for amending the Directive on Trafficking in Human Beings[52] constitutes an exception. In that Proposal, the Commission introduces a proportionality justification of newly proposed offences for attaining an appropriate response to emerging security issues in the field.[53] Therefore, it appears to attribute a broader scope to proportionality under Article 5(4) TEU, thus implying a scrutiny of criminalisation choices. However, this proposal is the only example: future legislative practice may show whether it would pave the way to a more proficient proportionality assessment of the Union criminalisation under Article 5(4) TEU.

[50] Proposal for a Directive of the European Parliament and of the Council on Combating Fraud and Counterfeiting of Non-cash Means of Payments and Replacing Council Framework Decision 2001/413/JHA, COM(2017) 489 final, 9.

[51] Proposal for a Directive of the European Parliament and of the Council on the Protection of the Environment through Criminal Law, COM(2007) 51 final, 6.

[52] Proposal for a Directive of the European Parliament and of the Council amending Directive 2011/36/EU on Preventing and Combating Trafficking in Human Beings and Protecting its Victims, COM(2022) 732 final.

[53] *ibid*, 6: 'In order to address forms of exploitation which are currently not explicitly mentioned in the Anti-trafficking Directive, it is proposed to explicitly add forced marriage and illegal adoption. The proposed addition of these forms of exploitation, which are already mentioned in the recitals of the Directive, is deemed as a proportionate response to the increase in the percentage of trafficking cases for purposes other than sexual and labour exploitation'.

ii. The Rising Role of the Fundamental Rights Dimension of Proportionality under Article 52(1) of the Charter

Compared to Article 5(4) TEU, the fundamental rights dimension of proportionality appears more promising. Any harmonisation of offences and penalties entails fundamental rights implications,[54] since it establishes positive obligations to criminalise upon the Member States. Being criminal law the most intrusive public interference in the individual sphere,[55] individual rights protection under the Charter is crucial in shaping harmonised offences. In that context, Article 52(1) of the Charter plays a key role. Each interference with fundamental rights shall not only be provided for by the law but also respect the essence of the right at stake and, subject to the principle of proportionality, be 'necessary and genuinely meet objectives of general interest recognised by the Union or the need to protect the rights and freedoms of others'.

The fundamental rights dimension of proportionality has only recently started influencing EU criminalisation. Only post-Lisbon legislative proposals in substantive criminal law enshrine an assessment of their interference with the enjoyment of fundamental rights.[56] This evaluation is substantially absent from pre-Lisbon legislative initiatives, which just affirm that the proposal's content complies with the proportionality principle underpinning the exercise of Union competencies.[57] What is more, some pre-Lisbon legislative proposals do not provide any proportionality justification of the envisaged criminalisation.[58]

This different approach may be explained by the Charter acquiring primary law value only after Lisbon. However, fundamental rights protection was an obligation upon EU institutions even before. As shown in Chapter 1, fundamental rights have been qualified as general principles of the Union legal order since 1969,

[54] Some elements in the practice confirm that assumption. To provide just one explicative example, see European Parliament Resolution of 22 May 2012 on an EU Approach to Criminal Law cit, para 2 of the operative part.

[55] Among many, see Monar (n 25) 360. See also M Kaiafa-Gbandi, 'The Importance of Core Principles of Substantive Criminal Law for a European Criminal Policy Respecting Fundamental Rights and the Rule of Law' (2011) 1 *European Criminal Law Review* 6, 33.

[56] This aspect constitutes just one result of the evolutive process which gradually led the Commission to assess the impact of legislative proposals on the enjoyment of fundamental rights secured by the Charter. For a broader assessment of this phenomenon, see N Lazzerini, 'Le clausole generali della Carta dei diritti fondamentali nel law-making europeo: codificazione e innovazione nella determinazione del livello di tutela' in A Annoni, S Forlati and F Salerno (eds), *La codificazione nell'ordinamento internazionale e dell'Unione europea* (Napoli, Editoriale Scientifica, 2019) 519–523.

[57] Among potential examples in the legislative practice, see Proposal for a Council Framework Decision on the Fight Against Organised Crime, COM(2005) 6 final, 10, recitals 7–8; Proposal for a Council Framework Decision on Combating Racism and Xenophobia, COM(2001) 664 final, 7. In that regard, it should be noted that a formal obligation to extensively justify compliance of each legislative proposal with the principle of subsidiarity and proportionality has been imposed on the Commission only by the Treaty of Lisbon, as set forth in Art 5 of Protocol (No 2) on the Application of the Principles of Subsidiarity and Proportionality [2016] OJ C202/206.

[58] In particular, see the Proposal for a Council Framework Decision on Combating Terrorism, COM(2001) 521 final.

when the ECJ rendered its judgment in *Stauder*.[59] Subsequent case-law of the Court developed an assessment for the legitimacy of Union measures interfering with the enjoyment of fundamental rights.[60]

Nowadays, the Commission is conscious of the critical role proportionality plays under Article 52(1) of the Charter in EU substantive criminal law. The 2016 Proposal for a Directive on Countering Money Laundering by Criminal Law is quite explicative of this trend.[61] Its Explanatory Memorandum affirms that

> the respect of fundamental rights in general and the principle of proportionality is respected in limiting the scope of offences to what strictly necessary to allow for the effective prosecution of acts that pose a particular threat to the EU's internal security.[62]

The same findings emerge from both the 2017 Proposal for a Directive on Combating Fraud and Counterfeiting of Non-Cash Means of Payment[63] and the 2015 Proposal for a Directive on Combating Terrorism.[64]

The fundamental rights dimension of proportionality unveils a more articulated balancing than Article 5(4) TEU. Indeed, the Commission's reasoning based on Article 52(1) of the Charter elucidates not only the interests warranting criminalisation – in the case of money laundering, the protection of the EU's internal security – but also the proportionality standard of assessment employed ('strictly necessary'). This proportionality scheme acquires prominence in the legislative practice over Article 5(4) TEU, as showed by the 2012 Proposal for a Directive on the Fight Against Fraud to the Union's Financial Interests.[65] Articles 5(4) TEU and 52(1) of the Charter are both considered in the same section of the Proposal's Explanatory Memorandum. However, the proportionality assessment encapsulated therein only focuses on the offences' interference with fundamental rights under the Charter. After acknowledging that harmonised offences interfere with the enjoyment of several individual rights,[66] the Proposal clarifies that these limitations 'are justified because they meet the objectives of general interest recognised by the Union'[67] as required by Article 52(1) of the Charter. The Commission pledges that 'it has been carefully ensured that these measures do not go beyond what is necessary to achieve this objective, and are thus proportionate'.[68]

[59] Case 29/69 *Stauder v Stadt Ulm* ECLI:EU:C:1969:57, para 7.

[60] Further on this topic, see Section III(C)(ii) of Chapter 1.

[61] Proposal for a Directive of the European Parliament and of the Council on Countering Money Laundering by Criminal Law cit.

[62] *ibid*, 10.

[63] Proposal for a Directive of the European Parliament and of the Council on Combating Fraud and Counterfeiting of Non-Cash Means of Payment cit 15.

[64] Proposal for a Directive of the European Parliament and of the Council on Combating Terrorism and Replacing Council Framework Decision 2002/475/JHA on Combating Terrorism, COM(2015) 625 final, 14. Terrorism represents an emblematic example of global security threats tackled by the EU under securitised criminalisation (see Section II above in this chapter).

[65] Proposal for a Directive of the European Parliament and of the Council on the Fight Against Fraud to the Union's Financial Interests by Means of Criminal Law, COM(2012) 363 final.

[66] *ibid*, 8.

[67] *ibid*.

[68] *ibid*.

These examples from legislative practice show that Article 52(1) of the Charter provides a suitable balancing rule for shaping harmonised criminal offences vis-à-vis the protection of fundamental rights. Moreover, the practice shows that the fundamental rights dimension of proportionality has a more profound influence on EU criminalisation than Article 5(4) TEU. This difference is not surprising since these two paradigms should not be conceived as alternatives. While both shape the EU legislative action in the substantive criminal law field, they impose different limits on the legislature's discretion. On the one hand, Article 5(4) TEU is invoked to justify EU intervention as such in the given domain. On the other hand, the specific criminalisation choices must be justified vis-à-vis their impact on fundamental rights under Article 52(1) of the Charter.

B. Prospective and Retrospective Proportionality in the Definition of Harmonised Criminal Offences

The examples outlined so far highlight the insufficiency of the threefold proportionality test alone in shaping EU legislative action. Relying solely on the proportionality primary scheme makes it challenging to define in which cases the scope of harmonised offences is suitable and necessary. This is because harmonised offences should be evaluated according to their prospective and retrospective features.

Legislative practice evidences the critical role played by the secondary schemes of the principle of proportionality of offences. Prospective and retrospective considerations emerge from the general policy indications provided by the Commission and the European Parliament, as well as the *travaux préparatoires* of individual pieces of legislation on substantive criminal law.

Focusing firstly on policy orientations, four documents shall be recalled here: the 2011 Commission Communication 'Towards an EU Criminal Policy',[69] the 2012 European Parliament Resolution on an EU Approach to Criminal Law,[70] the 2009 Council Conclusions on Model Provisions, Guiding the Council's Criminal Law Deliberations',[71] and the 2024 Council Conclusions 'The Future of EU Criminal Law: Recommendations on the Way Forward'.[72] According to these soft-law instruments, harmonised offences 'should be introduced when they

[69] Communication from the Commission to the European Parliament, the Council, the European Economic and Social Committee and the Committee of the Regions – Towards an EU Criminal Policy: Ensuring the Effective Implementation of EU Policies Through Criminal Law, COM(2011) 573 final. For a comprehensive analysis, see A Weyembergh and I Wieczorek, 'Is There an EU Criminal Policy?' in R Colson and S Field (eds), *EU Criminal Justice and the Challenges of Legal Diversity: Legal Cultures in the Area of Freedom, Security and Justice* (Cambridge, Cambridge University Press, 2016).

[70] European Parliament Resolution of 22 May 2012 on an EU Approach to Criminal Law cit.

[71] Council Conclusions on Model Provisions, Guiding the Council's Criminal Law Deliberations, 30 November 2009.

[72] Council Conclusions on 'The Future of EU Criminal Law: Recommendations on the Way Forward', 10984/24, 14 June 2024.

are considered essential in order for the interests to be protected',[73] by tackling conducts 'which cannot be addressed effectively by less severe measures'.[74] In the context of that assessment, 'the seriousness and character of the breach of law must be taken into account'.[75] Therefore, the justification of EU criminalisation shall be evaluated on a retrospective account by verifying whether 'the crime involved is of a particularly serious nature'.[76] At the same time, the proposed harmonisation of offences shall also be assessed from a prospective point of view, as recourse to criminalisation 'may be chosen when it is considered important to stress strong disapproval *in order to ensure deterrence* (emphasis added)'.[77]

As far as the liability of legal persons is concerned, the EU's general policy documents take a nuanced approach. In principle, harmonised offences also apply to legal entities.[78] Indeed, their liability is vital to ensure the effective attainment of the objectives underlying supranational criminalisation,[79] especially in those areas of serious crime where 'legal entities play a particularly important role as perpetrators'.[80] On those grounds, the Council Conclusions on Model Provisions stipulates that legal entities should be liable for offences committed for their benefit by any person holding a leading position therein, as well as for offences committed due to that person's lack of supervision or control.[81] Still, criminal liability regimes against legal persons are not established in all Member States.[82] Therefore, EU provisions usually leave the domestic legislature

[73] Council Conclusions on Model Provisions, Guiding the Council's Criminal Law Deliberations cit, para 1.

[74] *ibid*, para 2. This point is reaffirmed by the 2024 Council Conclusions, which states that 'criminal law instruments and provisions should only be adopted when necessary to achieve the objective behind those instruments and provisions, when that objective cannot be achieved through other means' (Council Conclusions on 'The Future of EU Criminal Law: Recommendations on the Way Forward' cit, para 2).

[75] Communication from the Commission to the European Parliament, the Council, the European Economic and Social Committee and the Committee of the Regions – Towards an EU Criminal Policy: Ensuring the Effective Implementation of EU Policies Through Criminal Law cit 11.

[76] European Parliament Resolution of 22 May 2012 on an EU Approach to Criminal Law cit, para 3, alinea 3; Council Conclusions on Model Provisions, Guiding the Council's Criminal Law Deliberations cit, para 2, letter a).

[77] Communication from the Commission to the European Parliament, the Council, the European Economic and Social Committee and the Committee of the Regions – Towards an EU Criminal Policy: Ensuring the Effective Implementation of EU Policies through Criminal Law cit 11.

[78] *ibid*, 9.

[79] In literature, see N Selvaggi, '*Ex Crimine* Liability of Legal Persons in EU. An Overview of Substantive Criminal Law' in A Fiorella (eds), *Corporate Criminal Liability and Compliance Programs. Vol. II: Towards a Common Model in the European Union* (Napoli, Jovene, 2012) 10.

[80] Communication from the Commission to the European Parliament, the Council, the European Economic and Social Committee and the Committee of the Regions – Towards an EU Criminal Policy: Ensuring the effective implementation of EU policies through criminal law cit 8.

[81] Council Conclusions on Model Provisions, Guiding the Council's Criminal Law Deliberations cit 5. For some examples in the legislative practice, see Proposal for a Directive of the European Parliament and of the Council on Countering Money Laundering by Criminal Law cit 14–15; Proposal for a Directive of the European Parliament and of the Council on the Protection of the Environment through Criminal Law and Repealing Directive 2008/99/EC, COM(2021) 851 final 18.

[82] *ibid*. On this point, see n 51 of the Introduction to this book.

choosing whether to provide a 'criminal or non-criminal fine' together with accessory sanctions.[83] This approach envisages a certain discretion towards qualifying actions attributable to legal entities as criminal offences, and it has remained constant even in the most recent legislative initiatives.[84] At the same time, Member States are still required to establish administrative sanctioning schemes whenever they opt for non-criminal fines against offences committed by legal entities.

Concerning the scope of harmonised offences, the *travaux préparatoires* of single pieces of legislation further confirm the general policy orientations just outlined. As the following subsections will analyse in better detail, the EU legislature constantly relies on prospective (i) and retrospective (ii) proportionality schemes.

i. Prospective Proportionality of Harmonised Criminal Offences and its Intersection with Censure and General Prevention

When presenting a legislative proposal establishing minimum rules for the definition of offences, the Commission appears aware that criminalisation may serve both punitive and dissuasive purposes.[85] This consideration paves the way to evaluating the deterrent effect inherent in criminalising a given behaviour. In that context, the prospective scheme requires assessing the suitability and necessity of the proposed criminalisation to attain a genuinely dissuasive effect.

To that aim, some legislative proposals put forward a thorough analysis. That is the case, for instance, of the 2022 Proposal for Amending the Directive on Trafficking in Human Beings. The criminalisation of the use of services which are the object of exploitation is regarded as 'a proportionate legislative measure aimed at preventing and combating trafficking in human beings more effectively *by discouraging demand* (emphasis added)'.[86] The 2012 Proposal for a Directive on the Fight Against Fraud to the Union's Financial Interests by Means of Criminal

[83] Council Conclusions on Model Provisions, Guiding the Council's Criminal Law Deliberations cit 5. According to that policy document, accessory sanctions may include '(a) exclusion from entitlement to public benefits or aid; (b) temporary or permanent disqualification from the practice of commercial activities; (c) placing under judicial supervision; (d) a judicial winding-up order; (e) temporary or permanent closure of establishments which have been used for committing the offence' (*ibid*).

[84] While most recent legislative proposals envisaged an evolution towards better detailed and restrictive provisions on sanctions for legal persons, that development did not affect the possibility for domestic authorities to opt between criminal and non-criminal fines (on this point, see C Brière, 'Proportionality of Penalties in EU Substantive Criminal Law Legislative Instruments' in L Grossio, S Montaldo and V Mitsilegas (eds), *Proportionality of Criminal Penalties in EU Law* (Oxford, Hart Publishing, 2025) 107).

[85] In that regard, see Proposal for a Council Framework Decision on Combating Racism and Xenophobia cit 5: 'apart from their punitive aspect, criminal law measures have a significant dissuasive force'. The cited consideration horizontally underpins the harmonisation of both offences and penalties.

[86] Proposal for a Directive of the European Parliament and of the Council Amending Directive 2011/36/EU on Preventing and Combating Trafficking in Human Beings and Protecting its Victims cit 7.

Law constitutes a further example of this approach.[87] The Impact Assessment justifies the necessity of newly introduced offences on prospective proportionality grounds.[88] Interestingly, this document also crystallises the Commission's own understanding of the concept of 'deterrence', defined as the influence exercised by criminal provisions over individuals 'which results in voluntary refraining from the commission of illegal acts'.[89]

The 2003 Proposal for a Directive on Ship-Source Pollution[90] provides insightful guidance on how the Commission balances deterrence under the prospective proportionality. Indeed, the Commission clarifies therein that:

> in line with its policy on offences against environmental crime, [...] only criminal sanctions will be sufficiently effective for ensuring the effects of ship-source pollution rules. A measure of penal nature will serve as a Community-wide application of a deterrent sanction for those involved in the transport of polluting goods by sea. *Sufficiently dissuasive effects will only be achieved by establishing that illegal discharges is a criminal offence*, which demonstrates *a social disapproval of qualitatively different nature compared to compensation mechanisms under civil law or administrative measures*. It therefore sends a *strong signal, with a greater dissuasive effect, to potential offenders* (emphasis added).[91]

It follows that achieving 'sufficient dissuasive effects' constitutes the reference parameter for justifying supranational criminalisation from a general prevention perspective. Harmonised criminalisation choices are proportionate under the prospective scheme only if less intrusive options – such as allowing Member States to apply administrative penalties – would be insufficient.

A comparison between criminalisation and administrative sanctioning has been sometimes put forward in the legislative practice. An example may be found in the 2007 Proposal for a Directive on the Protection of Environment Through

[87] In that regard, see Proposal for a Directive of the European Parliament and of the Council on the Fight Against Fraud to the Union's Financial Interests by Means of Criminal Law cit. In that context, the Commission highlighted that potential interferences with the Charter would be justified on a proportionality basis since the Proposal puts forward 'effective and deterring measures for the protection of Union financial interests' (*ibid*, 8).

[88] Commission Staff Working Paper – Impact Assessment Accompanying the Proposal for a Directive of the European Parliament and of the Council on the Fight Against Fraud to the Union's Financial Interests by Means of Criminal Law (Part I), SWD(2012) 195 final, 20: differences among Member States' definition of 'professional secrecy' for the purposes of its breach create 'deterrence and enforcement gaps'; *ibid*, 20–21: concerning abuse of public tenders procedures, 'the non-existence of this offence type as a matter of criminal law thus leads to a lack of deterrent effect'; *ibid*, 21: the absence of the favouritism/abuse of powers offence in some domestic criminal systems gives rise to 'some deterrence gaps and enforcement difficulties'.

[89] Commission Staff Working Paper – Impact Assessment Accompanying the Proposal for a Directive of the European Parliament and of the Council on the Fight Against Fraud to the Union's Financial Interests by Means of Criminal Law cit 11.

[90] Proposal for a Directive of the European Parliament and of the Council on Ship-source Pollution and on the Introduction of Sanctions, Including Criminal Sanctions, for Pollution Offences, COM(2003) 92 final.

[91] *ibid*, 5.

Criminal Law.[92] According to the Commission's analysis, 'only criminal penalties will have a sufficiently dissuasive effect for several reasons'.[93] Among the latter, 'administrative or other financial penalties may not be dissuasive in cases where the offenders are impecunious or, on the contrary, financially very strong'.[94]

As the 2003 Proposal for a Directive on Ship-Source Pollution shows, sufficient deterrent effects may be attained thanks to the censure inherent in criminalisation. Provided that the qualification of illegal discharges as a criminal offence implies particularly intense social disapproval, the latter is functional to attaining deterrence. Indeed, criminalisation addresses 'a strong signal, with a greater dissuasive effect, to potential offenders'.[95] The 2007 Proposal for a Directive on the Protection of Environment Through Criminal Law further confirms the legislative approach just highlighted. Social disapproval inherent in criminal law – which is 'of a qualitatively different nature compared to administrative sanctions'[96] – is one of the reasons why only criminalisation would attain the purported deterrent effects.[97]

The enhancement of censure in EU criminalisation is unsurprising. Social disapproval is indissociable from the concept of criminal, as it is one of the elements differentiating criminal sanctions from administrative ones.[98] This consideration is crystallised in the 2004 Green Paper on the Approximation, Mutual Recognition and Enforcement of Criminal Sanctions. The Commission underlined that EU criminalisation conveys 'a symbolic message [as it would] be a clear signal that certain forms of conduct are unacceptable and punished on

[92] Proposal for a Directive of the European Parliament and of the Council on the Protection of the Environment through Criminal Law cit.

[93] *ibid*, 2. See also the Proposal for a Directive of the European Parliament and of the Council on the Definition of Criminal Offences and Penalties for the Violation of Union Restrictive Measures, COM(2022) 684 final, according to which 'harmonisation would also increase the deterrent effect of penalties for the violation of Union restrictive measures' (*ibid*, 8). The Proposal highlights that violation of restrictive measures does not constitute a criminal offence in all Member States, as some of them only provide for administrative penalties (*ibid*, 2–3). In the Commission's view, an EU obligation to criminalise these conducts may be justified since it enhances deterrence, thus contributing to the effective protection of the EU criminalisation objective.

[94] *ibid*, 2.

[95] Proposal for a Directive of the European Parliament and of the Council on Ship-source Pollution cit 5. The deterrent function of social disapproval has also been put forward in the Commission Staff Working Paper – Impact Assessment Accompanying the Proposal for a Directive of the European Parliament and of the Council on the Fight Against Fraud to the Union's Financial Interests by Means of Criminal Law cit 11.

[96] Proposal for a Directive of the European Parliament and of the Council on the Protection of the Environment through Criminal Law cit 2.

[97] *ibid*.

[98] Among extensive literature, see M Kettunen, *Legitimizing European Criminal Law*, vol 2 (Cham, Springer, 2020) 50. For further references on the topic, see: S Miettinen, *Criminal Law and Policy in the European Union* (Oxon, Routledge, 2013) 119; M Luisa Cesoni, 'Droit pénal européen : une harmonisation périlleuse' in G De Kerchove and A Weyembergh (eds), *L'espace pénal européen : enjeux et perspectives* (Bruxelles, Editions de l'Université de Bruxelles, 2002) 155; S Bonini, *La funzione simbolica nel diritto penale del bene giuridico* (Napoli, Editoriale Scientifica, 2018) 220; T Elholm, 'The Emotional Component of Proportionality' in E Billis, N Knust and JP Rui (eds), *Proportionality in Crime Control and Criminal Justice* (Oxford, Hart Publishing, 2021).

an equivalent basis'.[99] In that regard, scholars have argued that social blame has sometimes been purportedly regarded as functional to developing an EU-own political identity, thus reinforcing citizens' solidarity bonds and sense of affiliation to the Union.[100]

Still, the Commission's reliance on criminal law symbolism under prospective proportionality is peculiar. Criminal law scholarship traditionally conceives social disapproval as a corollary of deontological theories of punishment, which imply a retrospective rather than prospective account of the conduct.[101] The symbolic dimension of criminal law implies censure towards the proscribed action or omission, constituting an essential element of any retributive theory.[102] Against that theoretical understanding, the Commission shapes social disapproval in criminal law in a functional perspective, different from the one emerging from the predominant criminal law scholarship. From that viewpoint, censure in the EU legislative practice comes as a tool to enhance deterrence in a prospective dimension.

The practice analysed so far shows that the EU legislature relies on prospective proportionality from a general prevention viewpoint. Conversely, special prevention is absent from the proportionality assessment of EU criminalisation. No single document in the legislative practice suggests the need to limit the Union's action to conducts that effectively require criminal sanctions to re-socialise the offender. Therefore, while recent scholarship has highlighted that the offenders' rehabilitation paradigm is currently gaining importance under EU law,[103] it seems that EU criminalisation has not been permeated by that development.

ii. Retrospective Proportionality of Harmonised Criminal Offences between Harmfulness and Ordinal Proportionality

Proportionality of criminal offences requires EU criminalisation not only to be necessary to attain sufficient dissuasive effects but also to reflect the seriousness of the wrongdoing. Not every type of behaviour may be so serious as to require EU criminalisation. This finding follows from the wording of Article 83 TFEU,

[99] Green Paper on the Approximation, Mutual Recognition and Enforcement of Criminal Sanctions in the European Union, COM(2004) 334 final, 81. In that regard, see T Elholm and R Colson, 'The Symbolic Purpose of EU Criminal Law' in R Colson and S Field (eds), *EU Criminal Justice and the Challenges of Legal Diversity: Legal Cultures in the Area of Freedom, Security and Justice* (Cambridge, Cambridge University Press, 2016) 56.

[100] R Colson and S Field, 'Legal Cultures in Europe: Brakes, Motors and the Rise of EU Criminal Justice' in R Colson and S Field (eds), *EU Criminal Justice and the Challenges of Legal Diversity: Legal Cultures in the Area of Freedom, Security and Justice* (Cambridge, Cambridge University Press, 2016) 58.

[101] See Section III(B)(ii) of Chapter 2.

[102] F Viganò, *La proporzionalità della pena: profili di diritto penale e costituzionale* (Torino, Giappichelli, 2021) 136.

[103] S Montaldo, 'Offenders' Rehabilitation: Towards a New Paradigm for EU Criminal Law?' (2018) 8 *European Criminal Review* 222.

which clarifies that minimum rules for the definition of offences may be adopted only in the 'areas of *particularly serious* crime (emphasis added)'. This affirmation is followed by the enumeration of the areas of serious crime potentially subject to harmonisation.[104] It appears that the Treaties themselves encapsulate a judgement on the seriousness of these categories of conduct.[105] Moreover, the last paragraph of Article 83(1) TFEU allows the Council, acting unanimously upon the consent of the European Parliament, to extend the list to further areas of crime 'that meet the criteria specified in this paragraph', among which seriousness plays a key role. This possibility has been recently relied upon to allow the harmonisation of offences and penalties for violating CFSP restrictive measures.[106] Conversely, a Commission initiative to extend the EU competence in substantive criminal law to hate speech and hate crime is still pending before the Council.[107]

Should a given behaviour fall under the scope of an area of serious crime under Article 83 TFEU, this circumstance does not relieve the EU legislature from assessing whether it is sufficiently serious to warrant EU criminalisation. Some examples may explain this point. The previously cited 2007 Proposal for a Directive on the Protection of the Environment through Criminal Law stresses that 'criminal sanctions are not in force in all Member States for all *serious* environmental offences'.[108] The Commission thus affirms that the serious nature of specific conducts justifies the EU legislative intervention.[109] In the same perspective, the 2021 Proposal for a Directive on the Protection of the Environment through Criminal Law points out that offences shall be 'limited to *serious breaches* of environmental law, *and thus respect proportionality* (emphasis added)'.[110] Conversely, 'minor nuisances or disruptions […] should not be considered as fulfilling the threshold of seriousness',

[104] These are terrorism, trafficking in human beings and sexual exploitation of women and children, illicit drug trafficking, illicit arms trafficking, money laundering, corruption, counterfeiting of means of payment, computer crime and organised crime (Art 83(1), second para, TFEU).

[105] N Peršak, 'Criminalising Hate Crime and Hate Speech at EU Level: Extending the List of Eurocrimes Under Article 83(1) TFEU' (2022) 33 *Criminal Law Forum* 85, 111.

[106] Council Decision (EU) 2022/2332 of 28 November 2022 on Identifying the Violation of Union Restrictive Measures as an Area of Crime that Meets the Criteria Specified in Article 83(1) of the Treaty on the Functioning of the European Union [2022] OJ L308/18.

[107] Communication from the Commission to the European Parliament and the Council – A More Inclusive and Protective Europe: Extending the List of EU Crimes to Hate Speech and Hate Crime cit. The European Parliament in 2024 has backed the Commission initiative and urged the Council to adopt that proposal (European Parliament Resolution of 18 January 2024 on Extending the List of EU Crimes to Hate Speech and Hate Crime (2023/2068(INI) [2024] OJ C5733).

[108] Proposal for a Directive of the European Parliament and of the Council on the Protection of the Environment through Criminal Law cit 2.

[109] A similar retrospective account also emerges from the Impact Assessment accompanying the 2009 Proposal for a Framework Decision on Combating Sexual Abuse, Sexual Exploitation and Child Pornography (Commission Staff Working Document – Impact Assessment Accompanying the Proposal for a Council Framework Decision on Combating the Sexual Abuse, Sexual Exploitation of Children and Child Pornography, Repealing Framework Decision 2004/68/JHA, SEC(2009) 335, 18: 'serious forms of child sexual abuse and exploitation are currently not covered by EU legislation').

[110] Proposal for a Directive of the European Parliament and of the Council on the Protection of the Environment through Criminal Law and Repealing Directive 2008/99/EC cit 4.

as clarified by the 2002 Proposal for a Framework Decision on Attacks Against Information Systems.[111]

How does the EU legislature frame the concept of 'seriousness'? A definition can be derived from the 2002 Proposal for a Council Framework Decision on Attacks Against Information Systems.[112] By analysing the offence of 'illegal interference with information systems', the Commission outlines that the proposed provision 'uses the word "serious hindering or interruption" as a constituent element of the offence *in order to describe the effects of such an attack* (emphasis added)'.[113] Therefore, the seriousness of the conduct is the result of its harmfulness to the legal interests the EU legislature aims to protect.[114]

Two further elements in the legislative practice may help understand the concept of 'harmfulness' in EU criminalisation. On the one hand, the violence inherent in the abstract behaviour tackled by the offence may amount to the parameter of reference for assessing its harmfulness. This point emerges from the 2001 Proposal for a Council Framework Decision on Terrorism. To justify the criminalisation of cyberterrorism, the proposal points out that 'although terrorist offences committed by computer or electronic devices are apparently less *violent* they can be as threatening as the offences previously mentioned, *endangering not only life, health or safety of people but the environment as well* (emphasis added)'.[115]

On the other hand, the Impact Assessment accompanying the 2012 Proposal for a Directive on the Fight Against Fraud to the Union's Financial Interests by Means of Criminal Law clarifies that embezzlement and misappropriation warrant criminalisation as they are 'equally reprehensible and equally harmful to the EU budget'[116] compared to fraud. This finding has a double significance for the concept of 'harmfulness' in EU substantive criminal law. Firstly, it implies a judgement of moral disapproval, an aspect inherent in qualifying the conduct as sufficiently reprehensible. This finding is not isolated in the practice. The very same assumption may be found within the already mentioned 2021 Proposal for a Directive on the Protection of the Environment through Criminal Law, according to which

> establishing criminal offences for serious breaches of Union rules, which [...] contribute to the Union policy of protecting the environment, sets clear boundaries for types of behaviours that are considered to be particularly unacceptable and sends a message

[111] Proposal for a Council Framework Decision on Attacks Against Information Systems, COM(2002) 173 final, 12.

[112] *ibid.*

[113] *ibid.*

[114] In that regard, see P Asp, *The Substantive Criminal Law Competence of the EU* (Stockholm, Stiftelsen Skrifter utgivna av Juridiska fakulteten vid Stockholms Universitet, 2012) 190; Peršak, 'Criminalising Hate Crime and Hate Speech at EU Level: Extending the List of Eurocrimes Under Article 83(1) TFEU' (n 105) 111.

[115] Proposal for a Council Framework Decision on Combating Terrorism cit 5.

[116] Commission Staff Working Paper – Impact Assessment Accompanying the Proposal for a Directive of the European Parliament and of the Council on the Fight Against Fraud to the Union's Financial Interests by Means of Criminal Law cit 19.

> to the public and to potential offenders that competent authorities take such behaviour very seriously.[117]

Therefore, the symbolic dimension of criminal law is not only functional to attaining general prevention under the prospective scheme.[118] Censure also reflects the seriousness of the criminalised conduct, aligning with the well-established criminal law scholarship.[119]

Secondly, the finding under analysis demonstrates that retrospective proportionality may entail comparing the conduct to a different offence taken as a benchmark on a seriousness scale.[120] Indeed, it affirms that criminalisation of embezzlement and misappropriation is justified since 'the behaviour sanctioned [...] is very close to fraud'.[121] This comparison bears some similarities to the concept of ordinal proportionality derived from criminal law scholarship and analysed above in Chapter 2.[122] That notion, however, cannot apply here in its proper sense since it postulates a legal relationship between a given offence and the respective penalty.

It appears that the EU legislative practice features reliance on the retrospective scheme as a secondary assessment under the principle of proportionality of criminal offences. That evaluation entails that the scope of harmonised offences shall be limited to serious conduct, namely behaviours sufficiently harmful to the relevant protected interests and reprehensible from a moral point of view. To evaluate the degree of harmfulness of a given conduct, the EU legislature may compare the latter to a different behaviour already subject to criminalisation. In that perspective, an equivalent or superior degree of harmfulness may justify the proposed criminalisation under retrospective proportionality.

IV. Assessing the EU Legislative Approach: Proportionality in the Definition of Harmonised Criminal Penalties

The following sections, mirroring the analysis of the proportionality of offences, explore the normative grounds for proportionality in defining harmonised criminal penalties (A) and the role played by prospective and retrospective schemes in that regard (B).

[117] Proposal for a Directive of the European Parliament and of the Council on the Protection of the Environment through Criminal Law and Repealing Directive 2008/99/EC cit 6–7.

[118] In that regard, see Section III(B)(i) of Chapter 2.

[119] See Section III(B)(ii) above in Chapter 2 of this book.

[120] Therefore, ordinal proportionality may be called into question only with respect to the principle of proportionality of penalties.

[121] Commission Staff Working Paper – Impact Assessment Accompanying the Proposal for a Directive of the European Parliament and of the Council on the Fight Against Fraud to the Union's Financial Interests by Means of Criminal Law cit 19.

[122] See Section IV(B)(i) above in Chapter 2 of this book.

A. The Neglected (with Good Reason) Role of Article 49(3) of the Charter

The EU legislature does not frame a separate proportionality paradigm for, respectively, the scope of offences and the type and level of penalties. Instead, the primary proportionality scheme previously analysed – grounded on either Article 5(4) TEU or Article 52(1) of the Charter – applies to both offences and penalties.

This conclusion stems quite evidently from the practice. For instance, the proportionality assessment advanced in the 2012 Proposal for a Directive on the Fight against Fraud to the Union's Financial Interests by Means of Criminal Law refers to criminal 'measures' in general, thus encompassing both the scope of harmonised offences and the type and amount of the relevant penalties.[123] In the same line of reasoning, the 2017 Proposal for a Directive on Combating Fraud and Counterfeiting of Non-Cash Means of Payment states that, under Article 52(1) of the Charter, any of the proposed criminal provision shall respect 'the principle that criminal *offences and penalties* must be set out in law and be proportionate (emphasis added)'.[124] Therefore, the main features of the proportionality paradigm applicable to the harmonisation of offences shall be entirely recalled here concerning the proportionality of harmonised penalties.

Article 52(1) of the Charter constitutes the key dimension also for the proportionality of harmonised penalties in the EU legislative practice. This aspect is indicative of the EU institutions' understanding of the principle. While proportionality of offences does not enjoy a specific legal basis in primary law – thus requiring a reference to Article 52(1) of the Charter and, more scarcely, to Article 5(4) TEU – Article 49(3) of the Charter may well serve as a normative foundation for the proportionality assessment of harmonised penalties. As previously recalled, that provision states that 'the severity of penalties must not be disproportionate to the criminal offence', and it codifies retrospective proportionality under EU law.[125]

Conversely, the Commission and EU legislature rely on Article 52(1) of the Charter even to define harmonised penalties. As a result, the role of Article 49(3) of the Charter is somewhat neglected: that provision is usually cited among the fundamental rights to respect when legislating in the substantive criminal law domain.[126] That approach does not seem fully coherent from a theoretical point

[123] Proposal for a Directive of the European Parliament and of the Council on the Fight Against Fraud to the Union's Financial Interests by Means of Criminal Law cit 8.

[124] Proposal for a Directive of the European Parliament and of the Council on Combating Fraud and Counterfeiting of Non-Cash Means of Payment cit 15. See also the Proposal for a Directive of the European Parliament and of the Council on Criminal Sanctions for Insider Dealing and Market Manipulation, COM(2011) 654 final, which specifies that the principle of proportionality as enshrined in Art 5(4) TEU 'has guided the process from the identification and evaluation of alternative policy options to the drafting of this proposal' (*ibid*, 5).

[125] See Section III(C)(iii) of Chapter 1 and the literature cited therein.

[126] See, for instance, the Proposal for a Directive of the European Parliament and of the Council on Combating Terrorism cit 14, as well as the Proposal for a Directive of the European Parliament and of the Council on the Fight Against Fraud to the Union's Financial Interests by Means of Criminal Law

of view. Article 49(3) of the Charter cannot be merely regarded as one of the fundamental rights whose enjoyment shall be balanced under Article 52(1) against attaining the objectives warranting EU criminalisation. Rather, Article 49(3) provides a retrospective proportionality standard for assessing the interference of criminal law on individual rights.

Notwithstanding this aspect, the EU legislature's choice not to rely exclusively on Article 49(3) of the Charter in assessing the proportionality of harmonised penalties is commendable. Indeed, a different approach would have reduced the principle's scope to its retrospective dimension. In line with the principle's hybrid theorisation, reliance on Article 52(1) of the Charter paves the way for a broader theoretical understanding that combines the threefold proportionality test with prospective and retrospective schemes. As argued in Chapter 2, the proportionality of criminal offences and penalties enjoys multiple normative foundations. Concerning harmonised criminal penalties, Articles 52(1) of the Charter and 5(4) TEU frame the proportionality primary scheme, consisting of the threefold test. Conversely, Article 49(3) of the Charter amounts to the legal basis of the retrospective secondary scheme, as the following analysis will show.[127]

B. The Role of Prospective and Retrospective Proportionality of Criminal Penalties in the Legislative Practice

The EU legislature employs prospective and retrospective assessments under the edge of the threefold proportionality test. The relationship between the secondary schemes and the latter is of a functional nature, as some examples show. According to the Commission, the 2017 Proposal for a Directive on Combating Fraud and Counterfeiting of Non-Cash Means of Payment 'introduces minimum rules on the level of sanctions in accordance with the principle of proportionality, *having regard to the nature of the offence* (emphasis added)'.[128] This finding implies that a retrospective assessment of the offence's nature is necessary to fulfil the proportionality requirement. In the same vein, the 2013 Proposal for a Directive on the Protection of the Euro and Other Currencies against Counterfeiting by Criminal Law outlines that interferences with the enjoyment of individual rights deriving from harmonised penalties 'are justified because they serve to meet the objectives of general interest recognised by the Union […], *and in particular to provide effective and deterring measures* (emphasis added)'.[129] In this regard, the 2003 Proposal

cit 8, and the Proposal for a Directive of the European Parliament and of the Council on the Protection of the Euro and Other Currencies against Counterfeiting by Criminal Law, and Replacing Council Framework Decision 2000/383/JHA cit 8.

[127] See Section IV(B) below in this chapter.

[128] Proposal for a Directive of the European Parliament and of the Council on Combating Fraud and Counterfeiting of Non-Cash Means of Payment cit 15.

[129] Proposal for a Directive of the European Parliament and of the Council on the Protection of the Euro and Other Currencies against Counterfeiting by Criminal Law, and Replacing Council Framework

for a Directive on Ship-source Pollution better specifies that 'sanctions against the offences shall be adequate as to their dissuasive nature, which is of evident importance if the discharge prohibitions are to be effective'.[130] This affirmation postulates a link between deterrence and the effectiveness of the relevant Union policy, namely, the goal whose realisation is subject to scrutiny under the threefold proportionality test. Therefore, prospective and retrospective schemes constitute the necessary concretisation of the proportionality assessment of harmonised penalties.

Moreover, prospective and retrospective schemes are complementary. The 2001 Proposal for a Council Framework Decision on combating trafficking in human beings is quite explicative in that regard, as it clarifies that 'possible penalties for trafficking should *reflect the seriousness of the crime* and have a *strong deterrent effect* (emphasis added)'.[131] The necessary combination of prospective and retrospective assessments on harmonised penalties also emerges from the subsequent 2010 Proposal for a Directive on the same topic. Indeed, the Explanatory Memorandum affirms that the proposal is intended to define '*precise level of penalties adapted to the severity of the offences* (emphasis added)',[132] thus postulating a retrospective secondary assessment. At the same time, recital 6 of the same legislative proposal specifies that penalty levels 'reflect the growing concern among Member States about increased trafficking in human beings', thus advancing a complementary prospective account.

Given their complementarity, the application of prospective (i) and retrospective (ii) schemes of the principle of proportionality of criminal penalties in the EU legislative practice shall now be separately considered.

i. Harmonised Penalties shall be the Lowest Possible Entailing a Sufficient Deterrent Effect

The harmonisation of criminal penalties has been called upon addressing 'inadequate sanction types and levels'[133] to achieve 'foreseeable and sufficiently

Decision 2000/383/JHA cit 8. The very same formula is also reproduced in the Proposal for a Directive of the European Parliament and of the Council on the Fight Against Fraud to the Union's Financial Interests by Means of Criminal Law cit 8.

[130] Proposal for a Directive of the European Parliament and of the Council on Ship-source Pollution and on the Introduction of Sanctions, Including Criminal Sanctions, for Pollution Offences cit 9.

[131] Proposal for a Council Framework Decision on Combating Trafficking in Human Beings, attached to the Communication from the Commission to the Council and the European Parliament – Combating Trafficking in Human Beings and Combating the Sexual Exploitation of Children and Child Pornography, COM(2000) 854 final/2, 10 and 24.

[132] Proposal for a Directive of the European Parliament and of the Council on Preventing and Combating Trafficking in Human Beings, and Protecting Victims, Repealing Framework Decision 2002/629/JHA, COM(2010) 95 final, 7.

[133] Commission Staff Working Paper – Impact Assessment accompanying the Proposal for a Directive of the European Parliament and of the Council on the Fight against Fraud to the Union's Financial Interests by Means of Criminal Law (Part I) cit 14. More recently, this justification for EU intervention has been reproduced in the 2021 Proposal for a Directive on the Protection of the Environment through

significant, though not excessive, consequences'.[134] In this way, the EU legislature aims to deter potential offenders, 'which results in voluntary refraining from the commission of illegal acts'.[135] Conversely, special prevention is not considered in the legislative practice on harmonised penalties. As for the approximation of offences, there is no reference to offenders' rehabilitation as a prospective aim for tailoring harmonised standards on criminal sanctions.

As legislative practice shows, the need to prospectively achieve deterrence usually entails a rise in the penalty levels because of harmonisation. Increased repression may stem from the choice between financial and custodial penalties, as well as their respective amount. The EU legislator generally considers the option for imprisonment rather than alternative measures as 'to send a strong message of disapproval that could increase the dissuasiveness of sanctions'.[136]

Concerning penalty scales, attaining a sufficient deterrent effect usually results in the provision of harsh sanctioning levels. From a first point of view, severe sanctions are seen as dissuasive per se, as they convey strong stigmatisation to the public.[137] The desired deterrent effect may also stem indirectly from the applicability of judicial cooperation instruments. Indeed, a sanctioning level meeting the penalty thresholds required for triggering the European Arrest Warrant (EAW)[138] or other judicial cooperation instruments strengthens the deterrence of harmonised penalties. Judicial cooperation mechanisms would prevent offenders from escaping from domestic authorities by fleeing to different Member States.[139] This rationale emerges from the Impact Assessment accompanying the 2012 Proposal for a Directive on the Fight against Fraud to the Union's Financial Interests by Means of Criminal Law, as it clarifies that 'any sentencing range which [...] do not entail a risk of extradition or surrender under the

Criminal Law, according to which 'sanction levels are not effective and dissuasive in all Member States' (Proposal for a Directive of the European Parliament and of the Council on the Protection of the Environment through Criminal Law and Repealing Directive 2008/99/EC cit 11).

134 Commission Staff Working Paper – Impact Assessment accompanying the Proposal for a Directive of the European Parliament and of the Council on the Fight against Fraud to the Union's Financial Interests by Means of Criminal Law (Part I) cit 14. In the same perspective, see also the Proposal for a Directive of the European Parliament and of the Council on the Protection of the Environment through Criminal Law and Repealing Directive 2008/99/EC cit 9, which outlines that one of the main objectives of the proposal is to 'improve availability of dissuasive and comparable sanction types and levels'.

135 Commission Staff Working Paper – Impact Assessment Accompanying the Proposal for a Directive of the European Parliament and of the Council on the Fight Against Fraud to the Union's Financial Interests by Means of Criminal Law (Part I) cit 11.

136 Proposal for a Directive of the European Parliament and of the Council on Criminal Sanctions for Insider Dealing and Market Manipulation cit 2.

137 In that regard, see for instance the Proposal for a Directive of the European Parliament and of the Council on Ship-source Pollution and on the Introduction of Sanctions, Including Criminal Sanctions, for Pollution Offences cit 9: 'grossly negligent conduct leading up to major oil spills and significant damage needs to be very severely penalised in order to have the intended dissuasive effects'.

138 Art 2(1) of Council Framework Decision 2002/584/JHA of 13 June 2002 on the European Arrest Warrant and the Surrender Procedures Between Member States cit.

139 On the principle of mutual recognition of judicial decisions in criminal matters, see Section VI of Chapter 4.

European Arrest Warrant system, can be regarded as *ineffective from a deterrence point of view* (emphasis added)'.[140]

The EU legislature typically harmonises the maximum term of a given penalty scale to set common sanctioning levels. More specifically, EU law defines a minimum threshold for the maximum penalty which can be imposed by Member States. The establishment of minimum maximum penalties enhances deterrence,[141] and it constitutes the main strategy employed by the EU legislature to attain sufficient prospective consequences on the public at large.[142]

The Commission has seldom considered the possibility of harmonising not only the maximum but also the minimum term of the penalty scale.[143] This option has been mooted in the 2013 Proposal for a Directive on the Protection of the Euro and Other Currencies against Counterfeiting by Criminal Law.[144] According to the Commission, 'since in practice the minimum standard for the maximum penalty is rarely imposed, a minimum penalty can be considered as a more dissuasive and of great practical value for the protection of the euro'.[145] However, the harmonisation of minimum sanctions has been opposed by Member States and then discarded from the finally adopted legislation. On the occasion of the 2021 Proposal for a Directive on the Protection of the Environment through Criminal Law, the Commission acknowledged that since

> such minimum threshold would meet constitutional problems as they do not allow the judge to remain below that level even if that would be justified in a given case [...], a possible option to propose minimum sanction levels was dismissed from the start.[146]

[140] Commission Staff Working Paper – Impact Assessment Accompanying the Proposal for a Directive of the European Parliament and of the Council on the Fight Against Fraud to the Union's Financial Interests by Means of Criminal Law (Part I) cit 22.

[141] In that regard, see the Proposal for a Directive of the European Parliament and of the Council on Countering Money Laundering by Criminal Law cit 14: 'setting a minimum level of the maximum penalty at EU level will facilitate international police and judicial cooperation and enhance deterrence'.

[142] In literature, see A Weyembergh, 'Le rapprochement des législations pénales au sein de l'Union européenne : les difficultés et leurs conséquences' in G De Kerchove and A Weyembergh (eds), *L'espace pénal européen : enjeux et perspectives* (Bruxelles, Editions de l'Université de Bruxelles, 2001) 134; W De Bondt, 'The Missing Link between 'Necessity' and 'Approximation of Criminal Sanctions' in the EU' (2014) 4 *European Criminal Law Review* 147, 152.

[143] In that regard, see: W De Bondt and S Miettinen, 'Minimum Criminal Penalties in the European Union: In Search of a Credible Justification' (2015) 21 *European Law Journal* 722.

[144] Proposal for a Directive of the European Parliament and of the Council on the Protection of the Euro and Other Currencies Against Counterfeiting by Criminal Law, COM(2013) 042 final.

[145] *ibid*, 3. That finding is corroborated by a comparative analysis, disclosing that a number of Member States do not provide for a minimum penalty with respect to counterfeiting offences. The Impact Assessment accompanying the Proposal clarifies that 'a minimum sanction of at least six months of imprisonment for production and distribution of counterfeit currency will have a beneficial deterrent effect in the nine Member States where there is no minimum sanction' (Commission Staff Working Document – Impact Assessment accompanying the Proposal for a Directive of the European Parliament and of the Council on the Protection of the Euro and Other Currencies Against Counterfeiting by Criminal Law, and Replacing Framework Decision 2000/383/JHA cit 31).

[146] Commission Staff Working Document – Impact Assessment Report accompanying the Proposal for a Directive of the European Parliament and of the Council on the Protection of the Environment through Criminal Law and Replacing Directive 2008/99/EC, SWD(2021) 465 final, 48-49.

Deterrence can also be enhanced by harmonising aggravating circumstances and accessory sanctions. Indeed, they 'contribute to more effective and dissuasive and proportionate sanctions, as they provide the criminal judge with a toolbox from which it could choose the most appropriate and dissuasive ones adapted to the individual case (emphasis added)'.[147] This statement is insightful, as it shows that deterrence may also be pursued by leaving domestic criminal courts enough room for choosing the most appropriate penalty *in concreto*.

It appears that the EU legislature relies on several techniques to enhance the deterrence of harmonised penalties. However, proportionality poses a limit in that regard. Under its prospective scheme, the type and level of penalties shall be adequate and necessary to attain genuinely dissuasive effects. Therefore, should the availability of surrender procedures be sufficient to attain the desired deterrence, the lowest sanctioning level 'which still allows a practical prospect of permitting surrender among EU Member States' shall be regarded as proportionate.[148] Alternatively, a comparative analysis of existing Member States' provisions may help to define 'the lowest realistic penalty which still exerts a deterring effect in the sense of stigmatising and disrupting effect'.[149] Therefore, domestic criminalisation plays a key role in defining a harmonised penalty threshold compliant with the prospective proportionality of penalties.

ii. Harmonised Penalties shall Reflect the Seriousness of the Offence

Distinct from prospective proportionality, the retrospective scheme postulates a complementary balancing rule for the definition of harmonised penalties. The latter shall reflect the seriousness of the wrongdoing, framed by the EU legislature as the abstract behaviour's harmfulness.[150] This requirement is encapsulated in Article 49(3) of the Charter and represents a constant scheme in the EU legislative practice.[151]

[147] *ibid*, 52.

[148] Commission Staff Working Paper – Impact Assessment Accompanying the Proposal for a Directive of the European Parliament and of the Council on the Fight Against Fraud to the Union's Financial Interests by Means of Criminal Law (Part I) cit 35.

[149] *ibidem*. For a comparative assessment of sanctioning levels in the Member States, see the Final Report of the 2015 ECLAN Research Project on Minimum Sanctions in the EU Member States (R Kert, B Slot, G Vernimmen, A Lehner and J Schellekens, *Study on Minimum Sanctions in the EU Member States: Final Report* (Brussels, European Commission, 2015).

[150] Among various potential examples in the practice, see the Commission Staff Working Document – Impact Assessment Report accompanying the Proposal for a Directive of the European Parliament and of the Council on the Protection of the Environment through Criminal Law and Replacing Directive 2008/99/EC cit which clarifies that 'minimum maximum sanction levels ensure that a common sanction level is available in the Member States *that appropriately reflects the harmfulness of environmental crime* (emphasis added)' (*ibid*, 56).

[151] For instance, see the Proposal for a Directive of the European Parliament and of the Council on the Definition of Criminal Offences and Penalties for the Violation of Union Restrictive Measures cit 13, and the Proposal for a Directive of the European Parliament and of the Council on the Protection of the Environment through Criminal Law and Repealing Directive 2008/99/EC cit 18, according to which '[t]he categorisation proposed reflects the seriousness of the offences'.

Given the variety of elements to be considered and the vagueness of offences' definitions in EU secondary law, quantifying their harmfulness could prove particularly challenging. What is more, that concept may be conceived in different ways. As the practice shows, criminal behaviour may harm the victim or the society at large, as it endangers the public interest.[152] In an attempt to provide a systematisation, early in 2002 the Council adopted Conclusions on the Approach Towards the Approximation of Penalties.[153] According to this instrument, whenever the Council concludes that criminal penalties for a given offence shall be approximated, it may opt between four distinct levels of penalties:

> Level 1: Penalties of a maximum of at least between 1 and 3 years of imprisonment
> Level 2: Penalties of a maximum of at least between 2 and 5 years of imprisonment
> Level 3: Penalties of a maximum of at least between 5 and 10 years of imprisonment
> Level 4: Penalties of a maximum of at least 10 years of imprisonment (cases where very serious penalties are required).[154]

Notwithstanding rigid categorisation, the 2002 Council Conclusions do not indicate which criterion the EU legislature shall employ for choosing between the four sanctioning levels.[155] In fact, the option between these levels may be based on either prospective or retrospective assessments. Moreover, this categorisation only considers custodial penalties without providing any guidance regarding financial or alternative sanctions.

The inherent weakness of the 2002 Council Conclusions is testified by its scarce success in the practice. Only two legislative proposals adopted by the Commission in 2003[156] and 2007[157] refer to the four levels just outlined. On both occasions, the EU legislature followed the guidance of the 2002 Council Conclusions for retrospectively assessing the proportionality of penalties. For example, the 2003 Proposal for a Framework Decision on Ship-Source Pollution contends that 'the

[152] Proposal for a Directive of the European Parliament and of the Council on Combating the Sexual Abuse, Sexual Exploitation of Children and Child Pornography, Repealing Framework Decision 2004/68/JHA, COM(2010) 94 final, 6: 'to determine the degree of seriousness and attach penalties proportional to it, consideration is given to different factors', among them: 'degree of harm to the victim' and 'the level of risk posed to the society'.

[153] Council Conclusions on the Approach to Apply Regarding Approximation of Penalties, 9141/02 LIMITE DROIPEN 33.

[154] *ibid*, 4.

[155] Against this background, an alternative categorisation of offences based on their relative seriousness has been advanced in literature by Satzger (H Satzger, 'The Harmonisation of Criminal Sanctions in the European Union – A New Approach' (2019) *eucrim – The European Criminal Law Associations' Forum* 115). Differently from the 2002 Council Conclusions, this model does not define uniform penalty threshold. In fact, while the EU legislature defines the level of seriousness of the harmonised offence, 'it is the task of the Member States to provide for a sanction specific to their own national legal order, which – in relation to severity – corresponds to the chosen EU category' (*ibid*, 118).

[156] Proposal for a Council Framework Decision to Strengthen the Criminal-law Framework for the Enforcement of the Law against Ship-source Pollution, COM(2003) 227 final, 5.

[157] Proposal for a Directive of the European Parliament and of the Council on the Protection of the Environment through Criminal Law cit 8.

seriousness of imprisonable offences is such [...] that it would seem right to set a harmonisation threshold corresponding to level 3'.[158]

The critical issue for retrospective proportionality consists of the inherent difficulty in the commensuration of penalty levels vis-à-vis an abstract concept such as the harmfulness of criminal behaviour. However, the absence of indications from general policy instruments[159] has not prevented the EU legislature from developing some techniques. In particular, the EU legislature has sometimes quantified the harmfulness of the conduct by referring to the expected damage or turnout generated by the offence. That is the case, for instance, of the 2002 Proposal for a Framework Decision on Attacks Against Information Systems. Having established a minimum maximum term of imprisonment of at least one year for 'serious cases', the Proposal further clarifies that this category 'shall be understood as excluding cases where the conduct resulted in no damage or economic benefit'.[160] This penalty level would be disproportionate vis-à-vis these more lenient conducts, as it would not reflect their lower harmfulness.

A quantitative approach has also led to the definition of monetary thresholds corresponding to a different level of penalties. This technique has been employed for distinguishing between financial and custodial penalties, as well as between different terms of imprisonment. In this perspective, the 2013 Proposal for a Directive on Counterfeiting the Euro holds that

> in order to guarantee that the severity of penalties is not disproportionate to the criminal offence, a specific safeguard for cases of lower amounts of counterfeits is being proposed, i.e. one threshold below which a lower penalty of imprisonment can be imposed and another one below which also a fine can be imposed, unless the case features particularly serious circumstances.[161]

Monetary thresholds are also provided to distinguish between different maximum terms of detention for sanctioning violations of CFSP restrictive measures. In fact, the 2022 Proposal for a Directive on the Definition of Criminal Offences and Penalties for the Violation of Union Restrictive Measures sets a monetary

[158] Proposal for a Council Framework Decision to Strengthen the Criminal-law Framework for the Enforcement of the Law against Ship-source Pollution cit 5.

[159] With particular emphasis on the already cited Council Conclusions on Model Provisions, Guiding the Council's Criminal Law Deliberations cit; European Parliament Resolution of 22 May 2012 on an EU approach to criminal law cit; Communication from the Commission to the European Parliament, the Council, the European Economic and Social Committee and the Committee of the Regions – Towards an EU Criminal Policy: Ensuring the Effective Implementation of EU Policies Through Criminal Law cit.

[160] Proposal for a Council Framework Decision on Attacks Against Information Systems cit 13. The same formula has been upheld by the EU legislature and included in Art 6 of Council Framework Decision 2005/222/JHA of 24 February 2005 on Attacks Against Information Systems cit.

[161] Proposal for a Directive of the European Parliament and of the Council on the Protection of the Euro and Other Currencies against Counterfeiting by Criminal Law, and Replacing Council Framework Decision 2000/383/JHA cit 7.

threshold of EUR 100 000 to distinguish more serious offences – punishable by a maximum term of imprisonment of at least 5 years – from minor conducts.[162]

As far as the definition of financial penalties is concerned, a reference to percentages of the offence's turnover has sometimes been envisaged. That is the case of the 2003 Proposal for a Council Framework Decision on Ship-Source Pollution, which underlines that fixed financial penalties 'could evolve as a result of index-linking and [their adoption] by definition would not be in accordance with the proportionality requirement'.[163] The cited Proposal introduces a system of calculating financial penalties based on a certain percentage of turnover or assets. According to the Commission, that system 'is inspired by different instruments of Community law, in the field of competition law in particular'.[164] In particular, a reference is made to Article 23 of Regulation (EC) No 1/2003,[165] which includes a similar calculation system for fines against violations of Articles 101 and 102 TFEU.[166]

The very same approach has been recently envisaged for criminal or non-criminal financial sanctions against legal entities, as witnessed by the 2021 Proposal for a Directive on the Protection of the Environment through Criminal Law,[167] the 2022 Proposal for a Directive on the Definition of Criminal Offences and Penalties for the Violation of Union Restrictive Measure[168] and the 2023 Proposal on Facilitation of Unauthorised Entry, Transit and Stay in the Union.[169] As underlined by Brière, the adoption of turnover-based fines in this domain is evidence of a shift in the practice of the EU legislature towards more prescriptive provisions

[162] Proposal for a Directive of the European Parliament and of the Council on the Definition of Criminal Offences and Penalties for the Violation of Union Restrictive Measures cit 13.

[163] Proposal for a Council Framework Decision to Strengthen the Criminal Law Framework for the Enforcement of the Law Against Ship-Source Pollution cit 6.

[164] *ibid.*

[165] Council Regulation (EC) No 1/2003 on the Implementation of the Rules on Competition Laid Down in Articles 81 and 82 of the Treaty [2003] OJ L1/1.

[166] This is not the only example. For instance, a similar system of calculation of fines has also been envisaged in the context of EU environmental law (Art 18 of Directive (EU) 2016/802 of the European Parliament and of the Council relating to a Reduction in the Sulphur Content of Certain Liquid Fuels [2016] OJ L132/58).

[167] Proposal for a Directive of the European Parliament and of the Council on the Protection of the Environment through Criminal Law and Repealing Directive 2008/99/EC cit Art 7(4)–(5). Still, the finally adopted Directive leaves the Member States free to impose penalties corresponding to a percentage of the turnover or a fixed financial sanction (Art 7(3) of Directive (EU) 2024/1203 of the European Parliament and of the Council on the Protection of the Environment through Criminal Law and Replacing Directives 2008/99/EC and 2009/123/EC [2024] OJ L 2024/1203).

[168] Proposal for a Directive of the European Parliament and of the Council on the Definition of Criminal Offences and Penalties for the Violation of Union Restrictive Measures cit 14 and Art 7(2)–(3) therein.

[169] Proposal for a Directive of the European Parliament and of the Council Laying Down Minimum Rules to Prevent and Counter the Facilitation of Unauthorised Entry, Transit and Stay in the Union, and Replacing Council Directive 2002/90/EC and Council Framework Decision 2002/946 JHA, COM(2023) 755 final, 13 and Art 7(3) therein.

on sanctions against legal entities.[170] However, as observed by Caeiro, this fining method obliterates retrospective proportionality: the sanction *in concreto* would mainly depend on the offender's turnover and only to a minimal extent on the seriousness of the wrongdoing.[171]

Quantitative assessments do not constitute the panacea for ensuring retrospective proportionality. It is not always possible to easily translate the inherent harmfulness of criminal behaviour into monetary or quantitative thresholds. In this case, ordinal proportionality may constitute a valuable option. The EU legislature has sometimes established a comparison between distinct forms of wrongdoings characterised by different levels of harmfulness. Should the proposed new offence be equally harmful to a criminal behaviour already subject to approximation, a comparable sanctioning level may be proportionate. That is the case, for instance, of the 2001 Proposal for a Council Framework Decision on Drug Trafficking: minimum maximum penalties have been defined therein by reference to custodial terms already provided at the EU level for money laundering.[172] A similar comparison has also been employed to distinguish between different offences defined by the same piece of legislation to justify the provision of distinct penalty levels. Indeed, they are meant to reflect the degree of harmfulness of the wrongdoing, which may stem from the inherent characteristics of the conduct[173] or, in the case of associative crimes, 'the degree of participation in the criminal organisation'.[174]

Therefore, retrospective proportionality implies that the type and level of harmonised standards on criminal penalties – comprising minimum maximum penalties, aggravating circumstances, and accessory sanctions – shall reflect the harmfulness of the offence. The EU legislature may develop quantitative thresholds to account for minor or trivial cases and rely on ordinal proportionality techniques to assess the wrongdoing's degree of harmfulness.

[170] Brière (n 84) 108.

[171] P Caeiro, 'Broadly Unknown, but Deservedly Unloved? Turnover-based Fines and their Transplant from Competition Law to EU Criminal Law' in L Grossio, S Montaldo and V Mitsilegas (eds), *Proportionality of Criminal Penalties in EU Law* (Oxford, Hart Publishing, 2025) 154–155.

[172] Proposal for a Council Framework Decision Laying Down Minimum Provisions on the Constituent Elements of Criminal Acts and Penalties in the Field of Illicit Drug Trafficking, COM(2001) 259 final, 4.

[173] Proposal for a Directive of the European Parliament and of the Council on Combating the Sexual Abuse, Sexual Exploitation of Children and Child Pornography, Repealing Framework Decision 2004/68/JHA cit 6–7.

[174] Proposal for a Council Framework Decision on the Fight Against Organised Crime, COM(2005) 6 final, 5. See also recital 3 of the mentioned proposal, according to which '*penalties corresponding to the seriousness of these offences* should be envisaged (emphasis added)'. For a discussion of the legislative debate concerning different penalties for different forms of participation in the criminal organisation, see M Fichera, 'Organised Crime: Developments and Challenges for an Enlarged European Union' in C Eckes and T Konstadinides (eds), *Crime Within the Area of Freedom, Security and Justice: A European Public Order* (Cambridge, Cambridge University Press, 2011) 173–177.

V. A Consistent EU Legislative Practice with Limited Room for ECHR Proportionality Standards

The EU legislative practice is characterised by a certain degree of consistency in the application of the principle of proportionality of criminal offences and penalties. In fact, the Commission and the EU legislature justify their actions by parameterising the scope of harmonised offences and the type and level of harmonised penalties to attaining the objectives driving supranational criminalisation.

As previous sections showed, this assessment is mainly grounded on Article 52(1) of the Charter. As the fundamental rights dimension of proportionality is prominent in EU criminalisation, the ECtHR case-law may constitute an important source, under Article 52(3) of the Charter, for shaping legislative balancing. However, the EU legislative practice leaves almost no room for proportionality standards derived from the ECHR. Indeed, references to the Convention and Strasbourg Court case-law are extremely scarce in this context, and they fall short of influencing the positive proportionality assessment of offences and penalties carried out by the EU legislature.

Against the limited range of examples available, ECHR standards have been employed in a twofold way. On the one hand, provisions of the ECHR have been invoked to justify criminalisation on grounds of positive obligations incumbent on Member States and deriving from the Convention itself. This is the case, for instance, of the 2022 Proposal for a Directive on Gender Based Violence.[175] As violence against women constitutes an assault on the rights to life, integrity, private and family life and the prohibition of inhuman or degrading treatment, the Impact Assessment accompanying the cited Proposal observes that 'the ECtHR has established comprehensive obligations on states parties to prevent, investigate and punish this kind of violence'.[176] Against that background, EU criminalisation shall provide for deterring offences and effective penalties, as 'the ECtHR considers that this is a key part of Member States' obligations to ensure protection of the abovementioned rights'.[177] Therefore, the obligations imposed on EU Member States because they are party to the ECHR are here invoked as a driver for criminalisation.

ECHR positive obligations have also been recalled in the recent Proposal for Extending the List of EU Crimes to Hate Speech and Hate Crime.[178] To justify the

[175] Proposal for a Directive of the European Parliament and of the Council on Combating Violence Against Women and Domestic Violence, COM(2022) 105 final.

[176] Commission Staff Working Document – Impact Assessment Report accompanying the Proposal for a Directive of the European Parliament and of the Council on Combating Violence Against Women and Domestic Violence, SWD(2022) 62 final, 46.

[177] *ibid*, 47. In particular, the Commission refers therein to the ECtHR findings according to which cyberviolence conducts may be sufficiently serious, from a retrospective point of view, to warrant criminalisation. In that regard, see *Volodina v Russia* App No 40419/19 (ECtHR, 14 September 2021), para 57, *Buturugă v Romania*, App No 56967/15 (ECtHR, 11 February 2020), para 68.

[178] Communication from the Commission to the European Parliament and the Council – A More Inclusive and Protective Europe: Extending the List of EU Crimes to Hate Speech and Hate Crime cit 8.

addition of these two areas of crime to Article 83 TFEU, the Commission established a direct reference to the case-law of the Strasbourg Court. In particular, much emphasis is posed upon those judgments outlining the existence of a positive obligation for Contracting Parties to take steps to 'sanction or even prevent all forms of expression which spread, incite, promote or justify hatred based on intolerance'.[179] The ECtHR case-law is here invoked to demonstrate the necessity of EU criminalisation, as the Strasbourg Court 'considered [...] that criminal law measures are required with respect to direct verbal assaults and physical threats motivated by discriminatory attitudes'.[180]

On the other hand, the ECtHR case-law has sometimes been employed to further substantiate the scope of individual rights enshrined in the Charter, thereby limiting EU criminalisation. This is the approach featuring, for instance, the 2010 Proposal for a Directive on Sexual Abuse, Sexual Exploitation of Children and Child Pornography, which clarifies that proposed offences and penalties 'were specially scrutinised with regard to the right to respect for private and family life and the protection of personal data'[181] stemming not only from Articles 7 and 8 of the Charter but also from Article 8 ECHR.[182]

The complementarity between the Charter and the ECHR is acknowledged by the Commission when proposing new legislation in the substantive criminal law field. The 2015 Proposal for a Directive on Combating Terrorism constitutes an example in that regard, as it outlines that

> the Union's approach [...] must respect and promote fundamental rights, as set out in the Charter of Fundamental Rights, which reaffirms [...] the rights as they result, in particular, from the constitutional traditions and international obligations common to the Member States, including [...] the European Convention for the Protection of Human Rights and Fundamental Freedoms, and the case-law of the Court of Justice of the European Communities and of the European Court of Human Rights.[183]

The approach just outlined is commendable. Indeed, a reference to the European Convention appears consistent with Article 52(3) of the Charter, according to

[179] *Erbakan v Turkey* App No 59405/00 (ECtHR, 6 July 2006), para 56.

[180] Communication from the Commission to the European Parliament and the Council – A More Inclusive and Protective Europe: Extending the List of EU Crimes to Hate Speech and Hate Crime cit 8. In that regard, a reference may be established to the Strasbourg Court judgments in *Beizaras and Levickas v Lithuania* App No 41288/15 (ECtHR, 14 January 2020), para 111; *Identoba and Others v Georgia* App No 73235/12 (ECtHR, 12 May 2015), para 86; *R.B. v Hungary* App No 64602/12 (ECtHR, 12 April 2016), paras 80 and 84–85; *Király and Dömötör v Hungary* App No 10851/13 (ECtHR, 17 January 2017), para 76; *Alković v Montenegro* App No 66895/10 (ECtHR, 5 December 2017), paras 8, 11, 65 and 69.

[181] Proposal for a Directive on Sexual Abuse, Sexual Exploitation of Children and Child Pornography cit 4.

[182] That assessment is reflected in recital 13 of the same legislative proposal, which provides that 'any such developments must take account of the rights of the end users, adhere to existing legal and judicial procedures and *comply with the European Convention on Human Rights and the Charter of Fundamental Rights of the European Union* (emphasis added)'.

[183] Proposal for a Directive of the European Parliament and of the Council on Combating Terrorism and Replacing Council Framework Decision 2002/4757JHA on Combating Terrorism cit 13.

which Charter rights corresponding to ECHR ones shall be interpreted as providing at least the same level of protection. In this perspective, ECHR provisions and the ECtHR case-law clarifying their meaning and scope constitute a key integrative source.

At the same time, references to the ECHR and Strasbourg Court case-law in the EU legislative practice are scarce and particularly generic in their content. Consequently, their impact on the scrutiny carried out by the Commission and EU legislature is remarkably reduced. Indeed, they fall short of indicating in which way the cited ECHR provision or ECtHR case-law could enrich the guarantees afforded by the Charter in the given domain. Moreover, even if ECHR provisions effectively complemented the content of relevant individual rights, the fact would remain that the proportionality schemes applied by the EU legislature are not subject to any influence by ECHR proportionality standards. There is no reference among EU legislative practice to the proportionality paradigms inherent in the ECtHR case-law. It follows that the proportionality of criminal offences and penalties in EU criminalisation is based upon EU-own proportionality paradigms – with particular emphasis on Article 52(1) of the Charter – without any meaningful influence from the ECHR.

Notwithstanding this conclusion, proficient interaction between the two proportionality standards in EU criminalisation is not impossible from a theoretical point of view. Evidence of that may be found in the already cited 2021 Proposal for the Extension of the List of EU Crimes to Hate Speech and Hate Crime. Having relied upon ECtHR case-law to recognise the existence of a positive obligation to criminalise, the Commission also recalls that, according to the Strasbourg Court, 'criminal sanctions, including against the individuals responsible for the most serious expressions of hatred, inciting others to violence, could be invoked only as an *ultima ratio* measure'.[184] This finding entails reliance on the ECtHR case-law to conclude that the EU legislature should exercise a strict necessity assessment when defining the extent of criminalisation of hate speech and hate crime.

That example is isolated in the EU legislative practice on substantive criminal law, but it fuels further reflection on potential developments. Indeed, references to the ECHR proportionality standards are scarce since the Union is still not a Party to the Convention. Consequently, the latter is not directly binding upon the EU legislature, and the Union cannot be held accountable before the Strasbourg Court for any inconsistency in this respect. Still, standards deriving from the ECHR indirectly permeate the Union's legal order, as they qualify as general principles under Article 6 TEU and integrative sources for interpreting fundamental rights under Article 52(3) of the Charter. Therefore, the EU legislature may incorporate them in its reasoning: the motivations behind the different approach described above amount to a policy choice.

[184] *Beizaras and Levickas v Lithuania* App No 41288/15 (ECtHR, 14 January 2020), para 111; *Vona v Hungary* App No 35943/10 (ECtHR, 9 July 2013), para 42.

Against this background, the EU's accession to the ECHR may lead to a change of approach. In that potential circumstance, any incompliance with the Strasbourg Court's proportionality standards could entail a violation of the European Convention attributable to the Union. That risk would probably be a pulling factor for the EU legislature, driving it to a deeper consideration of ECHR standards for justifying the harmonisation of substantive criminal law. In this line of reasoning, the Strasbourg Court's case-law may play a broader role in shaping the EU legislative approach.

VI. Proportionality in the Judicial Review of Harmonised Offences and Penalties

The ECJ is entitled to review the proportionality of harmonised standards on offences and penalties in the context of actions for annulment or preliminary reference procedures. In that case, the Court would exercise a negative proportionality scrutiny, thereby assessing whether the EU legislature exceeded the limits of its discretion by exercising disproportionate criminalisation choices.

To frame the ECJ proportionality scrutiny, the standard of review shall be defined. However, for a long time, no proportionality contestation had been addressed against EU substantive criminal law provisions. The ECJ has been confronted with validity pleas against EU substantive criminal law instruments only in two actions for annulment previously recalled: the 2005 Environmental Crimes and 2007 Ship-Source Pollution cases.[185] However, the judgments rendered by the Court – concerning the 2003 Framework Decision on Environmental Crimes[186] and the 2005 Framework Decision on Ship-Source Pollution[187] – focused on the division of competencies between the EC and the EU rather than the proportionality of harmonised offences and penalties.[188]

Despite the longstanding absence of proportionality pleas, a recent referral for a preliminary ruling by the Tribunale di Bologna (Italy) has brought a paradigm shift.[189] Indeed, this development in the judicial practice shows that the proportionality of EU criminalisation does not constitute an exclusively theoretical issue deprived of practical relevance. This case paves the way for future litigation, thus

[185] Case C-176/03 *Commission v Council* ECLI:EU:C:2005:542; Case C-440/05 *Commission v Council* ECLI:EU:C:2007:625.

[186] Council Framework Decision 2003/80/JHA on the Protection of the Environment through Criminal Law cit.

[187] Council Framework Decision 2005/667/JHA to Strengthen the Criminal-Law Framework for the Enforcement of the Law against Ship-Source Pollution cit.

[188] For an analysis of the Court's reasoning in the mentioned judgments and their implications, see A Klip, *European Criminal Law: An Integrative Approach*, 4th edn (Cambridge, Intersentia, 2021) 234–237.

[189] Case C-460/23 *Kinsa*.

making the proportionality review of harmonised offences and penalties one of the most topical issues in the EU criminal law field.[190]

For the purposes of the present analysis, the lack of a substantial body of case-law – which several reasons can explain (A) – prevents the definition of the standard of review in a *de iure condito* perspective. Therefore, some *de iure condendo* reflections appear necessary to frame the standard of review for the retrospective (B) and the prospective (C) assessments exercised by the EU legislature.

A. The Reasons for the Lack of Proportionality Pleas against EU Substantive Criminal Law before the *Kinsa* Case

In the recent *Kinsa* case, the Tribunale di Bologna seeks to ascertain whether EU provisions on facilitating illegal immigration, with particular emphasis on Framework Decision 2002/946/JHA,[191] are compatible with fundamental rights under the Charter insofar as they do not provide that humanitarian assistance purposes may exclude criminal liability. Based on Article 52(1) of the Charter, the preliminary questions raise the issue of excessive criminalisation at the EU level, entailing a potentially disproportionate interference with the rights to liberty (Article 6), property (Article 17), life (Article 2), physical integrity (Article 3), asylum (Article 18) and respect for family life (Article 7).

This case, still pending at the time of writing, comes after a longstanding absence of similar proportionality pleas against EU substantive criminal law instruments. Indeed, *Kinsa* constitutes the very first preliminary ruling in that regard, while no action for annulment against harmonised offences and penalties based on proportionality grounds has been lodged so far. This circumstance derives from both structural and contingent reasons. Concerning actions for annulment, their absence from the case-law on substantive criminal law stems from different grounds depending on potential applicants. Indeed, Article 263(2)–(4) TFEU distinguishes between privileged (Member States, the European Parliament, the Council and the Commission), quasi-privileged (the Court of Auditors, the European Central Bank and the Committee of Regions) and non-privileged applicants (any natural or legal person), whose legal standing before the ECJ is subject to different conditions.[192]

The possibility of quasi-privileged applicants lodging an action against harmonised offences and penalties shall be excluded from the outset. Under

[190] Among the scholarly debate on the topic, see: V Mitsilegas, 'Reforming the "Facilitators' Package" through the Kinsa litigation: Legality, Effectiveness and Taking International Law Into Account' (2024) *Eurojus* 155; E Pistoia, 'La facoltá di non incriminare il "favoreggiamento umanitario" al confronto con alcuni diritti di cittadini di Stati terzi sanciti nella Carta' in *Sistema penale*, 18 October 2024.

[191] Council Framework Decision 2002/946/JHA on the Strengthening of the Penal Framework to Prevent the Facilitation of Unauthorised Entry, Transit and Residence [2002] OJ L328/1.

[192] In that regard, among many, see P Craig and G de Búrca, *EU Law: Text, Cases and Materials*, 7th edn (Oxford, Oxford University Press, 2020) 545–563; R Baratta, *Institutions of EU Law*, 2nd edn (Milano, Wolters Kluwer, 2024) 290–297; G Strozzi and R Mastroianni, *Diritto dell'Unione europea. Parte istituzionale*, 9th edn (Torino, Giappichelli, 2023) 377–388.

Article 263(3) TFEU, they may institute proceedings only to defend their prerogatives. However, the Court of Auditors, the European Central Bank, and the Committee of Regions do not have any prerogative in substantive criminal law. Therefore, they are prevented from lodging actions for annulment against harmonising provisions on offences and penalties.

The legal standing of privileged applicants is not subject to any condition. However, legal proceedings instituted by the European Parliament, the Council or the Commission against substantive criminal law provisions appear quite unlikely after the Treaty of Lisbon's entry into force. Indeed, the abolition of the dichotomy between the First and Third Pillar has overcome the previous duplication of legal bases that led the Commission to contest the 2003 Framework Decision on Environmental Crimes and the 2005 Framework Decision on Ship-Source Pollution. As a result of extending the ordinary legislative procedure, the European Parliament and the Council now have an equal say in the legislative process for adopting substantive criminal law instruments.[193] Therefore, proportionality contestations may now be absorbed by the interaction between the European Parliament and the Council within the legislative procedure. This finding may also apply to the Commission, as the practice of the ordinary legislative procedure envisages strict coordination between the latter and legislators within informal fora known as trilogues.[194] The possibility of proportionality pleas lodged by the Commission cannot be ruled out at the outset. Still, trilogues allow raising and dealing with such issues in the context of the legislative process.

Member States may eventually advance proportionality pleas. However, in the substantive criminal law field, they are provided with an additional tool for conveying contestations against (draft) legislative acts: the so-called 'emergency brake' established by Article 83(3) TFEU. Should a Member State in the Council consider that a draft directive for the approximation of offences and penalties affects 'fundamental aspects of its criminal justice system',[195] this issue shall be referred to the European Council. The legislative procedure is suspended and will be resumed only after a solution has been reached by Member States' Heads of State or Government. Clearly enough, the emergency brake does not constitute an alternative instrument to judicial redress. It does not entail the draft directive to be set aside but rather a temporary burden on the legislative process. At the same time, it may strengthen the position of Members States alongside the procedure.

[193] Among many, see Mitsilegas, *EU Criminal Law after Lisbon. Rights, Trust and the Transformation of Justice in Europe* (n 1) 5–7.

[194] On the role and implications of trilogues in the EU decision-making process, see C Roederer-Rynning and J Greenwood, 'The Culture of Trilogues' (2015) 22 *Journal of European Public Policy* 1148; P Recaldini, 'I triloghi all'ora della riforma dei Trattati: come bilanciare flessibilità e trasparenza in un tentativo di costituzionalizzazione?' (2024) *Rivista Quaderni AISDUE* 1.

[195] Art 83(3) TFEU. For an analysis of the meaning of that concept, see K Rosin and M Kärner, 'The Limitations of the Harmonisation of Criminal Law in the European Union Protected by Articles 82(3) and 83(3) TFEU' (2018) 26 *European Journal of Crime, Criminal Law and Criminal Justice* 315.

Legal scholarship has pointed out that a threat of invoking the emergency brake can amount to a chilling instrument to drive consensus within the Council.[196] Therefore, the emergency brake may allow reluctant Member States to push the Council in the policy direction they desire, thus neutralising successive pleas for annulment.

The absence of similar actions lodged by non-privileged applicants may be explained by the restrictive conditions for legal standing provided by the Treaties before and after the 2007 reform. Under Article 35(6) of the pre-Lisbon TEU, actions for annulment against Third Pillar instruments may be filed by Member States and the Commission only.[197] This regime has been temporarily extended until 1 December 2014 by Article 10(1) of Protocol No 36 attached to the Treaty of Lisbon.[198] Therefore, non-privileged applicants were wholly precluded from attacking Third Pillar instruments.

Moreover, the rules for legal standing provided by Article 263(4) TFEU deeply narrow the scope for actions by non-privileged applicants. It is pretty challenging for private parties to plead that the approximation of offences and penalties is of 'direct and individual concern' for them. According to Article 83(1) TFEU, the Union is entitled to approximate domestic criminal systems only in some 'areas of particularly serious crime' traditionally subject to domestic criminalisation. Consequently, it is difficult to ascertain whether the prejudice for a given offender originates from EU harmonising provisions, its national implementation, or even purely domestic criminalisation. This circumstance may result in a considerable burden for a potential applicant willing to affirm that EU acts

> affect directly the legal situation of the individual and leave no discretion to its addressees, who are entrusted with the task of implementing it, such implementation being purely automatic and resulting from [EU] rules without the application of other intermediate rules.[199]

Even if a given EU harmonising provision directly affected the situation of a natural and legal person, the individual concern would be even more challenging to establish. Article 83 TFEU envisages 'minimum rules' only. This limit does not confine the EU competence to 'minimalist' harmonisation by adopting provisions

[196] In that regard, see J Öberg, 'Exit, Voice and Consensus – A Legal and Political Analysis of the Emergency Brake in EU Criminal Policy' (2021) 46 *European Law Review* 506.

[197] Art 35(6) of the Consolidated Version of the Treaty on the European Union [2006] OJ CE321/1. In literature, see Pistoia (n 7) 11; ME Bartoloni, 'La tutela giurisdizionale nell'ambito del secondo e terzo pilastro UE' (2005) 25 *Quaderni costituzionali* 170; L Daniele, 'Art 35 TUE' in A Tizzano (ed), *Trattati dell'Unione europea e della Comunità europea* (Milano, Giuffrè, 2004) 146; C Amalfitano, 'Scaduto il regime transitorio per gli atti del terzo pilastro. Da oggi in vigore il sistema "ordinario" di tutela giurisdizionale della Corte di giustizia' in *Eurojus*, 1 December 2014.

[198] Art 10(1) of the Consolidated Version of the Treaty on the Functioning of the European Union – Protocol (No 36) on Transitional Provisions [2016] OJ C202/321.

[199] Among many, see Case C-343/07 *Bavaria and Bavaria Italia* ECLI:EU:C:2009:415, para 43; Case C-404/96 P *Glencore Grain v Commission* ECLI:EU:C:1998:196, para 41; Case C-486/01 P *Front National v Parliament* ECLI:EU:C:2004:394, para 34; Case C-15/06 P *Regione Siciliana v Commission* ECLI:EU:C:2007:183, para 31.

reproducing the minimum common denominator in a given field.[200] However, the 2011 Communication 'Towards an EU Criminal Policy' acknowledges that 'minimum rules' preclude complete harmonisation of domestic criminal systems.[201] As scholars outlined, certain self-restraint characterises the approach of the EU legislature.[202] Therefore, the Member States enjoy a degree of discretion when transposing harmonised offences and penalties, and the latter may hardly affect natural or legal persons 'by reason of certain attributes which are peculiar to them or by reason of circumstances in which they are differentiated from all other persons'.[203] On top of that, even assuming that an EU substantive criminal law instrument is of direct and individual concern for a non-privileged applicant, that prejudice would hardly emerge within the two-month limitation period provided by Article 263(6) TFEU.

Secondly, proportionality contestations may be brought to the ECJ through preliminary references, like in the *Kinsa* case. However, the fact that no referral has occurred before is unsurprising since this possibility was remarkably reduced until 1 December 2014. Indeed, the pre-Lisbon regime – extended until the mentioned date by Protocol No 36[204] – only allowed preliminary references raised by the judicial authorities of Member States that expressly recognised the ECJ competence for adjudicating on acts of the Third Pillar.[205] Nothing prevents nowadays national courts from referring preliminary questions on the validity of harmonising provisions of offences and penalties. Therefore, while actions for annulment may still be quite rare in the future, different conclusions may be drawn for preliminary references, as *Kinsa* testifies.

B. The ECJ (Potential) Scrutiny Over Retrospective Proportionality: A Standard of Review Difficult to Grasp

When the Court is confronted with proportionality pleas against harmonised offences and penalties, which standard of review shall it apply? The ECJ case-law provides some limited indications in this regard. According to its reasoning in the 2005 Environmental Crimes and 2007 Ship-Source Pollution cases, the

[200] In that regard, see C Haguenau-Moizard, F Gazin and J Leblois-Happe, *Les fondements du droit pénal de l'Union européenne* (Bruxelles, Larcier, 2016) 152; Klip (n 188) 181.

[201] Communication from the Commission to the European Parliament, the Council, the European Economic and Social Committee and the Committee of the Regions – Towards an EU Criminal Policy: Ensuring the Effective Implementation of EU Policies Through Criminal Law cit 7.

[202] K Zoumpoulakis, 'Approximation of Criminal Sanctions in the European Union: A Wild Goose Chase?' (2022) 13 *New Journal of European Criminal Law* 333, 336.

[203] Among many, see Case C-309/89 *Codorniu v Council* ECLI:EU:C:1994:197, para 20; Case 25/62 *Plaumann v Commission of the EEC* ECLI:EU:C:1963:17, p 107.

[204] Consolidated Version of the Treaty on the Functioning of the European Union – Protocol (No 36) on Transitional Provisions cit.

[205] Art 35 of the Treaty on European Union (Consolidated version 2006) [2006] OJ C321E/5.

Union legislature may adopt harmonising provisions on offences and penalties when the latter are 'necessary in order to ensure that the rules which it lays down […] are fully effective'.[206] This finding confirms that the primary proportionality scheme shall be construed as a necessity assessment. However, these seminal indications fall short of clarifying the standard of review that the ECJ should apply when exercising proportionality scrutiny on harmonised offences and penalties.

Neither the Conclusions of Advocate General Richard de la Tour in the *Kinsa* case provide decisive insights. Against the referring court's questions on the validity of Article 1(1)(a) of Directive 2002/90/EC, paragraph 2 therein leaves the Member States free not to impose sanctions if the conduct was aimed at providing humanitarian assistance. According to the Advocate General, this legislative arrangement should be regarded as proportionate to combating the facilitation of illegal migration.[207] It would be for domestic authorities to assess whether the implementing criminal provisions leave enough room to

> balance the interests at stake and to differentiate between the criminalisation of a person who is shown to have acted out of humanity or necessity, in the sole interest of relatives, in particular his or her children, and that of a person who is motivated solely by the criminal intent to commit the very act prohibited by the law and to profit from it.[208]

To reach such a conclusion, the Advocate General does not clarify the standard of review to be applied in the proportionality assessment. Moreover, the reasoning proposed in his Conclusions incidentally recalls the prospective and retrospective schemes[209] but does not rely on them in the scrutiny. This approach is questionable since, as the practice shows, the EU legislature constantly relies on prospective and retrospective schemes to balance between conflicting interests under the proportionality of criminal offences and penalties. Therefore, judicial review by the ECJ should involve scrutinising these secondary assessments.

Further reflection is thus required to fine-tune the standard for reviewing the proportionality of harmonised offences and penalties. This section focuses on retrospective proportionality, while the following delves into the prospective scheme.

As codified in Article 49(3) of the Charter, the retrospective scheme requires the severity of criminal sanctions not to be disproportionate to the seriousness of the offence. While the legislative practice has mostly neglected this provision,[210]

[206] Case C-176/03 *Commission v Council* ECLI:EU:C:2005:542, para 48; Case C-440/05 *Commission v Council* ECLI:EU:C:2007:625, para 66.

[207] Case C-460/23 *Kinsa*, Opinion of AG Richard de la Tour, ECLI:EU:C:2024:941, para 87.

[208] *ibid*, para 111. See also para 113 therein.

[209] *ibid*, para 102.

[210] See Section IV(A) above in this chapter.

some recent preliminary rulings on the proportionality of domestic sanctioning systems envisage a bond between Articles 49(3) and 52(1) of the Charter. More specifically, in *Link Logistik* and *ECOTEX Bulgaria* the ECJ held that

> the severity of a penalty must correspond to the seriousness of the offence concerned, that requirement following both from Article 52(1) of the Charter and from the principle of proportionality of penalties in Article 49(3) of the Charter.[211]

This affirmation has a double significance. On the one hand, it confirms that the proportionality assessment under Article 52(1) of the Charter entails prospective and retrospective evaluations. On the other hand, it confers fundamental significance to Article 49(3) of the Charter for grounding the latter proportionality scheme when reviewing criminal sanctions. As clarified by the Court, that provision establishes a negative criterion or, more specifically, a 'prohibition on adopting disproportionate penalties'.[212]

Notwithstanding this seminal affirmation, the standard for the judicial review of retrospective proportionality of harmonised offences and penalties remains elusive. Indeed, any retrospective assessment is highly dependent upon moral judgements and assumptions.[213] That is the case, in particular, of cardinal proportionality. It entails determining which type – criminal or non-criminal, as well as custodial, financial or other forms – and amount of punishment would be appropriate in absolute terms to sanction a given wrongdoing in the light of its seriousness.[214] As recalled by Von Hirsch, cardinal proportionality 'cannot possibly tell us how much an offender deserves, but can only suggest certain upper and lower limits, beyond which punishment would be manifestly undeserved'.[215] Therefore, cardinal proportionality may pose a standard for reviewing legislative discretion. However, this standard is particularly difficult to grasp. Indeed, any relationship of commensurability between a given wrongdoing and the attached penalty is highly dependent upon the Court's perception of the seriousness of the conduct. Given the absence of a theoretical methodology for operating cardinal proportionality in the legislative process, the standard for judicial review of this assessment appears challenging to define in abstract terms.[216] This is why Asp contended that cardinal proportionality would be of little help for reviewing EU

[211] Case C-544/19 *ECOTEX Bulgaria* ECLI:EU:C:2021:803, para 97; Case C-384/17 *Link Logistik N&N* ECLI:EU:C:2018:810, para 42; Case C-537/16 *Garlsson Real Estate and Others* ECLI:EU:C:2018:193, para 56.

[212] Case C-205/20 *Bezirkshauptmannschaft Hartberg-Fürstenfeld (Effet direct)* ECLI:EU:C:2022:168, para 24.

[213] A von Hirsch, 'Proportionality in the Philosophy of Punishment: From 'Why Punish' to 'How Much'' (1991) 25 *Israel Law Review* 549, 574.

[214] See Section IV(B)(i) of Chapter 2.

[215] A von Hirsch, 'Proportionality in the Philosophy of Punishment' (1992) 16 *Crime and Justice* 55, 75.

[216] For an extensive analysis of the counterintuitive implications of absolute constraints on criminal punishment, see J Ryberg, 'Retributivism and the Proportionality Dilemma' (2021) 34 *Ratio* 158.

harmonised offences and penalties, as it consists of 'an obscure, tradition-bound standard for assessing sanctions if made part of the legal system'.[217]

Against these hurdles, a broader view of the ECJ case-law beyond substantive criminal law does not provide meaningful guidance. The Luxembourg Court developed a retrospective account when reviewing financial sanctions imposed by the Commission in the competition law domain. As clarified by Article 23(3) of Council Regulation (EC) No 1/2003[218] on anticompetitive agreements, decisions, concerted practices and abuses of dominant positions, and Article 14(3) of Council Regulation (EC) No 139/2004[219] on merger control, fines imposed by the Commission shall be commensurate to the nature, gravity, and duration of the infringement. Building upon these seminal provisions, the ECJ developed quite an extensive case-law on evaluating the seriousness of anti-competitive conduct. According to the Court's jurisprudence, the seriousness of the behaviour 'has to be determined by reference to numerous factors, such as the particular circumstances of the case, its context and the dissuasive effect of fines'.[220] This assessment allows the Court to verify whether the sanction is disproportionate not only from a prospective,[221] but also retrospective point of view.[222]

However, the peculiar features of the ECJ jurisdiction on competition law sanctions do not allow for reasoning by analogy. In fact, according to Article 261 TFEU,[223] the Court of Justice exercises 'unlimited jurisdiction' when reviewing penalties imposed for violations of Articles 101–102 TFEU. Judicial scrutiny is thus not limited to their legality, as Union courts have 'the power to assess the evidence, to annul the contested decision and to alter the amount of a fine'.[224] This is, in particular, the task of the General Court on first instance. But this scrutiny is not negative and, therefore, does not imply reliance on a standard of review. Indeed, the General Court is entitled to replace the Commission's assessment with

[217] Asp (n 114) 201.

[218] Council Regulation (EC) No 1/2003 of 16 December 2002 on the Implementation of the Rules on Competition Laid Down in Articles 81 and 82 of the Treaty cit.

[219] Council Regulation (EC) No 139/2004 of 20 January 2004 on the Control of Concentrations between Undertakings [2004] OJ L 24/1.

[220] Case C-219/95 P *Ferriere Nord v Commission* ECLI:EU:C:1997:375, para 33. In literature, see L Bernardeau and J-P Christienne, *Les amendes en droit de la concurrence: pratique décisionnelle et contrôle juridictionnel du droit de l'Union* (Bruxelles, Larcier, 2013) 648.

[221] H Gilliams, 'Proportionality of EU Competition Fines: Proposal for a Principled Discussion' (2014) 4 *World Competition* 435, 437.

[222] M Mezaguer, M Cartapanis, W Chaiehloudj, F Jacomino, J Malet-Vigneaux, F Marty and E Salemme, *Le droit antitrust de l'Union européenne. Tome I: Les dispositions générales* (Mehdi Mezaguer ed, Bruxelles, Éditions de l'Université de Bruxelles, 2022) 74; Gilliams (n 221) 438–439; J Steenbergen, 'Proportionality in Competition Law and Policy' (2008) 3 *Legal Issues of Economic Integration* 259, 260.

[223] As also further confirmed in secondary law by Art 31 of Council Regulation (EC) No 1/2003 and Art 16 of Council Regulation (EC) No 139/2004.

[224] Case C-389/10 P *KME Germany and Others v Commission* ECLI:EU:C:2011:816, para 133.

its own one. By so doing, the Court exercises positive balancing between conflicting interests.[225] Therefore, the General Court case-law on the proportionality of competition law sanctions may not provide guidance for defining the ECJ negative scrutiny on harmonised criminal penalties.

A negative standard of review is required when the ECJ assesses competition law sanctions on appeal against judgments of the General Court. In fact,

> it is not for the Court of Justice, when ruling on questions of law in the context of an appeal, to substitute, on grounds of fairness, its own assessment for that of the General Court exercising its unlimited jurisdiction to rule on the amount of fines.[226]

Therefore, should a proportionality plea against the fine arise as a ground for appeal, 'only inasmuch as the Court of Justice considers that the level of the penalty is not merely inappropriate, but also excessive to the point of being disproportionate, would it have to find that the General Court erred in law'.[227] However, this standard of review is not comparable to the one applicable to harmonising provisions on penalties. The intensity of the standard of review on competition law fines depends upon the breadth of the margin of discretion afforded to the General Court when exercising unlimited jurisdiction. Therefore, the ECJ standard on appeal reflects the peculiar relationship between the Court of Justice and the General Court. This aspect pertains to the internal division of tasks within the Union judiciary. Conversely, the severity of the ECJ review on retrospective proportionality of harmonised penalties reflects the margin of discretion recognised by Union Courts upon the legislature, which stems from different rationales.

Even assuming a commonality between the two margins of discretion and standards of review, the fact remains that, in the competition law domain, the ECJ exercises proportionality scrutiny *in concreto*. The Court reviews fines imposed for specific charges. Conversely, the ECJ review of harmonised penalties applies to abstract provisions. The same considerations hold true for other EU non-criminal sanctioning powers against individuals. That is the case of disciplinary measures under the EU Staff Regulations[228] and penalties adopted by the Commission upon

[225] Case C-3/06 P *Groupe Danone v Commission* ECLI:EU:C:2007:88, para 61; Joined Cases C-238/99 P, C-244/99 P, C-245/99 P, C-247/99 P, C-250/99 P to C-252/99 P and C-254/99 P *Limburgse Vinyl Maatschappij and Others v Commission* ECLI:EU:C:2002:582, para 692. In that regard, see C Prieto and D Bosco, *Droit européen de la concurrence* (Bruxelles, Bruylant, 2013) 1285–1286.

[226] Case C-89/11 P *E.ON Energie v Commission* ECLI:EU:C:2012:738, para 125; Case C-310/93 P *BPB Industries and British Gypsum v Commission* ECLI:EU:C:1995:101, para 34; Case C-248/98 P *KNP BT v Commission* ECLI:EU:C:2000:625, para 54. In literature, see L Calzolari, 'Sanctions in EU Competition Law: Ensuring Deterrence within the Decentralised Enforcement System of Articles 101 and 102 TFEU' in S Montaldo, F Costamagna and A Miglio (eds), *EU Law Enforcement. The Evolution of Sanctioning Powers* (Oxon-Torino, Routledge-Giappichelli, 2021) 249.

[227] Case C-89/11 P *E.ON Energie v Commission* ECLI:EU:C:2012:738, para 126. In literature, see Bernardeau and Christienne (n 220) 633.

[228] Regulation No 31 (EEC), 11 (EAEC), Laying Down the Staff Regulations of Officials and the Conditions of Employment of Other Servants of the European Economic Community and the European Atomic Energy Community [1963] OJ 45/1385. In literature, see J Pilorge-Vrancken, *Le droit de la fonction publique de l'Union européenne* (Bruxelles, Bruylant, 2017) 241.

recommendation by OLAF.[229] It thus appears that the ECJ case-law on neither competition law fines nor other EU sanctioning powers can provide meaningful guidance for defining the standard of review on retrospective proportionality of EU substantive criminal law.

Clearly enough, this consideration does not prevent the Court from finding the supranational criminalisation of a given conduct or the corresponding harmonised penalty disproportionate to the absolute seriousness of the wrongdoing.[230] However, a *de iure condendo* analysis falls short of elucidating the boundaries of the EU legislature's discretion posed by cardinal proportionality and, consequently, the pertinent standard of review. The latter would probably be highly dependent upon the circumstances of each case, thus allowing to tackle manifestly disproportionate provisions.

Slightly different considerations apply to ordinal proportionality, a retrospective technique based upon the comparison of conducts characterised by different levels of harmfulness.[231] Ranging offences on a seriousness-based scale does not constitute an intuitive operation, as various aspects shall be considered.[232] However, the ECJ may review the legislative application of ordinal proportionality. As shown in this chapter, the EU legislature has sometimes employed this criterion to establish a comparison between different harmonised offences and penalties.[233] The fact that a given conduct has been criminalised at the EU level justifies criminalising a behaviour characterised by a higher degree of seriousness. On the same line of reasoning, the harmonised type and level of penalties for a given wrongdoing justifies providing equally harsh punishments for equally serious offences. As underlined in literature, these comparisons shall be exclusively grounded in EU criminal law instruments. Taking into account the level of severity of penalties provided at the national level would be impracticable since 'there is simply no existing common starting or anchoring point for punishment'.[234]

However, should the ECJ review the reasonableness of these retrospective analyses, the applicable standard for this review is once again quite elusive. Indeed, fixing the limits of legislative discretion for determining that two wrongdoings are equally serious appears counterintuitive. It seems logical to expect the ECJ to

[229] In that regard, see L Kuhl, 'Des moyens à approfondir: les missions de l'OLAF' in D Berlin, F Martucci and F Picod (eds), *La fraude et le droit de l'Union européenne* (Bruxelles, Bruylant, 2017) 94. For a broader perspective on the role of EU agencies and bodies in the exercise of sanctioning powers by the Commission, see J Alberti, 'New Actors on the Stage: The Emerging Role of EU Agencies in Exercising Sanctioning Powers' in S Montaldo, F Costamagna and A Miglio (eds), *EU Law Enforcement. The Evolution of Sanctioning Powers* (Torino-Oxon, Giappichelli-Routledge, 2021) 25 *et seq.*

[230] In the same line of reasoning, see Asp (n 114) 200–201.

[231] See Section IV(B)(i) of Chapter 2 and literature cited therein.

[232] Viganò (n 102) 64–65.

[233] See Section III(B)(ii) above in this chapter.

[234] Asp (n 114) 201.

leave a certain margin of discretion to the EU legislature when exercising ordinal proportionality. At the same time, manifestly illogical reasoning based on ordinal proportionality may be subject to judicial review, thereby leading the Court to conclude that a given criminalisation choice is disproportionate.

C. The ECJ (Potential) Scrutiny Over Prospective Proportionality: Two Alternative Options

Against the elusiveness of retrospective review, the ECJ scrutiny over the prospective scheme is more promising. Indeed, the latter is based upon a finalistic assessment, which is mainstreamed in the ECJ case-law. Under this scheme, the scope of harmonised offences and the type and level of harmonised penalties are seen in relation to attaining a penological aim, namely, a sufficient dissuasive effect. Conversely, the EU legislature has never parameterised harmonised offences and penalties to special prevention – namely, offenders' rehabilitation – purposes so far.[235]

Against this background, the standard for judicial review shall be investigated. In the current absence of case-law on EU substantive criminal law provisions, and considering the elusive reasoning proposed on this point by Advocate General Richard de la Tour in *Kinsa*,[236] it seems appropriate to take a broader view by considering the depth of judicial scrutiny on EU acts at large. As shown in Chapter 1,[237] two main approaches have emerged in the Court's proportionality review of secondary law acts. The ECJ has traditionally applied quite a looser standard of review by recognising that 'the EU legislature has a broad discretion, [...] whereas review by the EU judicature has to be limited to verifying [...] whether the legislature has manifestly exceeded the limits of its discretion'.[238] At the same time, the recent stream of case-law on the compatibility of EU measures with fundamental rights has paved the way to a more severe approach. Should the contested provision entail 'a particularly serious interference with those rights',[239] the ECJ has exercised a strict necessity review.[240]

If the ECJ is confronted with a proportionality contestation against EU harmonised offences and penalties, it may choose between these two diverging approaches. The following sections outline alternative arguments supporting either a looser (i) or stricter (ii) standard of review and then discuss them (iii).

[235] See Section III(B)(i) and (ii) above in this chapter.

[236] See Section IV(B) above in this chapter.

[237] See Section IV(A)(ii) of Chapter 1.

[238] Case C-5/16 *Poland v Parliament and Council* ECLI:EU:C:2018:483, para 150.

[239] Joined Cases C-293/12 and C-594/12 *Digital Rights Ireland and Seitlinger and Others* ECLI:EU:C:2014:238, para 39.

[240] In the same stream of case-law, see also Joined Cases C-37/20 and C-601/20 *Luxembourg Business Registers* ECLI:EU:C:2022:912, para 64.

i. The Argument for a 'Manifestly Disproportionate' Standard of Review

Self-restraint by the ECJ in the review of EU acts stems from the 'broad legislative power'[241] conferred on the Union legislature, 'which involves political, economic and social choices on its part, and in which it is called on to undertake complex assessments'.[242] In similar circumstances,

> the criterion to be applied is not whether a measure adopted in such an area was the only or the best possible measure, since its legality can be affected only if the measure is *manifestly inappropriate* having regard to the objective which the competent institutions are seeking to pursue (emphasis added).[243]

The Court has recognised that various secondary law acts of different domains of EU law entail policy choices warranting self-restraint in the proportionality review.[244] Against this approach, it seems plausible that adopting harmonising provisions on offences and penalties may imply the exercise of broad discretion by the EU legislature. Criminalisation entails profound political choices, as recognised not only by well-established scholarship[245] but also by the Commission itself, which deemed it necessary to lay down extensive policy indications.[246]

In the same line of reasoning, an additional argument for recognising broad discretion upon the EU legislature has been recently advanced in literature. Indeed, Monar has suggested that

> [a]s the EU Member States, in full awareness of security as a fundamental public good, have explicitly reserved in the EU Treaties their national competences as primary providers of this fundamental good to their citizens, they should arguably be granted, when struggling in the EU Justice and Home Affairs Council to arrive at common

[241] Case C-176/09, *Luxembourg v Parliament and Council* ECLI:EU:C:2011:290, para 62.

[242] Case C-210/03 *Swedish Match* ECLI:EU:C:2004:802, para 48. On the same point, see: Case C-84/94 *United Kingdom v Council* ECLI:EU:C:1996:431, para 58; Case C-233/94 *Germany v Parliament and Council* ECLI:EU:C:1997:231, paras 55-56; Case C-157/96 *The Queen v Ministry of Agriculture, Fisheries and Food and Commissioners of Customs & Excise, ex parte National Farmers' Union and Others* ECLI:EU:C:1998:191, para 61; Case C-491/01 *British American Tobacco (Investments) and Imperial Tobacco* ECLI:EU:C:2002:741, para 123.

[243] Case C-151/17 *Swedish Match* ECLI:EU:C:2018:938, para 36; Case C-477/14 *Pillbox 38* ECLI:EU:C:2016:324, para 49.

[244] In that regard, see JW Ouwerkerk, 'Criminalisation Powers of the European Union and the Risks of Cherry-Picking between Various Legal Bases: The Case for a Single Legal Framework for EU-Level Criminalization' (2017) 23 *Columbia Journal of European Law* 503, 533–534.

[245] Regarding securitised criminalisation under Art 83(1) TFEU, among many, see: Klip (n 188) 181; I Wieczorek, 'The Emerging Role of the EU as a Primary Normative Actor in the EU Area of Criminal Justice' (2021) 27 *European Law Journal* 378, 389. On criminalisation as a tool functional to the effectiveness of EU policies under Art 83(2) TFEU, see Asp (n 114) 128.

[246] Communication from the Commission to the European Parliament, the Council, the European Economic and Social Committee and the Committee of the Regions – Towards an EU Criminal Policy: Ensuring the Effective Implementation of EU Policies Through Criminal Law cit. For a discussion on the actual existence of fully-fledged EU criminal policy, see Weyembergh and Wieczorek (n 69).

> approaches and measures to enhance security for EU citizens, a margin of discretion in the definition of what can be regarded as an EU internal security issue and what action, in the criminal justice domain or other, this may require.[247]

According to this position, a wide margin of discretion for the EU legislature – and, particularly, the Council – may indirectly stem from the Member States' retained competencies in the field of internal security recalled in Articles 4(2) TEU and 72 TFEU.[248]

Before discussing these contentions, the opposite argument for a strict necessity review shall be investigated.

ii. The Argument for a Strict Necessity Review

The recognition of broad discretion upon the EU institutions characterises the ECJ proportionality review based on Articles 5(4) TEU and 52(1) of the Charter. However, should EU acts interfere with enjoying the rights to respect for private life and data protection, the ECJ has recently taken a different stance.[249] After recognising that a given EU measure 'constitutes a particularly serious interference with those rights',[250] the ECJ has concluded that the proportionality scrutiny shall ascertain whether the interference is limited to what is *strictly necessary* for attaining a legitimate aim. More specifically,

> derogations from and limitations on the protection of personal data should apply only in so far as is strictly necessary, it being understood that where there is a choice between several measures appropriate to meeting the legitimate objectives pursued, recourse must be had to the least onerous.[251]

It thus seems that resorting to strict proportionality scrutiny in EU substantive criminal law depends upon the depth of interferences with fundamental rights caused by harmonised offences and penalties. May EU harmonising provisions on offences and penalties entail 'serious interferences' with the enjoyment of Charter rights, thus triggering strict necessity scrutiny? Defining that threshold is not intuitive, as the 'serious interferences' paradigm describes a clash characterised by a particular level of intensity. At the same time, this clash does not

[247] Monar (n 25) 360.

[248] On the meaning and role of the 'internal security' concept within the AFSJ, among many, see: A Hinarejos, 'Law and Order and Internal Security Provisions in the Area of Freedom, Security and Justice: Before and After Lisbon' in C Eckes and T Konstadinides (eds), *Crime Within the Area of Freedom, Security and Justice: A European Public Order* (Cambridge, Cambridge University Press, 2011) 263–269; A Adinolfi, 'La libertà di circolazione delle persone e la politica dell'immigrazione' in G Strozzi and R Mastroianni (eds), *Diritto dell'Unione europea. Parte speciale* (Torino, Giappichelli, 2021) 146–147; A Lang, 'Art. 72 TFUE' in A Tizzano (ed), *Trattati dell'Unione europea* (Milano, Giuffrè, 2014) 819.

[249] See Section IV(A)(ii) of Chapter 1.

[250] Joined Cases C-293/12 and C-594/12 *Digital Rights Ireland and Seitlinger and Others* ECLI:EU:C:2014:238, para 39.

[251] Case C-37/20 *Luxembourg Business Registers* ECLI:EU:C:2022:912, para 64.

qualify as a 'core interference',[252] amounting to a violation of the very essence of the right.[253]

Against this interrogative, the ECJ ruling in *Digital Rights Ireland* provides a useful benchmark for framing the Court's potential approach to reviewing harmonised offences and penalties. Indeed, the ECJ affirmed that the collection and storage of personal data, as well as the possibility for public authorities to access them for law enforcement purposes, constitutes a serious interference with Charter rights. Arguably, all EU measures entailing more serious interferences with individual rights than data retention techniques shall warrant strict necessity scrutiny by the ECJ. That should be the case of EU criminalisation. It is common ground that criminal punishment amounts to the most severe form of interference with individual rights.[254] Therefore, if EU acts in the field of data retention require strict necessity scrutiny, this standard of review would be even more justified for harmonising provisions on offences and penalties. Following this argument, the margin of appreciation left to the EU legislature under the prospective proportionality of offences and penalties would be remarkably reduced. The ECJ should verify whether less restrictive measures than criminalisation would be available to the EU legislature to ensure a sufficient deterrent effect. More specifically, as far as the proportionality of offences is concerned, the ECJ shall assess whether non-criminal sanctioning systems – such as administrative sanctions[255] – or limiting the scope of criminalisation to a narrower range of conducts would still ensure a sufficient level of deterrence. In the same line of reasoning, the ECJ would assess whether financial criminal penalties or other alternative measures to detention, as well as more lenient penalty scales, would adequately attain the required level of deterrence.

iii. Discussion: Why a Strict Necessity Review would be Advisable

The two arguments just presented are grounded on sound theoretical foundations. When confronted with proportionality contestations against EU harmonised offences and penalties, the ECJ would probably have good reasons for conducting either a 'manifestly inappropriate' or 'strict necessity' review.

Against this background, it is contended that this choice should depend on the different characteristics of the proportionality plea at issue. The latter may be

[252] M Husovec, 'The Essence of Intellectual Property Rights under Article 17(2) of the EU Charter' (2019) 20 *German Law Journal* 840, 848.

[253] For further analysis of the concept of 'essence of the right' in the light of the ECJ case-law, see Section IV(A)(iii) of Chapter 1.

[254] This point is particularly evident from the scholarly works on the *ultima ratio* principle of criminal law: among many, see N Jareborg, 'Criminalization as Last Resort (Ultima Ratio)' (2005) 2 *Ohio State Journal of Criminal Law* 521, 527; S Melander, 'Ultima Ratio in European Criminal Law' (2013) 3 *European Criminal Law Review* 45, 52.

[255] In that case, a different legal basis should have been employed by the EU legislature, as Art 83 TFEU only allows the harmonisation of criminal offences and penalties.

grounded either on Article 5(4) TEU, thus contending an excessive exercise of the EU criminalisation powers, or on Article 52(1) TFEU, which implies a review of the legitimacy of interferences with Charter rights. The option between the two dimensions is upon the applicant for an action for annulment or the national court referring a preliminary question. However, this choice implies profound consequences for the intensity of the ECJ scrutiny.

Should the proportionality plea be based exclusively on Article 5(4) TEU, Union courts should probably recognise certain discretion upon the EU legislator. The ECJ case-law on proportionality in exercising EU powers has constantly confined the scrutiny to 'manifestly inappropriate' legislative arrangements. Moreover, the arguments previously advanced disclose that there are sound theoretical grounds for applying the same standard of review to harmonised offences and penalties.

Conversely, the fundamental rights dimension of the proportionality of criminal offences and penalties may result in a stricter review. In cases like *Kinsa*, where the legitimacy of EU criminalisation is questioned for its interference with fundamental rights, the Luxembourg Court is confronted with a choice between the 'manifestly inappropriate' and 'strict necessity' standards of review. Against that dichotomy, it is contended here that the ECJ should opt for a strict necessity review. This option would uphold criminal law as a tool implying profound interferences with individual rights, which are at least comparable to those generated from data retention techniques previously scrutinised by the Luxembourg Court. Moreover, a strict necessity assessment would give significance to the 'defensive' function of fundamental rights against criminal law. In fact, according to well-established literature, individual rights constitute an essential burden on criminalisation.[256] Recognising broad discretion upon the EU legislature would fall short of enhancing a meaningful limit to EU criminalisation under the Charter. Should the ECJ be willing to take the defensive role of Charter rights seriously, a strict necessity review under the prospective scheme is required.

The argument proposed by Monar, according to whom Member States' competencies on internal security imply broad discretion for the Council, may not lead to a different conclusion. Member States are indeed primarily responsible for 'maintaining law and order and safeguarding national security' under Article 4(2) TEU, but upholding internal security is also one of the Union's objectives. This is apparent from Article 67(3) TFEU, according to which 'the Union shall endeavour to ensure a high level of security through measures to prevent and combat crime, racism and xenophobia'.[257] In response to this task, the Commission has developed

[256] Among many, see F Tulkens, 'The Paradoxical Relationship between Criminal Law and Human Rights' (2011) 9 *Journal of International Criminal Justice* 577.

[257] On the concept and implications of enhancing internal security under EU law, among many, see V Mitsilegas, J Monar and W Rees, *The European Union and Internal Security: Guardian of the People?* (Basingstoke, Palgrave Macmillan, 2003); J Monar, 'EU Internal Security Governance: The Case of Counter-Terrorism' (2014) 23 *European Security* 195. On the concept of 'internal security' in the context of Art 72 TFEU specifically, see n 248 above.

quite an extensive policy on internal security,[258] which includes adopting legislation in the substantive criminal law field.

Notwithstanding Member States' discretion in this field, that finding could hardly justify the application of a loose standard of review under Article 52(1) of the Charter. Indeed, the 'wide discretion' paradigm strengthens the EU political institution's prerogatives, not the Member States' ones. Therefore, recognising that Member States' competence on internal security entails broad discretion upon the EU legislature would give rise to a paradox. Should a Member State plea for the annulment of a directive harmonising offences and penalties, enhancing broad discretion would confine the ECJ scrutiny to 'manifestly inappropriate' legislative arrangements. Therefore, rather than easing Member States' proportionality contestations against EU substantive criminal law acts, a reference to domestic prerogatives on internal security would pose a considerable obstacle to these pleas. Given this paradox, the observations put forward by Monar could not lead to the conclusion that the EU legislature shall be endowed with broad discretion in assessing the prospective proportionality of harmonised criminal offences and penalties.

Therefore, the ECJ standard of review on the prospective proportionality scheme depends on whether the assessment is based on Article 5(4) TEU exclusively or involves Article 52(1) of the Charter. This choice is ultimately upon each applicant before the ECJ and for domestic courts referring preliminary questions on the validity of EU substantive criminal law provisions. However, a proportionality scrutiny vis-à-vis Charter rights, like the one sought by the referring court in *Kinsa*, may offer a greater opportunity for the ECJ to conduct a meaningful review. In a similar case, there are reasonable grounds for considering that the ECJ scrutiny of prospective proportionality should consist of a strict necessity assessment.

VII. Concluding Remarks

The analysis of the Union's legislative practice disclosed that the proportionality of criminal offences and penalties plays a crucial role in EU substantive criminal law. In this domain, the principle shapes harmonising provisions on the definition

[258] Most notably, see: Communication from the Commission to the Council and the European Parliament on Measures to be Taken to Combat Terrorism and Other Forms of Serious Crime, in Particular to Improve Exchanges of Information, COM(2004) 221 final; Communication from the Commission to the European Parliament, the Council, the European Economic and Social Committee and the Committee of Regions – The European Agenda on Security, COM(2015) 185 final; Communication from the Commission to the European Parliament, the European Council and the Council Delivering on the European Agenda on Security to Fight against Terrorism and Pave the Way Towards an Effective and Genuine Security Union, COM(2016) 230 final; Commission Staff Working Document – Implementation of Home Affairs Legislation in the Field of Internal Security – 2017–2020, SWD(2020) 135 final (Part 1/2); Communication from the Commission to the European Parliament, the European Council, the Council, the European Economic and Social Committee and the Committee of the Regions on the EU Security Union Strategy, COM(2020) 605 final.

of criminal offences and sanctions under Article 83 TFEU. Three declinations of the principle are relevant: proportionality as a limit to the exercise of EU legislative powers (Article 5(4) TEU), as a condition for the legitimacy of limitations to fundamental rights (Article 52(1) of the Charter) and, concerning harmonised penalties, retrospective proportionality under Article 49(3) of the Charter. As shown in this chapter, the fundamental rights dimension of proportionality prevails over the other two. According to most recent EU legislative practice, the Commission, the Parliament and the Council appear aware that harmonised criminal offences and penalties may burden the enjoyment of fundamental rights secured by the Charter. Therefore, the sacrifice for those rights shall be limited to what is necessary to attain the aim pursued. In line with the hybrid nature of the principle, the EU legislature relies on both prospective – although considering only deterrence under general prevention and not social rehabilitation purposes – and retrospective secondary assessments to justify that the proposed legislation meets this requirement. Conversely, proportionality under Article 5(4) TEU has limited influence on the EU legislative action in the substantive criminal law field.

Against the near absence of relevant case-law, the chapter also discussed the ECJ standard for proportionality scrutiny of harmonised offences and penalties. Given the critical role played by the secondary schemes of the hybrid principle, the standard for the review of both retrospective and prospective legislative assessments has been analysed. On the one hand, judicial scrutiny of retrospective proportionality remains particularly elusive. While the EU legislature enjoys discretion in employing ordinal and cardinal retrospective evaluations, the limits of that power of appreciation may hardly be established *a priori*. On the other hand, different conclusions have been drawn concerning prospective proportionality. Should Article 52(1) of the Charter be invoked as a ground for review, like in the *Kinsa* case, the Court should emphasise the profound interference that criminalisation entails for fundamental rights. On that basis, the ECJ should carry out a strict necessity review of harmonising provisions on offences and penalties.

4

Proportionality of Member States' Criminal Offences and Penalties in the ECJ Case-law

I. Introduction

Domestic substantive criminal law intersects with the EU legal order in two ways. On the one hand, domestic criminalisation may be warranted to punish wrongdoings that impair the effectiveness of EU law. On the other hand, national criminal measures may clash with the enjoyment of fundamental rights and internal market freedoms secured by the EU legal order (II).

Proportionality of criminal offences and penalties plays a crucial role in both circumstances, as it defines the boundaries of States' discretion in the exercise of *ius puniendi* vis-à-vis EU law. These limits are framed and refined by the case-law of the Luxembourg Court, which regularly reviews the compatibility of domestic offences and penalties with EU law. This balancing operation has distinct features explored and systematised throughout this chapter. The analysis firstly zooms in on the application of proportionality of offences and penalties in cases where EU law warrants domestic criminalisation (III). Secondly, the chapter focuses on the principle's role in the clash between domestic substantive criminal law and rights and freedoms secured by the EU legal order (IV). Following the approach framed in Chapter 2,[1] both sections compare the ECJ and ECtHR practice concerning the application of the hybrid principle. Indeed, a brief look at the Strasbourg Court's practice helps explain the reasons underpinning the ECJ case-law's peculiarities. Thirdly, the chapter considers the procedural dimension of the principle by analysing the uneasy role of proportionality of criminal penalties in EU judicial cooperation (V). The final section joins the dots of the analysis by advancing a systematisation of the multifaceted ECJ approach to the proportionality review of domestic offences and penalties, thereby confirming the principle's hybrid nature (VI).

[1] See Section V of Chapter 2.

II. The Twofold Domestic Interface of the EU Principle of Proportionality of Criminal Offences and Penalties

The principle's twofold domestic interface reflects the two distinct and opposite forms of influence the EU legal order exercises over national criminal systems. Indeed, EU law may either drive (A) or limit (B) the exercise of the domestic *ius puniendi*.

A. When EU Law Requires Domestic *Ius Puniendi*: Proportionality of Criminal Offences and Penalties under the *Greek Maize* Paradigm

The effective application of EU law at the domestic level may warrant recourse to criminalisation. That is the rationale, for instance, of harmonising Member States' substantive criminal law. Indeed, ensuring the effectiveness of EU law constitutes one of the goals underlying the approximation of offences and penalties under Article 83 TFEU.[2] Still, obligations to criminalise in EU law do not stem exclusively from harmonisation. Two additional forms of positive integration drive the exercise of domestic *ius puniendi*. These are the principle of assimilation and the *Greek Maize* paradigm.

The origins of the principle of assimilation trace back to the protection of the Community's financial interests before the adoption of the Treaty of Maastricht.[3] Without a legal basis for approximating substantive criminal law, the Commission relied on assimilation to seek the extension of the scope of domestic criminal provisions on frauds to the national budget to frauds against the EC financial interests.[4] In this light, Member States would have been compelled to consider the protection of the EC's financial interests equally worth criminalisation compared to safeguarding the domestic budget. Following this move by the Commission, the principle of assimilation was affirmed in broad terms by the ECJ in the *Greek Maize* case.[5] Building upon the principle of loyal cooperation enshrined in Article 5 EEC – now Article 4(3) TEU, which 'requires the Member States to take all measures

[2] See Section II of Chapter 3.

[3] D Flore, *Droit pénal européen: les enjeux d'une justice pénale européenne*, 3rd edn (Bruxelles, Larcier, 2009) 249. For a deeper account of the evolution in the protection of EU financial interests from Maastricht to Lisbon, among many, see A Damato, *La tutela degli interessi finanziari tra competenze dell'Unione e obblighi degli Stati membri* (Bari, Cacucci, 2018) 3–13.

[4] See Arts 14 and 15 of the Proposal for a Treaty Amending the Treaties Establishing the European Communities so as to Permit the Adoption of Common Rules on the Protection Under Criminal Law of the Financial Interests of the Communities and the Prosecution of Infringements of the Provisions of those Treaties [1976] OJ C222/2.

[5] Case 68/88 *Commission v Greece (Greek Maize)* ECLI:EU:C:1989:339.

necessary to guarantee the application and effectiveness of Community law'[6] – the Court recognised a duty upon the Member States to penalise violations of EC law analogously to violations of similar domestic provisions.[7] It follows that the principle of assimilation applies to any domain covered by EU law.[8] Moreover, it compels the Member States to criminalise violations of EC law even when secondary law already provides for administrative sanctions.[9] However, the principle of assimilation implies the mere equation of two distinct interests rather than the accommodation of conflicting ones;[10] therefore, it does not unveil a proportionality reasoning.

The *Greek Maize* ruling also established the duty upon Member States to sanction violations of EC law with 'effective, proportionate and dissuasive'[11] penalties. This obligation – best known as the *Greek Maize* paradigm – requires greater attention here. Since *Greek Maize*, the duty to sanction violations of Community law by 'effective, proportionate and dissuasive' penalties[12] has been mainstreamed. Indeed, this obligation has become a refrain in EU secondary law and an essential driver for Member States' sanctioning systems.[13]

The relevance of the *Greek Maize* paradigm is not limited to criminal law. In line with the Court's previous findings in *Amsterdam Bulb*,[14] Member States may choose between administrative and criminal sanctions provided that they are effective, proportionate, and dissuasive.[15] This choice – as well as the type and

[6] *ibid*, para 23.

[7] *ibid*, para 24.

[8] In literature, see V Mitsilegas, *EU Criminal Law after Lisbon. Rights, Trust and the Transformation of Justice in Europe* (Oxford, Hart Publishing, 2016) 75. F Giuffrida, 'Effectiveness, Dissuasiveness, Proportionality of Sanctions and Assimilation Principle: The Long-Lasting Legacy of the Greek Maize Case' in V Mitsilegas, A Di Martino and L Mancano (eds), *The Court of Justice and European Criminal Law. Leading Cases in a Contextual Analysis* (Oxford, Hart Publishing, 2019) 108.

[9] Case C-186/98 *Nunes and de Matos* ECLI:EU:C:1999:376, para 14.

[10] As underlined by Mitsilegas, assimilation derives not only from the principle of effectiveness, but also of equivalence (Mitsilegas (n 8) 75).

[11] Case 68/88 *Commission v Greece (Greek Maize)* ECLI:EU:C:1989:339, para 24.

[12] *ibid.* For subsequent references in case-law, see Case C-58/95 *Gallotti* ECLI:EU:C:1996:323, para 14; Case C-341/94 *Allain* ECLI:EU:C:1996:356, para 24; Case C-7/90 *Vandevenne* ECLI:EU:C:1991:363, para 11; Case C-326/88 *Hansen* ECLI:EU:C:1990:291, para 17; Case C-36/94 *Siesse v Director da Alfândega de Alcântara* ECLI:EU:C:1995:351, para 20; Case C-382/92 *Commission v United Kingdom* ECLI:EU:C:1994:233, para 55.

[13] Among many, see S Montaldo, 'Handle with Care! The Direct Effect of the Requirement of Proportionality of Sanctions and the Remedy of Disapplication: NE v. Bezirkshauptmannschaft Hartberg-Fürstenfeld' (2023) 60 *CML Rev* 863, 863. At the same time, Nuotio underlines that the relevance of the *Greek Maize* paradigm as an autonomous driver of criminalisation is reduced by the EU legislature's reliance on harmonisation techniques (K Nuotio, 'A Legitimacy-Based Approach to EU Criminal Law: Maybe We Are Getting There, After All' (2020) 11 *New Journal of European Criminal Law* 20, 23). While this formula is also reproduced in Directives and Framework Decisions adopted on the basis of Art 83 TFEU, these pieces of secondary law lay down clear and precise rules on the definition of offences and penalties, which supplement the 'effective, proportionate and dissuasive' paradigm.

[14] Case 50/76 *Amsterdam Bulb* ECLI:EU:C:1977:13, para 32.

[15] Nuotio (n 13) 22; H-H Jescheck, 'Possibilità e limiti di un diritto penale per la protezione dell'Unione europea' in L Picotti (ed), *Possibilità e limiti di un diritto penale dell'Unione europea* (Milano, Giuffrè, 1999) 21.

amount of the penalty – is subject to the limits dictated by the proportionality requirement.

Under the *Greek Maize* paradigm, proportionality must be read in conjunction with effectiveness and dissuasiveness. The meaning of 'dissuasiveness' has already been investigated in Chapter 2,[16] as it is inherently linked to the consequentialist criminal law theory. Dissuasiveness consists of offences and penalties' capability to influence the behaviour of the public at large, thereby acting as a deterrent from the commission of criminal wrongdoing. The concept of effectiveness, conversely, is much broader, as it embraces the whole spectrum of EU law. Effectiveness generally consists of the capacity of a legal arrangement to attain its underlying purposes.[17]

While effectiveness and dissuasiveness foster Member States' criminalisation under the *Greek Maize* paradigm, proportionality limits it.[18] Therefore, EU law requires recourse to criminal measures insofar as they are effective and dissuasive, to the extent that they do not exceed the limit of what is proportionate. Similarly, the severity of criminal penalties shall ensure adequate and deterring punishment while not amounting to disproportionate sanctions.

The meaning of 'proportionate' under the *Greek Maize* paradigm raises once again a crucial question: to what offences and penalties shall be proportionate? The ECJ provides some guidance. It regularly affirms that 'the administrative or punitive measures permitted under national legislation must not go beyond what is necessary in order to attain the objectives legitimately pursued by that legislation'.[19] This definition elicits two considerations.

Firstly, the *Greek Maize* paradigm entails a finalistic proportionality assessment: the severity of offences and penalties shall be commensurate to accomplishing the aim pursued. The specific aims attained by offences and penalties vary depending on the secondary law instrument at issue. However, these objectives converge to one common goal: the effectiveness of EU law. Under the *Greek Maize* paradigm,

[16] See Section III(B)(ii) of Chapter 2.

[17] Among many, see: M Accetto and S Zleptnig, 'The Principle of Effectiveness: Rethinking Its Role in Community Law' (2009) 11 *European Public Law* 375, 378–379; P Bilancia, 'L'effettività nello Spazio di libertà, sicurezza e giustizia tra realtà intergovernativa e prospettiva comunitaria' in A Catania (ed), *Dimensioni dell'effettività: Tra teoria generale e politica del diritto* (Milano, Giuffrè, 2005) 5. In this regard, Vitale contends that the ECJ case-law enshrines effectiveness itself as a general principle of EU law, entailing both the effective attainment of given objectives underlying the EU legal order and the effectiveness of judicial protection (G Vitale, *Principi generali e diritto derivato. Contributo allo studio del sistema delle fonti dell'Unione europea* (Torino, Giappichelli, 2013) 113).

[18] M Dougan, 'From the Velvet Glove to the Iron Fist: Criminal Sanctions for the Enforcement of Union Law' in M Cremona (ed), *Compliance and the Enforcement of EU Law* (Oxford, Oxford University Press, 2012) 82.

[19] Among many, see: Case C-77/20 *K. M. (Sanctions infligées au capitaine de navire)* ECLI:EU:C:2021:112, para 37. Similarly, see: Case C-190/17 *Zheng* ECLI:EU:C:2018:357, para 41; Case C-255/14 *Chmielewski* ECLI:EU:C:2015:475, para 22; Case C-430/05 *Ntionik and Pikoulas* ECLI:EU:C:2007:410, para 54; Case C-210/10 *Urbán* ECLI:EU:C:2012:64, paras 24 and 53; Case C-210/91 *Commission v Greece* ECLI:EU:C:1992:525, para 20.

offences and penalties are meant to secure the effective implementation of EU legislation at the domestic level.[20]

Secondly, the definition framed by the ECJ focuses only on necessity, which is just one requirement for the threefold proportionality test. This is unsurprising: as Chapter 1 already disclosed, the ECJ approach towards proportionality *stricto sensu* is ambivalent since that step does not always play a central role in the Court's scrutiny.[21] For what concerns the suitability test, the *Greek Maize* formula implicitly requires domestic offences and penalties to be functional to attaining the effective enforcement of EU law. There would be no need to assess whether a criminal law measure is necessary to pursue that goal if it were not suitable to that aim.

This test only amounts to the primary proportionality scheme postulated by the *Greek Maize* paradigm. Further to that assessment, the ECJ consistently affirms that 'the severity of the sanctions must be commensurate with the seriousness of the breaches for which they are imposed, in particular by ensuring a genuinely dissuasive effect, while respecting the general principle of proportionality'.[22] This definition of the proportionate requirement follows the hybrid theoretical model theorised in Chapter 2. Indeed, prospective and retrospective assessments complement the proportionality evaluation required by the *Greek Maize* paradigm.

Once again, a distinction shall be drawn between the primary and secondary schemes of the principle of proportionality of criminal offences and penalties. The first implies that the scope of offences and the type and level of penalties shall be adequate, necessary and proportionate *stricto sensu* to secure the effective implementation of EU law at the domestic level. That assessment shall consider the prospective and retrospective secondary schemes, thereby evaluating whether offences and penalties attain a genuinely dissuasive effect while being commensurate to the seriousness of the wrongdoing.

Section III below better frames the place and role of secondary schemes under the *Greek Maize* paradigm. For the moment, it suffices to underline that the two other principles recalled therein – effectiveness and dissuasiveness – play different roles in the proportionality assessment. Effectiveness defines the general goal to which offences and penalties shall be commensurate under the suitability and necessity test. Dissuasiveness, conversely, constitutes the non-retributive goal of reference under the prospective proportionality scheme.

[20] S Montaldo, 'EU Sanctioning Power and the Principle of Proportionality' in S Montaldo, F Costamagna and A Miglio (eds), *EU Law Enforcement. The Evolution of Sanctioning Powers* (Torino-Oxon, Giappichelli-Routledge, 2021) 121–122.

[21] See Section IV(A)(iii) of Chapter 1.

[22] In case-law, among many, see Case C-77/20 *K. M. (Sanctions infligées au capitaine de navire)* ECLI:EU:C:2021:112, para 38. For further references in case-law, see: Case C-255/14 *Chmielewski* ECLI:EU:C:2015:475, para 23; Case C-81/12 *Asociaţia Accept* ECLI:EU:C:2013:275, para 63; Case C-565/12 *LCL Le Crédit Lyonnais* ECLI:EU:C:2014:190, para 45.

B. Proportionality of Domestic Offences and Penalties Interfering with Individual Rights Secured by EU Law

As disclosed in Chapter 2,[23] the proportionality of offences and penalties hinges upon various normative foundations in EU primary law. These multiple dimensions are crucial when domestic criminalisation clashes with EU fundamental rights and internal market freedoms. Either Treaty provisions on limitations to internal market freedoms, Article 52(1) or Article 49(3) of the Charter may apply. They may also apply simultaneously, as domestic offences and penalties can burden the enjoyment of both fundamental rights and internal market freedoms at one time.

Notwithstanding such a plurality of dimensions, the ECJ has followed a holistic approach. As far as the proportionality of offences is concerned, the Court has consistently assessed limitations to internal market freedoms and fundamental rights in a comparable manner.[24] In harmony with its case-law on the proportionality review of domestic acts,[25] the ECJ scrutiny is mainly grounded on a necessity assessment: the scope of the offence shall not go beyond what is necessary to attain the legitimate aim pursued.[26]

The Court has been even more explicit about the proportionality of criminal penalties. In a couple of recent rulings, the Luxembourg Court affirmed that this requirement 'follow[s] both from Article 52(1) of the Charter and from the principle of proportionality of penalties in Article 49(3) of the Charter'.[27] What is more, some judgments also suggest that the proportionality requirements flowing from Article 49(3) of the Charter and Treaty provisions on limitations to internal market freedoms overlap. To provide just one example, in *Landespolizeidirektion Steiermark and Others (Machines à sous)*[28] the Court has been confronted with a financial penalty related to illegal gaming activities entailing a burden on the provision of services under EU law. The referring Court sought to ascertain the proportionality of that sanction under Articles 49(3) of the Charter and 56 TFEU

[23] See Section II of Chapter 2.

[24] The two assessments may overlap in concrete cases. According to well-established case-law, the Charter applies to domestic limitations to the enjoyment of internal market freedoms (further on this point, see N Lazzerini, *La Carta dei diritti fondamentali dell'Unione europea. I limiti di applicazione* (Milano, Franco Angeli, 2018) 224–226). Therefore, the legitimacy of domestic criminal law interfering with internal market freedoms can be scrutinised under the Charter, as it falls under its scope of application pursuant to Art 51(1) therein (LS Rossi, 'I rapporti fra la Carta dei diritti fondamentali e la CEDU nella giurisprudenza delle rispettive Corti' in *Annali AISDUE* (Napoli, Editoriale Scientifica, 2020) 581, fn 16).

[25] See Section IV(A)(ii) of Chapter 1.

[26] In that regard, see: Case C-920/19 *Fluctus and Others* ECLI:EU:C:2021:395, para 29; Case C-482/18 *Google Ireland* ECLI:EU:C:2020:141, para 45; Case C-393/17 *Kirschstein* ECLI:EU:C:2019:563, para 80; Case C-49/16 *Unibet International* ECLI:EU:C:2017:491, para 37; Case C-46/08 *Carmen Media Group* ECLI:EU:C:2010:505, para 46.

[27] Case C-544/19 *ECOTEX Bulgaria* ECLI:EU:C:2021:803, para 97; Case C-537/16 *Garlsson Real Estate and Others* ECLI:EU:C:2018:193, para 56.

[28] Case C-231/20 *Landespolizeidirektion Steiermark e a. (Machines à sous)* ECLI:EU:C:2021:845.

on the free provision of services. The Court relied upon the latter provision alone, while Article 49(3) of the Charter was sporadically recalled throughout the proportionality assessment.[29] It thus appears that also Article 49(3) of the Charter and Treaty provisions on limitations to internal market freedoms entail interchangeable proportionality paradigms.

These considerations elicit a syllogism: if proportionality under Article 52(1) of the Charter is equivalent to the principle as enshrined in Article 49(3) therein, and the latter is equivalent to that postulated by Treaty provisions on limitations to internal market freedoms, it follows that the latter is also equal to Article 52(1) of the Charter. Therefore, the ECJ interprets the three dimensions of the principle as entailing a holistic proportionality assessment of domestic substantive criminal law.

Against this background, some clarifications are required concerning the proportionality of penalties specifically. Given the bond established by the Court between Article 49(3) of the Charter and the two other legal bases previously considered, one may assume that the principle shall be framed as an inherently retrospective assessment. However, a closer look at the relevant case-law unveils a different reality. Retrospective proportionality, as crystallised in Article 49(3) of the Charter, is part of a broader compound assessment. This aspect is well illustrated in *ECOTEX Bulgaria* where, in line with well-established case-law,[30] the Court framed the primary proportionality requirement as a finalistic assessment: 'the administrative or punitive measures permitted under national legislation must not go beyond what is necessary to attain the objectives legitimately pursued by that legislation'.[31] Therefore, prospective and retrospective proportionality operate in the framework of this broader criterion, in harmony with the hybrid double-layered model advanced in this book.[32] More specifically, 'the severity of the penalties imposed must also be commensurate with the seriousness of the infringements for which they are imposed, particularly by ensuring a genuinely deterrent effect, while not going beyond what is necessary to attain that objective'.[33] It follows that Article 49(3) does not constitute an autonomous normative foundation for the principle of proportionality of penalties. Conversely, it represents the legal basis for the principle's retrospective secondary scheme.

Building upon these considerations, the proportionality assessment shall now be framed. As previously underlined, the interference with fundamental rights and

[29] *ibid*, para 45.

[30] Among many, see Case C-255/14 *Chmielewski* ECLI:EU:C:2015:475, para 22; Case C-430/05 *Ntionik and Pikoulas* ECLI:EU:C:2007:410, para 54; Case C-210/10 *Urbán* ECLI:EU:C:2012:64, paras 24 and 53.

[31] Case C-544/19 *ECOTEX Bulgaria* ECLI:EU:C:2021:803, para 99.

[32] See Section III(A)(ii) of Chapter 2.

[33] Case C-231/20 *Landespolizeidirektion Steiermark e a. (Machines à sous)* ECLI:EU:C:2021:845, para 45. On the same point, see also: Case C-679/18 *OPR-Finance* ECLI:EU:C:2020:167, para 26; Case C-42/15 *Home Credit Slovakia* ECLI:EU:C:2016:842, para 63; Case C-565/12 *LCL Le Crédit Lyonnais* ECLI:EU:C:2014:190, para 45; Case C-418/11 *Texdata Software* ECLI:EU:C:2013:588, para 51.

internal market freedoms caused by offences and penalties shall be necessary to attain a legitimate aim. Differently from the *Greek Maize* paradigm, that objective is of a domestic nature. Criminal measures are not intended here to serve a supranational interest warranting a criminal law response from the Member States, such as the need to secure the effectiveness of EU law. Conversely, they materialise a domestic interest in criminalisation that the EU legal order considers worthy of protection or at least legitimate.

The scope of this category of objectives depends upon the distinct declination of the principle invoked. Three different cases may arise. Firstly, domestic criminal provisions may qualify as distinctly applicable measures burdening the enjoyment of EU internal market freedoms. In that circumstance, those criminal measures are legitimate only if suitable, necessary and proportionate *stricto sensu* to attain one of the objectives expressly listed by relevant Treaty provisions. Secondly, should offences and penalties amount to indistinctly applicable measures, they are justified insofar as suitable, necessary and proportionate *stricto sensu* to pursue an 'overriding reason in the general interest'.[34] Finally, whenever offences and penalties impair a fundamental right secured by the Charter, the aim they pursue shall be of general interest and recognised by the Treaties.[35]

III. The ECJ Proportionality Review of Domestic Offences and Penalties under the *Greek Maize* Paradigm

Having framed the twofold interaction between EU and domestic criminal law, it is now time to turn attention to the principle's application. This section delves into the proportionality of criminal offences and penalties under the *Greek Maize* paradigm. The analysis reveals a diverging approach from the Court between the review of offences (A) and penalties (B) implementing EU law. Still, in both circumstances the *Greek Maize* paradigm postulates upper and lower limits to domestic criminalisation. This aspect is profoundly different compared to the approach emerging from the ECtHR case-law on obligations to criminalise (C).

A. A Partial Proportionality Limit to Member States' Criminalisation Choices under the *Greek Maize* Paradigm

Whenever EU secondary law requires the establishment of 'effective, proportionate and dissuasive' penalties for violations of EU law provisions, this formula implies a pre-determination of the essential elements of the offence.[36] At the same

[34] See Section III(B) of Chapter 1.
[35] For an analysis of the meaning of these expressions, see Section III(C)(ii) of Chapter 1.
[36] Montaldo, 'EU Sanctioning Power and the Principle of Proportionality' (n 20) 123.

time, this paradigm does not compel Member States to automatically resort to criminal sanctions. As clarified in *Wijsenbeek*,[37] in the absence of harmonisation, 'Member States retain the power to choose the sanctions which seem to them to be appropriate, provided that they exercise that power in accordance with EU law and its general principles'.[38] In particular, the Member States may establish criminal penalties even when that possibility is not expressly recalled by EU secondary law. Since the *Greek Maize* paradigm 'does not specify the nature of the penalties that the Member States must adopt [...] Member States remain free to determine the nature of the penalties applicable and may, in consequence, lay down criminal penalties'.[39]

EU secondary law may pose constraints to the Member States' discretion by defining which sanctions shall be implemented at the national level.[40] Even in those cases, the *Greek Maize* paradigm does not nullify the possibility for Member States to opt for either administrative or criminal penalties. Indeed, EU secondary law usually qualifies criminalisation as a complementary or alternative measure to administrative sanctioning schemes.[41] In those cases, whether to criminalise a given conduct under the *Greek Maize* paradigm is subject to the limits dictated by the general principles of EU law, with particular emphasis on proportionality.[42]

Against the prevailing approach, the Court's case-law on the protection of the EU financial interests constitutes an exception. In this domain,

> [w]hile the Member States have [...] a freedom to choose the applicable penalties, which may take the form of administrative penalties, criminal penalties or a combination of the two, *they must nonetheless ensure that cases of serious fraud or any other serious illegal activity affecting the financial interests of the Union in customs matters are punishable by criminal penalties* (emphasis added).[43]

This obligation to criminalise is emphasised in even more explicit terms in the context of VAT frauds, an area where it proves 'essential to combat certain serious cases of VAT evasion in an effective and dissuasive manner'.[44] Similarly,

[37] Case C-378/97 *Wijsenbeek* ECLI:EU:C:1999:439, para 44.

[38] This finding has been recently confirmed in Case C-35/20 *A (Franchissement de frontières en navire de plaisance)* ECLI:EU:C:2021:813, para 57.

[39] Case C-137/17 *Van Gennip and Others* ECLI:EU:C:2018:771, para 96. On the same issue, see: Case C-367/09 *SGS Belgium and Others* ECLI:EU:C:2010:648, para 41; Case C-186/98 *Nunes and de Matos* ECLI:EU:C:1999:376, paras 12 and 14.

[40] For some examples in the EU legislative practice, see Montaldo, 'EU Sanctioning Power and the Principle of Proportionality' (n 20) 122–123.

[41] This is, for instance, the EU legislature's approach in the Common Fisheries Policy. In that regard, see Art 90(5) of Council Regulation (EC) No 1224/2009 of 20 November 2009 Establishing a Community Control System for Ensuring Compliance with the Rules of the Common Fisheries Policy [2009] OJ L343/1; Art 44(3) of Council Regulation (EC) No 1005/2008 of 29 September 2008 Establishing a Community System to Prevent, Deter and Eliminate Illegal, Unreported and Unregulated Fishing [2008] OJ L286/1.

[42] Case C-77/20 *K. M. (Sanctions infligées au capitaine de navire)* ECLI:EU:C:2021:112, para 36.

[43] Case C-612/15 *Kolev and Others* ECLI:EU:C:2018:392, para 54.

[44] Case C-105/14 *Taricco and Others* ECLI:EU:C:2015:555, para 39. For further references, see Case C-42/17 *M.A.S. and M.B.* ECLI:EU:C:2017:936, paras 34-35; Case C-524/15 *Menci* ECLI:EU:C:2018:197, para 20; Case C-574/15 *Scialdone* ECLI:EU:C:2018:295, paras 34–35.

establishing criminal penalties may be necessary to tackle serious frauds affecting the Union's financial interests under Art. 325 TFEU, with particular emphasis on frauds concerning VAT revenues.[45]

These findings reduce Member States' discretion but still warrant a proportionality evaluation to assess whether a given behaviour qualifies as 'serious'. *Scialdone* is illustrative in this regard. In that ruling, the Court affirmed that criminal penalties are not necessary to sanction failures to pay declared VAT.[46] To reach this conclusion, the ECJ relied on an ordinal proportionality reasoning, thus arguing that the offence under analysis is less harmful than serious VAT frauds.[47] While these latter deserve criminalisation, criminal offences punishing failures to pay declared VAT would be disproportionate.

It follows that criminalisation under the *Greek Maize* paradigm is a discretionary choice of Member States subject to the limits dictated by EU law and, in particular, by the proportionality of criminal offences. Under the principle's threefold test, the scope of criminalised conduct shall be adequate, necessary, and proportionate *stricto sensu* to secure the effective implementation of EU law at the domestic level.

A proportionality limit to domestic criminal offences may apply in two ways: by curtailing the scope of the criminalised conduct or by setting conditions for its criminalisation. Concerning the first aspect, in some cases the ECJ concluded that the offences' scope was excessive. For instance, in *Commission v Hungary (Incrimination de l'aide aux demandeurs d'asile)* the Court held that the definition of the 'Facilitating illegal immigration' offence 'goes beyond what may be regarded as necessary to attain the objective of preventing fraudulent or abusive practices'.[48] In fact, this offence made punishable any individual providing assistance to asylum seekers on the sole ground that the alleged offender was aware that the asylum application could not be accepted.[49] The Court concluded that this provision was liable to 'strongly discourage[e] any person wishing to provide any assistance whatsoever for the purposes of making or lodging an application for asylum'.[50] This reasoning discloses reliance on a prospective proportionality scheme: the offence's conduct amounts to an excessive deterrent, thus being disproportionate vis-à-vis the attainment of its ultimate goal.

[45] Among many, see Case C-105/14 *Taricco and Others* ECLI:EU:C:2015:555, para 39; Case C-42/17 *M.A.S. and M.B.* ECLI:EU:C:2017:936, para 34; Case C-574/15 *Scialdone* ECLI:EU:C:2018:295, para 35. In literature, see Damato (n 3) 43.

[46] Case C-574/15 *Scialdone* ECLI:EU:C:2018:295, para 43.

[47] *ibid*, para 41.

[48] Case C-821/19 *Commission v Hungary (Incrimination de l'aide aux demandeurs d'asile)* ECLI:EU:C:2021:930, para 133.

[49] For an analysis of the judgment, see L Pascual Matellán, 'La criminalización de la asistencia a los solicitantes de asilo en Hungría (a propósito de la sentencia Comisión/Hungría, C-821/19)' (2022) 71 *Revista de Derecho Comunitario Europeo* 169.

[50] Case C-821/19 *Commission v Hungary (Incrimination de l'aide aux demandeurs d'asile)* ECLI:EU:C:2021:930, para 132.

Concerning the second profile – the establishment of proportionality limitations to domestic criminalisation – judicial practice unveils a looser approach. In most cases, the ECJ proportionality review of offences under the *Greek Maize* paradigm falls short of setting a meaningful limit to the Member States' discretion in choosing between criminal and administrative penalties. Even where excessive sanctions may ultimately hinder the exercise of EU internal market freedoms, the Court has recognised that Member States are allowed to resort to criminal penalties. The judgment in *A (Franchissement de frontières en navire de plaisance)* testifies this approach.[51] In that case, the Court recognised that Member States may criminalise the violations of formal requirements established by Article 5(1) of Directive 2004/38/EC[52] for the exercise of the right to free movement, such as the obligation to hold a valid identity card or passport.[53]

It follows that the ECJ's application of the proportionality of criminal offences under the *Greek Maize* paradigm limits only partially domestic criminalisation choices. Except for limited cases – such as frauds affecting EU financial interests – the ECJ restrains itself from limiting Member States' discretion in criminalising. However, the Court's proportionality assessment sometimes focuses on the scope of the prohibition stemming from offences' definition.

B. The Directly Enforceable *Greek Maize* Proportionality Requirement of Penalties

Looking at the case-law on the *Greek Maize* paradigm, it appears that the proportionality requirement of penalties has received much more attention compared to the review of offences. Most recently, the Luxembourg Court has recognised in *Bezirkshauptmannschaft Hartberg-Fürstenfeld (Effet direct)* – a case commonly known as *NE* – that the proportionality of criminal penalties under the *Greek Maize* paradigm is endowed with direct effect.[54] Should domestic provisions entail the imposition of disproportionate sanctions, the competent

[51] In particular, see Case C-35/20 *A (Franchissement de frontières en navire de plaisance)* ECLI:EU:C:2021:813, para 79.

[52] Directive 2004/38/EC of the European Parliament and of the Council of 29 April 2004 on the Right of Citizens of the Union and Their Family Members to Move and Reside Freely Within the Territory of the Member States [2004] OJ L158/77.

[53] Similarly, see Case 8/77 *Sagulo and Others* ECLI:EU:C:1977:131, para 12.

[54] Case C-205/20 *Bezirkshauptmannschaft Hartberg-Fürstenfeld (Effet direct)* ECLI:EU:C:2022:168. For a thorough analysis of this judgment and its implications for the understanding of proportionality of penalties under the *Greek Maize* paradigm, see Montaldo, 'Handle with Care! The Direct Effect of the Requirement of Proportionality of Sanctions and the Remedy of Disapplication: NE v. Bezirkshauptmannschaft Hartberg-Fürstenfeld' (n 13); M Lanotte, 'La proporzionalità della sanzione: un principio ritrovato? Note a margine della sentenza NE' in *Quaderni AISDUE – Serie Speciale, Atti del Convegno 'Ambiente, digitale, economia: l'Unione europea verso il 2030' Bari 3-4 novembre 2022* (Napoli, Editoriale Scientifica, 2023).

court is required to set aside that provision and to redetermine the penalty to be imposed *in concreto*.[55] According to the Court, a total disapplication of the sanction would be at odds with the principle of effectiveness, which requires that conducts impairing the application of EU law shall be penalised. Therefore, the domestic court shall 'disregard that part of the national legislation from which the disproportionate nature of the penalties stems in such a way as to result in the imposition of proportionate penalties, which are at the same time effective and dissuasive'.[56]

The direct effect of proportionality of penalties entails the essential premise that the principle postulates a clear, precise and unconditional requirement. However, this stance is not self-evident. On the same issue, the ECJ itself came to the opposite conclusion just a few years before in *Link Logistik*.[57] Therefore, the key features of the *Greek Maize* proportionality of penalties require closer attention. Three aspects shall be considered: the role played by the prospective and retrospective schemes in the structure of the proportionality test (i), the standard of review (ii), and the limits posed by the principles of effectiveness and legality to disapplying criminal measures under the *Greek Maize* paradigm (iii).

i. The Prominence of Prospective Proportionality in the ECJ Review

To review the type and level of penalties under the *Greek Maize* paradigm, regard must be had to whether the sanction is 'commensurate with the seriousness of the breaches for which they are imposed, in particular by ensuring a genuinely dissuasive effect, while respecting the general principle of proportionality'.[58] This finding, which constitutes a refrain in all ECJ judgments on the *Greek Maize* paradigm,[59] encapsulates both prospective and retrospective proportionality. From a retrospective standpoint, the penalty shall be proportionate to the seriousness of the wrongdoing. From a prospective viewpoint, the penalty shall ensure a genuinely dissuasive effect while not overstepping the limits dictated by the principle of proportionality. More specifically, the type and amount of the penalty shall ensure a level of deterrence that does not exceed what is necessary to attain the objective pursued, namely, the effectiveness of EU law.

In principle, the two secondary schemes are complementary. However, they have a different influence on the Court's scrutiny. Indeed, prospective

[55] Case C-205/20 *Bezirkshauptmannschaft Hartberg-Fürstenfeld (Effet direct)* ECLI:EU:C:2022:168, para 44.

[56] *ibid*, para 42.

[57] Case C-384/17 *Link Logistik N&N* ECLI:EU:C:2018:810.

[58] Case C-77/20 *K. M. (Sanctions infligées au capitaine de navire)* ECLI:EU:C:2021:112, para 38.

[59] For some (although not exhaustive) references, see: Case C-452/20 *Agenzia delle dogane e dei monopoli and Ministero dell'Economia e delle Finanze* ECLI:EU:C:2022:111, para 39; Case C-565/12 *LCL Le Crédit Lyonnais* ECLI:EU:C:2014:190, para 45; Case C-493/21 *K.M. (Sanctions infligées au capitaine de navire – II)* ECLI:EU:C:2022:191, para 15; Case C-255/14 *Chmielewski* ECLI:EU:C:2015:475, para 23.

proportionality constitutes the crucial step for the Court to assess whether the penalty is proportionate to the aim pursued. In the context of the preliminary ruling procedure, it is ultimately for the domestic courts to determine whether a given penalty is excessively dissuasive vis-à-vis the objective pursued. However, according to the guidance provided by the ECJ case-law, deterrence is crucial in the context of penalties adopted under the *Greek Maize* paradigm. As criminal measures are adopted to secure the effectiveness of EU law, their capability to dissuade potential offenders from committing similar wrongdoings shall be taken into due regard within the proportionality assessment.[60]

Following this approach, defining the level of deterrence required for a given wrongdoing becomes crucial, and the ECJ usually demands a particularly cautious approach. Should domestic authorities opt for financial penalties, 'account should also be taken of the relationship between the amount of the fine that may be imposed and the economic benefit derived from the infringement committed'.[61] At the same time, the Court highlighted that financial penalties whose amount corresponds to the value of goods forming the object of the crime would be disproportionate from a prospective viewpoint.[62]

Against the Court's cautious approach, there is at least one case where the ECJ interpreted prospective proportionality as a strict necessity test. When reviewing the proportionality of the Austrian sanctioning scheme for violations of rules on the posting of workers, the Court affirmed in *Bezirkshauptmannschaft Hartberg-Fürstenfeld* that 'effective implementation [...] could be achieved through less restrictive measures, such as a lower fine or the introduction of an upper limit on such fines, and without necessarily imposing a custodial sentence as an alternative penalty'.[63]

The ECJ scrutiny of penalties also relies on retrospective proportionality but to a narrower extent. Indeed, the Luxembourg Court generally limits its review to verifying whether the domestic sanctioning system is *in abstracto* capable of ensuring a relationship of commensurability between the penalty and the wrongdoing. It is, therefore, pivotal that domestic sanctioning provisions allow the trial court to graduate the penalty imposed *in concreto* in the light of the wrongdoing's seriousness. The trial court shall be in the position to impose a given type and amount of penalty depending upon the circumstances of the case.[64] In the same vein, criminal law provisions imposing a high minimum penalty for a broad category of wrongdoings is not retrospectively proportionate, as this minimum threshold may be excessive to the seriousness of the conduct *in concreto*.[65]

[60] Among many, see: Joined Cases C-357/19, C-379/19, C-547/19, C-811/19 and C-840/19 *Euro Box Promotion and Others* ECLI:EU:C:2021:1034, paras 191–192.

[61] Case C-77/20 *K. M. (Sanctions infligées au capitaine de navire)* ECLI:EU:C:2021:112, para 49.

[62] Case C-655/18 *Schenker* ECLI:EU:C:2020:157, para 44.

[63] Joined Cases C-64/18, C-140/18, C-146/18 and C-148/18 *Maksimovic* ECLI:EU:C:2019:723, para 47. On the same point, see Case C-645/18 *Bezirkshauptmannschaft Hartberg-Fürstenfeld* ECLI:EU:C:2019:1108, para 40.

[64] Case C-384/17 *Link Logistik* ECLI:EU:C:2018:810, para 45.

[65] Case C-655/21 *G. ST. T. (Proportionnalité de la peine en cas de contrefaçon)* ECLI:EU:C:2023:791, para 81.

These findings only tackle manifestly disproportionate sanctioning arrangements and, therefore, provide domestic courts with minimum guidance concerning the upper and lower limits of domestic penalty scales. Within these limits, retrospective proportionality still requires assessing whether the penalty imposed is commensurate to the wrongdoing in the cardinal sense. However, the ECJ has rarely considered the absolute worthiness of the penalty from a retributive perspective. Save for some limited cases where the sanctioning system at issue entailed an evidently disproportionate penalty,[66] the assessment of cardinal proportionality is generally reserved for referring courts. This is not surprising, as this approach reflects the peculiar position of the ECJ in the context of the preliminary reference procedure. The Court's ruling is intended to provide domestic courts with all necessary guidance in applying the proportionality of penalties without supplementing or replacing the judicial determination of sanctions. Moreover, in preliminary rulings, the ECJ is, in principle, prevented from adjudicating the facts in the main proceedings, which is crucial for assessing the absolute worthiness of the penalty. Consequently, the Court may rely on the cardinal proportionality technique only in cases where penalties' disproportion is manifest upon examination of domestic provisions.

ii. The 'Prohibition on Adopting Disproportionate Penalties': Is there a Clear, Precise and Unconditional Standard of Review?

The *Greek Maize* paradigm entails proportionality scrutiny of domestic provisions, which usually warrants the ECJ exercising a strict necessity review.[67] On criminal penalties specifically, the Court clarified that the *Greek Maize* paradigm establishes a 'prohibition on adopting disproportionate penalties',[68] which is 'imperative in nature'.[69] By so doing, the ECJ framed the proportionality requirement of penalties as a negative provision, a crucial finding for recognising it as directly applicable. Indeed, negative provisions generally meet the clearness, preciseness and unconditional requirements needed for direct effect.[70]

On those grounds, one may assume that the ECJ exercises a rigorous assessment when reviewing Member States' adherence to the 'prohibition on adopting disproportionate penalties'. The ECJ case-law, however, depicts a different approach.

[66] Such as, for instance, the establishment of a financial penalty *in abstracto* without a predefined maximum amount and the provision of a fixed additional penalty in case of dismissal of the defendant's appeal, even if qualified as a contribution to the costs of the procedure (Case C-645/18 *Bezirkshauptmannschaft Hartberg-Fürstenfeld* ECLI:EU:C:2019:1108, para 43; Joined Cases C-64/18, C-140/18, C-146/18 and C-148/18 *Maksimovic* ECLI:EU:C:2019:723, para 50).

[67] See Section IV(A)(ii) of Chapter 1.

[68] Case C-205/20 *Bezirkshauptmannschaft Hartberg-Fürstenfeld (Effet direct)* ECLI:EU:C:2022:168, para 24.

[69] *ibid*, para 31.

[70] D Gallo, 'Rethinking Direct Effect and Its Evolution: A Proposal' (2022) 1 *European Law Open* 576, 597.

The principle's prospective scheme requires a necessity assessment, but it is not so strict as to decisively curtail the domestic authorities' margin of appreciation. As previously outlined, the Court demands caution when assessing the level of deterrence required for securing the effectiveness of EU law. The constant emphasis on deterrence ultimately blurs the standard of review, as it suggests a rise in the dissuasiveness threshold above which penalties would be disproportionate. This finding is further confirmed by the fact that only a few cases entailed the ECJ carrying out a 'least restrictive means' test.[71] It follows that the proportionality review of penalties implementing EU law features in theory a necessity assessment, but this scrutiny in practice does not result in a strict necessity evaluation.

Following these considerations, is it possible to conclude that the *Greek Maize* proportionality of criminal penalties entails a clear, precise and unconditional requirement? This issue is particularly tricky. Notwithstanding the negative understanding of the principle advanced by the Court in *Bezirkshauptmannschaft Hartberg-Fürstenfeld (Effet direct)*, applying this paradigm in concrete cases still leaves some margin of ambiguity. After all, proportionality is a legal principle: it entails different degrees of realisation and an ineradicable element of abstraction.[72] However, this characteristic does not prevent general principles of EU law from being translated into unconditional rules warranting direct effect.[73] On this point, Advocate General Bobek argued in its Opinion in *Bezirkshauptmannschaft Hartberg-Fürstenfeld (Effet direct)* that the extensive ECJ case-law on the proportionality of penalties provides domestic courts with sufficient guidance for applying the principle in concrete cases.[74] However, this chapter shows that the Court's guidance in this respect is only partial. More specifically, a distinction shall be drawn between manifestly disproportionate sanctioning schemes that allow the Court to elaborate in-depth retrospective considerations and the ones which do not reach this threshold.

In the first category of cases, the possibility to rely on the retrospective scheme has resulted in the Court translating the proportionality requirement into more precise assessment rules. As previously recalled, domestic sanctioning systems shall allow trial courts to graduate the penalty imposed *in concreto* according to the seriousness of the wrongdoing. Moreover, domestic provisions preventing trial courts from imposing a penalty below an exceptionally high threshold are disproportionate, as they lead to the imposition of harsh sanctions even for trivial cases. The same considerations apply to criminal systems providing for fixed penalties or unlimited cumulation of sanctions. These findings stem from cases where the

[71] In particular, see n 63 above in this chapter.

[72] See Section I(A) of the Introduction to this book.

[73] On this point, see B de Witte, 'Direct Effect, Primacy, and the Nature of the Legal Order' in P Craig and G de Búrca, *The Evolution of EU Law*, 3rd edn (Oxford, Oxford University Press, 2021) 202.

[74] Case C-205/20 *Bezirkshauptmannschaft Hartberg-Fürstenfeld (Effet direct)*, Opinion of AG Bobek, ECLI:EU:C:2021:759, para 38.

manifest disproportion of sanctioning schemes allowed the ECJ to thoroughly apply retrospective proportionality in the context of preliminary references. This assessment resulted in the Court elaborating clear and precise rules susceptible to being applied by domestic courts to set aside disproportionate provisions.

The second category of cases warrants partially different considerations. When domestic provisions do not amount to manifestly disproportionate sanctioning regimes, the ECJ usually abstains from in-depth retrospective assessments. Conversely, it provides guidance under the prospective scheme, thereby evaluating whether the level of deterrence characterising the penalty exceeds what is necessary to secure the effective implementation of EU law. That threshold shall be cautiously assessed by domestic authorities in light of the circumstances of each case.[75]

Compared to the retrospective proportionality rules previously analysed, this proportionality criterion is inevitably more blurred. It amounts to a standard of review to be adapted to the specific features of each case rather than a rule endowed with all constituent elements. The retrospective rules of assessment previously considered already encapsulate the threshold for recognising penalties as disproportionate. Conversely, the prospective standard requires domestic courts to identify that threshold in light of the specific circumstances of each case. Moreover, should the retrospective rules for manifestly disproportionate penalties previously considered not apply, the domestic court must investigate alone whether the sanction under scrutiny exceeds what is deserved for the seriousness of the wrongdoing.[76]

Still, the margin of appreciation left to domestic courts does not prevent proportionality from fulfilling the requirements for direct effect. Concerning the unconditional nature, the Court in *Bezirkshauptmannschaft Hartberg-Fürstenfeld (Effet direct)* clarified that the prohibition on adopting disproportionate penalties 'does not require the adoption of any measure of the EU institutions and […] does not in any way confer on Member States the right to limit the scope of that prohibition'.[77] Regarding clarity and preciseness, Advocate General Bobek insightfully recalled that

> a provision can meet those requirements whilst containing undefined or even vague concepts or indeterminate legal notions. […] Proportionality of penalties is a prime example in that regard. Irrespective the number of guidelines or judgments there may be on the interpretation of that concept, some degree of indeterminacy in terms of its application will remain as a consequence of the specific circumstances of each individual case.[78]

[75] See Section III(B)(i) of this Chapter.

[76] On the coexistence between prospective and retrospective schemes in the directly enforceable proportionality requirement of criminal penalties, see Montaldo, 'Handle with Care! The Direct Effect of the Requirement of Proportionality of Sanctions and the Remedy of Disapplication: NE v. Bezirkshauptmannschaft Hartberg-Fürstenfeld' (n 13) 875.

[77] Case C-205/20 *Bezirkshauptmannschaft Hartberg-Fürstenfeld (Effet direct)* ECLI:EU:C:2022:168, para 24.

[78] Case C-205/20 *Bezirkshauptmannschaft Hartberg-Fürstenfeld (Effet direct)*, Opinion of AG Bobek, ECLI:EU:C:2021:759, paras 36 and 38.

These findings appear convincing from a theoretical viewpoint. At the same time, it shall be underlined that applying this proportionality standard in concrete cases may still result in hurdles for domestic courts. Notwithstanding the precise and unconditional nature of the proportionality criterion, the ECJ only sometimes had the occasion to translate it into specific rules that domestic courts can apply without further assessment. Whenever these few rules do not apply or are not sufficient, it is for the domestic courts to translate the prospective and retrospective standards in the case at hand, thus identifying the threshold above which penalties are to be regarded as disproportionate. Given these difficulties, it is reasonable to expect that domestic courts will increasingly seek the assistance of the Court of Justice through the preliminary reference procedure to clarify the application of the proportionality requirement in concrete cases.

iii. Direct Effect the Remedy of Disapplication: Squaring Proportionality with the Principles of Effectiveness and Legality

Should domestic courts conclude that domestic rules on sanctions implementing the *Greek Maize* paradigm clash with the proportionality requirement, the principle of primacy requires them to set aside conflicting provisions.[79] However, the remedy of disapplication in substantive criminal law is a delicate task, as trial courts are kept between two opposing principles. On the one hand, the need to ensure the effectiveness of EU law prevents the total disapplication of domestic sanctioning schemes.[80] The opposite solution would lead to a legal void in criminal law enforcement against behaviours impairing the effective application of EU law.[81] Therefore, domestic courts shall selectively disapply those components of substantive criminal law provisions that lead to imposing disproportionate penalties. This approach is consistent with well-settled case-law, according to which the scope of disapplication shall coincide with the profile of incompatibility with EU law.[82]

[79] Case C-205/20 *Bezirkshauptmannschaft Hartberg-Fürstenfeld (Effet direct)* ECLI:EU:C:2022:168, para 39. Among extensive literature on the relationship between direct effect, primacy and the remedy of disapplication, see de Witte (n 73); D Gallo, *L'efficacia diretta del diritto dell'Unione europea negli ordinamenti nazionali. Evoluzione di una dottrina ancora controversa* (Milano, Giuffrè, 2018); M Dougan, 'Primacy and the Remedy of Disapplication' (2019) 56 *CML Rev* 1456; M Dougan, 'The Primacy of Union Law Over Incompatible National Measures: Beyond Disapplication and Towards a Remedy of Nuly?' (2022) 59 *CML Rev* 1301; E Cannizzaro, 'La dottrina degli effetti diretti in taluni dei suoi sviluppi più recenti' in M Distefano (ed), *L'effetto diretto delle fonti dell'ordinamento giuridico dell'Unione europea* (Napoli, Editoriale Scientifica, 2017); G Contaldi, 'Effetto diretto e primato' in S Cassese (ed), *Dizionario di diritto pubblico* (Milano, Giuffrè, 2006).

[80] Case C-205/20 *Bezirkshauptmannschaft Hartberg-Fürstenfeld (Effet direct)* ECLI:EU:C:2022:168, para 44.

[81] Among many, see Montaldo, 'Handle with Care! The Direct Effect of the Requirement of Proportionality of Sanctions and the Remedy of Disapplication: NE v. Bezirkshauptmannschaft Hartberg-Fürstenfeld' (n 13) 881; R Palladino, *Il principio di proporzionalità nel diritto dell'Unione europea* (Bari, Cacucci, 2024) 157.

[82] Among many, see Case C-226/97 *Lemmens* ECLI:EU:C:1998;296, paras 34–35. In literature, see Montaldo, 'Handle with Care! The Direct Effect of the Requirement of Proportionality of Sanctions

On the other hand, the remedy of disapplication is limited by the principle of legality, which is of fundamental importance for substantive criminal law. That principle, also recognised by Article 49(1) of the Charter,[83] implies that 'legislation must clearly define offences and the penalties which they attract'.[84] On this point, the ECJ in *Bezirkshauptmannschaft Hartberg-Fürstenfeld (Effet direct)* ruled out possible interferences with the principle of legality because the disapplication of disproportionate penalties would apply *in bonam partem*.[85] That consideration distinguishes the direct effect of the proportionality of criminal penalties from Article 325 TFEU as interpreted in *Taricco*[86] and later refined in *M.A.S. e M.B.*[87]

This stance from the Court discloses a narrow understanding of the principle of legality in EU law, construed as a mere prohibition for the judiciary to aggravate the individuals' criminal liability and penalties imposed on them.[88] However, the principle of legality has a broader meaning since it is inherently entrenched with the principles of legal certainty and separation of powers.[89] In particular,

and the Remedy of Disapplication: NE v. Bezirkshauptmannschaft Hartberg-Fürstenfeld' (n 13) 880; Dougan, 'Primacy and the Remedy of Disapplication' (n 79) 1463.

[83] For an analysis, see: R Sicurella, 'Legalità e proporzionalità nel diritto penale sostanziale' in R Mastroianni, O Pollicino, S Allegrezza, F Pappalardo and O Razzolini (eds), *Carta dei diritti fondamentali dell'Unione europea* (Milano, Giuffrè, 2017); V Mitsilegas and E Billis, 'Article 49 – Principles of Legality and Proportionality of Criminal Offences and Penalties' in S Peers, T Hervey, J Kenner and A Ward (eds), *The EU Charter of Fundamental Rights: A Commentary*, 2nd edn (Oxford, Hart Publishing, 2021).

[84] Among extensive case-law, see Case C-205/20 *Bezirkshauptmannschaft Hartberg-Fürstenfeld (Effet direct)* ECLI:EU:C:2022:168, para 47; Case C-623/22 *Belgian Association of Tax Lawyers and Others* ECLI:EU:C:2024:639, para 39; Case C-655/21 *G. ST. T. (Proportionnalité de la peine en cas de contrefaçon)* ECLI:EU:C:2023:791, para 50.

[85] S Montaldo, 'Domestic Sanctions and the Greek Maize Obligation to Impose Effective, Proportionate and Dissuasive Penalties: Empowering National Courts' in L Grossio, S Montaldo and V Mitsilegas (eds), *Proportionality of Criminal Penalties in EU Law* (Oxford, Hart Publishing, 2025) 228.

[86] Case C-105/14 *Taricco and Others* ECLI:EU:C:2015:555.

[87] Case C-42/17 *M.A.S. and M.B.* ECLI:EU:C:2017:936. On the legal aspects raised by disapplication *in malam partem* in the Taricco saga, among many, see C Amalfitano, 'Primato del diritto dell'Unione vs identità costituzionale o primato del diritto dell'Unione e identità nazionale?' in A Bernardi and C Cupelli (eds), *Il caso Taricco e il dialogo tra le Corti. L'ordinanza 24/2017 della Corte costituzionale* (Napoli, Jovene, 2017) 5–8; G Di Federico, 'La "saga Taricco": il funzionalismo alla prova dei controlimiti (e viceversa)' in C Amalfitano (eds), *Primato del diritto dell'Unione europea e controlimiti alla prova della 'saga Taricco'* (Milano, Giuffrè, 2018) 112–115; R Sicurella, 'Effectiveness of EU Law and Protection of Fundamental Rights: The Questions Settled and the New Challenges After the ECJ Decision in the *M.A.S. and M.B.* case' (2018) 9 *New Journal of European Criminal Law* 24; G Vitale, 'L'attesa sentenza "Taricco bis": brevi riflessioni' (2018) 3 *European Papers* 445.

[88] Case C-205/20 *Bezirkshauptmannschaft Hartberg-Fürstenfeld (Effet direct)* ECLI:EU:C:2022:168, para 48.

[89] C Peristeridou, *The Principle of Legality in European Criminal Law* (Cambridge, Intersentia, 2015) 48–54, 58. On the principle of legal certainty, among extensive scholarly analysis, see T Tridimas, *The General Principles of EU Law*, 2nd edn (Oxford, Oxford University Press, 2007) 242 *et seq*; C Amalfitano, 'La certezza del diritto nel diritto dell'Unione europea' in E Triggiani, F Cherubini, I Ingravallo, E Nalin and R Virzo (eds), *Dialoghi con Ugo Villani* (Bari, Cacucci, 2017). On the principle of separation of powers in EU law, among extensive scholarship, see K Lenaerts, 'Some Reflections on the Separation of Powers in the European Union' (1991) 28 *CML Rev* 11; F Fabbrini, 'La separazione dei poteri nell'Unione europea' (2023) 73 *Rivista trimestrake di diritto pubblico* 45.

Article 49(1) of the Charter entails that criminal provisions shall not only be precise but also 'comply with certain requirements of accessibility and foreseeability, as regards both the definition of the offence and the determination of the penalty'.[90] In particular, a broader understanding of the principle of legality would entail that courts are prevented from discretionally defining appropriate penalty scales independently from the balancing between opposing interests inherent in substantive criminal law provisions. This different dimension of the principle of legality may limit the toolbox available to domestic courts for shaping proportionate penalties after setting aside domestic provisions.[91]

It follows that the scope of judicial intervention for disapplying disproportionate sanctions lies between the principles of effectiveness and legality. Their accommodation elicits two different scenarios.

Firstly, legal scholarship has underlined that the law of criminal sanctions is often composed of a conundrum of different provisions entailing, for instance, accessory penalties, aggravating circumstances and specific rules of cumulation which apply in conjunction with the offence's penalty scale.[92] Moreover, sanctions may be severed by derogatory schemes prevailing on the ordinary penalty scale on grounds of speciality. Should the alleged disproportion of the sanction derive from one or more of these ancillary provisions, domestic courts may well have recourse to selective disapplication. That was the case in *Bezirkshauptmannschaft Hartberg-Fürstenfeld (Effet direct)*, where multiple normative sources provided for the automatic cumulation of fixed penalties and an additional sanction in case of dismissal of appeal. In a similar situation, the legal void created by selective disapplication is filled by applying provisions already existent in the domestic legal order. The same solution can be extended to the disapplication of special sanctioning schemes: the criminal case will be settled based on the ordinary regime. In this scenario, domestic courts do not exercise any discretional choice for crafting new sanctioning criteria in contrast with the principle of legality. The penalty following disapplication will result from other provisions already enacted in the domestic legal order. Moreover, national courts may seek the assistance of the ECJ through the preliminary reference procedure to ascertain which element of the sanctioning regime causes disproportionate penalties in circumstances such as those at issue and shall thus be disapplied.

[90] Case C-42/17 *M.A.S. and M.B.* ECLI:EU:C:2017:936, para 55. On the same point, see also Case C-460/23 *Kinsa*, Opinion of AG Richard de la Tour, ECLI:EU:C:2024:941, para 58. This finding by the ECJ follows from extensive case-law of the Strasbourg Court on Article 7(1) ECHR which, pursuant to Article 52(3) of the Charter, corresponds to Article 49(1) therein. In particular, see *Cantoni v France* ECHR 1996–V, para 29; *OAO Neftyanaya Kompaniya Yukos v Russia* App No 14902/04 (ECtHR, 20 September 2011), para 568. On the scope and implications of the principle of legality in EU criminal law, among many, see Peristeridou (n 89); A Barletta, *La legalità penale tra diritto dell'Unione europea e Costituzione* (Napoli, Jovene, 2011); C Grandi, *Riserva di legge e legalità penale europea* (Milano, Giuffrè, 2010).

[91] Montaldo, 'Domestic Sanctions and the Greek Maize Obligation to Impose Effective, Proportionate and Dissuasive Penalties: Empowering National Courts' (n 85) 228.

[92] *ibid.*

Secondly, there may be cases where selective disapplication is not available to the trial court. For instance, that situation may happen when all relevant domestic provisions lead to the imposition of disproportionate criminal penalties. The same issue also arises from fixed penalties leaving no room for their individualisation or even forms of penalties that are per se disproportionate vis-à-vis the wrongdoing. As recently argued in literature, the principle of proportionality of criminal penalties requires the complete disapplication of these sanctioning schemes.[93] However, the principle of effectiveness requires filling the resulting legal void. This is a tricky task, as domestic courts may have no legislative point of reference for determining the penalty to be imposed *in concreto*.[94] Therefore, disapplication in similar cases may put domestic courts in the uncomfortable situation of exercising discretional choices that pertain to the legislature under the principle of legality.

Whenever the disapplication of criminal law provisions goes into tension with the principle of legality, the ECJ ruling in *M.A.S. and M.B.* provides the ultimate way out.[95] In that ruling, the Court of Justice held that domestic courts are not obliged to disapply national provisions if that operation would contrast with the principle of legality.[96] Should the *M.A.S. and M.B.* doctrine apply, the principle of primacy would still require the judiciary to remedy the disproportion by means alternative to disapplication. The available tools mostly depend upon the specific feature of each Member State's judicial system. Whenever domestic legal orders so provide, criminal judges may consider referring the matter to domestic constitutional adjudication for a review of the relevant national provisions' legitimacy vis-à-vis EU law.[97]

[93] Montaldo, 'Handle with Care! The Direct Effect of the Requirement of Proportionality of Sanctions and the Remedy of Disapplication: NE v. Bezirkshauptmannschaft Hartberg-Fürstenfeld' (n 13) 881.

[94] The same issue may arise from sanctioning schemes composed uniquely by a penalty scale ranging between a minimum and a maximum. Should the former be disapplied and no other provision be applicable in this respect, the judicial determination of the minimum penalty may imply discretionary choices in contrast with the principle of legality. For an in-depth analysis of hurdles that domestic courts may encounter in the disapplication of domestic provisions on criminal penalties, see M Pelissero, 'The Influence of Proportionality of Penalties Derived from EU Law on Domestic Criminal Legislation and Sentencing' in L Grossio, S Montaldo and V Mitsilegas (eds), *Proportionality of Criminal Penalties in EU Law* (Oxford, Hart Publishing, 2025).

[95] Case C-42/17 *M.A.S. and M.B.* ECLI:EU:C:2017:936.

[96] See n 87 above.

[97] Montaldo, 'Domestic Sanctions and the Greek Maize Obligation to Impose Effective, Proportionate and Dissuasive Penalties: Empowering National Courts' (n 85) 229. For instance, that possibility is provided by the Italian legal order, from which the *Taricco* saga originated. As a result of a turn in the constitutional case-law following the ruling C. Cost. No 269/2017, the Constitutional Court has affirmed that the Italian judiciary may consider referring the case for a review of the constitutional legitimacy of domestic provisions even if the conditions for their disapplication are met. That solution may be envisaged whenever the domestic court considers that the same clash with directly enforceable EU law provisions may emerge in other cases, thus soliciting the eradication *erga omnes* of that contrast through the intervention of the Constitutional Court. Thus construed, the review of constitutional legitimacy triggered by a clash with EU law and the remedy of disapplication amount to alternative and complementary tools in the hands of domestic courts. On this point, see: O Porchia, 'Il dialogo tra Corte costituzionale e Corte di giustizia' in L Delli Priscoli (ed) *La Costituzione vivente* (Milano, Giuffrè, 2023) 311–314; C Favilli, 'La possibile convivenza tra disapplicazione e questione di

These considerations show that the scope for disapplying substantive criminal law breaching proportionality largely depends upon the peculiar features of the criminal sanctioning scheme at issue. Should selective disapplication not be possible, potential tensions with the principle of legality may be avoided by invoking the *M.A.S and M.B.* doctrine and contextually relying on alternative remedies, such as constitutional adjudication.

C. A Look at the Broader European Context: Upper and Lower Limits to the Domestic *Ius Puniendi* between the ECJ and ECtHR Case-law

As anticipated in Chapter 2, the hybrid conceptualisation of the principle of proportionality of criminal offences and penalties characterises both EU law and the ECHR. Given the relationship and differences between the two legal systems, looking at the Strasbourg Court's practice may provide a term of reference to better understand the underlying reasons driving the ECJ's approach.[98]

However, in the domain under analysis, the Luxembourg and Strasbourg Courts' proportionality assessments are radically different since they imply divergent constraints upon domestic authorities' discretion. On the one hand, the proportionality requirement enshrined in the *Greek Maize* paradigm postulates an *upper* limit to Member States' criminalisation choices and imposition of penalties. On the other hand, the proportionality of criminal offences and penalties under ECHR positive obligations consists of an opposite constraint. The Strasbourg Court's jurisprudence has framed proportionality as a *lower* limit to the severity of Contracting Parties' sanctioning regimes. That is the case of some human rights requiring domestic authorities to establish offences and penalties to punish certain harmful behaviour.[99] In particular, the Strasbourg Court has developed similar obligations from a variety of rights secured by the ECHR, including the right to life (Article 2 ECHR), the prohibition of torture and inhuman or degrading treatments and punishments (Article 3 ECHR), the prohibition of slavery and forced labour (Article 4 ECHR), and the right to respect for private and family life (Article 8 ECHR).[100] In this context, the case-law unveils two rationales driving

legittimità costituzionale dopo la sentenza n. 15 del 2024 del giudice delle leggi' (2024) 2 *Rivista del contenzioso europeo* 37; R Mastroianni, 'Sui rapporti tra Carte e Corti: nuovi sviluppi nella ricerca di un sistema rapido ed efficace di tutela dei diritti fondamentali' (2020) 5 *European Papers* 493; F Spitaleri, 'Doppia pregiudizialità e concorso di rimedi per la tutela dei diritti fondamentali' (2019) *Il Diritto dell'Unione europea* 729; P Mori, 'La Corte costituzionale e la Carta dei diritti fondamentali dell'UE: dalla sentenza 269/2017 all'ordinanza 117/2019. Un rapporto in mutazione?' in *Annali AISDUE*, vol 1 (Bari, Cacucci, 2020).

[98] As argued in Section V of Chapter 2.

[99] F Bestagno, *Diritti umani e impunità: obblighi positivi degli Stati in materia penale* (Milano, Vita e pensiero, 2003) 27.

[100] For an assessment of the relevant case-law, see among many: A Ashworth, *Positive Obligations in Criminal Law* (Oxford, Hart Publishing, 2013) 196–211; C Paonessa, *Gli obblighi di tutela penale: la discrezionalità legislative nella cornice dei vincoli costituzionali e comunitari* (Pisa, ETS, 2009) 167–192.

domestic criminalisation. From one perspective, the latter may be required to ensure effective deterrence, as the dissuasive nature of criminal punishment prevents violations of fundamental rights.[101] From a complementary viewpoint, criminalisation may be warranted to express censure towards the conduct. The severity of public authorities' response shall thus reflect the seriousness of the wrongdoing.[102]

When adjudicating over positive obligations, the Strasbourg Court employs prospective and retrospective assessments to define the threshold required for States' action.[103] This examination is composed of two stages. First, the ECtHR assesses the intensity of the wrongdoing's negative impact on the right invoked. In this regard, a distinction may be drawn between absolute and conditional rights. The former – such as Articles 3 ECHR (prohibition of torture and inhuman or degrading treatment and punishment), 4 ECHR (prohibition of slavery), 7 ECHR (right to no punishment without law) and 4 of Protocol No 4 (prohibition of collective expulsion of aliens) – often materialise 'the basic values of the democratic societies making up the Council of Europe'.[104] Given the importance of these rights in the ECHR legal system, the seriousness of any behaviour impairing their enjoyment is almost self-evident. The reasoning is more articulated for conditional rights, such as the protection of private life under Article 8 ECHR. In this case, the Contracting Parties are not bound by a general positive obligation of prevention. Instead, criminalisation is warranted insofar as the conduct touches upon 'a particularly important facet of an individual's existence or identity [...], or where [it involves] a most intimate aspect of private life'.[105]

The second (and crucial) step of the Strasbourg Court's assessment consists of verifying – in the light of the peculiar circumstances of the case – whether criminal law is necessary to comply with the positive duty flowing from the right

[101] In this regard, see *X and Y v The Netherlands* Series A No 91 (1985), para 27; *E.S. v Sweden* App No 5786/08 (ECtHR, 21 June 2012), para 58; *Siliadin v France* ECHR 2005-VII, para 144; *Ageyevy v Russia* App No 7075/10 (ECtHR, 18 April 2013), paras 195–196; *M. C. v Bulgaria* ECHR 2003-XII, para 150; *K.U. v Finland* App No 2872/02 (ECtHR, 2 December 2008), para 43.

[102] In this regard, see *Barovov v Russia* App No 9183/09 (ECtHR, 15 June 2021), para 38; *Gäfgen v Germany* App No 22978/05 (ECtHR, 1 June 2010), para 124; *Külah and Koyuncu v Turkey* App No 24827/05 (ECtHR, 23 April 2013), para 41; *Kasap and Others v Turkey* App No 8656/10 (ECtHR, 14 January 2014), para 59; *Leparskienė v Lithuania* App No 4860/02 (ECtHR, 7 July 2009), para 52; *Nikolova and Velichkova v Bulgaria* App No 7888/03 (ECtHR, 20 December 2007), para 62; *Myumyun v Bulgaria* App No 67258/13 (ECtHR, 3 November 2015), para 67.

[103] Among many, see *M. C. v Bulgaria* ECHR 2003-XII, para 150; *Kurt v Austria* App No 62903/15 (ECtHR, 15 June 2021), para 163; *Öneryildiz v Turkey* ECHR 2004-XII, para 89; *K.U. v Finland* App No 2872/02 (ECtHR, 2 December 2008), para 43. In literature, see V Stoyanova, *Positive Obligations under the European Convention on Human Rights. Within and Beyond Boundaries* (Oxford, Oxford University Press, 2023) 176.

[104] Among many, see *Calvelli and Ciglio v Italy* ECHR 2002-I, para 48; *Siliadin v France* ECHR 2005-VII, para 82; *L.C.B. v The United Kingdom* ECHR 1998-III, para 36; *Fernandes de Oliveira v Portugal* App No 78103/14 (ECtHR, 31 January 2019), para 104.

[105] *Söderman v Sweden* App No 5786/08 (ECtHR, 12 November 2013), para 79. According to Bestagno, this reasoning implies the existence of an abstract ranking between different facets of individual rights as inherent in the ECHR legal system (Bestagno (n 99) 37).

invoked. The ECtHR's reasoning on this point is straightforward, as it regularly holds that criminal law is indispensable insofar as it constitutes the only way to ensure effective deterrence.[106] In other words, recourse to criminal law is necessary when alternative measures, such as civil and administrative law measures, prove insufficient.[107] This evaluation depends upon the detriment caused by the conduct, which involves not only the importance of the right's facet impaired but also the abstract seriousness of the wrongdoing per se. An example of this approach may be found in *E.S. v Sweden*:

> while recourse to the criminal law is not necessarily the only answer, effective deterrence against *grave acts* where fundamental values and essential aspects of private life are at stake requires efficient criminal law provisions [...]. As to *lesser grave acts*, the protection afforded by civil law may be sufficient (emphasis added).[108]

ECHR's positive obligations to criminalise also require Contracting Parties to impose proportionate penalties. Similarly to the proportionality of offences, this declination of the principle of proportionality of penalties does not pose an *upper* limit to Contracting Parties' *ius puniendi*. Conversely, it seeks to ascertain whether the criminal sanction is *insufficient* to protect the right. As Viganò pointed out, proportionality of penalties may be framed here as *'l'exigence de l'infliction [...] d'une peine non disproportionnée par défaut'*.[109]

Whenever confronted with the proportionality of criminal penalties under positive obligations, the Strasbourg Court assesses whether the sentence imposed suffices or not to protect the right invoked.[110] The relevant jurisprudence of the Strasbourg Court is mainly centred on Articles 2 and 3 ECHR and follows a coherent approach. The ECtHR is aware of the need to recognise a margin of discretion upon domestic authorities and, consequently, to exercise self-restraint in assessing the proportionality of penalties. In particular, the ECtHR regularly recalls that it does not seek to determine the appropriate sentence for an offender[111] and,

[106] Among many, see *M.C. v Bulgaria* ECHR 2003-XII, para 150; *Ageyevy v Russia* App No 7075/10 (ECtHR, 18 April 2013), para 195–196; *Beganović v Croatia* App No 46423/06 (ECtHR, 25 June 2009), para 56; *Y.G. v Russia* App No 8647/12 (ECtHR, 30 August 2022), para 43; *Tyagunova v Russia* App No 19433/07 (ECtHR, 31 July 2012), para 63; *C.A.S. and C.S. v Romania* App No 26692/05 (ECtHR, 20 March 2012), para 71.

[107] *X and Y v The Netherlands* (1985) Series A No 91, para 27.

[108] *E.S. v Sweden* App No 5786/08 (ECtHR, 21 June 2012), para 58; *Söderman v Sweden* App No 5786/08 (ECtHR, 12 November 2013), para 85; *K.U. v Finland* App No 2872/02 (ECtHR, 2 December 2008), para 47. In literature, see V Scalia, 'Una proposta di ricostruzione degli obblighi positivi di tutela penale nella giurisprudenza della Corte europea dei diritti dell'uomo. L'esempio degli obblighi di protezione del diritto alla vita (I Parte)' (2020) *Archivio penale* 1, 31.

[109] F Viganò, 'Les obligations de protection pénale des droits fondamentaux' in G Giudicelli-Delage, S Manacorda and J Tricot (eds), '*Devoir de punir?' - Le système pénal face à la protection internationale du droit à la vie* (Paris, Société de législation comparée, 2013) 68.

[110] *Myumyun v Bulgaria* App No 67258/13 (ECtHR, 3 November 2015), para 75.

[111] Among many, see: *Gäfgen v Germany* App No 22978/05 (ECtHR, 1 June 2010), para 123; *Stübing v Germany* App No 43547/08 (ECtHR, 12 April 2012), para 62; *Austrianu v Romania* App No 16117/02 (ECtHR, 12 February 2013), para 73.

consequently, 'to rule on the degree of individual guilt'.[112] At the same time, the Strasbourg Court 'must still exercise a certain power of review and intervene in cases of *manifest disproportion between the gravity of the act and the punishment imposed* (emphasis added)'.[113]

Should a domestic penalty be manifestly disproportionate to the seriousness of the offence, this sanction 'does not have the necessary deterrent effect to prevent further violations'.[114] This finding discloses the Court's view on the relationship between prospective and retrospective proportionality: the latter scheme – namely, the manifest disproportion between the penalty and the wrongdoing – is intended as the key assessment, as it is functional to assess whether the penalty imposed ensures the deterrent effect required. Should a punishment be manifestly disproportionate from a retrospective viewpoint, the same conclusion will follow from a prospective standpoint.[115]

This brief analysis shows that the proportionality of criminal offences and penalties under ECHR positive obligations consists of a *by default* evaluation. It does not amount to a guarantee for the offender against excessive criminalisation; conversely, it secures the rights of victims of committed offences. This approach marks a clear difference with the EU legal order. While the proportionality of offences and penalties under the *Greek Maize* paradigm seeks to define whether criminalisation is excessive for ensuring the effectiveness of EU law, the same criterion under ECHR positive obligations establishes whether domestic sanctioning schemes are insufficient to protect the rights secured by the Convention.

These diverging perspectives result from the different institutional features underlying the *Greek Maize* paradigm and ECHR positive obligations. The former entails compound obligations upon Member States: they shall adopt effective and dissuasive penalties, which, however, shall not amount to disproportionate sanctions. Therefore, the *Greek Maize* orients and limits national *ius puniendi* simultaneously. In a human rights instrument such as the ECHR, upper and lower limits to *ius puniendi* enjoy different sources. Indeed, positive duties tackle the risk of insufficient protection of individual rights through criminal law. Conversely, negative obligations imposed on Contracting Parties entail upper proportionality limits to the severity of domestic criminal measures and aim to prevent excessive criminalisation.

[112] Among many, see: *Gäfgen v Germany* App No 22978/05 (ECtHR, 1 June 2010), para 123; *Öneryıldız v Turkey* ECHR 2004-XII, para 116.

[113] *Ali and Ayşe Duran v Turkey* App No 42942/02 (ECtHR, 8 April 2008), para 66; *Nikolova and Velichkova v Bulgaria* App No 7888/03 (ECtHR, 20 December 2007), para 62.

[114] *Gäfgen v Germany* App No 22978/05 (ECtHR, 1 June 2010), para 124.

[115] This conclusion flows evidently from the Court's reasoning: having established a manifest disproportion between the sanction and the wrongdoing, the ECtHR concludes that a similar penalty 'could not be regarded as having the necessary dissuasive effect' (*Myumyun v Bulgaria* App No 67258/13 (ECtHR, 3 November 2015), para 75; *Gäfgen v Germany* App No 22978/05 (ECtHR, 1 June 2010), para 124; *Austrianu v Romania* App No 16117/02 (ECtHR, 12 February 2013), para 74).

IV. The ECJ Proportionality Scrutiny of Domestic Criminal Offences and Penalties vis-à-vis Fundamental Rights and Internal Market Freedoms

Domestic substantive criminal law may interfere with the enjoyment of fundamental rights secured by the Charter or internal market freedoms. One of the core tools to settle this conflict is the hybrid principle of proportionality of criminal offences and penalties. Prospective and retrospective proportionality schemes allow for assessing whether measures pursuing domestic criminal policy aims are necessary and proportionate *stricto sensu* to attain a legitimate objective.

In that context, the Court of Justice adopts different approaches to reviewing criminal offences (A) and penalties (B). Moreover, the ECJ appears to assign different weights to prospective and retrospective proportionality, but consideration of the ECtHR case-law provides insights into the reasons for this differentiated approach (C).

A. The ECJ Reticent Approach Towards Prospective and Retrospective Proportionality of Offences

As explained in Chapter 2,[116] the proportionality of criminal offences entails two prongs. On the one hand, it postulates a limit to the scope of the abstract definition of an offence. On the other hand, it is a benchmark for reviewing whether the criminalisation choice is legitimate.

Against this dichotomy, the ECJ case-law mostly concerns limitations to internal market freedoms and entails the Court reviewing the scope of criminalised conduct. Interestingly, in these cases, the Court does not assess whether the offence's conduct is prospectively or retrospectively worth criminalisation. Conversely, the ECJ considers whether the prohibition of a given conduct – irrespective of whether criminally sanctioned or not – is necessary vis-à-vis attaining the purported aim. It follows that the reasoning of the Court does not feature any prospective or retrospective assessment. The ECJ sporadically refers to the concept of deterrence when assessing the suitability of the offence to attain the aim pursued. In *ZW*, for instance, the ECJ underlines that criminalisation per se ensures deterrence and, therefore, qualifies as a suitable measure.[117] However, this finding does not yield a prospective proportionality review of Member States' discretion. Indeed, the necessity test applied in that case does not enshrine any penological consideration. On these grounds, the Court sticks to the scrutiny defined by the threefold test characterising the general principle of proportionality.[118]

[116] See Section IV(A)(i) of Chapter 2.

[117] Case C-454/19 *ZW* ECLI:EU:C:2020:947, para 43.

[118] Among many, see Case C-137/17 *Van Gennip and Others* ECLI:EU:C:2018:771, para 80; Case C-393/17 *Kirschstein* ECLI:EU:C:2019:563, para 80.

Regarding the intensity of the review, ECJ usually conducts a strict necessity assessment. The criminal measure hampering internal market freedoms shall constitute the least restrictive means to attain the aim pursued. In particular, the Court regularly verifies whether the scope of the offence's definition 'does not appear to be absolutely necessary'[119] to attain a legitimate objective at the expense of free movement of persons,[120] goods,[121] capitals[122] and free provision of services.[123]

Concerning the second prong of proportionality of offences – namely the choice between criminalisation and alternative regimes – the ECJ case-law is very scarce and seems unable to limit Member States' discretion on this core dilemma. Instead, the justification for criminal sanctions is usually assessed through the proportionality of penalties.[124] Among the few exceptions, the *Skanavi and Chryssanthakopoulos* case deserves consideration.[125] This case concerned the imposition of financial penalties for driving in Germany without exchanging the licence issued by another Member State. The Court carried out an ordinal proportionality assessment to determine whether such a sanctioning system may be proportionate vis-à-vis the free movement of persons. The domestic offence under scrutiny was so broad that it made criminal penalties applicable to both unlicensed drivers and those who failed to exchange their foreign licences. The Court underlined that these two offences entail a different degree of seriousness; therefore, the imposition of criminal penalties on drivers who did not exchange their foreign licence is disproportionate from a retrospective point of view.[126]

B. The Emergence of Prospective and Retrospective Schemes in the ECJ Review of Domestic Penalties

Compared to the approach analysed in the preceding section, the ECJ's scrutiny of penalties clashing with EU rights and freedoms is characterised by an increasing emphasis on retrospective (i) and prospective (ii) schemes. In this context, the Court has developed a peculiar assessment for reviewing the legitimacy of

[119] Among many, see: Case C-265/88 *Messner* ECLI:EU:C:1989:632, para 11.

[120] *ibid.*

[121] See, in particular: Case 25/88 *Wurmser and Others* ECLI:EU:C:1989:187, paras 13 and 17; Case C-243/01 *Gambelli and Others* ECLI:EU:C:2003:597, para 74; Case C-137/17 *Van Gennip and Others* ECLI:EU:C:2018:771, paras 55 and 64; Case C-5/11 *Donner* ECLI:EU:C:2012:370, para 36; Case C-12/02 *Grilli* ECLI:EU:C:2003:538, para 47; Case C-42/90 *Bellon* ECLI:EU:C:1990:475, para 14.

[122] See, in particular, Case C-544/19 *ECOTEX Bulgaria* ECLI:EU:C:2021:803, para 68.

[123] See, in particular: Joined Cases C-338/04, C-359/04 and C-360/04 *Placanica and Others* ECLI:EU:C:2007:133, paras 48 and 53; Case C-920/19 *Fluctus and Others* ECLI:EU:C:2021:395, para 29; Case C-3/17 *Sporting Odds* ECLI:EU:C:2018:130, para 22; Joined Cases C-72/10 and C-77/10 *Costa and Cifone* ECLI:EU:C:2012:80, para 63; Case C-49/16 *Unibet International* ECLI:EU:C:2017:491, para 40; Case C-339/15 *Vanderborght* ECLI:EU:C:2017:335, paras 65 and 75.

[124] See Section IV(B) below in this chapter.

[125] Case C-193/94 *Skanavi and Chryssanthakopoulos* ECLI:EU:C:1996:70.

[126] *ibid*, para 37.

double-track administrative and criminal sanctioning schemes vis-à-vis *ne bis in idem* under Article 50 of the Charter. This test requires separate consideration since it has been profoundly influenced by the ECtHR case-law (iii).

i. Retrospective Proportionality as a Tool for Providing Domestic Courts with Broad Guidance

When penalties impair the enjoyment of individual freedoms secured by EU law, earlier case-law relied heavily on retrospective proportionality. The Court referred to a peculiar declination of that scheme, particularly when penalties clash with internal market freedoms. More specifically, the ECJ required that any criminal sanction is not '*so disproportionate to the gravity of the infringement* that it becomes an *obstacle to the freedoms enshrined in the Treaty* (emphasis added)'.[127] This finding exemplifies the functional bond between the secondary schemes and the threefold proportionality test. Should the penalty be particularly disproportionate to the gravity of the offence – in light of the nature and seriousness of the wrongdoing[128] – it shall also be regarded as an unlawful obstacle to exercising EU internal market freedoms.

The ECJ made extensive application of this declination of the retrospective scheme.[129] In particular, the Court's jurisprudence on the free movement of persons entails the most insightful examples. While domestic authorities may apply criminal penalties for violating formalities to exercise free movement rights, the ECJ consistently recognises that these offences shall be considered minor. Therefore, custodial sanctions would be disproportionate to the seriousness of similar wrongdoings.[130]

Most recent jurisprudence, however, features an evolution in the ECJ approach. Both prospective and retrospective schemes now complement the primary scheme – namely, the threefold test – of the principle of proportionality of criminal penalties, thus following the hybrid model theorised in this book. More specifically,

> the severity of the penalties imposed must […] be commensurate with the seriousness of the infringements for which they are imposed, in particular by ensuring a genuinely deterrent effect, while not going beyond what is necessary to attain that objective.[131]

[127] Case C-210/91 *Commission v Greece* ECLI:EU:C:1992:525, para 20.

[128] Joined Cases C-482/01 and C-493/01 *Orfanopoulos and Oliveri* ECLI:EU:C:2004:262, para 99; Case C-156/04 *Commission v Greece* ECLI:EU:C:2007:316, para 72; Case C-262/99 *Louloudakis* ECLI:EU:C:2001:407, paras 69-70; Case C-315/13 *De Clercq and Others* ECLI:EU:C:2014:2408, para 73.

[129] In that regard, see: Case C-193/94 *Skanavi and Chryssanthakopoulos* ECLI:EU:C:1996:70, para 36; Case C-127/08 *Metock and Others* ECLI:EU:C:2008:449, para 97.

[130] Case 157/79 *Regina v Pieck* ECLI:EU:C:1980:179, para 19; Case C-265/88 *Messner* ECLI:EU:C:1989:632, para 14.

[131] Case C-231/20 *Landespolizeidirektion Steiermark e a. (Machines à sous)* ECLI:EU:C:2021:845, para 45. On the same point, see: Case C-544/19 *ECOTEX Bulgaria* ECLI:EU:C:2021:803, para 100.

At the same time, the ECJ's application of the two secondary schemes discloses some noteworthy differences. Similarly to the review of criminal penalties under *Greek Maize*, the Luxembourg Court exercises self-restraint when assessing retrospective proportionality. The ECJ relies on this scheme only to verify whether the domestic sanctioning system allows the penalties imposed *in concreto* to be graduated according to the seriousness of the wrongdoing.[132] Therefore, abstract penalty levels established by domestic provisions shall leave sufficient discretion to the trial court.

On that basis, retrospective proportionality results in a tool for the Court to tackle manifestly disproportionate arrangements and dictate general guidance to the referring Court on reviewing the proportionality of criminal penalties. In particular, the impossibility of imposing fines below a predetermined minimum threshold shall be cautiously considered, as it 'might lead to their being imposed where it has not been established that the offence at issue is particularly serious'.[133] However, a minimum threshold for the penalty may be justified by the particular seriousness of the wrongdoing it seeks to penalise.[134] In that regard, the harmfulness of the conduct is assessed by reference not only to the nature of the behaviour but also to the personal characteristics of the offender, thus ensuring appropriate individualisation of the penalty.[135] Symmetrically, the Court has also emphasised the critical role vested by the upper penalty threshold for the retrospective proportionality of punishment. The absence of an upper limit in the domestic penalty scale leads to disproportionate penalties *in concreto*, thus violating the proportionality requirement.[136] Further to these general indications, the retrospective proportionality of the penalty shall ultimately be verified by domestic courts in the light of the specific circumstances of each case.[137]

ii. *The Leading Role of Prospective Proportionality*

The prospective scheme, on its part, has been employed in a twofold manner. On the one hand, the ECJ resorts to prospective proportionality to provide domestic courts with guidance on reviewing penalties *in concreto*. To establish the maximum

[132] In this regard, see Joined Cases C-64/18, C-140/18, C-146/18 and C-148/18 *Maksimovic* ECLI:EU:C:2019:723, para 41; Case C-544/19 *ECOTEX Bulgaria*, ECLI:EU:C:2021:803, para 104; Case C-255/14 *Chmielewski* ECLI:EU:C:2015:475, para 26.

[133] Joined Cases C-64/18, C-140/18, C-146/18 and C-148/18 *Maksimovic* ECLI:EU:C:2019:723, para 43.

[134] In this regard, see Case C-231/20 *Landespolizeidirektion Steiermark e a. (Machines à sous)* ECLI:EU:C:2021:845, para 46.

[135] Case C-544/19 *ECOTEX Bulgaria* ECLI:EU:C:2021:803, para 105.

[136] Joined Cases C-64/18, C-140/18, C-146/18 and C-148/18 *Maksimovic* ECLI:EU:C:2019:723, para 42.

[137] J Öberg, 'Conceptualising Proportionality and Criminal Sanctions in EU Law: Three Different Visions' in L Grossio, S Montaldo and V Mitsilegas (eds), *Proportionality of Criminal Penalties in EU Law* (Oxford, Hart Publishing, 2025) 22.

level of dissuasiveness required, in the case of financial penalties, regard must be had to the

> relationship between the amount of the fine that may be imposed and the economic benefit derived from the infringement committed, *in order to deter offenders.* [...] *It must, however, ensure*, taking account of all the circumstances of the case, *that the minimum amount thus imposed is not disproportionate to that benefit* (emphasis added).[138]

In the same vein, while an offence entailing a remarkable benefit for the wrongdoer justifies in principle the imposition of heavy financial penalties,[139] 'a fine corresponding to 100% of the total amount [...] would go beyond what is necessary in order to ensure compliance'[140] (ie, to deter potential offenders).

These general criteria are similar to those stemming from the proportionality review of criminal penalties through the prism of the *Greek Maize* paradigm, with a noteworthy difference.[141] When criminal penalties clash with individual rights secured by EU law, the ECJ does not advance a particularly cautious approach in determining the maximum deterrence threshold under prospective proportionality. This difference is unsurprising: in the domain at issue, criminal penalties serve purely domestic policy aims and are not meant to secure the effectiveness of EU law.[142] Therefore, there is no need to warrant due regard from the national authorities that sanctions are sufficiently dissuasive.

On the other hand, the prospective scheme sometimes amounts to the decisive argument for the ECJ to hold a given penalty as disproportionate. The ECJ ruling in *Maksimovic* is illustrative of this approach. Like *Bezirkshauptmannschaft Hartberg-Fürstenfeld (Effet direct)*,[143] this case concerns the Austrian sanctioning scheme for violating provisions on the posting of workers, although assessed through the prism of free provision of services. National provisions in question stipulated that penalties could not be lower than a given minimum amount and apply cumulatively without a maximum limit. Moreover, in case of dismissal of the appeal, the fine was increased by a contribution to court costs of 20% of the sanction and the total amount could be replaced by custodial sentences in the event of non-payment.[144] In the proportionality review, the Court first relied on retrospective proportionality. However, the latter scheme only allowed the Court to provide domestic authorities with abstract guidance. In particular, the judgment recalls that 'legislation providing for penalties of which the amount varies depending on the number of workers affected by non-compliance with certain labour law

[138] Case C-231/20 *Landespolizeidirektion Steiermark e a. (Machines à sous)* ECLI:EU:C:2021:845, para 47.

[139] Case C-544/19 *ECOTEX Bulgaria* ECLI:EU:C:2021:803, para 107.

[140] *ibid*, para 110. In this regard, see also Case C-190/17 *Zheng* ECLI:EU:C:2018:357, para 45.

[141] See Section III(B) above in this chapter.

[142] That was the case, conversely, of criminal penalties established under the *Greek Maize* paradigm: in that regard, see Section III(B)(ii) above in this chapter.

[143] Case C-205/20 *Bezirkshauptmannschaft Hartberg-Fürstenfeld (Effet direct)* ECLI:EU:C:2022:168.

[144] Joined Cases C-64/18, C-140/18, C-146/18 and C-148/18 *Maksimovic* ECLI:EU:C:2019:723, para 24.

obligations does not, in itself, appear to be disproportionate'.[145] Therefore, the ECJ went further in the assessment by applying prospective proportionality. The Court exercised a strict necessity assessment, then concluding that 'effective implementation of the obligations, non-compliance with which carries penalties under such legislation, could be achieved through less restrictive measures'.[146]

To sum up, the ECJ application of the principle of proportionality of penalties interfering with the enjoyment of EU rights and freedoms entails prospective and retrospective assessments. Under the retrospective scheme, the type and level of the penalties shall not be disproportionate to the seriousness of the wrongdoing, such as to amount to an obstacle to the exercise of EU internal market freedoms or an illegitimate restriction of fundamental rights secured by the Charter. This assessment is primarily reserved for domestic authorities, subject to the general guidance provided by the ECJ. As far as the level of penalties is concerned, the abstract penalty scale shall leave sufficient room for the trial court to graduate the sanction *in concreto*. Under the prospective scheme, the type and level of penalties shall not exceed what is necessary to ensure a genuinely dissuasive effect. Whenever less restrictive penalties – concerning either their type or amount – suffice to dissuade potential offenders from committing the offence, the criminal sanctions under scrutiny shall be regarded as disproportionate.

iii. The Enhancement of Retrospective Proportionality of Criminal Penalties in the Ne Bis in Idem *Framework*

Among fundamental rights secured by EU law, *ne bis in idem* constitutes a traditional criminal law guarantee according to which nobody can be tried and punished twice for the same act.[147] This principle is codified in Article 50 of the Charter, Article 54 CISA and Article 4 of Protocol No 7 of the ECHR. The scope of *ne bis in idem* in principle extends to double-track sanctioning systems, where a given conduct may amount to both a criminal and an administrative offence. Should the administrative penalty qualify as criminal in nature,[148] the duplication of proceedings and sanctions may be contrary to *ne bis in idem*.

That conclusion is reached when two conditions are met. Firstly, the two proceedings shall amount to a duplication (*bis*) as one already led to a final decision.[149] Secondly, the two proceedings and the sanctions must be imposed

[145] *ibid*, para 41.

[146] *ibid*, para 47.

[147] Among extensive literature, see E Śliwiński, 'Principle of Proportionality as a Threat to Criminal-Law-Related Fundamental Rights' (2023) 14 *New Journal of European Criminal Law* 327, 328.

[148] In that regard, see Section III of the Introduction to this book.

[149] As underlined in literature, *ne bis in idem* constitutes not only an individual guarantee against excessive exercise of *ius puniendi*, since it also protects the authority of *res judicata* (in this regard, see M Vetzo, 'The Past, Present and Future of the Ne Bis In Idem Dialogue between the Court of Justice of the European Union and the European Court of Human Rights: The Cases of Menci, Garlsson and Di Puma' (2019) 11 *Review of European Administrative Law* 55, 55.

for the same act (*idem*). Concerning the *idem* requirement, two approaches have emerged in the case-law.[150] On the one hand, the *idem* concept may be construed as *idem crimen*, thus requiring identity between the abstract offences forming the object of the two proceedings. According to this approach, two parallel sanctions for the same material conduct do not constitute an *idem* if the two offences secure different legal interests[151] or entail different essential elements.[152] On the other hand, the term *idem* may be understood as meaning *idem factum*: if the facts forming the object of the two proceedings are identical, they tackle the same wrongdoing irrespective of their legal qualification.[153]

In the area of criminal law, both the ECJ and the ECtHR adhere to the *idem factum* criterion. This convergence constitutes the outcome of judicial dialogue and cross-fertilisation between the law of the EU and ECHR. Indeed, the ECJ jurisprudence on Article 54 CISA[154] exercised a profound influence on the Strasbourg Court, which initially applied the *idem crimen* criterion in the framework of Article 4 of Protocol No 7.[155] By reverting this previous approach, the ECtHR in *Sergey Zolotukhin v Russia* aligned itself on the *idem factum* interpretation.[156]

Concerning the *bis* requirement, the 2016 judgment in *A and B v Norway* marked a new shift.[157] The ECtHR clarified that two parallel proceedings for the same acts do not violate Article 4 of Protocol No 7 if they are 'sufficiently closely connected in substance and in time'.[158] To assess this bond, the Strasbourg Court advanced several criteria. In particular, the two proceedings shall address different aspects of the wrongdoing; the duplication of sanctioning schemes shall be

[150] In this regard, see Case C-117/20 *bpost*, Opinion of AG Bobek, ECLI:EU:C:2021:680, para 39.

[151] That was the approach followed by the ECJ before the *bpost* judgment in cases involving the application of competition law fines, where the same conduct may be prosecuted by both the Commission and National Competition Authorities. In particular, in *Toshiba* (Case C-17/10 *Toshiba Corporation and Others* ECLI:EU:C:2012:72, para 97) and, more recently, in *Slovak Telecom* (Case C-857/19 *Slovak Telecom* ECLI:EU:C:2021:139, para 43) the Luxembourg Court held the *ne bis in idem* principle applicable whereas the two proceedings concern the same offender, the same material facts and secure the same legal interest.

[152] That was the approach followed by the ECtHR before the *Sergey Zolotukhin v Russia* judgment (*Sergey Zolotukhin v Russia* App No 14939/03 (ECtHR, 10 February 2009)).

[153] This approach has been consistently followed by the ECJ when interpreting *ne bis in idem* within the AFSJ. For some references, see: Case C-436/04 *Van Esbroeck* ECLI:EU:C:2006:165, para 27; Case C-150/05 *Van Straaten* ECLI:EU:C:2006:614, para 41; Case C-261/09 *Mantello* ECLI:EU:C:2010:683, paras 39–40; Case C-665/20 PPU *X (Mandat d'arrêt européen – Ne bis in idem)* ECLI:EU:C:2021:339, para 71.

[154] For an analysis, see C Brière and A Weyembergh, 'Article 50 – Droit à ne pas être jugé ou puni pénalement deux fois pour une même infraction' in F Picod, C Rizcallah and S Van Drooghenbroeck (eds), *Charte des droits fondamentaux de l'Union européenne. Commentaire article par article*, 3rd edn (Bruxelles, Bruylant, 2023) 1297.

[155] Case C-617/10 *Åkerberg Fransson*, Opinion of AG Cruz Villalón, ECLI:EU:C:2012:340, para 77, as recalled in Case C-117/20 *bpost*, Opinion of AG Bobek, ECLI:EU:C:2021:680, para 62.

[156] *Sergey Zolotukhin v Russia* App No 14939/03 (ECtHR, 10 February 2009), para 82. In literature, among many, see: J Callewaert, 'The European Convention on Human Rights and European Union Law: A Long Way to Harmony' (2009) *European Human Rights Law Review* 768.

[157] *A and B v Norway* App Nos 24130/11 and 29758/11 (ECtHR, 15 November 2016).

[158] *ibid*, para 130.

foreseeable for the wrongdoer; the proceedings shall be conducted in a coordinated manner, thus avoiding duplications in the collection and assessment of evidence; and most importantly, the first sanction imposed shall be taken into account when determining the penalty to be pronounced in the second proceedings, to ensure 'that the overall quantum of any penalties imposed is proportionate'.[159] Should these criteria be complied with, the ECtHR considers that the two proceedings do not constitute an unlawful duplication but complementary and coherent sanctioning responses to the wrongdoing.[160]

This approach paved the way for applying proportionality of penalties in the context of *ne bis in idem*.[161] In fact, retrospective proportionality of the overall sanction constitutes an essential criterion for assessing whether the two proceedings are sufficiently closely connected. Contracting Parties enjoy a margin of appreciation in establishing dual-track sanctioning schemes, provided that their simultaneous application leads to an overall sanctioning response proportionate to the seriousness of the offence.[162] Subsequent case-law featured a consistent approach in this regard. Usually, the Court first verifies whether the second decision has considered the penalty previously imposed when determining the new sanction. A failure to meet this requirement – defined in *Galović v Croatia* as 'the principle of deduction'[163] – sometimes sufficed to hold the total penalty amount as disproportionate.[164] However, in some cases this circumstance was not enough to reach that conclusion. The overall sanction may be nonetheless proportionate if the second penalty is particularly low compared to the statutory maximum[165] or has been reduced on appeal.[166]

The renewed ECtHR approach profoundly influenced the EU legal order, as the ECJ followed a comparable – although different – path. In *Menci*,[167] *Garlsson Real Estate and Others*[168] and *Di Puma*[169] the Luxembourg Court developed its own test to assess whether the double imposition of criminal and administrative penalties may be legitimate under Article 50 of the Charter. A dual-track sanctioning scheme shall pursue a legitimate aim[170] based on 'clear and precise rules allowing

[159] *ibid*, para 132.
[160] *ibid*, para 133.
[161] As underlined in the literature, *ne bis in idem* and proportionality of sanctions serve, at least in part, similar goals. On this point, see A Turmo, 'The Proportionality of Criminal Sanctions and Ne Bis in Idem', in L Grossio, S Montaldo and V Mitsilegas (eds), *Proportionality of Criminal Penalties in EU Law* (Oxford, Hart Publishing, 2025) 201.
[162] G Coffey, 'An Interpretative Analysis of the European Ne Bis in Idem Principle through the Lens of ECHR, CFR and CISA Provisions: Are Three Streams Flowing in the Same Channel?' (2023) 14 *New Journal of European Criminal Law* 345, 370.
[163] *Galović v Croatia* App No 45512/11 (ECtHR, 31 August 2021), para 121.
[164] In this regard, see *Goulandris and Vardinogianni v Greece* App No 1735/13 (ECtHR, 16 June 2022), paras 77-78; *Milošević v Croatia* App No 12022/16 (ECtHR, 31 August 2021), para 41.
[165] *Bajčić v Croatia* App No 67334/13 (ECtHR, 8 October 2020), para 44.
[166] *Nodet v France* App No 47342/14 (ECtHR, 6 June 2019), para 50.
[167] Case C-524/15 *Menci* ECLI:EU:C:2018:197.
[168] Case C-537/16 *Garlsson Real Estate* ECLI:EU:C:2018:193.
[169] Case C-596/16 *Di Puma* ECLI:EU:C:2018:192.
[170] Case C-524/15 *Menci* ECLI:EU:C:2018:197, para 63, first indent.

individuals to predict which acts or omissions are liable to be subject to such a duplication of proceedings and penalties'[171] and limit the disadvantages for the offender deriving from the duplication of proceedings to what is strictly necessary for attaining the aim pursued.[172] In the context of the latter assessment, it shall be ensured that 'the severity of the sum of all of the penalties imposed corresponds with the seriousness of the offence concerned'.[173] Following the recent rulings in *bpost*[174] and *Nordzucker and Others*,[175] this test has become a uniform standard for assessing the legitimacy of limitations to *ne bis in idem* under EU law.[176]

In line with the Strasbourg Court's approach, retrospective proportionality plays a key role also in the context of the ECJ test. The existence of a relationship of commensurability between the seriousness of the wrongdoing and the severity of the total amount of penalties constitutes the ultimate requirement for duplication of sanctioning proceedings to be compatible with Article 50 of the Charter. This assessment is primarily for the domestic courts. The Luxembourg Court, however, has provided them with some guidance. In particular, a sanctioning scheme establishing the automatic cumulation of penalties, thus excluding any proportionality evaluation, would be in contrast with Article 50 of the Charter.[177] Moreover, when assessing retrospective proportionality, domestic authorities shall consider all the penalties imposed, irrespective of their nature.[178] In particular, considering the statutory maximum of the harshest penalty imposed as a limit for the overall sanction does not suffice as such to guarantee a proportionate sanctioning response.[179] These findings entail general guidance for the domestic courts. However, the ECJ has sometimes taken a bolder stance, thus conducting a cardinal proportionality assessment. In some cases, the Luxembourg Court has considered whether 'the cumulative effect of those measures may exceed the seriousness of the offence committed by the applicant in the main proceedings and contravene the requirements of the principle of proportionality'.[180] It thus seems that the profound emphasis put by the Strasbourg Court on retrospective proportionality in the context of *ne bis in idem*, later upheld by the ECJ, has led the EU Court to refine and deepen the retrospective balancing between the seriousness of the wrongdoing and the severity of penalties.

[171] Case C-537/16 *Garlsson Real Estate* ECLI:EU:C:2018:193, para 51.
[172] Case C-524/15 *Menci* ECLI:EU:C:2018:197, para 53.
[173] Case C-537/16 *Garlsson Real Estate* ECLI:EU:C:2018:193, para 56.
[174] Case C-117/20 *bpost* ECLI:EU:C:2022:202.
[175] Case C-151/20 *Nordzucker and Others* ECLI:EU:C:2022:203.
[176] In particular, the two judgments extended this test to the competition law domain. In fact, under the Court's previous approach, two parallel sanctioning schemes for violations of competition law provisions had to secure the same legal interests to fulfil the *idem* requirement. In literature, see P Van Cleynenbreugel, 'BPost and Nordzucker: Searching for the Essence of Ne Bis in Idem in European Union Law' (2022) 18 *European Constitutional Law Review* 357.
[177] Case C-97/21 *MV – 98* ECLI:EU:C:2023:371, para 54.
[178] Case C-570/20 *Direction départementale des finances publiques de la Haute-Savoie* ECLI:EU:C:2022:348, para 50.
[179] *ibid*, para 52.
[180] Case C-97/21 *MV – 98* ECLI:EU:C:2023:371, para 62.

Against this background, one may conclude that the ECJ and ECtHR case-law feature a true convergence on the proportionality of penalties. This finding is only partially correct. The Strasbourg and Luxembourg Courts are driven by two radically different understandings of the clash between domestic penalties and *ne bis in idem*. On the one hand, the ECtHR conceives double-track sanctioning schemes as an exception to the *bis* requirement: insofar as the two proceedings are closely connected in substance and time, there is no duplication under Article 4 of Protocol No 7. On the other hand, the ECJ construes the duplication of criminal and administrative proceedings as an interference with Article 50 of the Charter, which shall be justified under Article 52(1) therein. In this different understanding, the ECJ adheres to the hybrid double-layered model featuring the principle of proportionality of criminal penalties. Indeed, retrospective proportionality is not conceived as a stand-alone paradigm, whereas it constitutes the secondary scheme of the proportionality assessment enshrined in Article 52(1) of the Charter.

C. Towards the Direct Effect of Article 49(3) of the Charter: Prospects and Implications

As previously affirmed in this chapter,[181] the *Bezirkshauptmannschaft Hartberg-Fürstenfeld (Effet direct)* ruling brought a paradigm shift by holding that the *Greek Maize* proportionality requirement of sanctions has direct effect. This conclusion is limited to the proportionality of criminal penalties implementing EU law. However, this ruling may pave the way for recognising the direct enforceability of the principle of proportionality of penalties as a whole. Indeed, in *Bezirkshauptmannschaft Hartberg-Fürstenfeld (Effet direct)* the ECJ avoided to rule that Article 49(3) of the Charter as such is directly enforceable. Still, a closer look at the Court's reasoning discloses that this provision played a crucial role in reaching such a conclusion. In particular, the Luxembourg Court established a robust legal connection between Article 49(3) of the Charter and the *Greek Maize* paradigm. The former amounts to the unifying paradigm that all other normative foundations for the proportionality of criminal penalties merely reiterate.[182] This proportionality requirement 'is imperative in nature',[183] thus meeting the conditions for being directly invoked.[184] Provided that the *Greek Maize* proportionality requirement recalls Article 49(3) of the Charter and has direct effect, the same conclusion may thus potentially be drawn for said provision.

It thus appears that the *Bezirkshauptmannschaft Hartberg-Fürstenfeld (Effet direct)* ruling paves the way for soon recognising that Article 49(3) of the Charter

[181] See Section III(B)(ii) of the present chapter.

[182] Case C-205/20 *Bezirkshauptmannschaft Hartberg-Fürstenfeld (Effet direct)* ECLI:EU:C:2022:168, para 31.

[183] *ibid.* On the implications of the imperative nature of fundamental rights in the ECJ reasoning on their direct effect, see F Costamagna, *Diritti fondamentali e rapporti tra privati nell'ordinamento dell'Unione europea* (Torino, Giappichelli, 2022) 96 *et seq.*

[184] See Section III(B)(ii) of the present chapter.

is directly enforceable.[185] Should the ECJ reach this conclusion, what would be the consequences for the proportionality of criminal penalties clashing with rights and freedoms secured by EU law? Three different cases should be considered.

Considering first those sanctions entailing disproportionate interferences with internal market freedoms, the direct effect of Article 49(3) of the Charter would hardly entail novelties. Indeed, Treaty provisions on internal market freedoms are themselves directly enforceable, thus warranting the disapplication of any domestic rule posing illegitimate obstacles to their exercise.[186] Criminal penalties are not an exception in this respect. Advocate General Bobek relied exactly on this point to argue that the *Greek Maize* proportionality requirement should be endowed with direct effect. Provided that criminal penalties which are disproportionate vis-à-vis internal market freedoms shall be set aside,

> it would be paradoxical, to say the least, to consider that the national provisions regarding sanctions shall be set aside because they are contrary to the general prohibition to introduce disproportionate obstacles to free movement […], but to conclude that the more specific provision regarding the proportionality of penalties within the more specific directive on the issue of the posting of workers is not directly effective.[187]

It thus appears that the disapplication of penalties disproportionately interfering with internal market freedoms is already a reality under EU law.

Second, the proportionality of criminal penalties may be invoked against sanctions hindering the enjoyment of fundamental rights under the Charter. In similar cases, both Articles 49(3) and 52(1) of the Charter apply in the review of the type and level of the sanction. As the ECJ recalled in *ECOTEX Bulgaria* and *Garlsson Real Estate*, the principle of proportionality of criminal penalties follows from both provisions.[188] This stance implies a holistic understanding of the principle: Article 49(3) of the Charter is a unifying paradigm for the proportionality of criminal penalties under both Article 52(1) of the Charter and Treaty provisions on internal market freedoms.[189] Therefore, should the ECJ rule that Article 49(3) of the Charter is directly enforceable, that provision would exercise a key role in fundamental rights adjudication. By complementing the assessment enshrined in Article 52(1) of the Charter, Article 49(3) would confer direct effect to the proportionality of criminal penalties also this context, thus ensuring that sanctions qualifying as disproportionate could be set aside.

[185] On this point, see Palladino (n 81) 156; Montaldo, 'Handle with Care! The Direct Effect of the Requirement of Proportionality of Sanctions and the Remedy of Disapplication: NE v. Bezirkshauptmannschaft Hartberg-Fürstenfeld' (n 13) 873; Pelissero (n 94) 242.

[186] In this regard, among many, see L Daniele, *Diritto del mercato unico europeo e dello Spazio di libertà, sicurezza e giustizia* (Milano, Giuffrè, 2019) 30–31.

[187] Case C-205/20 *Bezirkshauptmannschaft Hartberg-Fürstenfeld (Effet direct)*, Opinion of AG Bobek, ECLI:EU:C:2021:759, para 51.

[188] Case C-544/19 *ECOTEX Bulgaria* ECLI:EU:C:2021:803, para 97; Case C-537/16 *Garlsson Real Estate and Others* ECLI:EU:C:2018:193, para 56.

[189] See n 182 above.

Thirdly, consider the situation of a domestic sanctioning scheme providing for draconian penalties which, however, neither implement EU law nor interfere with internal market freedoms or Charter rights different from Article 49(3). In principle, such penalties fall outside the scope of EU law and, consequently, are not subject to the hybrid principle of proportionality. However, let us imagine the existence of a link between the committed offence in question and EU law under Article 51(1) of the Charter, thus leading the defendant to invoke Article 49(3) of the Charter.[190] A similar scenario has never occurred in judicial practice, and it also appears hardly conceivable. In the presence of a link between EU law and the criminal case, the sanctioning scheme would arguably be established to secure the effectiveness of EU law or clash with rights and freedoms secured by the Treaties as in the cases previously analysed in this book. However, should a different link be hypothetically envisaged, a case like that would envisage Article 49(3) of the Charter applying alone rather than in conjunction with the *Greek Maize* paradigm, Treaty provisions on internal market freedoms, or even Article 52(1) of the Charter. Being a declination of the principle of proportionality of penalties itself, Article 49(3) is not subject to proportionality limitations based on Article 52(1) of the Charter. Therefore, what should be the meaning of the proportionality of criminal penalties if invoked in this hypothetical situation? Despite the retrospective wording of Article 49(3) of the Charter, the ECJ case-law previously analysed suggests that the provision is part of a broader and holistic understanding of the proportionality of criminal penalties to which it refers.[191] As this book showed, its theorisation amounts to a hybrid model combining EU and criminal law proportionality, including both prospective and retrospective schemes. Since that Charter provision has emerged as a unifying paradigm for the proportionality of criminal penalties, hypothetical reliance on Article 49(3) of the Charter in isolation should not entail any narrower or different understanding of the principle under EU law.

D. A Look at the Broader European Context: The ECtHR Approach Towards Criminal Measures Clashing with the Enjoyment of Fundamental Rights

As shown in Section IV(B)(iii) above, *ne bis in idem* constitutes an example of cross-fertilisation between EU law and the ECHR on the proportionality of criminal penalties. Notwithstanding the link between the Convention and the Charter

[190] For an analysis of the uneasy definition of the scope of application of EU law and potential links between the latter and domestic actions or omissions, among many, see ME Bartoloni, *Ambito d'applicazione del diritto dell'Unione europea e ordinamenti nazionali: una questione aperta* (Napoli, Edizioni Scientifiche Italiane, 2018) 221 *et seq*.

[191] See Section II(B) of the present chapter.

established by Article 52(3) therein, there is no further example of convergence between the two systems in the application of the hybrid principle. When domestic substantive criminal law clashes with the enjoyment of individual rights, the Strasbourg Court relies heavily on the retrospective scheme rather than the prospective one (i). What is more, the ECtHR advances retrospective proportionality as a stand-alone paradigm to censure manifestly disproportionate sentences through the prism of the prohibition of inhuman or degrading treatments or punishments as established by Article 3 ECHR (ii).

i. The Enhancement of Retrospective Proportionality in the ECtHR Review of Domestic Criminal Measures vis-à-vis Conditional Rights

The ECtHR standard of review on criminal measures is generally looser than the ECJ one, as it reflects the margin of appreciation recognised by the Strasbourg Court to domestic authorities. Still, the scope of legitimate discretion left to Contracting Parties differs depending on the peculiarities of the wrongdoing. Should the offence impair one of the most intimate facets of individuals' life, the margin of discretion would usually be reduced.[192] Conversely, when there is no consensus among Contracting Parties on the weight of the interests at stake and how to accommodate them, the national authorities are granted broader leeway.[193] The discretion of domestic authorities is also broad when the imposition of offences and penalties addresses sensitive moral or ethical issues.[194] Depending upon the margin of manoeuvre in question, the ECtHR standard of review may be looser or stricter accordingly.[195]

This finding entails one noteworthy consequence for the Strasbourg Court's approach. While the necessity assessment represents the crucial step of the ECJ reasoning, proportionality *stricto sensu* constitutes the very heart of the ECtHR assessment of criminal offences and penalties. In this respect, the ECtHR carries out an in-depth retrospective proportionality assessment. *Grigoriades v Greece* is

[192] That is the case, for instance, of the criminalisation of homosexual activities. In that respect, see *Dudgeon v The United Kingdom* Series A No 45 (1981), para 52; *Norris v Ireland* Series A No 142 (1988), para 46. In similar situations, 'there must exist particularly serious reasons before interferences on the part of the public authorities can be legitimate' (*Stübing v Germany* App no 43547/08 (ECtHR, 12 April 2012), para 52). In literature, among many, see F Sudre, L Milano, B Pastre-Belda and A Schahmaneche, *Droit européen et international des droits de l'homme*, 16th edn (Paris, Presses Universitaires de France, 2023) 220.

[193] *Stübing v Germany* App no 43547/08 (ECtHR, 12 April 2012), para 60; *Otto-Preminger-Institut v Austria* (1994) Series A No 295–A, para 56; *Leyla Şahin v Turkey* ECHR 2005–XI, para 116; *Lautsi and Others v Italy* App No 30814/06 (ECtHR, 18 March 2011), paras 68–69.

[194] *Stübing v Germany* App No 43547/08 (ECtHR, 12 April 2012), para 60.

[195] In literature, see Sudre, Milano, Pastre-Belda and Schahmaneche (n 192) 219; C Pitea, 'Art 8' in S Bartole, P De Sena and V Zagrebelsky (eds), *Commentario breve alla Convenzione europea dei diritti dell'uomo* (Padova, CEDAM, 2012) 309; S Van Drooghenbroeck, *La proportionnalité dans le droit de la Convention européenne des droits de l'homme : prendre l'idée simple au sérieux* (Bruxelles, Presses de l'Université Saint-Louis, 2001) 510.

an insightful example. This case concerned the criminal conviction of a military officer on charges of desertion and insulting the army, as he sent a letter to his commander denouncing abuses against other officers. To balance the public interest to protect the discipline and reputation of the military and the exercise of freedom of expression, the Court considered 'the objective impact on military discipline to have been insignificant'.[196] In fact, the letter had not been disseminated among the public, nor had it contained any insult to the addressee.[197] Accordingly, in *Manoussakis v Greece* the Strasbourg Court held that a criminal conviction for establishing an unauthorised place of worship could not follow the applicant's failure to comply with a legal formality, such as obtaining an authorisation from the competent domestic authority.[198] The enforcement of that offence did not fit the seriousness of the conduct and disproportionately interfered with freedom of religion under Article 9 ECHR.

On some occasions, the Strasbourg Court has complemented its retrospective assessment with a prospective analysis. However, this scheme is scarcely used, and its influence on the Court's reasoning appears limited. For instance, the *Laskey, Jaggard and Brown v The United Kingdom* judgment[199] witnesses the Court's awareness that deterrence constitutes an inherent component of criminal offences. That was one of the rationales behind the criminalisation of violence and bodily injuries during sexual acts, even if consensual. According to the Court, the dissuasiveness inherent in this offence shall be balanced against the individual personal autonomy protected by Article 8 ECHR.[200] Still, the Strasbourg Court considered this assessment as a complement to the retrospective scheme, thereby framing a 'level of harm that should be tolerated by the law in situations where the victim consents'.[201]

The same emphasis on the retrospective secondary scheme characterises the ECtHR proportionality review of the type and amount of criminal penalties. As the Strasbourg Court regularly recalls, 'in assessing the proportionality of the interference, *the nature and severity of the penalties imposed are also factors to be taken into account* (emphasis added)'.[202] This scheme is reproduced in every judgment of the Strasbourg Court dealing with the proportionality of criminal penalties. Its most insightful applications may be traced within the jurisprudence on freedom of expression and assembly under Articles 10 and 11 ECHR. In these two streams of case-law, the Strasbourg Court has developed few but critical limits to domestic authorities' discretion in the sentencing domain. These pertain to the choice between custodial or financial penalties and their amount.

[196] *Grigoriades v Greece* ECHR 1997–VII, para 47.
[197] *ibid.*
[198] *Manoussakis and Others v Greece* ECHR 1996–IV, para 52.
[199] *Laskey, Jaggard and Brown v The United Kingdom* ECHR 1997–I.
[200] *ibid*, para 44.
[201] *ibid.*
[202] Among many, see: *Tammer v Estonia* ECHR 2001–I, para 69; *Skałka v Poland* App No 43425/98 (ECtHR, 27 May 2003), para 38; *Kincses v Hungary* App No 66232/10 (ECtHR, 27 January 2015), para 42; *Krasulya v Russia* App No 12365/03 (ECtHR, 22 February 2007), para 44.

Regarding the type of criminal penalties, the ECtHR regularly holds that prison sanctions 'will be compatible with journalists' freedom of expression as guaranteed by Article 10 of the Convention only in exceptional circumstances, notably where other fundamental rights have been seriously impaired'.[203] The Strasbourg Court has applied this paradigm in cases involving, among others, political speech,[204] defamation,[205] and media-related offences.[206] Therefore, the imposition of custodial measures shall be confined to cases involving particularly harmful wrongdoings, such as to cause a severe prejudice to other human rights. This is the case, for instance, of offences qualifying as hate speech or incitement to violence.[207] The paradigm under analysis unveils a retrospective proportionality scheme, as it poses a minimum threshold of seriousness below which recourse to detention would be disproportionate.

The Strasbourg Court thoroughly applies retrospective proportionality also to review the amount of the penalty imposed. To that aim, the circumstances of the wrongdoing and the offender's culpability shall be considered. The ECtHR jurisprudence on freedom of assembly is particularly instructive in this regard, as it usually features an in-depth examination of the factual circumstances of mass protest offences to assess the proportionality of penalties. The Court exercises strict scrutiny in cases where the protest involves a matter of public interest and results in minor disruptions.[208] The offenders' minor involvement may also indicate that their conduct is not harmful enough to justify a heavy penalty.[209] In defamation cases, the Strasbourg Court has clarified that the seriousness of the wrongdoing may be measured by referring to the offence's detrimental impact on the victim's reputation.[210] Following this reasoning, an insult made in front of many people is more serious than an identical remark made in front of a limited audience.[211] This approach entails an ordinal proportionality argument since it compares two distinct wrongdoings featuring different levels of seriousness.

[203] Among many, see *Cumpănă and Mazăre v Romania* ECHR 2004-XI, para 115.

[204] *Otegi Mondragon v Spain* App No 2034/07 (ECtHR, 15 March 2011), para 59.

[205] In this regard, see: *Mariapori v Finland* App No 37751/07 (ECtHR, 6 July 2011), para 67; *Balaskas v Greece* App No 73087/17 (ECtHR, 5 November 2020), para 61; *Matalas v Greece* App No 1864/18 (ECtHR, 25 March 2021), para 59.

[206] *Sallusti v Italy* App No 22350/13 (ECtHR, 7 March 2019), para 59; *Cumpănă and Mazăre v Romania* ECHR 2004-XI, para 115; *Atamanchuk v Russia* App No 4493/11 (ECtHR, 11 February 2020), para 67; *Mukhin v Russia* App No 3642/10 (ECtHR, 14 December 2021), para 143.

[207] For an analysis of the ECtHR approach towards balancing freedom of expression against public interests in the context of hate speech and incitement to violence, among many, see A Buyse, 'Dangerous Expressions: The ECHR, Violence and Free Speech' (2014) 63 *International and Comparative Law Quarterly* 491.

[208] SJ Summers, *Sentencing and Human Rights* (Oxford, Oxford University Press, 2022) 144.

[209] In this regard, see *Yaroslav Belousov v Russia* App Nos 2653/13 and 60980/14 (ECtHR, 4 October 2016), para 180; *Barabanov v Russia* App Nos 4966/13 and 5550/15 (ECtHR, 30 January 2018), para 75; *Lutskevich v Russia* App Nos 6312/13 and 60902/14 (ECtHR, 15 May 2018), para 101.

[210] Among many, see *Raichinov v Bulgaria* App No 47579/99 (ECtHR, 20 April 2006), para 48.

[211] *ibid.*

Retrospective proportionality of financial penalties deserves closer attention. For the sole reason of their imposition, they interfere with the right to peaceful enjoyment of one's properties under Article 1(1) of the First Additional Protocol to the ECHR.[212] In that context, the Strasbourg Court relies on retrospective proportionality to verify whether the financial penalty under analysis constitutes an 'excessive burden' on the offender. This requirement is satisfied, for instance, when the penalty corresponds to the benefit that the offender obtained from the crime.[213]

Against the central role played by retrospective proportionality, the prospective scheme's influence is more nuanced. The Strasbourg Court relies upon a peculiar declination of prospective proportionality: the 'chilling effect' doctrine.[214] According to this argument, the domestic measure shall not amount to an excessive deterrent, thus discouraging the public from exercising the rights and freedoms secured by the ECHR.[215] In the context of criminal penalties, the Strasbourg Court employed this paradigm mainly to review offences clashing with Article 10 ECHR.[216] Regarding press offences, in the landmark *Cumpănă and Mazăre* ruling the ECtHR recognised that custodial sentences entail an evident chilling effect on the exercise of media freedom of expression, 'a factor which goes to the proportionality, and thus the justification, of the sanctions imposed'.[217] The same paradigm has also been applied to speech offences that do not necessarily involve the exercise of journalistic freedoms, thus affirming that the imposition of custodial penalties 'will inevitably have a chilling effect on public debate'.[218] This finding reinforces and complements the retrospective argument previously analysed, according to which custodial sentences may be justified only insofar as the wrongdoing materialises a serious breach of other fundamental rights. Beyond cases involving penalties in contrast with Article 10 ECHR, the ECtHR has scarcely applied the chilling effect paradigm.[219] That circumstance further

[212] Among many, see *Insanov v Azerbaijan* App No 16133/08 (ECtHR, 14 March 2013), para 180.

[213] *Phillips v The United Kingdom* ECHR 2001–VII, para 53.

[214] Further on this topic, see T Baumbach, 'Chilling Effect as a European Court of Human Rights' Concept in Media Law Cases' (2018) 6 *Bergen Journal of Criminal Law & Criminal Justice* 92.

[215] Among many, see RÓ Fathaigh, 'Article 10 and the Chilling Effect Principle' (2013) *European Human Rights Law Review* 304, 305.

[216] Among many, see *Perinçek v Switzerland* App No 27510/08 (ECtHR, 15 October 2015), paras 127 and 129; *Öztürk v Turkey* ECHR 1999–VI, para 70; *Bodrozic and Vujin v Serbia* App No 38435/05 (ECtHR, 23 June 2009), para 39; *Krasulya v Russia App* No 12365/03 (ECtHR, 22 February 2007), para 44; *Atamanchuk v Russia* App No 4493/11 (ECtHR, 11 February 2020), para 66.

[217] *Cumpănă and Mazăre v Romania* ECHR 2004–XI, para 114. For a scholarly analysis, see: F Viganò, *La proporzionalità della pena: profili di diritto penale e costituzionale* (Torino, Giappichelli, 2021) 94–96; M Oetheimer and A Cardone, 'Art. 10' in S Bartole, P De Sena and V Zagrebelsky (eds), *Commentario breve alla Convenzione europea dei diritti dell'uomo* (Padova, CEDAM, 2012) 409.

[218] *Mariapori v Finland* App No 37751/07 (ECtHR, 6 July 2010), para 68.

[219] Further judgments include the concept of chilling effect in the proportionality assessment. That is the case, for instance, of offences related to the involvement in mass protests: the imposition of heavy penalties may discourage the public at large from participating in political debate (see *Yaroslav Belousov v Russia* App Nos 2653/13 and 60980/14 (ECtHR, 4 October 2016), para 181).

confirms that – differently from the ECJ approach – retrospective proportionality constitutes the heart of the ECtHR scrutiny on criminal penalties.

ii. The ECtHR Review of 'Manifestly Disproportionate' Penalties under Article 3 ECHR

As Chapter 1 showed, the proportionality reasoning is not entirely absent from adjudicating on absolute rights under the European Convention. Indeed, the *proportionnalité-interprétation* technique allows the Strasbourg Court to delimit the scope of the right invoked in a given case.[220] In criminal law, this issue came to the fore only under the prohibition of inhuman and degrading treatments or punishments under Article 3 ECHR.[221] That provision designs an abstract category of punishments which shall be prohibited in the light of the suffering and humiliation they cause. The Court shall thus verify whether the criminal measure at stake attains a level of severity which goes 'beyond that inevitable element of suffering or humiliation connected with a given form of legitimate treatment or punishment'.[222]

The Strasbourg Court has translated this abstract threshold into a standard for judicial review in two distinct streams of cases. On the one hand, Article 3 ECHR has been invoked to contest the legitimacy of capital, corporal and life sentences. However, this case-law does not yield any proportionality assessment. Firstly, the Strasbourg Court recognised the illegitimacy of death sentences by interpreting the Convention in the light of the two Protocols on the abolition of the death penalty entered into force, respectively, in 1985 and 2003.[223] Indeed, the ECtHR held that this development amounts to an implicit amendment of the permission for death sentences enshrined in Article 2(1) ECHR.[224] Secondly, the ECtHR relied on an evolutionary interpretation of the Convention to hold corporal punishments as

[220] See Section III(C)(i) of Chapter 1.

[221] While Art 5 ECHR provides several grounds for assessing the legitimacy of custodial measures, the Strasbourg Court has never translated them into proportionality arguments. Under Art 5 ECHR, 'the lawfulness of punishment is considered to be guaranteed by the lawfulness of the judgment of the sentencing court' (Summers (n 208) 123).

[222] Among many, see *A v The United Kingdom* ECHR 1998–VI, para 127.

[223] Protocol No 6 to the Convention for the Protection of Human Rights and Fundamental Freedoms Concerning the Abolition of the Death Penalty [1983] CETS No 114; Protocol No 13 to the Convention for the Protection of Human Rights and Fundamental Freedoms, Concerning the Abolition of the Death Penalty in All Circumstances [2002] CETS No 187. In literature, see: A Mowbray, 'The European Convention on Human Rights: The Abolition of Capital Punishment and Recent Cases' (2002) 2 *Human Rights Law Review* 311.

[224] *Al-Saadoon and Mufdhi v The United Kingdom* App No 61498/08 (ECtHR, 2 March 2010), para 120. In literature, see F Vecchio, *L'Europa e la pena di morte: comparazione giuridica e strategie abolizioniste* (Milano, CEDAM-Wolters Kluwer, 2017) 274. This approach has been criticised in literature as in contrast with the rules of international law on the application of successive treaties relating to the same subject matter (see, in particular, Art 30(3) of the Vienna Convention on the Law of Treaties [1969] UNTS No 1155). In particular, Citroni and Scovazzi contended that the ECtHR could have better relied upon Art 62 of the cited Convention, thereby affirming that the provision at issue has been terminated by reason of a fundamental change of circumstances (G Citroni and T Scovazzi, *Corso di diritto internazionale. Parte III – La tutela internazionale dei diritti umani*, 3rd edn (Milano, Giuffrè, 2013) 226).

prohibited under Article 3 ECHR. As recognised in *Tyrer v The United Kingdom*,[225] current standards in Contracting Parties' sanctioning policies imply that corporal punishments overstep the minimum severity required to qualify as 'degrading punishment'.[226] Once again, no balancing between conflicting interests was exercised by the Court.[227] Finally, in *Kafkaris v Cyprus*[228] and *Vinter and Others v The United Kingdom*[229] the Strasbourg Court held that life sentences not affording any prospect of future release are contrary to Article 3 ECHR. However, this conclusion is not the consequence of a proportionality assessment. As underlined by Viganò, the necessity of a review of life sentences is a direct consequence of the need to enhance the rehabilitation purposes of criminal penalties.[230]

On the other hand, the Strasbourg Court has advanced an inherently retrospective proportionality test for assessing whether a given penalty is 'grossly disproportionate', thereby violating Article 3 ECHR. This approach dates back to the practice of the European Commission of Human Rights. In principle, 'the nature of any offence allegedly committed by the applicant is [...] irrelevant for the purposes of Article 3'.[231] At the same time, some decisions issued by the CoE Commission affirmed that exceptionally harsh penalties may be incompatible with Article 3 ECHR if imposed for minor offences.[232] This finding has been confirmed and refined by the ECtHR jurisprudence. In particular, in *Harkins and Edwards v The United Kingdom* the Court affirmed that 'while, in principle, matters of appropriate sentencing largely fall outside the scope of Convention [...], a *grossly disproportionate sentence* could amount to ill-treatment contrary to Article 3 (emphasis added)'.[233]

[225] *Tyrer v The United Kingdom* Series A No 26 (1978), para 31.

[226] *ibid*, para 35. In fact, as the Court further stressed, '[the] very nature of judicial corporal punishment is that it involves one human being inflicting physical violence on another human being. Furthermore, it is institutionalised violence that is in the present case violence permitted by the law, ordered by the judicial authorities of the State and carried out by the police authorities of the State' (*ibid*, para 33).

[227] Some authors have sought to frame the Court's reasoning on capital and corporal punishments in proportionality terms (in particular, see Summers (n 208) 99, 103–104). However, the mere fact that an argument may potentially be translated in proportionality terms does not mean that the Court employed this legal technique.

[228] *Kafkaris v Cyprus* App No 21906/04 (ECtHR, 12 February 2008).

[229] *Vinter and Others v The United Kingdom* App Nos 66069/09, 130/10 and 3896/10 (ECtHR, 9 July 2013).

[230] Viganò (n 217) 93.

[231] Among many, see: *Al-Saadoon and Mufdhi v The United Kingdom* App No 61498/08 (ECtHR, 2 March 2010), para 122; *Saadi v Italy* App No 37201/06 (ECtHR, 28 February 2008), para 127.

[232] *X v Germany* (dec) App No 7057/75 (1976); *X v The United Kingdom* (dec) App No 5871/72 (1974). For an analysis of these decisions, see Summers (n 208) 110–111.

[233] *Harkins and Edwards v The United Kingdom* App Nos 9146/07 and 32650/07 (ECtHR, 17 January 2012), para 133. This test has been also evocated by the Court in *Vinter and Others v The United Kingdom*: 'while, in principle, matters of appropriate sentencing largely fall outside the scope of Convention [...], a grossly disproportionate sentence could amount to ill-treatment contrary to Article 3 at the moment of its imposition' (*Vinter and Others v The United Kingdom* App Nos 66069/09, 130/10 and 3896/10 (ECtHR, 9 July 2013), para 103).

On that basis, the Strasbourg Court set a highly demanding threshold for a penalty to qualify as inhuman or degrading, thus meeting the minimum level of severity required to fall under Article 3 ECHR. The disproportionate nature shall be manifest, as it may occur only in rare and unique circumstances.[234] That was not the case in *Harkins and Edwards v The United Kingdom*, even if the applicants faced a life sentence without parole. While that penalty 'is much more likely to be grossly disproportionate than any of the other types of life sentence',[235] life without parole does not amount to a disproportionate criminal sanction *per se*. Following this case, the 'grossly disproportionate' test has been applied in a couple of subsequent judgments.[236] However, in no case the Strasbourg Court found a penalty to be grossly disproportionate under Article 3 ECHR.[237]

As result, the relevant case-law offers very few indications on how the 'grossly disproportionate' paradigm shall be interpreted. As a retrospective assessment, it entails a relationship of commensurability between the sanction and a parameter of reference. The second term of this proportionality relationship is 'the gravity of the crime committed'.[238] The latter shall be assessed by reference not only to the circumstances of the conduct but also to the offender's personal characteristics. For instance, in *Harkins and Edwards v The United Kingdom* the Strasbourg Court affirmed that a life without parole sentence would violate Article 3 ECHR if imposed for a crime 'in respect of which there was no real culpability on the part of the defendant'.[239]

The absence of a coherent sentencing practice among Contracting Parties can explain the Court's reluctance to hold a domestic penalty as grossly disproportionate. The ECtHR cannot resort to ordinal proportionality techniques, as 'there would often be legitimate and reasonable differences between States as to the length of sentences which were imposed, even for similar offences'.[240] The only option available is to conduct a cardinal retrospective proportionality assessment to verify whether the relevant penalty is undeserved in absolute terms. However, the ECtHR seems willing to censure under Article 3 ECHR only those penalties whose disproportionate nature is manifestly and uncontestably evident in the light

[234] *Harkins and Edwards v The United Kingdom* App Nos 9146/07 and 32650/07 (ECtHR, 17 January 2012), para 133.

[235] *ibid*, para 138.

[236] In particular, see: *Aswat v The United Kingdom* App No 17299/12 (ECtHR, 16 April 2014), para 58; *Babar Ahmad and Others v The United Kingdom* App Nos 24027/07, 11949/08, 36742/08, 66911/09 and 67354/09 (ECtHR, 10 April 2012), paras 235–242.

[237] Summers (n 208) 121.

[238] *Soering v The United Kingdom* (1989) Series A No 161, para 104; *Öcalan v Turkey* ECHR 2005-IV, para 168.

[239] *Harkins and Edwards v The United Kingdom* App Nos 9146/07 and 32650/07 (ECtHR, 17 January 2012), para 139. This finding fits the retributive theory underlying retrospective proportionality: offenders shall be treated as moral agents, thereby imposing penalties commensurate to their culpability (N Mavronicola, 'Crime, Punishment and Article 3 ECHR: Puzzles and Prospects of Applying an Absolute Right in a Penal Context' (2015) 15 *Human Rights Law Review* 721, 733).

[240] *Willcox and Hurford v The United Kingdom* App Nos 43759/10 and 43771/12 (ECtHR, 8 January 2013), para 74.

of the circumstances of the case. Only a self-evident disproportion may overstep the margin of appreciation domestic authorities enjoy in sanctioning matters, thus allowing judicial intervention by the Strasbourg Court.

V. Proportionality of Non-Criminal Penalties: The Spill-Over Effect of the Hybrid Principle

This book focuses exclusively on offences and penalties which are criminal in nature, defined by the threefold criteria advanced by the Strasbourg Court in *Engel* and adopted by the ECJ.[241] While approaching the conclusion of this analysis, a glimpse at the proportionality of non-criminal sanctioning measures provides insights into the reach of the hybrid principle in EU law. Especially when confronted with financial penalties, the ECJ does not always assess whether they entail genuinely punitive features or their severity is enough to qualify as criminal under the *Engel* criteria. Still, the Luxembourg Court usually resorts to prospective and retrospective paradigms, thus suggesting that – at least for what concerns reviewing the type and amount of sanctions – the hybrid EU and criminal principle of proportionality may have a spill-over to non-criminal sanctions.

The recent ECJ ruling in *Agenţia Naţională de Integritate* confirms this finding.[242] The case stems from a preliminary ruling on the interpretation of Commission Decision 2006/928/EC on a Mechanism for Cooperation and Verification of Progress in Romania in Judicial Reforms and the Fight Against Corruption in the light, in particular, of Article 49(3) of the Charter.[243] In this respect, the Romanian legislation imposes an additional sanction for individuals holding elective public offices who are found in situations of conflict of interests, consisting of a three-year foreclosure from holding similar positions. Among the questions raised, the referring court sought a proportionality review of that measure under Article 49(3) of the Charter, insofar as the penalty in question qualifies as criminal. On that point, the Court concluded in the negative;[244] therefore, Article 49(3) of the Charter is not applicable.

However, 'in so far as it implements EU law, […] the national legislation at issue in the main proceedings must, in any event, observe the principle of proportionality, as a general principle of EU law'.[245] On those grounds – and against the inapplicability of Article 49(3) of the Charter – the Court still held that 'the severity of the penalty must be commensurate with the seriousness of the breach which

[241] See Section III of the Introduction to this book.

[242] Case C-40/21 *Agenţia Naţională de Integritate* ECLI:EU:C:2023:367.

[243] Commission Decision 2006/928/EC Establishing a Mechanism for Cooperation and Verification of Progress in Romania to Address Specific Benchmarks in the Areas of Judicial Reform and the Fight Against Corruption [2006] OJ L354/56.

[244] Case C-40/21 *Agenţia Naţională de Integritate* ECLI:EU:C:2023:367, para 44.

[245] *ibid*, para 48.

it is intended to suppress'.[246] It thus appears that the non-criminal nature of the sanction at issue did not prevent the ECJ from adhering to the hybrid proportionality assessment derived from the intersection between EU and criminal law paradigms. The ECJ thus concluded that a fixed-term exclusion from holding public offices in principle is not disproportionate insofar as that length is not excessive vis-à-vis the seriousness of the wrongdoing committed *in concreto*. It is for the referring Court to verify that aspect, a conclusion in line with the Court of Justice's self-restraint approach to retrospective proportionality.[247]

This ruling confirms that prospective and retrospective proportionality may extend beyond the criminal law domain in the framework of the general principle of proportionality.[248] This finding is remarkable, as it shows that the hybrid proportionality of criminal offences and penalties has the potential to hybridise the general principle of proportionality concerning non-criminal sanctions. Therefore, an osmotic interaction between the hybrid and general principles of proportionality can be framed. The former emerged by specification from the general principle but, in turn, can influence the latter's theorisation outside the criminal law domain.

The remedies against violations of the principle of proportionality of criminal penalties or the general proportionality requirement of non-criminal sanctions appear different. The measure at issue in *Agenţia Naţională de Integritate* was meant to implement EU law. Indeed, effective and dissuasive penalties against conflict of interests are required by Commission Decision 2006/928/EC. However, contrary to the solution proposed by Advocate General Emiliou,[249] the ECJ did not recall the remedy of disapplication as advanced in *Bezirkshauptmannschaft Hartberg-Fürstenfeld (Effet direct)* about the *Greek Maize* paradigm.[250] The ECJ only referred to the referring court's duty to interpret domestic provisions consistently with EU law.[251]

Two critical remarks may be addressed to the ECJ's stance. From a practical viewpoint, the duty of consistent interpretation may prove ineffective in circumstances such as those in the case at issue. Indeed, the three-year exclusion from elective public offices amounts to a fixed penalty, which leaves a very narrow scope for hermeneutic exercises by the referring court. From a theoretical viewpoint, it may be questioned whether the choice not to reiterate the direct effect of the proportionality requirement for non-criminal sanctions is justified by solid arguments.

[246] *ibid*, para 51.
[247] *ibid*, para 69.
[248] Palladino (n 81) 150.
[249] Case C-40/21 *Agenţia Naţională de Integritate*, Opinion of AG Emiliou, ECLI:EU:C:2022:873.
[250] Case C-205/20 *Bezirkshauptmannschaft Hartberg-Fürstenfeld (Effet direct)* ECLI:EU:C:2022:168.
[251] Case C-40/21 *Agenţia Naţională de Integritate* ECLI:EU:C:2023:367, para 70–71. However, there are different readings in the literature. According to Zemskova, the Court's exclusive focus on the duty of consistent interpretation does not imply ruling out the possibility of invoking the direct effect of the principle of proportionality (A Zemskova, 'Op-Ed: C-40/21 Agenţia Naţională de Integritate: Another Chapter in an Ongoing Battle Against Corruption in the Member States?' (2023) *EU Law Live*).

The conclusions of Advocate General Emiliou in that case, which focused extensively on the legacy of the *Bezirkshauptmannschaft Hartberg-Fürstenfeld (Effet direct)* ruling and its implications for *Agenţia Naţională de Integritate*, expressly invited the ECJ to indicate disapplication as the appropriate remedy if the sanction at issue is disproportionate *in concreto*.[252] This position is commendable: provided that the hybridisation of general proportionality leads to relying on the hybrid principle's schemes as interpreted in *Bezirkshauptmannschaft Hartberg-Fürstenfeld (Effet direct)*, one may argue that the requirements for direct effect are satisfied even for the proportionality of non-criminal sanctions. On those grounds, a clear, precise and unconditional prohibition on imposing disproportionate penalties would emerge even in this domain. Still, the Court's more reticent position can be read as evidence that the hybridisation of the general principle is incomplete: a dividing line between the proportionality of criminal offences and penalties and general proportionality applied to non-criminal sanctions remains in place.

VI. The Uneasy Place of the Proportionality of Penalties in EU Judicial Cooperation in Criminal Matters

In addition to non-criminal penalties, the hybrid principle has a further potential spillover in EU judicial cooperation in criminal matters. Most notably, the issue of proportionality of criminal penalties has emerged concerning the EAW system established by Framework Decision 2002/584/JHA.[253] The European Arrest Warrant is a mechanism of streamlined surrender of individuals for prosecution or execution of custodial sentences which replaced extradition between the Member States. The system is grounded on the principle of mutual recognition of national judicial decisions, which the 1999 Tampere European Council Conclusions framed as 'the cornerstone of judicial cooperation […] within the Union'.[254] Mutual recognition has been subject to extensive scholarly analysis[255]

[252] Case C-40/21 *Agenţia Naţională de Integritate*, Opinion of AG Emiliou, ECLI:EU:C:2022:873, paras 48–49.

[253] Council Framework Decision 2002/584/JHA on the European Arrest Warrant and the Surrender Procedures between Member States [2002] OJ L190/1.

[254] Tampere European Council – Presidency Conclusions, para 33. The Tampere conclusions mark the transposition of mutual recognition as framed by the ECJ in the context of internal market regulation (Case 120/78 *Rewe v Bundesmonopolverwaltung für Branntwein* ECLI:EU:C:1979:42, para 8 of the Grounds of judgment) to the Third Pillar. On this point, see A Damato, 'L'incidenza sul terzo pilastro dell'applicazione di principi e regole di diritto comunitario' in *Studi in onore di Vincenzo Starace*, vol 2 (Napoli, Editoriale Scientifica, 2008) 1010–1011.

[255] Among many, see C Janssens, *The Principle of Mutual Recognition in EU Law* (Oxford, Oxford University Press, 2013); JW Ouwerkerk, *Quid pro Quo? A Comparative Law Perspecitve on the Mutual Recognition of Judicial Decisions in Criminal Matters* (Cambridge, Intersentia, 2011); C Amalfitano, *Conflitti di giurisdizione e riconoscimento delle decisioni penali nell'Unione europea* (Milano, Giuffrè, 2006) 331–337; A Damato, 'La cooperazione giudiziaria in materia penale' in G Tesauro, *Manuale di Diritto dell'Unione europea*, vol 2 (P De Pasquale and F Ferraro eds, Napoli, Editoriale Scientifica, 2021) 342.

and an in-depth examination of that principle would exceed the scope of this book. Only its key features shall be recalled here to frame the peculiar nature of the EAW system, which is 'the first concrete measure in the field of criminal law implementing the principle of mutual recognition'.[256]

The latter entails the imperative execution of judicial decisions imposing custodial measures in all the Member States,[257] in principle with the same effects as national ones.[258] That obligation hinges upon the principle of mutual trust, which constitutes the necessary premise for mutual recognition. As codified by the ECJ in Opinion 2/13, mutual trust implies a presumption that 'each Member State shares with all the other Member States, and recognises that they share with it, a set of common values on which the EU is founded, as stated in Article 2 TEU'.[259] On that basis, the principle of mutual trust requires all domestic authorities, 'save in exceptional circumstances, to consider all the other Member States to be complying with EU law and particularly with the fundamental rights recognised by EU law'.[260] Thus construed, mutual trust presupposes that all Member States share a common legal culture, fostered and secured by EU law itself.[261] That finding – together with the presumption that mutual trust entails – justifies swift cooperation between Member States' authorities within the AFSJ by recognising and executing foreign judicial decisions.[262]

Because of the operation of mutual recognition and mutual trust, the execution of foreign EAWs shall be dealt with as a matter of urgency[263] through a mechanism involving judicial authorities only,[264] thus avoiding any room for political discretion in deciding over surrender. Moreover, execution is tendentially automatic while subject to certain minimum formalities.[265] On the one hand, mutual recognition in the EAW system entails partially overcoming some traditional bars to extradition, such as the dual criminality requirement,[266] the political exception

[256] Council Framework Decision 2002/584/JHA on the European Arrest Warrant and the Surrender Procedures between Member States [2002] OJ L190/1, recital 6.

[257] Ouwerkerk (n 255) 175–184.

[258] Janssens (n 255) 175–183.

[259] Opinion 2/13 *Adhésion de l'Union à la CEDH* ECLI:EU:C:2014:2454, para 168.

[260] *ibid*, para 191.

[261] R Sicurella, 'Fostering a European Criminal Law Culture: In Trust We Trust' (2018) 9 *New Journal of European Criminal Law* 308, 311.

[262] For further analysis on the principle of mutual trust, see A Willems, *The Principle of Mutual Trust in EU Criminal Law* (Oxford, Hart Publishing, 2021); M Schwarz, 'Let's Talk about Trust, Baby! Theorizing Trust and Mutual Recognition in the EU's Area of Freedom, Security and Justice' (2018) 24 *European Law Journal* 124.

[263] S Montaldo, 'On a Collision Course! Mutual Recognition, Mutual Trust and the Protection of Fundamental Rights in the Recent Case-Law of the Court of Justice' (2016) 1 *European Papers* 965, 968.

[264] Janssens (n 255) 188.

[265] Mitsilegas (n 8) 127.

[266] Dual criminality is not a precondition for execution of warrants provided that the relevant offence as framed in the issuing Member State's legal order falls within the list provided for in Art 2(2) of Framework Decision 2002/584/JHA.

and the prohibition to surrender nationals.[267] On the other hand, surrender can be halted only on the basis of an exhaustive list of compulsory[268] or facultative[269] grounds for refusal, which do not include proportionality considerations.

The irrelevance of the principle of proportionality for eventually refusing the execution of arrest warrants sparked extensive scholarly analysis over the last two decades.[270] This issue has emerged in a twofold dimension, fuelling debate on whether surrender may be halted for the alleged disproportion affecting the recourse to the EAW mechanism or the severity of the penalty for which the warrant has been issued.[271]

The first profile unveils a longstanding issue for EU judicial cooperation in criminal matters. The absence of a proportionality check at the executing stage of the surrender procedure is a consequence of the principle of mutual recognition, which prevents domestic authorities from questioning the warrant's justification as assessed by the issuing court. On that basis, the fact that other judicial cooperation instruments based on mutual recognition do not foresee similar proportionality assessments[272] is no surprise. The only condition in this regard is provided by Article 2(1) of Framework Decision 2002/584/JHA: warrants may be issued only for facts which are punishable in the issuing Member State's legal order for a maximum term of imprisonment of at least twelve months or, should the sentence be imposed, for custodial penalties of at least four months. These penalty thresholds are particularly low and fail to ensure that recourse to the EAW is proportionate.[273] Indeed, surrender has sometimes been requested for petty or trivial offences. Well renowned in the EAW practice is the case of the Polish surrender request for the

[267] In that circumstance, under Art 4(6) of Framework Decision 2002/584/JHA Member States may provide for the possibility of nationals and residents serving the sentence in the executing Member States or, in case of EAWs issued for prosecution, being sent back to the latter State to serve the penalty eventually imposed.

[268] Art 3 of Framework Decision 2002/584/JHA.

[269] Art 4 of Framework Decision 2002/584/JHA.

[270] For some non-exhaustive references, see: E Xanthopoulou, 'The Quest for Proportionality for the European Arrest Warrant: Fundamental Rights Protection in a Mutual Recognition Environment' (2015) 6 *New Journal of European Criminal Law* 32; D Helenius, 'Mutual Recognition in Criminal Matters and the Principle of Proportionality: Effective Proportionality or Proportionate Effectiveness?' (2014) 3 *New Journal of European Criminal Law* 349; T Ostropolski, 'The Principle of Proportionality Under the European Arrest Warrant – With an Excursus on Poland' (2014) 5 *New Journal of European Criminal Law* 167; L Marin, 'Effective and Legitimate?' Learning from the Lessons of 10 Years of Practice with the European Arrest Warrant' (2014) 5 *New Journal of European Criminal Law* 327, in particular 335–339.

[271] On that dichotomy, see E Pistoia, 'Proportionality of Criminal Penalties and EU Judicial Cooperation' in L Grossio, S Montaldo and V Mitsilegas (eds), *Proportionality of Criminal Penalties in EU Law* (Oxford, Hart Publishing, 2025) 168.

[272] On this point, see A Rosanò, 'The EU-UK Extradition Arrangement and the Principle of Proportionality: Some Hints from the Practice of EU Institutions and Italian and UK Legislation and Case-law on the EAW' in L Grossio, S Montaldo and V Mitsilegas (eds), *Proportionality of Criminal Penalties in EU Law* (Oxford, Hart Publishing, 2025) 186.

[273] Among many, see E Xanthopoulou, *Fundamental Rights and Mutual Trust in the Area of Freedom, Security and Justice: A Role for Proportionality?* (Oxford, Hart Publishing, 2020) 117–118; Pistoia (n 271) 171.

theft of piglets.[274] These cases were ultimately liable to undermine substantive trust between the EU Member States,[275] an essential element for reinforcing the operation of mutual trust in the AFSJ.[276] Most notably, in 2014 the UK unilaterally decided to amend the Extradition Act 2003 in the part transposing the EAW Framework Decision to introduce a proportionality check on surrender requests as a precondition for their execution.[277]

Against this backdrop, the Council[278] and Commission[279] clarified that the requesting judicial authority shall always check whether recourse to surrender under the EAW constitutes a proportionate option before issuing the warrant. As affirmed by the latest edition of the EAW Handbook, several factors shall be considered. These include '(a) the seriousness of the offence (for example, the harm or danger it has caused); (b) the likely penalty imposed if the person is found guilty of the alleged offence (for example, whether it would be a custodial sentence); (c) the likelihood of detention of the person in the issuing Member State after surrender; (d) the interests of the victims of the offence'.[280] Moreover, the issuing judicial authority shall consider whether recourse to less coercive EU judicial cooperation instruments would be sufficient in the case at hand.[281]

The need for checking compliance with the principle of proportionality when issuing an EAW has been further confirmed by the ECJ case-law.[282] As recently underlined in literature, the relevant proportionality test appears to cover both the necessity step – that is, the availability of alternative measures – and proportionality *stricto sensu*, as it involves a comprehensive assessment of the worthiness of surrender in the light of different elements.[283] However, as argued by Pistoia, this assessment is not a manifestation of the principle of proportionality of criminal penalties. Indeed, the object of proportionality scrutiny is the recourse to

[274] Ostropolski (n 270) 174; Xanthopoulou (n 273) 116.

[275] Report from the Commission to the European Parliament and the Council on the Implementation since 2007 of the Council Framework Decision of 13 June 2002 on the European Arrest Warrant and the Surrender Procedures Between Member States COM(2011) 175 final – SEC(2011) 430 final, 7.

[276] Sicurella (n 261).

[277] Section 21A(1)(b) of Extradition Act 2003 as amended by Section 157 of Anti-Social Behaviour, Crime and Policing Act 2014. For an analysis of the subsequent UK practice in surrender, see Rosanò (n 272).

[278] Council, Revised Version of the European Handbook on How to Issue a European Arrest Warrant, 17195/1/10 REV 1, 14.

[279] See the last revision of the Handbook, published in the Commission Notice – Handbook on How to Issue and Execute a European Arrest Warrant – C/2023/7782, 18.

[280] *ibid.*

[281] *ibid.*

[282] Joined Cases C-508/18 and C-82/19 PPU *OG and PI* ECLI:EU:C:2019:456, paras 71, 75; Case C-414/20 PPU *MM* ECLI:EU:C:2021:4, paras 65-66. In other rulings, the ECJ relied on the principle of proportionality to interpret the provisions of Framework Decision 2002/584/JHA on the duration of custody while awaiting surrender (Case C-237/15 PPU *Lanigan* ECLI:EU:C:2015:474, paras 57–58; Case C-640/15 *Vilkas* ECLI:EU:C:2017:34, para 43) as well as on the calculation of the penalty to be served in case of previous coercive measures (Case C-294/16 *JZ* ECLI:EU:C:2016:610, para 42). For deeper analysis, see Rosanò (n 272).

[283] Pistoia (n 271) 173.

surrender under the EAW, and surrender does not amount to a form of sanction.[284] In that regard, the retrospective worthiness of sentences only amounts to one of the elements to be considered within the proportionality assessment, together with the seriousness of the offence for which they are (or they will be) imposed.

The question of potential proportionality checks on criminal penalties as a precondition for surrender solicits different considerations and constitutes the second dimension of the debate under analysis. However, this topic has received far less attention in legal scholarship. Looking at the judicial practice, the question has been earlier mooted by Advocate General Sharpston in *Radu*, as her Opinion hypothetically (and only incidentally) considered whether Article 49(3) of the Charter may entail an implicit ground for refusing the execution of the EAW in case of disproportionate sentences.[285] The same issue emerged in a couple of domestic cases concerning the execution of EAWs; among them, the 2010 ruling of the Higher Regional Court of Stuttgart (Germany) is the most notable example. In that case, the domestic court carried out a proportionality scrutiny of the penalty to be served by taking corresponding German penalty scales as a benchmark.[286]

Surprisingly, the Stuttgart court did not refer the question to the ECJ for a preliminary ruling. Years later, in *Procureur général près la cour d'appel d'Angers* the Court of Justice had been finally provided with the occasion to rule on a similar issue.[287] The case arose from the verification of dual criminality by the French *Cour de cassation* while deciding on the surrender of KL, convicted in Italy to a cumulative sentence of 12 years and 6 months for four offences committed on the occasion of the tragic protests against the 2001 G8 summit. These offences do not fall under the list of crimes for which the double criminality requirement is waived.[288] Concerning the offence of 'devastation and looting', the executing authority considered that only some of the acts for which KL has been convicted may meet the condition of double criminality. Therefore, the *Cour de cassation* sought to ascertain whether the provisions of Framework Decision 2002/584/JHA read in the light of Article 49(3) of the Charter may allow refusal of surrender on the grounds of a potential disproportion of the overall penalty vis-à-vis the seriousness of the wrongdoing, if only those acts meeting the double criminality requirement are considered in that proportionality assessment.[289]

[284] *ibid*, 169.

[285] Case C-396/11 *Radu*, Opinion of AG Sharpston, ECLI:EU:C:2012:648, para 103. In literature, see Mitsilegas (n 8) 144; M Ramat, 'The Court of Justice and the Assessment of Double Criminality Under the European Arrest Warrant Framework Decision: KL' (2022) 7 *European Papers* 993, 1002.

[286] For an analysis, among many, see J Vogel, 'Introduction to the Ruling of the Higher Regional Court of Stuttgart of 25 February 2010 – The Proportionality of a European Arrest Warrant' (2010) 1 *New Journal of European Criminal Law* 145.

[287] Case C-168/21 *Procureur général près la cour d'appel d'Angers* ECLI:EU:C:2022:558. For a comprehensive analysis of the ruling, see Ramat (n 285); G Bondi, 'Double Criminality and the European Arrest Warrant: Current Trends and Future Developments in Light of the KL Case' (2024) 15 *New Journal of European Criminal Law* 99.

[288] Art 2(2) of Framework Decision 2002/584/JHA.

[289] Case C-168/21 *Procureur général près la cour d'appel d'Angers* ECLI:EU:C:2022:558, para 25.

The ECJ replicated the same interpretation of the Framework Decision advanced for the proportionate use of the EAW. By reiterating that 'observance of the rights of the person whose surrender is sought falls primarily within the responsibility of the issuing Member State',[290] the Court concluded that the proportionality of criminal penalties cannot be assessed at the executing stage of the procedure. Only the issuing authority can undergo that verification as part of the checks it shall perform before requesting surrender.[291]

On this point, it has been argued that assigning the verification of the proportionality of the sentence to the issuing authority may be unsatisfactory. Indeed, a scenario where the issuing authority puts into question the worthiness of a final sentence issued by a fellow court within the same judicial system is hardly conceivable.[292] Therefore, the executing authority would be in a better position than the issuing one for assessing the proportionality of the criminal penalty for which surrender is sought. While the latter contention is convincing, an overruling of *Procureur général près la cour d'appel d'Angers* is quite unlikely. The ECJ jurisprudence on this point is monolithic: circumstances which do not amount to a ground for refusal of execution under Framework Decision 2002/584/JHA cannot be invoked by the executing authority for halting surrender. Just one exception is provided in this regard. Should the issuing Member State be affected by systemic or generalised deficiencies in the protection of a fundamental right, thus entailing that there are substantial grounds for believing that, in case of surrender, the individual sought will be subject to a real risk of a similar violation, that circumstance may exceptionally halt the execution of the warrant. Following the landmark *Aranyosi and Căldăraru* judgment[293] and subsequent case-law,[294] that double condition gives rise to exceptional circumstances capable of rebutting the mutual trust presumption.[295] This is the only assessment potentially leading to the refusal to execute the arrest warrant if no ground codified in the Framework Decision applies.[296]

[290] *ibid*, para 65.

[291] *ibid*, para 68.

[292] Pistoia (n 271) 181–182.

[293] Joined Cases C-404/15 e C-659/15 PPU *Aranyosi and Căldăraru* ECLI:EU:C:2016:198.

[294] On the potential violation of Art 4 of the Charter as a result of surrender, see also Case C-220/18 PPU *Generalstaatsanwaltschaft (Conditions of detention in Hungary)* ECLI:EU:C:2018:589; Case C-128/18 *Dorobantu* ECLI:EU:C:2019:857. On the risks of violation of the right secured by Art 47 of the Charter, see Case C-216/18 PPU *Minister for Justice and Equality (Deficiencies in the system of justice)* ECLI:EU:C:2018:586; Joined Cases C-354/20 PPU and C-412/20 PPU *Openbaar Ministerie (Independence of the issuing judicial authority)* ECLI:EU:C:2020:1033; Joined Cases C-562/21 PPU and C-563/21 PPU *Openbaar Ministerie (Tribunal Established by Law in the Issuing Member State)* ECLI:EU:C:2022:100; Case C-480/21 *Minister for Justice and Equality (Tribunal établi par la loi dans l'État membre d'émission – II)* ECLI:EU:C:2022:592. Concerning risks of violation of the right to private and family life (Art 7 of the Charter), as well as of the best interest of the child (Art 24 of the Charter), see Case C-261/22 *GN (Motif de refus fondé sur l'intérêt supérieur de l'enfant)* ECLI:EU:C:2023:1017.

[295] On the wide-ranging scholarly debate on this topic, see n 62 of Chapter 1.

[296] On this point, see L Grossio and M Rosi, 'The Ultimate (but Not the Only) Remedy for Securing Fundamental Rights in the EAW System? Some Reflections on Puig Gordi and E. D. L.' (2023) 8 *European Papers* 547, 558.

As argued by Pistoia, the *Aranyosi and Căldăraru* test may apply to violations of the right not to be subject to disproportionate criminal penalties as secured by Article 49(3) of the Charter. In particular, the existence of 'systemic or generalised' deficiencies concerning the proportionality of criminal sanctions may be deduced from substantive criminal law provisions of the issuing Member State. Should the latter provide for draconian penalties for minor offences, that circumstance would allow the executing judicial authority to perform the second step of the test, thus verifying whether that deficiency extends to the case at hand.[297] Arguably, the assessment of 'systemic or generalised' deficiencies should be limited to the category of offences of relevance for the case at issue. This finding ultimately eases the executing court's task, since it would not be required to undergo an overall evaluation of the level of penalties provided by the issuing Member State's criminal system as a whole.

This argument is commendable and may constitute a valuable way out from the issues deriving from a proportionality check on penalties performed exclusively by the issuing judicial authority. However, to what extent can the executing court scrutinise the proportionality of criminal penalties as provided by the legal order of the Member State requesting surrender? The answer is far from evident since that review may clash with the obligations flowing from mutual trust. In principle, the executing authority shall presume that the issuing Member State's criminal law system complies with Article 49(3) of the Charter, save for exceptional circumstances. At the same time, the Strasbourg Court's case-law may provide a way out from the limits derived from the principle of mutual trust. Should the disproportionate nature of the criminal law provisions at issue already be ascertained by the ECtHR, the executing judicial authority may rely on this information in the context of the first step of the *Aranyosi and Căldăraru* test.[298]

However, since refusal of surrender takes place only on an exceptional basis,[299] the executing authority would be prevented from conducting an in-depth proportionality review. Therefore, only a manifest disproportion of penalties may amount to exceptional circumstances capable of rebutting the mutual trust presumption. In that assessment, domestic courts may well rely on the guidance provided by the ECJ concerning sanctioning schemes which are evidently disproportionate from a retrospective viewpoint. For instance, a particularly high minimum penalty for a broadly defined offence covering petty conduct may be tackled in this context. Conversely, prospective proportionality should arguably be cautiously employed under the *Aranyosi and Căldăraru* test. Indeed, assessing whether the penalty exceeds the

[297] Pistoia (n 271) 178.

[298] As recognised by the ECJ itself in Joined Cases C-404/15 e C-659/15 PPU *Aranyosi and Căldăraru* ECLI:EU:C:2016:198, para 89.

[299] Among many, see Case C-216/18 PPU *Minister for Justice and Equality (Deficiencies in the system of justice)* ECLI:EU:C:2018:586, para 59; Case C-128/18 *Dorobantu* ECLI:EU:C:2019:857, para 83; Joined Cases C-562/21 PPU and C-563/21 PPU *Openbaar Ministerie (Tribunal established by law in the issuing Member State)* ECLI:EU:C:2022:100, para 46; Case C-158/21 *Puig Gordi and Others* ECLI:EU:C:2023:57, paras 72, 74.

level of dissuasiveness required may pave the way to a far more profound assessment of the issuing Member State's criminal system, in contrast with the principle of mutual trust. Only a self-restraint approach by executing judicial authorities may allow for a proportionality check of the severity of the sentence within the *Aranyosi and Căldăraru* test without neglecting the principles of mutual recognition and mutual trust, which lie at the heart of EU judicial cooperation in criminal matters.

VII. Concluding Remarks: A Systematisation of the ECJ Approach in the Proportionality Review of Domestic Criminal Offences and Penalties

This chapter has demonstrated that whenever domestic criminal measures are meant to secure the effectiveness of EU law or clash with the enjoyment of rights and freedoms granted by the Treaties, the Luxembourg Court exercises a hybrid proportionality review hinging on the double-layered model theorised in Chapter 2. Therefore, prospective and retrospective proportionality integrate the threefold test deriving from the *Greek Maize* paradigm, Treaty provisions on internal market freedoms, as well as Articles 52(1) and 49(3) of the Charter.

However, depending on the specific declination of the principle involved, the case-law discloses a different approach to applying these proportionality schemes. As a result, the ECJ proportionality review of domestic offences and penalties amounts to a complex patchwork in search of systematisation. To that end, the chapter's concluding section identifies trends and tendencies from the Court of Justice's case-law on domestic offences (A) and penalties (B).

A. The ECJ Nuanced Assessment of the Proportionality of Criminal Offences

The proportionality of offences is the first aspect to be considered. Chapter 2 showed that such an assessment may take place in two directions: by reviewing either the scope of the abstract behaviour described by the criminal offence or the choice to punish the same behaviour by recourse to criminal law.[300] In the context of preliminary references, the Court of Justice relies on the two possibilities to a different extent.

Under the *Greek Maize* paradigm, the ECJ sometimes posed proportionality constraints on the scope of offences' abstract conduct. On those occasions, the Court relied on a prospective reasoning construed in general (and not special) prevention terms. More specifically, it tackled offences that exceed the scope of

[300] See Section IV(A)(i) of Chapter 2.

behaviours that undermine the effective implementation of EU law since they result in unnecessary deterrence against the public. Conversely, the Court usually restrains itself from limiting the Member States' discretion in resorting to criminal law for punishing a given conduct.

Frauds affecting the EU's financial interests are an exception. This is unsurprising since that stream of case-law is the only one that enshrines criminalisation duties upon the Member States. While the *Greek Maize* paradigm usually leaves domestic authorities free to decide whether to employ criminal or administrative penalties, the ECJ's well-established jurisprudence requires *serious* frauds affecting the Union's financial interests to be punished under criminal law. This finding implies both a driver and a retrospective limit to criminalisation: other abstract behaviours which do not meet that minimum level of seriousness shall not be punished under criminal law. This threshold can hardly be theorised in a cardinal sense; therefore, the Court relies on a comparison between different offences based on the ordinal proportionality technique, as the ruling in *Scialdone* shows.[301] This approach is inevitably casuistic but is probably the only way out from the inherent elusiveness of the 'serious' concept.

The same reticence on limiting domestic criminalisation choices features in the ECJ approach to reviewing domestic offences interfering with rights and freedoms secured by EU law. The Court's review in the context of preliminary rulings mostly focuses on the extent of the abstract behaviour rather than its criminalisation. Moreover, the ECJ appears to review the proportionality of prohibiting a certain conduct per se and does not consider that the prohibition is punished through criminal sanctions. This approach differs from the proportionality review under the *Greek Maize* paradigm, where the Court treats the abstract behaviour under scrutiny as part of a criminal offence, thus applying the hybrid principle. Against this discrepancy, the ECJ approach to reviewing offences interfering with individual rights and freedoms seems not justified by sound theoretical reasons. Moreover, this choice is regrettable from a conceptual viewpoint. Treating the definition of criminal offences as any non-criminal provision neglects those criminal law peculiar features deserving particular attention in the proportionality scrutiny and giving rise to the prospective and retrospective review.

B. The Shifting Balance between Prospective and Retrospective Proportionality in the ECJ Review of Domestic Criminal Penalties

The analysis has identified a twofold approach concerning the proportionality of the type and amount of penalties. The ECJ relies on both prospective and

[301] See Section III(A) of this chapter.

retrospective assessments to evaluate whether a given criminal sanction is necessary to attain the aim pursued. However, the influence of the two schemes on the Court's review varies according to the specific features of the domestic penalties. More specifically, a dividing line shall be drawn between sanctioning provisions that the Court considers as evidently disproportionate and those which do not appear *prima facie* in contrast with the principle of proportionality of criminal penalties.

That distinction characterises primarily the ECJ approach towards retrospective proportionality. When confronted with particularly draconian sanctioning schemes, the ECJ appears more eager to rely on retrospective proportionality to conclude that they exceed the seriousness of the wrongdoing. That is the case, for instance, of domestic criminal law provisions which do not leave any room to trial courts for graduating penalties *in concreto* in the light of the seriousness of the wrongdoing. However, these are extreme cases. In all other circumstances, the Court of Justice exercises self-restraint in applying retrospective proportionality. In fact, this assessment is generally reserved for the referring court based on general guidance provided by ECJ.

The case-law on *ne bis in idem* constitutes a partial exception to this approach. The ECJ test for assessing the proportionality of limitations to Article 50 of the Charter enhances retrospective proportionality as the critical secondary scheme. However, the reason for this single divergence from the Court of Justice's general trend is easily explained by the genesis of that test. As previously shown,[302] the latter has been inspired by the ECtHR jurisprudence on Article 4 of Protocol No 7, which enhances retrospective proportionality of the overall sanction imposed as a key step for verifying whether dual-track sanctioning systems comply with *ne bis in idem*.

The ECJ construes prospective proportionality in general prevention terms exclusively, and the impact of this evaluation on the Court's review depends on the other scheme's intensity. In the case of evidently disproportionate sanctioning schemes, the two proportionality assessments' influence is rather balanced. Conversely, whenever domestic criminal law provisions are not evidently disproportionate, the retrospective scheme only allows the ECJ to provide the referring court with general guidance. Consequently, the outcome of the prospective assessment becomes decisive. That scheme's application is also influenced by the standard of review, which depends on whether penalties implement or clash with EU law. In the first circumstance, the Court's approach is quite cautious, as adequate deterrence is necessary to secure the effective implementation of EU law. In the second circumstance, a strict review is warranted: criminal sanctions shall not exceed what is strictly necessary for attaining a genuinely dissuasive effect. On that basis, they are disproportionate if less severe penalties could be sufficient to that end.

Overall, this approach appears justified by solid theoretical premises. Firstly, the looser or stricter standard of review reflects the different functions carried out

[302] See Section IV(B)(iii) of this chapter.

by domestic criminalisation vis-à-vis EU law. Should the former implement the latter, the penalties' dissuasiveness is a question of concern for EU law and shall cautiously be considered in the proportionality assessment. Conversely, deterrence amounts to a purely domestic concern in case of criminal sanctions hampering individual rights secured by the EU legal order. Therefore, the need to shield the enjoyment of those liberties from excessive penalisation justifies recourse to strict proportionality scrutiny.

Secondly, the prominent role of prospective proportionality is the consequence of that scheme's theoretical structure. As shown in Chapter 2, the threefold proportionality test and the prospective scheme are both finalistic. In criminal law, dissuasiveness is the purpose that offences and penalties pursue to attain the policy interest driving criminalisation. Given their theoretical proximity, it is pretty easy for the Court to move its reasoning from the threefold test to the prospective scheme. Moreover, the very fact that finalistic assessments are streamlined in the ECJ case-law on proportionality gives leeway for employing the prospective scheme as the critical assessment in the review of domestic criminal measures.

Concerning retrospective proportionality, the reasons for self-restraint shall be traced to the ECJ's peculiar position vis-à-vis domestic courts in the context of preliminary references, the latter representing most of the relevant case-law. In-depth retrospective assessments require the judiciary to elaborate extensively on the factual circumstances of the case. This task cannot be fulfilled by the Court of Justice and shall be reserved to the referring court. Indeed, only domestic courts are provided with the entire factual background of the case, thus being in a better position than the ECJ for assessing the retrospective proportionality of the penalty.

A glimpse into the ECtHR practice validates this conclusion. Contrary to the Court of Justice's approach, the Strasbourg Court relies heavily on retrospective proportionality when reviewing domestic criminal measures. However, the ECtHR pursues different tasks and has a different position than the ECJ vis-à-vis the domestic judiciaries. The Strasbourg Court reviews the proportionality of penalties imposed *in concreto* when all domestic remedies have been exhausted. The criminal case is settled: the only question left is whether the penalty imposed constitutes a disproportionate interference with the enjoyment of ECHR fundamental rights. From this viewpoint, the ECtHR can rely on a wide range of factual circumstances, allowing it to firmly ground an in-depth proportionality assessment of the penalty. Therefore, that diversity of approach comes as no surprise.

Clearly enough, this finding does not prevent the ECJ from relying on retrospective proportionality to provide referring courts with general guidance. In the same vein, the Court of Justice can itself hold that an evidently disproportionate sanctioning scheme is incompatible with EU law from a retrospective viewpoint. In such particular cases, that conclusion can be easily drawn from examining the provision in question without the need to assess the facts of the case in the main proceedings.

5

Conclusion: Reconstructing the Proportionality of Criminal Offences and Penalties in EU Law

I. The Principle in Theory

As this book aims to assess the theorisation and application of the proportionality of criminal offences and penalties in EU law, it is now time to connect the dots of the analysis to conceptualise the principle. This section focuses on theoretical profiles, while the following deals with the application of proportionality of criminal offences and penalties in practice.

The work has advanced a key argument: in the EU legal order, the proportionality of criminal offences and penalties amounts to a hybrid principle, as its theoretical structure combines the EU and criminal law different understandings of proportionality. This research hypothesis has been preliminarily framed in Chapters 1 and 2 by discussing the intersection between the EU legal order and criminal law. Chapters 3 and 4 have provided arguments to demonstrate this hypothesis through the analysis of legislative and judicial practice. On the one hand, the EU institutions constantly employ the prospective and retrospective paradigms when positively assessing the proportionality of harmonising provisions on offences and penalties. On the other hand, the hybrid nature of the proportionality of criminal offences and penalties is reflected in the Court of Justice's reliance on prospective and retrospective schemes in the negative review of domestic substantive criminal law measures. Therefore, the principle shall be construed as inherently hybrid, since it postulates a compound assessment resulting from the intersection between the EU and criminal law concepts of proportionality.

The principle's hybrid nature entails noteworthy implications from a theoretical viewpoint. On the one hand, it unveils that EU law can harmonically interact with other legal sciences – such as criminal law – without losing its distinct and autonomous nature (A). On the other hand, the very same finding questions the place of the proportionality of criminal offences and penalties within the EU legal order and its relationship with the general principle of proportionality (B).

A. A Hybrid Principle of the EU Legal Order

The book depicted a theoretical pattern featuring a complex intersection between the EU and criminal law dimensions of proportionality. When dealing with criminal measures, the EU concept of proportionality inevitably bumps into the criminal law understanding of the principle, thus giving rise to a compound theorisation. The suitability, necessity and proportionality *stricto sensu* test acquires a peculiar shape in EU criminal law, as it is complemented by two secondary schemes derived from the criminal law dimension of proportionality. The latter involves an assessment of the proportionality of criminal offences and penalties vis-à-vis, respectively, the attainment of a genuinely dissuasive effect (prospective proportionality) and the seriousness of the wrongdoing (retrospective proportionality).[1] From a theoretical viewpoint, the prospective scheme could also be construed in special prevention terms, thus evaluating offences and penalties in light of their capacity to attain offenders' social rehabilitation. However, this facet is absent from the EU legislative practice and the ECJ case-law on the proportionality of substantive criminal law, which constantly refer to the prospective scheme as a tool to assess the deterrence of offences and penalties from a general prevention perspective.

The principle's hybrid nature entails systemic implications for the EU legal order as a whole. In the context of the proportionality of criminal offences and penalties, the intensity of the interaction between EU law and substantive criminal law is so deep as to influence the principle's theoretical structure. The latter is not based on the threefold test alone, like all the multiple dimensions of proportionality in EU law.[2] Conversely, the proportionality of criminal offences and penalties combines theoretical schemes derived from different legal sciences. This characteristic elicits two considerations.

Firstly, the EU proportionality's hybridisation in the substantive criminal law domain further evidences the peculiar features of EU criminal law. As previously recalled, the European integration process and the consequent erosion of the former 'secret garden' of national sovereignty[3] gave rise to an area of criminal justice within the EU legal order. The very same development has paved the way for criminal law paradigms to permeate the EU legal order. To deal with criminal justice, the Union's legal order shall employ the 'vocabulary' of criminal law while still 'speaking the language' of EU law. In other words, EU criminal law entails the EU legal order interacting with criminal law paradigms and techniques without losing the distinctive identity and autonomy of EU law. The elaboration of

[1] See Section III(B) of Chapter 2.

[2] For an analysis of the various dimensions of the general principle of proportionality in EU law, see Section III of Chapter 1.

[3] See n 3 of the Introduction to this book.

autonomous notions is one of the tools available to achieve this goal: in the AFSJ, the ECJ takes criminal law understandings as a source of inspiration and reworks them to shape original concepts.[4] The hybrid nature of the proportionality of criminal offences and penalties marks an even more evident manifestation of this broader phenomenon. In fact, the criminal law understanding of proportionality does not simply influence the principle's structure: the latter results from integrating the EU proportionality technique with prospective and retrospective schemes.

Against this finding, one point shall be particularly emphasised. Hybridisation does not amount to EU law abdicating its understanding of proportionality in favour of criminal law paradigms. The threefold structure of the EU proportionality assessment remains constant even in the substantive criminal law domain. At the same time, prospective and retrospective schemes enrich the EU proportionality technique, thus providing indispensable tools for assessing whether offences and penalties are suitable, necessary and proportionate *stricto sensu*. By so doing, the EU legal order not only employs the 'vocabulary' of criminal law without mutating its distinctive language; it also manages typical phenomena of that field of law – like criminalisation choices and sentencing – by integrating and reworking criminal law techniques within the EU proportionality toolbox. This development results in the hybrid nature of the proportionality of criminal offences and penalties: a principle capable of combining the EU and criminal law understandings of proportionality without neglecting the distinctive features of the EU legal order.

Secondly, and from a broader perspective, the hybrid reconstruction of the principle highlights the peculiar relationship between EU law and other legal sciences. The distinct identity and autonomy of EU law[5] do not prevent the latter from proficiently interacting with other legal sciences and relying on their theoretical paradigms when required. From that perspective, the hybrid nature of the principle of proportionality of criminal offences and penalties discloses the potential openness of EU law towards other legal sciences. This posture results in legal cross-fertilisation. Paradigms and techniques derived from other legal disciplines do permeate and integrate EU law, as sometimes they represent the essential tools for the EU legal order to deal with legal phenomena typical of other fields of law. As this book demonstrated, that is the case of the interaction between EU and criminal law. However, it may be questioned whether the same phenomenon emerges from other domains of EU law. Considering the broad material scope of the European integration process, close interaction with other legal sciences appears almost unavoidable in certain circumstances.

[4] To provide just one example in the field of EU criminal law, that is the case of the concept of detention. In this regard, see S Montaldo and M Ramat, 'El concepto autónomo de "detención" en el Derecho penal de la UE. De la orden de detención europea a la necesidad de una apreciación sistémica del concepto' (2024) 83 *Revista de estudios europeos* 361.

[5] On the principle of autonomy of the EU legal order, see n 114 of Chapter 2.

B. Differentiation from and Osmosis with the EU General Principle of Proportionality

The hybrid nature of the proportionality of criminal offences and penalties depicted in this book raises issues on the principle's place in the EU legal order. Is it distinct and autonomous from the EU general principle of proportionality? Or is it just one of its dimensions?

Against these interrogatives, it shall be underlined that the hybrid theorisation of the principle analysed in this book entails a dividing line from all other dimensions of proportionality considered in Chapter 1.[6] When invoked as a limit to either the exercise of EU powers, derogations from fundamental rights or domestic obstacles to internal market freedoms, the principle of proportionality features a coherent theorisation codified in the threefold suitability, necessity and proportionality *stricto sensu* test. The proportionality of criminal offences and penalties is an exception in this regard. In this domain, the intersection between EU and criminal law is so profound that it results in the hybridisation of the EU conceptualisation of proportionality. While the threefold test remains the primary scheme of the principle, the latter is complemented by prospective and retrospective assessments. These secondary schemes become the proportionality test's key components, thereby mutating its theoretical structure into a compound – hybrid – paradigm.

The hybrid nature constitutes the unifying and distinctive feature of the principle of proportionality of offences and penalties, the theoretical element which characterises and differentiates it from the other manifestations of proportionality in EU law. On the one hand, the intersection between EU and criminal law paradigms underlies the proportionality of both offences and penalties. Therefore, even if only the proportionality of sanctions has been recognised as directly enforceable by the ECJ, the two prongs share the same conceptual nature and shall thus be considered together. On the other hand, the hybrid nature entails a theoretical diversity from the various dimensions that compose the EU general principle of proportionality. The interaction between EU and criminal law paradigms results in the specification of proportionality of criminal offences and penalties from general proportionality. Therefore, the former shall be considered distinct from the latter. Indeed, a different conclusion would neglect its unique conceptual peculiarities, manifested by its hybrid conceptualisation. This is the finding leading to the book's title: 'A Hybrid Principle'. The hybrid nature is liable to capture the proportionality of criminal offences and penalties in its individuality and, therefore, frames it as a 'principle' in itself.

Still, the hybrid principle maintains a close and indisputable bond with the general principle of proportionality underpinning the EU legal order. Firstly, it should be recalled that theoretical diversity between the two principles is

[6] See Section III of Chapter 1.

only partial. The hybridisation by criminal law paradigms does not neglect the conceptual foundations of the principle of proportionality in the EU legal order. The double-layered theorisation of the proportionality of criminal offences and penalties witnesses this finding, as it still envisages the threefold test as its primary scheme. While distinct, the proportionality of criminal offences and penalties is still proximate and profoundly shaped by the EU general principle. The latter represents the primary theoretical roots from which the principle of proportionality of criminal offences and penalties has acquired distinctive hybrid features. Secondly, the hybrid principle entails spillovers beyond the criminal law domain, influencing the general proportionality principle. That is the case, in particular, of the review of non-criminal penalties. In this domain, the ECJ applies the general principle of proportionality by borrowing the prospective and retrospective schemes which characterise the hybrid principle and derive from criminal law.

The two elements disclose an osmotic interaction between the proportionality of criminal offences and penalties and the EU general principle of proportionality. The latter profoundly influences the hybrid principle, which, in turn, expand its reach to the review of non-criminal sanctions by hybridising the general principle of proportionality.

It follows that differentiation and osmosis are the keywords that characterise the relationship between the EU general principle of proportionality and the proportionality of criminal offences and penalties. The latter entails a peculiar conceptual structure that differentiates it from the general principle. Still, the proportionality of criminal offences and penalties enjoys a close theoretical bond with the general principle of proportionality, thus preventing it from being framed as a completely autonomous general principle of the EU legal order.

II. The Principle in Action: How the Institutional Features of the EU Legal Order Shape the Interaction between Prospective and Retrospective Proportionality

The analysis of legislative and judicial practice not only witnessed the principle's hybrid nature, but also disclosed the interaction between prospective and retrospective schemes and their respective influence on proportionality scrutiny.

When harmonising offences and penalties, the proportionality limits to the exercise of EU powers stemming from Article 5(4) TEU fall short of posing meaningful limits to supranational criminalisation. Conversely, the EU legislature employs both prospective and retrospective schemes to assess whether the proposed minimum provisions entail a proportionate interference with fundamental rights within the meaning of Article 52(1) of the Charter. The *travaux préparatoires* of relevant Directives and Framework Decisions demonstrate that the two schemes exercise comparable influence on EU legislation.

However, judicial review of prospective and retrospective proportionality entails a different equilibrium. Save from cases of manifestly unreasonable arrangements, the discretion the EU legislature enjoys in the absence of a clear methodology for assessing the retributive worthiness of criminalisation poses hurdles to the ECJ for in-depth reviewing retrospective considerations.[7] Therefore, prospective proportionality would likely emerge as the critical tool for scrutinising the proportionality of harmonised offences and penalties vis-à-vis fundamental rights. In that regard, the book argued that the standard of review should be strict. Indeed, the recent ECJ case-law on the legitimacy of EU measures vis-à-vis the Charter clarifies that a strict necessity assessment is required insofar as the provisions in question amount to severe interference with rights secured therein. This approach shall extend to the harmonisation of offences and penalties, as criminal law represents the most intrusive form of interference with individual rights.[8]

The ECJ developed a coherent approach for the proportionality review of domestic criminal law measures either implementing or derogating from EU law. Article 49(3) of the Charter is the unifying paradigm between the proportionality assessment warranted by the *Greek Maize* paradigm, Treaty provisions on internal market freedoms and Article 52(1) of the Charter, thus giving rise to a holistic criterion for judicial review combining prospective and retrospective assessments. However, a self-restraint approach towards retrospective proportionality emerges also in this regard. Indeed, the Court relies on that scheme mainly to provide national judicial authorities with general guidance on retrospectively reviewing the worthiness of criminalisation or sanctions' type and amount. Should the criminal measure under scrutiny be manifestly disproportionate, the Court sometimes takes a bolder stance by coming to that conclusion on its own judgment. In all other cases, it is for the domestic courts to undergo an in-depth retrospective assessment based on the ECJ guidance.

Different considerations apply to prospective proportionality, usually being the decisive step in the Court's review. That technique allows the ECJ to hold a given offence or penalty disproportionate because it entails excessive deterrence, as the goal pursued could be attained through less restrictive measures. In that regard, the standard of review may vary depending on whether the offence or penalty under scrutiny implements or clashes with EU law. While the proportionality review of domestic measures – including criminal ones – under EU law warrants strict necessity scrutiny, this rigid approach is partially blurred towards offences and penalties established under the *Greek Maize* paradigm. Since they are meant to secure the effectiveness of EU law, the maximum level of deterrence permissible shall be carefully evaluated in light of the circumstances of each case.[9]

Therefore, a clear imbalance between the principle's secondary schemes has emerged from the case-law on domestic offences and penalties. This circumstance

[7] See Section VI(B) of Chapter 3.
[8] See Section VI(C)(iii) of Chapter 3.
[9] See Section III(B)(ii) of Chapter 4.

is not fortuitous, as it follows from the peculiar institutional characteristics of the EU legal order. Indeed, the ECJ's position vis-à-vis domestic courts prevents the former from undergoing an in-depth retrospective assessment, especially when proportionality pleas are raised in preliminary references. In the context of these procedures, the Court is meant to provide guidance to the national judicial authorities. Therefore, the ECJ is not always best placed to autonomously rule – even if 'subject to the verifications which it is for the referring court to carry out'[10] – that a given criminal measure is disproportionate. That conclusion can be reached based on a prospective analysis. This technique is grounded on a finalistic approach typical of the ECJ case-law and it does not entail profound factual assessments.

Conversely, retrospective proportionality usually demands similar evaluations, which the Luxembourg Court may hardly carry out. On that basis, the fact that the review of evidently disproportionate criminal measures features deeper reliance on the retrospective scheme is no surprise. In those circumstances, the Court is not required to exercise complex factual assessments to reach that conclusion. Therefore, the reason for the imbalanced influence of prospective and retrospective schemes on the proportionality scrutiny lies in the distinctive institutional features of the EU legal order, with particular emphasis on the Court of Justice's place and task.

A comparison with the ECtHR scrutiny further confirms this finding. Unlike the ECJ, the Strasbourg Court's assessment is mainly centred on retrospective proportionality. This approach characterises the case-law on both criminal measures securing the effectiveness of Convention rights – where retrospective proportionality establishes a lower limit to the severity of punitive responses – and those interfering with the same rights. This divergent attitude to the proportionality review can be explained by the ECtHR's different position vis-à-vis national authorities, compared to the ECJ: the Strasbourg Court's proportionality review occurs when all domestic remedies have been exhausted and the criminal case has been set. From that perspective, the ECtHR may rely on various factual circumstances to undergo retrospective scrutiny, whose intensity depends on the broader or narrower margin of appreciation domestic authorities enjoy under the Convention.

Therefore, the ECtHR case-law confirms that the relationship between prospective and retrospective proportionality highly depends upon the institutional characteristics of the respective legal system. That consideration leads to a final interrogative: may the potential EU accession to the ECHR overcome these differences? This question presupposes an extensive analysis – or even a different book – from a *de iure condendo* perspective. At the same time, the outcome of this study leaves room to advance at least a hypothesis in that regard. Convergence between EU law and the ECHR in applying the principle of proportionality of

[10] Case C-544/19 *ECOTEX Bulgaria* ECLI:EU:C:2021:803, para 83.

criminal offences and penalties may emerge in the EU legislative practice. As previously recalled, the *travaux préparatoires* of EU acts harmonising offences and penalties include scarce references to the ECHR proportionality standards.[11] The EU's accession to the ECHR may lead to a shift, as non-compliance with the Strasbourg Court's proportionality standards could entail a violation of the ECHR attributable to the Union. In this line of reasoning – and notwithstanding the unavoidable difference between the ECtHR negative scrutiny and the EU legislature's positive one – the Strasbourg Court's case-law may play a broader role in shaping the EU legislative approach for harmonising offences and penalties. Beyond this potential development, however, further approximation between the two legal systems is hardly conceivable. Although the EU's accession to the ECHR would surely enhance convergence of standards in fundamental rights protection, it would not obliterate the peculiar features of the EU legal order, upon which the principle's application depends. Therefore, even in the case of the EU's accession to the ECHR, any approximation between the ECJ and ECtHR standards of review may not be envisaged.

This final consideration further demonstrates a crucial finding. The interaction between EU law and theoretical paradigms of other legal sciences – such as criminal law – and legal systems – such as the ECHR – does not affect the distinctive and autonomous features of EU law. On the contrary, it is the institutional characteristics of the EU legal order that shape complex principles such as the proportionality of criminal offences and penalties.

[11] See Section V of Chapter 3.

BIBLIOGRAPHY

Monographs and Edited Books

Acosta Arcarazo, D, and Murphy, C (eds), *EU Security and Justice Law: After Lisbon and Stockholm* (Oxford, Hart Publishing, 2014)

Adam, R, and Tizzano, A, *Manuale di Diritto dell'Unione europea*, 4th edn (Torino, Giappichelli, 2024)

Alexy, R, *A Theory of Constitutional Rights* (Oxford, Oxford University Press, 2002)

Amalfitano, C, *Conflitti di giurisdizione e riconoscimento delle decisioni penali nell'Unione europea* (Milano, Giuffrè, 2006)

——, *General Principles of EU Law and the Protection of Fundamental Rights* (Cheltenham, Edward Elgar Publishing, 2018)

Amalfitano, C, and Condinanzi, M, *Unione europea: fonti, adattamento e rapporti tra ordinamenti* (Torino, Giappichelli, 2015)

Anrò, I, *L'adesione dell'Unione europea alla CEDU. L'evoluzione dei sistemi di tutela dei diritti fondamentali in Europa* (Milano, Giuffrè, 2015)

Arai-Takahashi, Y, *The Margin of Appreciation Doctrine and the Principle of Proportionality in the Jurisprudence of the ECHR* (Cambridge, Intersentia, 2002)

Arena, A, *Le "situazioni puramente interne" nel diritto dell'Unione europea* (Napoli, Editoriale Scientifica, 2019)

Ashworth, A, *Positive Obligations in Criminal Law* (Oxford, Hart Publishing, 2013)

Ashworth, A, and Roberts, JV, (eds), *Sentencing Guidelines: Exploring the English Model* (Oxford, Oxford University Press, 2013)

Asp, P, *The Substantive Criminal Law Competence of the EU* (Stockholm, Stiftelsen Skrifter utgivna av Juridiska fakulteten vid Stockholms Universitet, 2012)

Azoulai, L, *The Question of Competence in the European Union* (Oxford, Oxford University Press, 2014)

Barak, A, *Proportionality: Constitutional Rights and Their Limitations* (Cambridge, Cambridge University Press, 2012)

Baratta, R, *Institutions of EU Law*, 2nd edn (Milano, Wolters Kluwer, 2024)

Barents, R, *The Autonomy of Community Law* (The Hague, Kluwer Law International, 2004)

Barletta, A, *La legalità penale tra diritto dell'Unione europea e Costituzione* (Napoli, Jovene, 2011)

Barnard, C, *The Substantive Law of the EU: The Four Freedoms*, 2nd edn (Oxford, Oxford University Press, 2007)

Bartoloni, ME, *Ambito d'applicazione del diritto dell'Unione europea e ordinamenti nazionali: una questione aperta* (Napoli, Edizioni Scientifiche Italiane, 2018)

Bates, E, *The Evolution of the European Convention on Human Rights: From its Inception to the Creation of a Permanent Court of Human Rights* (Oxford, Oxford University Press, 2010)

Beccaria, C, *Edizione nazionale delle opere di Cesare Beccaria. 1: Dei delitti e delle pene* (L Firpo and G Francioni eds, Milano, Mediobanca, 1984)

Bernasconi, C, *La metafora del bilanciamento nel diritto penale. Ai confini della legalità* (Napoli, Jovene, 2019)

Bernardeau, L, and Christienne, J-P, *Les amendes en droit de la concurrence: pratique décisionnelle et contrôle juridictionnel du droit de l'Union* (Bruxelles, Larcier, 2013)

Bestagno, F, *Diritti umani e impunità: obblighi positivi degli Stati in materia penale* (Milano, Vita e pensiero, 2003)

Bestagno, F, Draetta, U, and Santini, A, *Elementi di Diritto dell'Unione europea. Profili istituzionali*, 8th edn (Milano, Giuffrè, 2024)

Bin, R, *Diritti e argomenti: il bilanciamento di interessi nella giurisprudenza costituzionale* (Milano, Giuffrè, 1992)

Bonini, S, *La funzione simbolica nel diritto penale del bene giuridico* (Napoli, Editoriale Scientifica, 2018)

Braum, S, and Weyembergh, A (eds), *Le contrôle juridictionnel dans l'espace pénal européen* (Bruxelles, Editions de l'Université de Bruxelles, 2009)

Calderoni, F, *Organized Crime Legislation in the European Union. Harmonization and Approximation of Criminal Law, National Legislations and the EU Framework Decision on the Fight Against Organized Crime* (Berlin, Springer-Verlag, 2010)

Cannizzaro, E, *Il principio della proporzionalità nell'ordinamento internazionale* (Milano, Giuffrè, 2000)

Christoffersen, J, *Fair Balance: Proportionality, Subsidiarity and Primarity in the European Convention on Human Rights* (Leiden, Brill-Nijhoff, 2009)

Ciciriello, MC, *Il principio di proporzionalità nel diritto comunitario* (Napoli, Editoriale Scientifica, 1999)

Citroni, G, and Scovazzi, T, *Corso di diritto internazionale. Parte III – La tutela internazionale dei diritti umani*, 3rd edn (Milano, Giuffrè, 2013)

Cognetti, S, *Principio di proporzionalità. Profili di teoria generale e di analisi sistematica* (Torino, Giappichelli, 2011)

Cohen-Eliya, M, and Porat, I, *Proportionality and Constitutional Culture* (Cambridge, Cambridge University Press, 2013)

Condinanzi, M, Nascimbene, B, and Lang, A, *Cittadinanza dell'Unione e libera circolazione delle persone* (Milano, Giuffrè, 2006)

Corstens, G, and Pradel, J, *European Criminal Law* (The Hague, Kluwer Law International, 2002)

Costamagna, F, *Diritti fondamentali e rapporti tra privati nell'ordinamento dell'Unione europea* (Torino, Giappichelli, 2022)

Craig, P, *EU Administrative Law*, 2nd edn (Oxford, Oxford University Press, 2012)

Craig, P, and de Búrca, G, *EU Law: Text, Cases and Materials*, 7th edn (Oxford, Oxford University Press, 2020)

Croquet, NAJ, *The Role and Extent of a Proportionality Analysis in the Judicial Assessment of Human Rights Limitations Within International Criminal Proceedings* (Leiden-Boston, Brill-Nijhoff, 2015)

Damato, A, *La tutela degli interessi finanziari tra competenze dell'Unione e obblighi degli Stati membri* (Bari, Cacucci, 2018)

Daniele, L, *Diritto del mercato unico europeo e dello Spazio di libertà, sicurezza e giustizia*, 3rd edn (Milano, Giuffrè, 2016)

De Pasquale, P, *Il principio di sussidiarietà nella Comunità europea* (Napoli, Editoriale Scientifica, 2000)

Delmas-Marty, M, and Teitgen-Colly, C, *Punir sans juger? De la répression administrative au droit administratif pénal* (Paris, Economica, 1992)

Duff, RA, *Trials and Punishments* (Cambridge, Cambridge University Press, 1986)

Duff, A, and Green, SP, *Philosophical Foundations of Criminal Law* (Oxford, Oxford University Press, 2011)

Dworkin, R, *Taking Rights Seriously* (Cambridge, Harvard University Press, 1977)

Emiliou, N, *The Principle of Proportionality in European Law: A Comparative Study* (London, Kluwer Law International, 1996)

Fiorella, A (ed), *Liability 'Ex Crimine' of Legal Entities in Member States*, vol 1 (Napoli, Jovene, 2012)

Fletcher, M, Lööf, R, and Gilmore, B, *EU Criminal Law and Justice* (Cheltenham, Edward Elgar Publishing, 2008)

Flore, D, *Droit pénal européen: les enjeux d'une justice pénale européenne*, 3rd edn (Bruxelles, Bruylant, 2009)

Franco, P, *Hegel's Philosophy of Freedom* (New Haven, Yale University Press, 1999)

Gallo, D, *L'efficacia diretta del diritto dell'Unione europea negli ordinamenti nazionali. Evoluzione di una dottrina ancora controversa* (Milano, Giuffrè, 2018)

Gallo, M, *Appunti di diritto penale. Vol II: Il reato. Parte I: La fattispecie oggettiva* (Torino, Giappichelli, 2007)

Garben, S, and Govaere, I (eds), *The Division of Competences Between the EU and the Member States* (Oxford, Hart Publishing, 2017)
Grandi, C, *Riserva di legge e legalità penale europea* (Milano, Giuffrè, 2010)
Grasso, G, *Comunità europee e diritto penale: i rapporti tra l'ordinamento comunitario e i sistemi penali degli Stati membri* (Milano, Giuffrè, 1989)
Grossio L, Montaldo S and Mitsilegas V (eds), *Proportionality of Criminal Penalties in EU Law* (Oxford, Hart Publishing, 2025)
Grosso, CF, Pelissero, M, Petrini, D, and Pisa, P, *Manuale di Diritto penale. Parte generale*, 2nd edn (Milano, Giuffrè, 2017)
Haguenau-Moizard, C, Gazin, F, and Leblois-Happe, J, *Les fondements du droit pénal de l'Union européenne* (Bruxelles, Larcier, 2016)
Harbo, TI, *The Function of Proportionality Analysis in European Law* (Leiden-Boston, Brill-Nijhoff, 2015)
Hart, HLA, *The Concept of Law* (Oxford, Clarendon Press, 1961)
Herlin-Karnell, E, *The Constitutional Dimension of European Criminal Law* (Oxford, Hart Publishing, 2012)
Herring, J, *Criminal Law* (Basingstoke, Palgrave Macmillan, 2005)
Husak, D, *The Philosophy of Criminal Law: Selected Essays* (Oxford, Oxford University Press, 2010)
Ippolito, F, *Fondamento, attuazione e controllo del principio di sussidiarietà nel diritto della Comunità e dell'Unione europea* (Milano, Giuffrè, 2007)
Janssens, C, *The Principle of Mutual Recognition in EU Law* (Oxford, Oxford University Press, 2013)
Kant, I, *Groundwork for the Metaphysics of Morals* (New Haven, Yale University Press, 2018)
Kert, R, Slot, B, Vernimmen, G, Lehner, A, and Schellekens, J, *Study on Minimum Sanctions in the EU Member States: Final Report* (Brussels, European Commission, 2015)
Kettunen, M, *Legitimizing European Criminal Law*, vol 2 (Cham, Springer, 2020)
Klatt, M, and Meister, M, *The Constitutional Structure of Proportionality* (Oxford, Oxford University Press, 2012)
Klip, A, *European Criminal Law: An Integrative Approach*, 4th edn (Cambridge, Intersentia, 2021)
Konstadinides, T, *Division of Powers in European Union Law: The Delimitation of Internal Competence Between the EU and the Member States* (Alphen aan den Rijn, Kluwer Law International, 2009)
Koutrakos, P, Nic Shuibhne, N, and Syrpis, P (eds), *Exceptions from EU Free Movement Law: Derogation, Justification and Proportionality* (Oxford, Hart Publishing, 2016)
Lattanzi, S, *I 'travaux préparatoires' del diritto dell'Unione europea: tassonomia, ruolo e funzioni* (Padova, CEDAM, 2022)
Lazzerini, N, *La Carta dei diritti fondamentali dell'Unione europea. I limiti di applicazione* (Milano, Franco Angeli, 2018)
Lavrysen, L, and Mavronicola, N (eds), *Coercive Human Rights: Positive Duties to Mobilise the Criminal Law under the ECHR* (Oxford, Hart Publishing, 2020)
Legg, A, *The Margin of Appreciation in International Human Rights Law* (Oxford, Oxford University Press, 2012)
Lenaerts, K, Gutman, K and Nowak, JT, *EU Procedural Law*, 3rd edn (Oxford, Oxford University Press, 2024)
Lenaerts, K, Van Nuffel, P and Corthaut, T, *EU Constitutional Law* (Oxford, Oxford University Press, 2022)
Lionello, L, *L'autonomia dell'ordinamento giuridico dell'Unione europea. Significato, portata e resistenze alla sua applicazione* (Torino, Giappichelli, 2024)
Lopera Mesa, GP, *Principio de proporcionalidad y ley penal. Bases para un modelo de control de constitucionalidad de las leyes penales* (Madrid, Centro de Estudios Políticos y Constitucionales, 2006)
Manes, V, and Caianiello, M, *Introduzione al diritto penale europeo* (Torino, Giappichelli, 2020)
Marinucci, G, Dolcini, E, and Gatta, GL, *Manuale di Diritto penale. Parte generale*, 10th edn (Milano, Giuffrè, 2021)

Marzal Yetano, A, *La dynamique du principe de proportionnalité : essai dans le contexte des libertés de circulation du droit de l'Union européenne* (Paris, Université de Paris I Panthéon-Sorbonne, 2013)
Mawbray, A, *The Development of Positive Obligations under the European Convention on Human Rights by the European Court of Human Rights* (Oxford, Hart Publishing, 2004)
Merle, R, and Vitu, A, *Traité de droit criminel. Problèmes généraux de la science criminelle. Droit pénal général* (Paris, Editions Cujas, 1984)
Mezaguer, M, Cartapanis, M, Chaiehloudj, W, Jacomino, F, Malet-Vigneaux, J, Marty, F, and Salemme, E, *Le droit antitrust de l'Union européenne. Tome I: Les dispositions générales* (M Mezaguer ed, Bruxelles, Éditions de l'Université de Bruxelles, 2022)
Miettinen, S, *Criminal Law and Policy in the European Union* (London, Routledge, 2013)
Mitsilegas, V, *Money Laundering Counter-Measures in the European Union: A New Paradigm of Security Governance versus Fundamental Legal Principles* (The Hague, Kluwer Law International, 2003)
——, *EU Criminal Law after Lisbon. Rights, Trust and the Transformation of Justice in Europe* (Oxford, Hart Publishing, 2016)
——, *EU Criminal Law*, 2nd edn (Oxford, Hart Publishing, 2022)
Mitsilegas, V, Bergström, M and Konstadinides, T (eds), *Research Handbook on EU Criminal Law* (Cheltenham, Edward Elgar Publishing, 2016)
Mitsilegas, V, Monar, J and Rees, W, *The European Union and Internal Security: Guardian of the People?* (Basingstoke, Palgrave Macmillan, 2003)
Montaldo, S, *I limiti della cooperazione in materia penale nell'Unione europea* (Napoli, Editoriale Scientifica, 2015)
Montaldo, S, Costamagna, F, and Miglio, A (eds), *EU Law Enforcement: The Evolution of Sanctioning Powers* (Torino-Oxon, Giappichelli-Routledge, 2021)
Morrone, A, *Il bilanciamento nello stato costituzionale: teorie e prassi delle tecniche di giudizio nei conflitti tra diritti e interessi costituzionali* (Torino, Giappichelli, 2014)
Nascimbene, B, and Rossi dal Pozzo, F, *Diritti di cittadinanza e libertà di circolazione nell'Unione europea* (Padova, CEDAM, 2012)
Neframi, E (ed), *Objectifs et compétences dans l'Union européenne* (Bruxelles, Bruylant, 2013)
Neves, M, *Constitutionalism and the Paradox of Principles and Rules* (Oxford, Oxford University Press, 2021)
Newton, M, *Proportionality in International Law* (Oxford, Oxford University Press, 2014)
Nicosia, E, *Convenzione europea dei diritti dell'uomo e diritto penale* (Torino, Giappichelli, 2006)
Oriolo, A, Castaldo, AR, Di Stasi, A and Nino, M (a cura di), *Criminalità transnazionale e Unione europea* (Napoli, Editoriale Scientifica, 2024)
Ottenhof, R (ed), *L'individualisation de la peine : de Saleilles à aujourd'hui* (Ramonville Saint-Agne, Érès, 2001)
Ouwerkerk, JW, *Quid pro Quo? A Comparative Law Perspective on the Mutual Recognition of Judicial Decisions in Criminal Matters* (Cambridge, Intersentia, 2011)
Öberg, J, *Limits to EU Powers: A Case Study of EU Regulatory Criminal Law* (Oxford, Hart Publishing, 2017)
——, *The Normative Foundations for EU Criminal Justice: Powers, Limits and Justifications* (Oxford, Hart Publishing, 2024)
Padovani, T, *Diritto penale*, 12th edn (Milano, Giuffrè, 2019)
Palladino, R, *Il principio di proporzionalità nel diritto dell'Unione europea* (Bari, Cacucci Editore, 2024)
Paonessa, C, *Gli obblighi di tutela penale: la discrezionalità legislativa nella cornice dei vincoli costituzionali e comunitari* (Pisa, ETS, 2009)
Parodi, M, *L'adesione dell'Unione europea alla CEDU: dinamiche sostanziali e prospettive formali* (Napoli, Edizioni Scientifiche Italiane, 2020)
Peristeridou, C, *The Principle of Legality in European Criminal Law* (Cambridge, Intersentia, 2015)
Petersen, N, *Proportionality and Judicial Activism: Fundamental Rights Adjudication in Canada, Germany and South Africa* (Cambridge, Cambridge University Press, 2017)

Pifferi, M, *L'individualizzazione della pena: difesa sociale e crisi della legalità penale tra Otto e Novecento* (Milano, Giuffrè, 2013)

Pilorge-Vrancken, J, *Le droit de la fonction publique de l'Union européenne* (Bruxelles, Bruylant, 2017)

Pirker, B, *Proportionality Analysis and Models of Judicial Review: A Theoretical and Comparative Study* (Groningen, Europa Law Publishing, 2013)

Pistoia, E, *Cooperazione penale nei rapporti fra diritto dell'Unione europea e diritto statale* (Napoli, Edizioni Scientifiche Italiane, 2008)

Pocar, F, and Baruffi, MC, *Commentario breve ai Trattati dell'Unione europea* (Padova, CEDAM, 2014)

Porchia, O, *Principi dell'ordinamento europeo. La cooperazione pluridirezionale* (Bologna, Zanichelli, 2008)

Pradel, J, *Droit pénal comparé*, 4th edn (Paris, Dalloz, 2016)

Prieto, C, and Bosco, D, *Droit européen de la concurrence* (Bruxelles, Bruylant, 2013)

Rawls, J, *A Theory of Justice* (Harvard, Harvard University Press, 1971)

Recchia, N, *Il principio di proporzionalità nel diritto penale. Scelte di criminalizzazione e ingerenza nei diritti fondamentali* (Torino, Giappichelli, 2020)

Romano, M, and Stella, F, *Teoria e prassi della prevenzione generale dei reati* (Bologna, Il Mulino, 1980)

Rosas, A, and Armati, L, *EU Constitutional Law: An Introduction*, 3rd edn (Oxford, Hart Publishing, 2018)

Rossi dal Pozzo, F, *Codice della concorrenza* (Milano, Giuffrè, 2019)

Ruggiero, G, *La proporzionalità nel diritto penale* (Napoli, Editoriale Scientifica, 2018)

Schütze, R, *EU Constitutional Law* (Cambridge, Cambridge University Press, 2012)

Sicurella, R, *Diritto penale e competenze dell'Unione europea: Linee guida di un sistema integrato di tutela dei beni giuridici sovrannazionali e dei beni giuridici di interesse comune* (Milano, Giuffrè, 2005)

Sicurella, R, Mitsilegas, V, and Parizot, R (eds), *General Principles for a Common Criminal Law Framework in the EU: A Guide for Legal Practitioners* (Milano, Giuffrè, 2017)

Scaccia, G, *Gli 'strumenti' della ragionevolezza nel giudizio costituzionale* (Milano, Giuffrè, 2000)

Stea, G, *I principi di diritto penale nella giurisdizione europea* (Pisa, Pisa University Press, 2014)

Stoyanova, V, *Positive Obligations under the European Convention on Human Rights. Within and Beyond Boundaries* (Oxford, Oxford University Press, 2023)

Strozzi, G, and Mastroianni, R, *Diritto dell'Unione europea. Parte istituzionale*, 9th edn (Torino, Giappichelli, 2023)

Sudre, F, Milano, L, Pastre-Belda, B, and Schahmaneche, A, *Droit européen et international des droits de l'homme*, 16th edn (Paris, Presses Universitaires de France, 2023)

Summers, SJ, *Sentencing and Human Rights* (Oxford, Oxford University Press, 2022)

Summers, S, Schwarzenegger, C, Ege, G, and Young, F, *The Emergence of EU Criminal Law: Cyber Crime and the Regulation of the Information Society* (Oxford, Hart Publishing, 2014)

Taupiac-Nouvel, G, *Le principe de reconnaissance mutuelle des décisions répressives dans l'Union européenne. Contribution à l'étude d'un modèle de libre circulation des décisions de justice* (Clermont-Ferrand, Institut Universitaire Varenne, 2011)

Tesauro, G, *La ragionevolezza nella giurisprudenza comunitaria* (Napoli, Editoriale Scientifica, 2012)

——, *Manuale di Diritto dell'Unione europea*, 4th edn (P De Pasquale and F Ferraro eds, Napoli, Editoriale Scientifica, 2023)

Tridimas, T, *The General Principles of EU Law*, 2nd edn (Oxford, Oxford University Press, 2007)

Urbina, FJ, *A Critique of Proportionality and Balancing* (Cambridge, Cambridge University Press, 2018)

Van Drooghenbroeck, S, *La proportionnalité dans le droit de la Convention européenne des droits de l'homme : Prendre l'idée simple au sérieux* (Bruxelles, Presses de l'Université Saint-Louis, 2001)

Van Raepenbusch, S, *Le contrôle juridictionnel dans l'Union européenne* (Bruxelles, Editions de l'Université de Bruxelles, 2018)

Vecchio, F, *L'Europa e la pena di morte: comparazione giuridica e strategie abolizioniste* (Milano, CEDAM-Wolters Kluwer, 2017)

Viganò, F, *La proporzionalità della pena: profili di diritto penale e costituzionale* (Torino, Giappichelli, 2021)
Villani, U, *Valori comuni e rilevanza delle identità nazionali e locali nel processo d'integrazione europea* (Napoli, Editoriale Scientifica, 2011)
Vitale, G, *Principi generali e diritto derivato. Contributo allo studio del sistema delle fonti dell'Unione europea* (Torino, Giappichelli, 2013)
Von Bogdandy, A, and Bast, J (eds), *Principles of European Constitutional Law* (Oxford-Munchen, Hart Publishing-Beck, 2009)
Von Hirsch, A, *Censure and Sanctions* (Oxford, Clarendon Press, 1993)
Von Hirsch, A, and Ashworth, A, *Proportionate Sentencing: Exploring the Principle* (Oxford, Oxford University Press, 2005)
Weyembergh, A, *L'harmonisation des législations : condition de l'espace pénal européen et révélateur de ses tensions* (Bruxelles, Editions de l'Université de Bruxelles, 2004)
Wieczorek, I, *The Legitimacy of EU Criminal Law* (Oxford, Hart Publishing, 2020)
Willems, A, *The Principle of Mutual Trust in EU Criminal Law* (Oxford, Hart Publishing, 2021)
Xanthopoulou, E, *Fundamental Rights and Mutual Trust in the Area of Freedom, Security and Justice: A Role for Proportionality?* (Oxford, Hart Publishing, 2020)
Xenos, D, *The Positive Obligations of the State under the European Convention of Human Rights* (London, Routledge, 2012)

Chapters in Edited Books

Adinolfi, A, 'La libertà di circolazione delle persone e la politica dell'immigrazione' in G Strozzi and R Mastroianni (eds), *Diritto dell'Unione europea. Parte speciale* (Torino, Giappichelli, 2021)
Alberti, J, 'New Actors on the Stage: The Emerging Role of EU Agencies in Exercising Sanctioning Powers' in S Montaldo, F Costamagna and A Miglio (eds), *EU Law Enforcement. The Evolution of Sanctioning Powers* (Torino-Oxon, Giappichelli-Routledge, 2021)
Alexy, R, 'Collisione e bilanciamento quale problema di base della dogmatica dei diritti fondamentali' in M La Torre and A Spadaro (eds), *Ragionevolezza del diritto* (Torino, Giappichelli, 2002)
Alix, J, 'Chapitre premier. Une liaison dangereuse. Dangerosité et droit pénal en France' in G Giudicelli-Delage and C Lazerges (eds), *La dangerosité saisie par le droit pénal* (Paris, Presses Universitaires de France, 2011)
Amadeo, S, 'Art 36' in A Tizzano (ed), *Trattati dell'Unione europea*, 2nd edn (Milano, Giuffrè, 2014)
Amalfitano, C, 'La certezza del diritto nel diritto dell'Unione europea' in E Triggiani, F Cherubini, I Ingravallo, E Nalin and R Virzo (eds), *Dialoghi con Ugo Villani* (Bari, Cacucci, 2017)
——, 'Primato del diritto dell'Unione vs identità costituzionale o primato del diritto dell'Unione e identità nazionale?' in A Bernardi and C Cupelli (eds), *Il caso Taricco e il dialogo tra le Corti. L'ordinanza 24/2017 della Corte costituzionale* (Napoli, Jovene, 2017)
Ambos, K, 'Omissions' in K Ambos, A Duff, J Roberts, T Weigend and A Heinze (eds), *Core Concepts in Criminal Law and Criminal Justice* (Cambridge, Cambridge University Press, 2019)
Arroyo Zapatero, L, and Muñoz de Morales Romero, M, 'Le contrôle des choix de pénalisation: effets directs et indirects' in G Giudicelli-Delage, S Manacorda and J Tricot (eds), *Cour de justice et justice pénale en Europe* (Paris, Société de législation comparée, 2010)
Bachmaier Winter, L, 'Dealing with European Legal Diversity at the Luxembourg Court: Melloni and the Limits of European Pluralism' in R Colson and S Field (eds), *EU Criminal Justice and the Challenges of Legal Diversity: Legal Cultures in the Area of Freedom, Security and Justice* (Cambridge, Cambridge University Press, 2016)
Bailleux, A, 'The Fiftieth Shade of Grey – Competition Law, Criministrative Law and Fairly Fair Trial' in A Weyembergh and F Galli (eds), *Do Labels Still Matter? Blurring Boundaries Between Criminal and Administrative Law. The Influence of the EU* (Bruxelles, Editions de l'Université de Bruxelles, 2014)

Barbe, E, 'Qu'attendre de la Convention pour les acteurs de l'espace pénal européen ?' in G De Kerchove and A Weyembergh (eds), *Quelles réformes pour l'espace pénal européen ?* (Bruxelles, Editions de l'Université de Bruxelles, 2003)

Barbou des Places, S, 'Revisiting Proportionality in Internal Market Law: Looking at the Unnamed Actors in the CJEU's Reasoning' in U Linderfalk and E Gill-Pedro, *Revisiting Proportionality in International and European Law: Interests and Interest-Holders* (Leiden-Boston, Brill Nijhoff, 2021)

Beauvais, P, and Dubos, O, 'Droit pénal et droit de l'Union européenne: vers un droit pénal fédéral?' in J-C Saint-Pau (ed), *Droit pénal et autres branches du droit* (Paris, Cujas, 2012)

Bernardi, A, 'La competenza penale accessoria dell'Unione europea: problemi e prospettive' in CE Paliero and F Viganò (eds), *Europa e diritto penale* (Milano, Giuffrè, 2013)

Bentham, J, 'An Introduction to the Principles of Morals and Legislation', in A Bailey (ed), *The Broadview Anthology of Social and Political Thought: From Machiavelli to Nietzsche* (Peterborough, Broadview Press, 2020)

Beauvais, P, and Dubos, O, 'Droit pénal et droit de l'Union européenne: vers un droit pénal fédéral?' in J-C Saint-Pau (ed), *Droit pénal et autres branches du droit* (Paris, Cujas, 2012)

Bilancia, P, 'L'effettività nello Spazio di libertà, sicurezza e giustizia tra realtà intergovernativa e prospettiva comunitaria' in A Catania (ed), *Dimensioni dell'effettività: Tra teoria generale e politica del diritto* (Milano, Giuffrè, 2005)

Billis, E, Knust, N, and Rui, JP, 'The Typology of Proportionality' in E Billis, N Knust and JP Rui (eds), *Proportionality in Crime Control and Criminal Justice* (Oxford, Hart Publishing, 2021)

Biondi, A, 'Subsidiarity in the Courtroom' in A Biondi, P Eeckhout and S Ripley (eds), *EU Law after Lisbon* (Oxford, Oxford University Press, 2012)

Bjorge, E, and Zglinski, J, 'The Principle of Proportionality in EU Law and Its Domestic Application: *ni tout à fait le même, ni tout à fait un autre*' in KS Ziegler, PJ Neuvonen and V Moreno-Lax (eds), *Research Handbook on General Principles in EU Law: Constructing Legal Orders in Europe* (Cheltenham, Edward Elgar Publishing, 2022)

Bothe, M, and Gillard, E-C, 'The Proportionality Principle in Comparative Public, European Union and International Law – Reflections on the "Proportionality Equation"' in E Billis, N Knust and JP Rui (eds), *Proportionality in Crime Control and Criminal Justice* (Oxford, Hart Publishing, 2021)

Brants, C, 'What Limits to Harmonising Justice?' in R Colson and S Field (eds), *EU Criminal Justice and the Challenges of Legal Diversity: Legal Cultures in the Area of Freedom, Security and Justice* (Cambridge, Cambridge University Press, 2016)

Brière, C, 'Proportionality of Penalties in EU Substantive Criminal Law Legislative Instruments' in L Grossio, S Montaldo and V Mitsilegas (eds), *Proportionality of Criminal Penalties in EU Law* (Oxford, Hart Publishing, 2025)

Brière, C, and Weyembergh, A, 'Article 50 – Droit à ne pas être jugé ou puni pénalement deux fois pour une même infraction' in F Picod, C Rizcallah and S Van Drooghenbroeck (eds), *Charte des droits fondamentaux de l'Union européenne. Commentaire article par article*, 3rd edn (Bruxelles, Bruylant, 2023)

Caeiro, P, 'Broadly Unknown, but Deservedly Unloved? Turnover-based Fines and their Transplant from Competition Law to EU Criminal Law' in L Grossio, S Montaldo and V Mitsilegas (eds), *Proportionality of Criminal Penalties in EU Law* (Oxford, Hart Publishing, 2025)

Calzolari, L, 'Sanctions in EU Competition Law: Ensuring Deterrence within the Decentralised Enforcement System of Articles 101 and 102 TFEU' in S Montaldo, F Costamagna and A Miglio (eds), *EU Law Enforcement. The Evolution of Sanctioning Powers* (Oxon-Torino, Routledge-Giappichelli, 2021)

Cannizzaro, E, 'La dottrina degli effetti diretti in taluni dei suoi sviluppi più recenti' in M Distefano (ed), *L'effetto diretto delle fonti dell'ordinamento giuridico dell'Unione europea* (Napoli, Editoriale Scientifica, 2017)

Cesoni, ML, 'Droit pénal européen: une harmonisation périlleuse' in G De Kerchove and A Weyembergh (eds), *L'espace pénal européen : enjeux et perspectives* (Bruxelles, Editions de l'Université de Bruxelles, 2002)

Colson, R, and Field, S, 'Legal Cultures in Europe: Brakes, Motors and the Rise of EU Criminal Justice' in R Colson and S Field (eds), *EU Criminal Justice and the Challenges of Legal Diversity: Legal Cultures in the Area of Freedom, Security and Justice* (Cambridge, Cambridge University Press, 2016)

Condinanzi, M, 'Diritti, principi e principi generali nell'ordinamento giuridico dell'Unione europea' in L D'Andrea, G Moschella, A Ruggeri and A Saitta (eds), *La Carta dei diritti dell'Unione Europea e le altre Carte (ascendenze culturali e mutue implicazioni)* (Torino, Giappichelli, 2016)

Contaldi, G, 'Effetto diretto e primato' in S Cassese (ed), *Dizionario di diritto pubblico* (Milano, Giuffrè, 2006)

Courakis, N, and Polyzoidou, V, 'The Principle of Proportionality: Tracing its Historical Evolution' in E Billis, N Knust and JP Rui (eds), *Proportionality in Crime Control and Criminal Justice* (Oxford, Hart Publishing, 2021)

Craig, P, 'General Principles of Law: Treaty, Historical and Normative Foundations' in KS Ziegler, PJ Neuvonen and V Moreno-Lax (eds), *Research Handbook on General Principles in EU Law: Constructing Legal Orders in Europe* (Cheltenham, Edward Elgar Publishing, 2022)

Damato, A, 'L'incidenza sul terzo pilastro dell'applicazione di principi e regole di diritto comunitario' in *Studi in onore di Vincenzo Starace*, vol 2 (Napoli, Editoriale Scientifica, 2008)

——, 'Art 325 TFUE' in F Pocar and MC Baruffi, *Commentario breve ai Trattati dell'Unione europea*, 2nd edn (Padova, CEDAM, 2014)

——, 'La cooperazione giudiziaria' in G Tesauro, *Manuale di Diritto dell'Unione europea*, vol 2 (P De Pasquale and F Ferraro eds, Napoli, Editoriale Scientifica, 2021)

Daniele, L, 'Carta dei diritti fondamentali dell'Unione europea e Trattato di Lisbona' in G Venturini and S Bariatti (eds), *Diritti individuali e giustizia internazionale – Individual Rights and International Justice – Droits individuels et justice international. Liber Fausto Pocar* (Milano, Giuffrè, 2009)

——, 'Art 35 TUE' in A Tizzano (ed), *Trattati dell'Unione europea e della Comunità europea* (Milano, Giuffrè, 2004)

De Kerchove, G, 'Améliorations institutionnelles à apporter au titre VI du traité sur l'Union européenne dans le domaine de la sécurité interne' in G De Kerchove and A Weyembergh (eds), *Quelles réformes pour l'espace pénal européen ?* (Bruxelles, Editions de l'Université de Bruxelles, 2003)

De Pasquale, P, 'Art 5 TUE' in A Tizzano (ed), *Trattati dell'Unione europea*, 2nd edn (Milano, Giuffrè, 2014)

De Vero, G, 'La giurisprudenza della Corte di Strasburgo' in G De Vero and G Panebianco (eds), *Delitti e pene nella giurisprudenza delle Corti europee* (Torino, Giappichelli, 2007)

De Witte, B, 'Direct Effect, Primacy, and the Nature of the Legal Order' in P Craig and G de Búrca (eds), *The Evolution of EU Law*, 3rd edn (Oxford, Oxford University Press, 2021)

Delage, P-J, 'Prolégomènes. Fragments archéologiques de la défense sociale' in G Giudicelli-Delage and C Lazerges (eds), *La dangerosité saisie par le droit pénal* (Paris, Presses Universitaires de France, 2011)

Delmas-Marty, M, 'La place d'un droit pénal commun dans la construction européenne' in *Mélanges offerts à Pierre Couvrat: la sanction du droit* (Paris, Presses Universitaires de France, 2001)

Di Federico, G, 'Fundamental Rights in the EU: Legal Pluralism and Multi-Level Protection After the Lisbon Treaty' in G Di Federico (ed), *The EU Charter of Fundamental Rights: From Declaration to Binding Instrument* (Dordrecht, Springer, 2011)

——, 'La "saga Taricco": il funzionalismo alla prova dei controlimiti (e viceversa)' in C Amalfitano (eds), *Primato del diritto dell'Unione europea e controlimiti alla prova della 'saga Taricco'* (Milano, Giuffrè, 2018)

Di Stasi, A, 'Introduzione – Spazio europeo, rivisitate priorità dell'UE e garanzia dei valori comuni. La cooperazione giudiziaria in materia penale per la repressione dei cross-border crimes' in A Oriolo, AR Castaldo, A Di Stasi and M Nino (eds), *Criminalità transnazionale e Unione europea* (Napoli, Editoriale Scientifica, 2024)

Dougan, M, 'From the Velvet Glove to the Iron Fist: Criminal Sanctions for the Enforcement of Union Law' in M Cremona (ed), *Compliance and the Enforcement of EU Law* (Oxford, Oxford University Press, 2012)

Dreyer, E, 'Droit pénal et droit européen des droits de l'homme' in J-C Saint-Pau (ed), *Droit pénal et autres branches du droit* (Paris, Cujas, 2012)

Duff, RA, 'Proportionality and the Criminal Law: Proportionality of What to What?' in E Billis, N Knust and JP Rui (eds), *Proportionality in Crime Control and Criminal Justice* (Oxford, Hart Publishing, 2021)

Edward, D, 'Subsidiarity as a Legal Concept' in P Cardonnel, A Rosas and N Wahl (eds), *Constitutionalising the EU Judicial System: Essays in Honour of Pernilla Lindh* (Oxford, Hart Publishing, 2012)

Elholm, T, 'The Emotional Component of Proportionality' in E Billis, N Knust and JP Rui (eds), *Proportionality in Crime Control and Criminal Justice* (Oxford, Hart Publishing, 2021)

Elholm, T, and Colson, R, 'The Symbolic Purpose of EU Criminal Law' in R Colson and S Field (eds), *EU Criminal Justice and the Challenges of Legal Diversity: Legal Cultures in the Area of Freedom, Security and Justice* (Cambridge, Cambridge University Press, 2016)

Feinberg, J, 'The Classic Debate' in J Feinberg and H Gross (eds), *The Philosophy of Law* (Belmont, Wadsworth Publishing, 1991)

Ferraro, F, and Lazzerini, N, 'Art 52 – Portata e interpretazione dei diritti e dei principi' in R Mastroianni, O Pollicino, S Allegrezza, F Pappalardo and O Razzolini (eds), *Carta dei diritti fondamentali dell'Unione europea* (Milano, Giuffrè, 2017)

Fichera, M, 'Organised Crime: Developments and Challenges for an Enlarged European Union' in C Eckes and T Konstadinides (eds), *Crime Within the Area of Freedom, Security and Justice: A European Public Order* (Cambridge, Cambridge University Press, 2011)

——, 'EU Fundamental Rights and the European Arrest Warrant' in S Douglas-Scott and N Hatzis (eds), *Research Handbook on EU Law and Human Rights*, 2nd edn (Cheltenham, Edward Elgar Publishing, 2019)

Fletcher, M, 'EU Criminal Justice: Beyond Lisbon' in C Eckes and T Konstadinides (eds), *Crime Within the Area of Freedom, Security and Justice: A European Public Order* (Cambridge, Cambridge University Press, 2011)

Flore, D, 'Droit pénal matériel et Union européenne' in G De Kerchove and A Weyembergh (eds), *Quelles réformes pour l'espace pénal européen ?* (Bruxelles, Editions de l'Université de Bruxelles, 2003)

Galetta, DU, 'The EU Law Principle of Proportionality and Judicial Review: Its Origin, Development, Dissemination and the Lessons to Be Learnt from the Court of Justice of the European Union', in *Continuity and Change – How the Challenges of Today Prepare the Ground for Tomorrow. ECB Legal Conference 2021* (Frankfurt, European Central Bank, 2022)

Geiger, R, 'Article 5 TEU' in R Geiger, D-E Khan and M Kotzur (eds), *European Union Treaties: A Commentary* (Munchen, Beck, 2015)

Giuffrida, F, 'Effectiveness, Dissuasiveness, Proportionality of Sanctions and Assimilation Principle: The Long-Lasting Legacy of the Greek Maize Case' in V Mitsilegas, A Di Martino and L Mancano (eds), *The Court of Justice and European Criminal Law. Leading Cases in a Contextual Analysis* (Oxford, Hart Publishing, 2019)

Grasso, G, 'Introduzione: diritto penale e integrazione europea' in G Grasso and R Sicurella (eds), *Lezioni di diritto penale europeo* (Milano, Giuffrè, 2007)

Hart, HLA, 'Prolegomenon to the Principles of Punishment' in HLA Hart (ed), *Punishment and Responsibility: Essays in the Philosophy of Law*, 2nd edn (Oxford, Oxford University Press, 2008)

Hervouët, F, 'Le droit communautaire, un ordre juridique pénalement sanctionné?' in *Mélanges offerts à Pierre Couvrat: La sanction du droit* (Paris, Presses Universitaires de France, 2001)

Hinarejos, A, 'Law and Order and Internal Security Provisions in the Area of Freedom, Security and Justice: Before and After Lisbon' in C Eckes and T Konstadinides (eds), *Crime Within the Area of Freedom, Security and Justice: A European Public Order* (Cambridge, Cambridge University Press, 2011)

Jarvis, M, 'The Proportionality Test: Constructive Dialogue between the English and Scottish Courts' in P Koutrakos, NN Shuibhne and P Syrpis (eds), *Exceptions from EU Free Movement Law: Derogation, Justification and Proportionality* (Oxford, Hart Publishing, 2016)

Jendly, M, and Delgrande, N, 'La valeur de la réhabilitation d'un point de vue criminologique' in PH van Kempen and W Young (eds), *Prevention of Reoffending: The Value of Rehabilitation and the Management of High Risk Offenders – Prévention de la récidive: valeur de la réhabilitation et gestion des délinquants à haut risque* (Cambridge, Intersentia, 2014)

Jescheck, H-H, 'Possibilità e limiti di un diritto penale per la protezione dell'Unione europea' in L Picotti (ed), *Possibilità e limiti di un diritto penale dell'Unione europea* (Milano, Giuffrè, 1999)

Kaiafa-Gbandi, M, 'The "Constitutional" CJEU Ruling on the Enforcement of Community Law (Case C-176/03) and Its Impact on EU Law' in V Mitsilegas, A Di Martino and L Mancano (eds), *The Court of Justice and European Criminal Law. Leading Cases in a Contextual Analysis* (Oxford, Hart Publishing, 2019)

Kellens, G, 'Quelle utilité pour l'harmonisation des sanctions au niveau européen?' in G De Kerchove and A Weyembergh (eds), *L'espace pénal européen: enjeux et perspectives* (Bruxelles, Editions de l'Université de Bruxelles, 2002)

Klip, A, 'Towards a General Part of Criminal Law for the European Union' in A Klip (ed), *Substantive Criminal Law of the European Union* (Antwerpen, Maklu, 2011)

Kuhl, L, 'Des moyens à approfondir: les missions de l'OLAF' in D Berlin, F Martucci and F Picod (eds), *La fraude et le droit de l'Union européenne* (Bruxelles, Bruylant, 2017)

Kurki, L, 'International Standards for Sentencing and Punishment' in M Tonry and R Frase (eds), *Sentencing and Sanctions in Western Countries* (Oxford, Oxford University Press, 2001)

Labayle, H, 'Instruments et procédures de l'espace de liberté, sécurité et justice: quelques réflexions critiques' in G De Kerchove and A Weyembergh (eds), *Quelles réformes pour l'espace pénal européen ?* (Bruxelles, Editions de l'Université de Bruxelles, 2003)

Lahti, R, 'Towards a Principled European Criminal Policy: Some Lessons from the Nordic Countries' in JB Banach-Gutierrez and C Harding (eds), *EU Criminal Law and Policy: Values, Principles and Methods* (London, Routledge, 2017)

Lambert-Abdelgawad, É, 'Tentative de modélisation' in M Delmas-Marty, G Giudicelli-Delage and É Lambert-Abdelgawad (eds), *L'harmonisation des sanctions pénales en Europe* (Paris, Société de législation comparée, 2003)

Lang, A, 'Art 72 TFUE' in A Tizzano (ed), *Trattati dell'Unione europea* (Milano, Giuffrè, 2014)

Lanotte, M, 'La proporzionalità della sanzione: un principio ritrovato? Note a margine della sentenza *NE*' in *Quaderni AISDUE – Serie Speciale: Atti del Convegno 'Ambiente, digitale, economia: l'Unione europea verso il 2030'* (Napoli, Editoriale Scientifica, 2023)

Lavrysen, L, 'Positive Obligations and the Criminal Law: A Bird's-Eye View on the Case Law of the European Court of Human Rights' in *Coercive Human Rights: Positive Duties to Mobilise the Criminal Law under the ECHR* (Oxford, Hart Publishing, 2020)

Lazzerini, N, 'Le clausole generali della Carta dei diritti fondamentali nel law-making europeo: codificazione e innovazione nella determinazione del livello di tutela' in A Annoni, S Forlati and F Salerno (eds), *La codificazione nell'ordinamento internazionale e dell'Unione europea* (Napoli, Editoriale Scientifica, 2019)

Lenaerts, K, 'Proportionality as a Matrix Principle Promoting the Effectiveness of EU Law and the Legitimacy of EU Action – Keynote Speech' in *Continuity and Change – How the Challenges of Today Prepare the Ground for Tomorrow. ECB Legal Conference 2021* (Frankfurt, European Central Bank, 2022)

Manacorda, S, 'Le contrôle des clauses d'ordre public : la "logique combinatoire" de l'encadrement du droit pénal' in G Giudicelli-Delage and S Manacorda (eds), *Cour de justice et justice pénale en Europe* (Paris, Société de législation comparée, 2010)

Manzini, P, 'La portata dei diritti garantiti dalla Carta dell'Unione europea: problemi interpretativi posti dall'art. 52' in LS Rossi (ed), *Carta dei diritti fondamentali e Costituzione dell'Unione europea* (Milano, Giuffrè, 2002)

Maresca, M, 'Il ruolo dei «principi» nel progetto di Trattato costituzionale e il diritto alla mobilità' in M Maresca (ed), *Valori e principi nella Costituzione europea. Il diritto alla mobilità* (Bologna, Il Mulino, 2004)

Martufi, A, 'Proportionality of Sanctions Under EU Law: Insights from Penal Theory' in L Grossio, S Montaldo and V Mitsilegas (eds), *Proportionality of Criminal Penalties in EU Law* (Oxford, Hart Publishing, 2025)

Maugeri, AM, 'Il principio di proporzionalità nelle scelte punitive del legislatore europeo: l'alternativa delle sanzioni amministrative comunitarie' in G Grasso, L Picotti and R Sicurella (eds), *L'evoluzione del diritto penale nei settori d'interesse europeo alla luce del Trattato di Lisbona* (Milano, Giuffrè, 2011)

Miglio, A, 'Autonomia dell'ordinamento dell'Unione europea e risoluzione delle controversie in materia di investimenti' in A Spagnolo and S Saluzzo (eds), *La responsabilità degli Stati e delle organizzazioni internazionali: nuove fattispecie e problemi di attribuzione e di accertamento* (Milano, Ledizioni, 2017)

Militello, V, *Prevenzione generale e commisurazione della pena* (Milano, Giuffrè, 1982)

Miller, RA, 'Proportionality Paradigm or Paradox? The Proportionality Principle in American and Germany Security Law Jurisprudence' in E Billis, N Knust and JP Rui (eds), *Proportionality in Crime Control and Criminal Justice* (Oxford, Hart Publishing, 2021)

Mitsilegas, V, 'Managing Legal Diversity in Europe's Area of Criminal Justice: The Role of Autonomous Concepts' in R Colson and S Field (eds), *EU Criminal Justice and the Challenges of Legal Diversity: Legal Cultures in the Area of Freedom, Security and Justice* (Cambridge, Cambridge University Press, 2016)

Mitsilegas, V, and Billis, E, 'Article 49 – Principles of Legality and Proportionality of Criminal Offences and Penalties' in S Peers, T Hervey, J Kenner and A Ward (eds), *The EU Charter of Fundamental Rights:A Commentary*, 2nd edn (Oxford, Hart Publishing, 2021)

Montaldo, S, 'EU Sanctioning Power and the Principle of Proportionality' in S Montaldo, F Costamagna and A Miglio (eds), *EU Law Enforcement. The Evolution of Sanctioning Powers* (Torino-Oxon, Giappichelli-Routledge, 2021)

——, 'Domestic Sanctions and the Greek Maize Obligation to Impose Effective, Proportionate and Dissuasive Penalties: Empowering National Courts' in L Grossio, S Montaldo and V Mitsilegas (eds), *Proportionality of Criminal Penalties in EU Law* (Oxford, Hart Publishing, 2025)

Moreno-Lax, V, and Ziegler, KS, 'Autonomy of the EU Legal Order a General Principle? On the Risks of Normative Functionalism and Selective Constitutionalisation' in KS Ziegler, PJ Neuvonen and V Moreno-Lax (eds), *Research Handbook on General Principles in EU Law* (Cheltenham, Elgar, 2022)

Mori, P, 'La 'qualità' della legge e la clausola generale di limitazione dell'art. 52, par. 1, della Carta dei diritti fondamentali dell'UE', in *Scritti in onore di Giuseppe Tesauro* (Napoli, Editoriale Scientifica, 2014)

Muñoz de Morales Romero, M, 'El principio de proporcionalidad en el derecho penal europeo: un puzle con muchas piezas' in JA Lascuraín Sánchez and M Adolfo Rusconi (eds), *El principio de proporcionalidad penal* (Buenos Aires, Ad Hoc, 2014)

Mylonopoulos, C, 'The Contribution of Fuzzy Logic and Comparative Concepts to the Rational Application of Proportionality *Stricto Sensu*' in E Billis, N Knust and JP Rui (eds), *Proportionality in Crime Control and Criminal Justice* (Oxford, Hart Publishing, 2021)

Nieto-Martin, A, 'Architectures judiciaires du droit pénal européen' in G Giudicelli-Delage and S Manacorda (eds), *Cour de justice et justice pénale en Europe* (Paris, Société de législation comparée, 2010)

Nuotio, K, 'On the Significance of Criminal Justice for a Europe – United in Diversity' in K Nuotio (ed), *Europe in Search of 'Meaning and Purpose'* (Helsinki, University of Helsinki, 2004)

Oetheimer, M, and Cardone, A, 'Art 10' in S Bartole, P De Sena and V Zagrebelsky (eds), *Commentario breve alla Convenzione europea dei diritti dell'uomo* (Padova, CEDAM, 2012)

Olinet, M, and Sebastien, S, 'Synthèse thématique' in M Delmas-Marty, G Giudicelli-Delage and É Lambert-Abdelgawad (eds), *L'harmonisation des sanctions pénales en Europe* (Paris, Société de législation comparée, 2003)

Ouwerkerk, JW, 'Evidence-Based Criminalisation in EU Law: Evidence of What Exactly?' in JW Ouwerkerk, J Altena, J Öberg and S Miettinen (eds), *The Future of EU Criminal Justice Policy and Practice: Legal and Criminological Perspectives* (Leiden-Boston, Brill-Nijhoff, 2019)

Öberg, J, 'Legal Diversity, Subsidiarity and Harmonization of EU Regulatory Criminal Law' in R Colson and S Field (eds), *EU Criminal Justice and the Challenges of Legal Diversity: Legal Cultures in the Area of Freedom, Security and Justice* (Cambridge, Cambridge University Press, 2016)

——, 'Conceptualising Proportionality and Criminal Sanctions in EU Law: Three Different Visions' in L Grossio, S Montaldo and V Mitsilegas (eds), *Proportionality of Criminal Penalties in EU Law* (Oxford, Hart Publishing, 2025)

Panebianco, G, 'La giurisprudenza della Corte di Lussemburgo' in G De Vero and G Panebianco (eds), *Delitti e pene nella giurisprudenza delle Corti europee* (Torino, Giappichelli, 2007)
Pelissero, M, 'The Influence of Proportionality of Penalties Derived from EU Law on Domestic Criminal Legislation and Sentencing' in L Grossio, S Montaldo and V Mitsilegas (eds), *Proportionality of Criminal Penalties in EU Law* (Oxford, Hart Publishing, 2025)
Peers, S, and Prechal, S, 'Article 52 – Scope and Interpretation of Rights and Principles' in S Peers, T Hervey, J Kenner and A Ward (eds), *The EU Charter of Fundamental Rights: A Commentary*, 2nd edn (Oxford, Hart Publishing, 2021)
Peršak, N, 'Positive Obligations in View of the Principle of Criminal Law as a Last Resort' in L Lavrysen and N Mavronicola (eds), *Coercive Human Rights: Positive Duties to Mobilise the Criminal Law under the ECHR* (Oxford, Hart Publishing, 2020)
Pirker, B, and Reitemeyer, S, 'Between Discursive and Exclusive Autonomy – Opinion 2/13, the Protection of Fundamental Rights and the Autonomy of EU Law' in *Cambridge Yearbook of European Legal Studies* (Cambridge, Cambridge University Press, 2015)
Pistoia, E, 'Proportionality of Criminal Penalties and EU Judicial Cooperation' in L Grossio, S Montaldo and V Mitsilegas (eds), *Proportionality of Criminal Penalties in EU Law* (Oxford, Hart Publishing, 2025)
Pitea, C, 'Art 8' in S Bartole, P De Sena and V Zagrebelsky (eds), *Commentario breve alla Convenzione europea dei diritti dell'uomo* (Padova, CEDAM, 2012)
Porchia, O, 'Il dialogo tra Corte costituzionale e Corte di giustizia' in L Delli Priscoli (ed) *La Costituzione vivente* (Milano, Giuffrè, 2023)
Poscher, R, 'Proportionality and the Bindingness of Fundamental Rights' in E Billis, N Knust and JP Rui (eds), *Proportionality in Crime Control and Criminal Justice* (Oxford, Hart Publishing, 2021)
Pradel, J, 'La réhabilitation des détenus – Introduction générale' in PH van Kempen and W Young (eds), *Prevention of Reoffending: The Value of Rehabilitation and the Management of High Risk Offenders – Prévention de la récidive: valeur de la réhabilitation et gestion des délinquants à haut risque* (Cambridge, Intersentia, 2014)
Roberts, JV, 'Promoting Retributive Proportionality through Sentencing Guidelines' in E Billis, N Knust and JP Rui (eds), *Proportionality in Crime Control and Criminal Justice* (Oxford, Hart Publishing, 2021)
Rosanò, A, 'The EU-UK Extradition Arrangement and the Principle of Proportionality: Some Hints from the Practice of EU Institutions and Italian and UK Legislation and Case-Law on the EAW' in L Grossio, S Montaldo and V Mitsilegas (eds), *Proportionality of Criminal Penalties in EU Law* (Oxford, Hart Publishing, 2025)
Rossi, LS, 'I rapporti fra la Carta dei diritti fondamentali e la CEDU nella giurisprudenza delle rispettive Corti' in *Annali AISDUE* (Napoli, Editoriale Scientifica, 2020)
Scaccia, G, 'Il principio di proporzionalità' in S Mangiameli (eds), *L'ordinamento europeo: l'esercizio delle competenze* (Milano, Giuffrè, 2006)
Selvaggi, N, '*Ex Crimine* Liability of Legal Persons in EU. An Overview of Substantive Criminal Law' in A Fiorella (eds), *Corporate Criminal Liability and Compliance Programs. Vol. II: Towards a Common Model in the European Union* (Napoli, Jovene, 2012)
Sicurella, R, 'La tutela "mediata" degli interessi della costruzione europea: l'armonizzazione dei sistemi penali nazionali tra diritto comunitario e diritto dell'Unione europea' in G Grasso and R Sicurella (eds), *Lezioni di diritto penale europeo* (Milano, Giuffrè, 2007)
——, 'Legalità e proporzionalità nel diritto penale sostanziale' in R Mastroianni, O Pollicino, S Allegrezza, F Pappalardo and O Razzolini (eds), *Carta dei diritti fondamentali dell'Unione europea* (Milano, Giuffrè, 2017)
Sotis, C, 'Le competenze penali dell'Unione previste nel Trattato di Lisbona: una lettura d'insieme' in CE Paliero and F Viganò (eds), *Europa e diritto penale* (Milano, Giuffrè, 2013)
Suominen, A, 'The Sensitive Relationship Between the Different Means of Legal Integration: Mutual Recognition and Approximation' in C Brière and A Weyembergh (eds), *The Needed Balances in EU Criminal Law: Past, Present and Future* (Oxford, Hart Publishing, 2018)

Syrpis, P, 'EU Secondary Legislation and Its Impact on Derogations from Free Movement' in P Koutrakos, NN Shuibhne and P Syrpis (eds), *Exceptions from EU Free Movement Law: Derogation, Justification and Proportionality* (Oxford, Hart Publishing, 2016)

Tesauro, G, 'Il ruolo della Corte di giustizia nell'elaborazione dei princìpi generali dell'ordinamento europeo e dei diritti fondamentali' in *La Costituzione europea. Annuario 1999. Atti del XIV Convegno Annuale (Perugia, 7-8-9 ottobre 1999)* (Padova, CEDAM, 2000)

——, 'Diritto comunitario, Corte di giustizia e diritto penale', in G Grasso and R Sicurella (eds), *Per un rilancio del progetto europeo. Esigenze di tutela degli interessi comunitari e nuove strategie di integrazione penale* (Milano, Giuffrè, 2008)

——, 'Art 19 TUE' in A Tizzano (ed), *Trattati dell'Unione europea*, 2nd edn (Milano, Giuffrè, 2014)

Timmermans, C, 'The Competence Divide of the Lisbon Treaty Six Years After' in S Garben and I Govaere (eds), *The Division of Competences between the EU and the Member States: Reflections on the Past, the Present and the Future* (Oxford, Hart Publishing, 2017)

Tridimas, T, 'Proportionality in Community Law: Searching for the Appropriate Standard of Scrutiny' in E Ellis (ed), *The Principle of Proportionality in the Laws of Europe* (Oxford, Hart Publishing, 1999)

Turmo, A, 'The Proportionality of Criminal Sanctions and Ne Bis In Idem', in L Grossio, S Montaldo and V Mitsilegas (eds), *Proportionality of Criminal Penalties in EU Law* (Oxford, Hart Publishing, 2025)

Tusseau, G, 'Theoretical Deflation: The EU Order of Competences and Power-Conferring Norms Theory' in L Azoulai (ed), *The Question of Competence in the European Union* (Oxford, Oxford University Press, 2014)

Van Drooghenbroeck, S, and Rizcallah, C, 'Article 52-1. Limitations aux droits garantis' in F Picod, C Rizcallah and S Van Drooghenbroeck (eds), *Charte de droits fondamentaux de l'Union européenne: Commentire article par article* (Bruxelles, Bruylant, 2023)

Van Kempen, PH, and Young, W, 'Obligations et Moyens de Prévention de La Récidive: Introduction, Contexte et Conclusions' in PH van Kempen and Warren Young (eds), *Prevention of Reoffending: The Value of Rehabilitation and the Management of High Risk Offenders – Prévention de la récidive: valeur de la réhabilitation et gestion des délinquants à haut risque* (Cambridge, Intersentia, 2014)

Vienne, R, 'De l'individualisation de la peine à la personnalisation de la mesure. À propos du soixante-quinzième anniversaire de la parution de l'ouvrage de Saleilles (1898–1973)' in *Aspects nouveaux de la pensée juridique. Recueil d'études en hommage à Marc Ancel*, vol 2 (Paris, Pedone, 1975)

Viganò, F, 'Les obligations de protection pénale des droits fondamentaux' in G Giudicelli-Delage, S Manacorda and J Tricot (eds), *'Devoir de punir ?' – Le système pénal face à la protection internationale du droit à la vie* (Paris, Société de législation comparée, 2013)

Weyembergh, A, 'Le rapprochement des législations pénales au sein de l'Union européenne: les difficultés et leurs conséquences' in G De Kerchove and A Weyembergh (eds), *L'espace pénal européen: enjeux et perspectives* (Bruxelles, Editions de l'Université de Bruxelles, 2001)

Weyembergh, A, and Wieczorek, I, 'Is There an EU Criminal Policy?' in R Colson and S Field (eds), *EU Criminal Justice and the Challenges of Legal Diversity: Legal Cultures in the Area of Freedom, Security and Justice* (Cambridge, Cambridge University Press, 2016)

Zedner, L, 'Ends and Means: Why Effective Counter-Terrorism Requires Respect for Proportionality and Rights' in E Billis, N Knust and JP Rui (eds), *Proportionality in Crime Control and Criminal Justice* (Oxford, Hart Publishing, 2021)

Articles and Contributions in Journals

Accetto, M, and Zleptnig, S, 'The Principle of Effectiveness: Rethinking Its Role in Community Law' (2009) 11 *European Public Law* 375

Adinolfi, A, 'I princìpi generali della giurisprudenza comunitaria e la loro influenza sugli ordinamenti degli Stati membri' (1994) *Rivista italiana di diritto pubblico comunitario* 521

Aleinikoff, TA, 'Constitutional Law in the Age of Balancing' (1987) 96 *The Yale Law Journal* 943
Alexy, A, 'On the Structure of Legal Principles' (2000) 13 *Ratio Juris* 294
Amalfitano, C, 'Scaduto il regime transitorio per gli atti del terzo pilastro. Da oggi in vigore il sistema "ordinario" di tutela giurisdizionale della Corte di giustizia' in *Eurojus*, 1 December 2014
Ambos, K, 'Is the Development of a Common Substantive Criminal Law for Europe Possible? Some Preliminary Reflections' (2005) 12 *Maastricht Journal of European and Comparative Law* 173
——, '*Ius Puniendi* and Constitution: A Comparative (Canadian-German) Perspective' (2020) 14 *Vienna Journal on International Constitutional Law* 253
Anagnostaras, G, 'Mutual Confidence is Not Blind Trust! Fundamental Rights Protection and the Execution of the European Arrest Warrant: Aranyosi and Căldăraru' (2016) 53 *Common Market Law Review* 1675
Anrò, I, 'Il parere 2/13 della Corte di giustizia sul progetto di accordo di adesione dell'Unione europea alla CEDU: una bocciatura senza appello?' (2014) *Eurojus* 1
Anrò, I, and Nascimbene, B, 'The Devil is in the Details: Does the End of Protocol N° 16 to the ECHR Lie in the Wrinkles of the EU Accession to the ECHR Process?' (2021) *Eurojus* 199
Arena, A, 'La Corte di giustizia sulla conservazione dei dati: quali conseguenze per le misure nazionali di recepimento? Note dall'Europa' (2014) 3 *Quaderni Costituzionali* 722
Ashworth, A, 'Prisons, Proportionality and Recent Penal History' (2017) 80 *Modern Law Review* 473
Asp, P, 'The Importance of the Principles of Subsidiarity and Coherence in the Development of EU Criminal Law' (2011) 1 *European Criminal Law Review* 43
——, 'Harmonisation of Penalties and Sentencing within the EU' (2013) 1 *Bergen Journal of Criminal Law & Criminal Justice* 53
Baker, E, 'What Price Criminal Justice in the EU?' (2016) 24 *European Journal of Crime, Criminal Law and Criminal Justice* 95
Banach-Gutierrez, JB, and Harding, C, 'Fundamental Rights in European Criminal Justice: An Axiological Perspective' (2012) 20 *European Journal of Crime, Criminal Law and Criminal Justice* 239
——, 'Exploring the Interface between EU and National Criminal Law' (2020) 11 *New Journal of European Criminal Law* 3
Bartoloni, ME, 'La tutela giurisdizionale nell'ambito del secondo e terzo pilastro UE' (2005) 25 *Quaderni costituzionali* 170
Baumbach, T, 'Chilling Effect as a European Court of Human Rights' Concept in Media Law Cases' (2018) 6 *Bergen Journal of Criminal Law & Criminal Justice* 92
Bedau, HA, 'Bentham's Utilitarian Critique of the Death Penalty' (1983) 74 *Journal of Criminal Law and Criminology* 1033
Belley, N, 'L'émergence d'un principe de proportionnalité' (1997) 38 *Les Cahiers de droit* 245
Bergamaschi, N, 'Prime considerazioni sul nuovo tentativo di adesione dell'Unione alla CEDU e sui suoi principali ostacoli' (2024) 1 *Rivista Quaderni AISDUE* 1
Bernardi, A, 'L'armonizzazione delle sanzioni in Europa: linee ricostruttive' (2008) 51 *Rivista italiana di diritto e procedura penale* 76
Borowski, M, 'Limiting Clauses: On the Continental European Tradition of Special Limiting Clauses and the General Limiting Clause of Art 52(1) Charter of Fundamental Richts of the European Union' (2007) 1 *Legisprudence* 197
——, 'Absolute Rights and Proportionality' (2013) 56 *German Yearbook of International Law* 385
Böse, M, 'The Principle of Proportionality and the Protection of Legal Interests (Verhältnismäßigkeit und Rechtsgüterschutz)' (2011) 1 *European Criminal Law Review* 34
Braum, S, '"Rechtsstaat" and European Criminal Law – From the End of Sovereignty' (2021) 12 *New Journal of European Criminal Law* 14
Brkan, M, 'The Essence of the Fundamental Rights to Privacy and Data Protection: Finding the Way through the Maze of the CJEU's Constitutional Reasoning' (2019) 20 *German Law Journal* 864
Bronsther, J, 'The Limits of Retributivism' (2021) 24 *New Criminal Law Review* 301

Buisman, SS, 'The Future of EU Substantive Criminal Law: Towards a Uniform Set of Criminalisation Principles at the EU Level' (2022) 30 *European Journal of Crime, Criminal Law and Criminal Justice* 161

Buyse, A, 'Dangerous Expressions: The ECHR, Violence and Free Speech' (2014) 63 *International and Comparative Law Quarterly* 491

Caeiro, P, 'Constitution and Development of the European Union's Penal Jurisdiction: Responsibility, Self-Reference and Attribution' (2022) 27 *European Law Journal* 441

Callewaert, J, 'The European Convention on Human Rights and European Union Law: A Long Way to Harmony' (2009) *European Human Rights Law Review* 768.

Carlsmith, KM, Darley, JM, and Robinson, PH, 'Why Do We Punish? Deterrence and Just Deserts as Motives for Punishment' (2002) 83 *Journal of Personality and Social Psychology* 284

Castiglione, JD, 'Qualitative and Quantitative Proportionality: A Specific Critique of Retributivism' (2010) 71 *Ohio State Law Journal* 71

Céré, J-P, and Grégoire, L, 'Nécessité et proportionnalité des peines' (2020) *Répertoire de droit pénal et de procédure pénale* 31

Christofi, A, 'La jurisprudence de la Cour et du Tribunal de l'Union européenne. Chronique des arrêts. Arrêt « Digital Rights Ireland »' (2014) *Revue du droit de l'Union européenne* 399

Cisotta, R, 'Brevi note sulla giurisprudenza sull'art. 52, par. 1 della Carta dei diritti fondamentali dell'UE in materia di limitazioni ai diritti fondamentali … con uno sguardo in avanti' (2021) 14 *Osservatorio sulle fonti* 19

Coffey, G, 'An Interpretative Analysis of the European Ne Bis in Idem Principle through the Lens of ECHR, CFR and CISA Provisions: Are Three Streams Flowing in the Same Channel?' (2023) 14 *New Journal of European Criminal Law* 345

Coppel, J, and O'Neill, A, 'The European Court of Justice: Taking Rights Seriously?' (1992) 12 *Legal Studies* 227

Corlett, JA, 'Making More Sense of Retributivism: Desert as Responsibility and Proportionality' (2003) 78 *Philosophy* 279

Davis, R, 'Citizenship of the Union … Rights for All?' (2002) 27 *European Law Review* 121

De Boer, N, and Van't Klooster, J, 'The ECB, the Courts and the Issue of Democratic Legitimacy after Weiss' (2020) 57 *Common Market Law Review* 1689

De Bondt, W, 'The Missing Link between "Necessity" and "Approximation of Criminal Sanctions" in the EU' (2014) 4 *European Criminal Law Review* 147

De Bondt, W, and Miettinenm, S, 'Minimum Criminal Penalties in the European Union: In Search of a Credible Justification' (2015) 21 *European Law Journal* 722

de Búrca, G, 'The Principle of Proportionality and its Application in EC Law' (1993) 13 *Yearbook of European Law* 105

De Pasquale, P, 'Sharing Is Caring: I primi trent'anni del principio di sussidiarietà nell'Unione europea' (2021) *Il Diritto dell'Unione europea* 429

De Pasquale, P, and Circolo, A, *Il criterio della ragionevolezza nella più recente giurisprudenza della Corte di giustizia* (2024) 2 *Il Diritto dell'Unione europea* 277

De Witte, B, 'European Union Law: How Autonomous is its Legal Order?' (2010) 65 *Zeitschrift für öffentliches Recht* 143

De Witte, B, and Imamović, Š, 'Opinion 2/13 on Accession to the ECHR: Defending the EU Legal Order against a Foreign Human Rights Court' (2015) 5 *European Law Review* 683

Delmas-Marty, M, 'The European Union and Penal Law' (1998) 4 *European Law Journal* 87

Dimock, S, 'Retributivism and Trust' (1997) 16 *Law and Philosophy* 37

Dolcini, E, 'La commisurazione della pena tra teoria e prassi' (1991) *Rivista italiana di diritto e procedura penale* 55

Donini, M, 'Per una concezione post-riparatoria della pena. Contro la pena come raddoppio del male' (2013) *Rivista italiana di diritto e procedura penale* 1162

Dougan, M, 'Primacy and the Remedy of Disapplication' (2019) 56 *Common Market Law Review* 1456

——, 'The Primacy of Union Law Over Incompatible National Measures: Beyond Disapplication and Towards a Remedy of Nuly?' (2022) 59 *Common Market Law Review* 1301

Durnescu, I, 'An Exploration of the Purposes and Outcomes of Probation in European Jurisdictions' (2008) 55 *Probation Journal* 273
Dworkin, R, 'The Model of Rules' (1967) 35 *The University of Chicago Law Review* 1
Duff, A, and von Hirsch, A, 'Responsibility, Retribution and the "Voluntary": A Response to Williams' (1997) 1 *Cambridge Law Journal* 103
Eckes, C, 'The Autonomy of the EU Legal Order' (2020) 4 *Europe and the World* 1
Elholm, T, 'Does EU Criminal Cooperation Necessarily Mean Increased Repression?' (2009) 17 *European Journal of Crime, Criminal Law and Criminal Justice* 191
Engle, E, 'The History of the General Principle of Proportionality: An Overview' (2012) 10 *Dartmouth Law Journal* 1
Fabbrini, F, 'La separazione dei poteri nell'Unione europea' (2023) 73 *Rivista trimestrake di diritto pubblico* 45
Fathaigh, RÓ, 'Article 10 and the Chilling Effect Principle' (2013) *European Human Rights Law Review* 304
Favilli, C, 'Il principio di sussidiarietà nel diritto dell'Unione europea' (2011) 231 *Archivio giuridico Filippo Serafini* 257
——, 'La possibile convivenza tra disapplicazione e questione di legittimità costituzionale dopo la sentenza n. 15 del 2024 del giudice delle leggi' (2024) 2 *Rivista del contenzioso europeo* 37
Feinberg, J, 'The Expressive Function of Punishment' (1965) 49 *The Monist* 397
Feix, M, 'Subsidiarité, proportionnalité et construction européenne' (2011) 267 *Revue d'éthique et de théologie morale* 59
Fiandaca, G, 'Considerazioni su colpevolezza e prevenzione' (1987) *Rivista italiana di diritto e procedura penale* 836
Fichera, M, and Herlin-Karnell, E, 'The Margin of Appreciation Test and Balancing in the Area of Freedom Security and Justice: A Proportionate Answer for a Europe of Rights?' (2013) 19 *European Public Law* 759
Finckenauer, JO, 'Public Support for the Death Penalty: Retribution as Just Deserts or Retribution as Revenge?' (1988) 5 *Justice Quarterly* 81
Flore, D, 'Un droit pénal européen : hasard ou nécessité' (2003) 9 *Revue de droit pénal et de criminologie* 5
Franssen, N, and Weyembergh, A, 'From Facts and Political Objectives to Legal Bases and Legal Provisions: Incremental European Integration in the Criminal Law Field' (2023) 27 *European Law Journal* 368
Frase, RS, 'Excessive Prison Sentences, Punishment Goals, and the Eighth Amendment: Proportionality Relative to What' (2005) 89 *Minnesota Law Review* 571
Galetta, DU, 'La proporzionalità quale principio generale dell'ordinamento' (2006) *Giornale di diritto amministrativo* 1106
——, 'Il principio di proporzionalità fra diritto nazionale e diritto europeo (e con uno sguardo anche al di là dei confini dell'Unione europea)' (2019) 6 *Rivista italiana di diritto pubblico comunitario* 903
Gallo, D, 'Rethinking Direct Effect and Its Evolution: A Proposal' (2022) 1 *European Law Open* 576
Gáspár-Szilágyi, S, 'Joined Cases Aranyosi and Căldăraru: Converging Human Rights Standards, Mutual Trust and a New Ground for Postponing a European Arrest Warrant' (2016) 24 *European Journal of Crime, Criminal Law and Criminal Justice* 197
Gilliams, H, 'Proportionality of EU Competition Fines: Proposal for a Principled Discussion' (2014) 4 *World Competition* 435
Giudicelli-Delage, G, 'Les eaux troubles du droit pénal de l'Union européenne' (2010) 53 *Archives de Philosophie du Droit* 130
Grasso, G, 'The Instruments of Harmonisation of National Criminal Law, Their Enforcement and the Role of the Court of Justice' (2015) 6 *New Journal of European Criminal Law* 494
Greene, J, 'Rights As Trumps ?' (2018) 1 *Harvard Law Review* 28
Grimm, D, 'Proportionality in Canadian and German Constitutional Jurisprudence' (2015) 57 *The University of Toronto Law Journal* 383
Grossio, L, and Rosi, M, 'The Ultimate (but Not the Only) Remedy for Securing Fundamental Rights in the EAW System? Some Reflections on Puig Gordi and E. D. L.' (2023) 8 *European Papers* 547

Groussot, X, and Minssen, T, 'Res Judicata in the Court of Justice Case-Law: Balancing Legal Certainty with Legality?' (2007) 3 *European Constitutional Law Review* 385

Guilmain, A, 'Sur les traces du principe de proportionnalité: une esquisse généalogique' (2016) 61 *McGill Law Journal* 87

Harbo, TI, 'The Function of the Proportionality Principle in EU Law' (2010) 16 *European Law Journal* 158

Harding, C, 'Exploring the Intersection Between European Law and National Criminal Law' (2000) 25 *European Law Review* 374

Helenius, D, 'Mutual Recognition in Criminal Matters and the Principle of Proportionality: Effective Proportionality or Proportionate Effectiveness?' (2014) 3 *New Journal of European Criminal Law* 349

Heringa, AW, and Verhey, L, 'The EU Charter: Text and Structure' (2001) 8 *Maastricht Journal of European and Comparative Law* 11

Herlin-Karnell, E, 'Recent Developments in the Area of European Criminal Law' (2007) 14 *Maastricht Journal of European and Comparative Law* 15

——, 'Subsidiarity in the Area of EU Justice and Home Affairs Law – A Lost Cause?' (2009) 15 *European Law Journal* 351

——, 'What Principles Drive (or Should Drive) European Criminal Law?' (2010) 11 *German Law Journal* 1115

——, 'Effectiveness and Constitutional Limits in European Criminal Law' (2014) 5 *New Journal of European Criminal Law* 267

Hogg, PW, and Bushell, AA, 'The Charter Dialogue between Courts and Legislatures (Or Perhaps the Charter of Rights Isn't Such a Bad Thing after All)' (1997) 35 *Osgoode Hall Law Journal* 187

Husovec, M, 'The Essence of Intellectual Property Rights under Article 17(2) of the EU Charter' (2019) 20 *German Law Journal* 840

Iannuccelli, P, 'La Corte di giustizia e l'autonomia del sistema giurisdizionale dell'Unione europea: *quousque tandem*?' (2018) *Il Diritto dell'Unione europea* 283

Iglesias Sánchez, S, 'The Court and the Charter: The impact of the entry into force of the Lisbon Treaty on the ECJ's approach to fundamental rights' (2012) 49 *Common Market Law Review* 1565

Ivaldi, P, and Tuo, CE, 'Diritti fondamentali e diritto internazionale privato dell'Unione europea nella prospettiva dell'adesione alla CEDU' (2012) 53 *Rivista di diritto internazionale private e processuale* 7

Jareborg, N, 'Criminalization as Last Resort (Ultima Ratio)' (2005) 2 *Ohio State Journal of Criminal Law* 521

Kaiafa-Gbandi, M, 'The Development towards Harmonization within Criminal Law in the European Union – A Citizen's Perspective' (2001) 9 *European Journal of Crime, Criminal Law and Criminal Justice* 239

——, 'The Importance of Core Principles of Substantive Criminal Law for a European Criminal Policy Respecting Fundamental Rights and the Rule of Law' (2011) 1 *European Criminal Law Review* 6

Klatt, M, 'Positive Obligations under the European Convention on Human Rights' (2011) 71 *Heidelberg Journal of International Law* 691

Koskas, M, 'Le dynamisme de la proportionnalité : enjeux de la fragmentation tripartite du principe dans le processus juridictionnel' (2019) 15 *Revue des droits de l'homme* 1

Lacey, N, and Pickard, H, 'The Chimera of Proportionality: Institutionalising Limits on Punishment in Contemporary Social and Political Systems' (2015) 78 *Modern Law Review* 216

Lamond, G, 'Legal Sources, the Rule of Recognition, and Customary Law' (2014) 59 *The American Journal of Jurisprudence* 25

Lasagni, G, and Mirandola, S, 'The European Ne Bis in Idem at the Crossroads of Administrative and Criminal Law' (2019) 13 *eucrim – The European Criminal Law Associations' Forum* 1

Lavrysen, L, 'Causation and Positive Obligations under the European Convention on Human Rights: A Reply to Vladislava Stoyanova' (2018) 18 *Human Rights Law Review* 705

Lazowski, A, 'The Sky Is Not the Limit: Mutual Trust and Mutual Recognition Après Aranyosi and Căldăraru' (2018) 14 *Croatian Yearbook of European Law and Policy* 2

Lazzerini, N, 'Gli obblighi in materia di protezione dei diritti fondamentali come limite all'esecuzione del mandato di arresto europeo: la sentenza Aranyosi e Căldăraru' (2016) 10 *Diritti umani e diritto internazionale* 445

Lenaerts, K, 'Some Reflections on the Separation of Powers in the European Communities' (1991) 28 *Common Market Law Review* 11
——, 'National Remedies for Private Parties in the Light of the EU Law Principles of Equivalence and Effectiveness (2011) 46 *Irish Jurist* 13
——, 'Exploring the Limits of the EU Charter of Fundamental Rights' (2012) 8 *European Constitutional Law Review* 375
——, 'The Principle of Mutual Recognition in the Area of Freedom, Security and Justice' (2015) *Il Diritto dell'Unione europea* 525
——, 'Limits on Limitations: The Essence of Fundamental Rights in the EU' (2019) 20 *German Law Journal* 779
Lenaerts, K, and Gutierrez-Fons, JA, 'The Constitutional Allocation of Powers and General Principles of EU Law' (2010) 47 *Common Market Law Review* 1629
Lo Schiavo, G, 'The Principle of Ne Bis in Idem and the Application of Criminal Sanctions: Of Scope and Restrictions' (2018) 14 *European Constitutional Law Review* 644
Lobba, P, 'Punishing Denialism beyond Holocaust Denial: EU Framework Decision 2008/913/JHA and Other Expansive Trends' (2014) 5 *New Journal of European Criminal Law* 58
Lock, T, 'Rights and Principles in the EU Charter of Fundamental Rights' (2019) 56 *Common Market Law Review* 1201
Luchtman, M, 'The CJEU's Recent Case Law on Ne Bis in Idem: Implications for Law Enforcement in a Shared Legal Order' (2018) 55 *Common Market Law Review* 1717
Lugato, M, 'Principio di proporzionalità e invalidità di atti comunitari nella giurisprudenza della Corte di giustizia delle Comunità europee' (1991) 30 *Diritto comunitario e degli scambi internazionali* 60
Lupo, E, 'La *primauté* del diritto dell'UE e l'ordinamento penale nazionale' (2016) *Diritto penale contemporaneo* 217
Mancano, L, 'A Theory of Justice? Securing the Normative Foundations of EU Criminal Law through an Integrated Approach to Independence' (2022) 27 *European Law Journal* 477
Marin, L, 'Effective and Legitimate? Learning from the Lessons of 10 Years of Practice with the European Arrest Warrant' (2014) 5 *New Journal of European Criminal Law* 327
Martinico, G, 'The "Polemical" Spirit of European Constitutional Law: On the Importance of Conflicts in EU Law' (2015) 16 *German Law Journal* 1343
Mastroianni, R, 'Sui rapporti tra Carte e Corti: nuovi sviluppi nella ricerca di un sistema rapido ed efficace di tutela dei diritti fondamentali' (2020) 5 *European Papers* 493
Maugeri, AM, 'Fundamental Rights in the European Legal Order, Both as a Limit on Punitive Power and as a Source of Positive Obligations to Criminalise' (2013) 4 *New Journal of European Criminal Law* 374
Mavronicola, N, 'Crime, Punishment and Article 3 ECHR: Puzzles and Prospects of Applying an Absolute Right in a Penal Context' (2015) 15 *Human Rights Law Review* 721
Melander, S, 'Effectiveness in EU Criminal Law and Its Effects on the General Part of Criminal Law' (2014) 5 *New Journal of European Criminal Law* 274
——, 'Ultima Ratio in European Criminal Law' (2013) 3 *European Criminal Law Review* 45
Micheletto, L, 'Towards an Integrated (and Possibly Pan-European?) Prima Facie Legitimacy Test: Merging the Rechtsgut Theory, the Offensività Principle, and the Harm Principle' (2021) 29 *European Journal of Crime, Criminal Law and Criminal Justice* 241
Militello, V, 'I diritti fondamentali fra limite e legittimazione di una tutela penale europea' (2004) *Ragion pratica* 139
Mitsilegas, V, 'The Transformation of Criminal Law in the Area of Freedom, Security and Justice' (2007) 26 *Yearbook of European Law* 1
——, 'The Third Wave of Third Pillar Law: Which Direction for EU Criminal Justice?' (2009) 34 *European Law Review* 523
——, 'Reforming the "Facilitators' Package" through the Kinsa Litigation: Legality, Effectiveness and Taking International Law Into Account' (2024) *Eurojus* 155
Molinarolli, A, 'Una possibile dimensione europea del principio di offensività' (2016) *Diritto penale contemporaneo* 19

Monar, J, 'EU Internal Security Governance: The Case of Counter-Terrorism' (2014) 23 *European Security* 195
——, 'Reflections on the Place of Criminal Law in the European Construction' (2021) 27 *European Law Journal* 356
Montaldo, S, 'On a Collision Course! Mutual Recognition, Mutual Trust and the Protection of Fundamental Rights in the Recent Case-Law of the Court of Justice' (2016) 1 *European Papers* 965
——, 'Offenders' Rehabilitation: Towards a New Paradigm for EU Criminal Law?' (2018) 8 *European Criminal Review* 222
——, 'Handle with Care! The Direct Effect of the Requirement of Proportionality of Sanctions and the Remedy of Disapplication: NE v. Bezirkshauptmannschaft Hartberg-Fürstenfeld' (2023) 60 *Common Market Law Review* 863
Montaldo, S, and Ramat, M, 'El concepto autónomo de "detención" en el Derecho penal de la UE. De la orden de detención europea a la necesidad de una apreciación sistémica del concepto' (2024) 83 *Revista de estudios europeos* 361
Mori, P, 'La Corte costituzionale e la Carta dei diritti fondamentali dell'UE: dalla sentenza 269/2017 all'ordinanza 117/2019. Un rapporto in mutazione?' in *Annali AISDUE*, vol 1 (Bari, Cacucci, 2020)
Mowbray, A, 'A Study of the Principle of Fair Balance in the Jurisprudence of the European Court of Human Rights' (2010) 10 *Human Rights Law Review* 289
——, 'The European Convention on Human Rights: The Abolition of Capital Punishment and Recent Cases' (2002) 2 *Human Rights Law Review* 311
Munari, F, 'I valori dell'Unione europea: una visione prospettica' in B Cortese (ed), *Il diritto dell'Unione europea nei rapporti tra ordinamenti: tra collaborazione, integrazione e identità* (2024) 1 *Rivista Quaderni AISDUE* 77
Nascimbene, B, and Anrò, I, 'La tutela dei diritti fondamentali nella giurisprudenza della Corte di giustizia: nuove sfide, nuove prospettive' (2017) 27 *Rivista italiana di diritto pubblico comunitario* 323
Nuotio, K, 'A Legitimacy-Based Approach to EU Criminal Law: Maybe We Are Getting There, after All' (2020) 11 *New Journal of European Criminal Law* 20
Ostropolski, T, 'The Principle of Proportionality Under the European Arrest Warrant – With an Excursus on Poland' (2014) 5 *New Journal of European Criminal Law* 167
Ouwerkerk, JW, 'Criminalisation as a Last Resort: A National Principle under the Pressure of Europeanisation?' (2012) 3 *New Journal of European Criminal Law* 228
——, 'Criminalisation Powers of the European Union and the Risks of Cherry-Picking between Various Legal Bases: The Case for a Single Legal Framework for EU-Level Criminalization' (2017) 23 *Columbia Journal of European Law* 503
——, 'The Potential of Mutual Recognition as a Limit to the Exercise of EU Criminalisation Powers' (2017) 7 *European Criminal Law Review* 5
——, 'Old Wine in a New Bottle: Shaping the Foundations of EU Criminal Law through the Concept of Legal Interests (*Rechtsgüter*)' (2022) 27 *European Law Journal* 426
Öberg, J, 'Union Regulatory Criminal Law Competence after Lisbon Treaty' (2011) 19 *European Journal of Crime, Criminal Law and Criminal Justice* 289
——, 'Do We Really Need Criminal Sanctions for the Enforcement of EU Law?' (2014) 5 *New Journal of European Criminal Law* 370
——, 'The Definition of Criminal Sanctions in the EU' (2014) 3 *European Criminal Law Review* 273
——, 'Subsidiarity as a Limit to the Exercise of EU Competences' (2017) 36 *Yearbook of European Law* 391
——, 'Guest Editorial: EU Agencies in Transnational Criminal Enforcement: From a Coordinated Approach to an Integrated EU Criminal Justice' (2021) 28 *Maastricht Journal of European and Comparative Law* 155
——, 'Exit, Voice and Consensus – A Legal and Political Analysis of the Emergency Brake in EU Criminal Policy' (2021) 46 *European Law Review* 506
Padovani, T, 'Teoria della colpevolezza e scopi della pena' (1987) *Rivista italiana di diritto e procedura penale* 798

Pagliaro, A, 'Empirical Verification of the Effects of General Prevention and Incapacitation' (2003) 4 *European Journal of Crime, Criminal Law and Criminal Justice* 398
Palmer, S, 'A Wrong Turning: Article 3 ECHR and Proportionality' (2006) 65 *Cambridge Law Journal* 438
Pascual Matellán, L, 'La criminalización de la asistencia a los solicitantes de asilo en Hungría (a propósito de la sentencia Comisión/Hungría, C-821/19)' (2022) 71 *Revista de Derecho Comunitario Europeo* 169
Pauley, MA, The Jurisprudence of Crime and Punishment from Plato to Hegel' (1994) 39 *American Journal of Jurisprudence* 97
Perillo, E, 'Adhésion à la Convention européenne des droits de l'homme, deux ans plus tard' (2016) 10 *Journal de droit européen* 377
Peršak, N, 'EU Criminal Law and its Legitimation: In Search for a Substantive Principle of Criminalisation' (2018) 26 *European Journal of Crime, Criminal Law and Criminal Justice* 20
——, 'Criminalising Hate Crime and Hate Speech at EU Level: Extending the List of Eurocrimes Under Article 83(1) TFEU' (2022) 33 *Criminal Law Forum* 85
——, 'Principles of EU Criminalisation and their Varied Normative Strength: Harm and Effectiveness' (2022) 27 *European Law Journal* 46
Pino, G, 'Conflitto e bilanciamento tra diritti fondamentali: una mappa dei problemi' (2007) 28 *Ragion Pratica* 219
Pistoia, E, 'Lo status del principio di mutua fiducia nell'ordinamento dell'Unione secondo la giurisprudenza della Corte di giustizia. Qual è l'intruso?' (2017) 2 *Freedom, Security & Justice: European Legal Studies* 26
——, 'La facoltá di non incriminare il "favoreggiamento umanitario" al confronto con alcuni diritti di cittadini di stati terzi sanciti nella Carta' in *Sistema penale*, 18 October 2024
Pollicino, O, 'Diritto all'oblio e conservazione di dati. La Corte di giustizia a piedi uniti: verso un *digital right to privacy*?' (2014) *Giurisprudenza costituzionale* 2946
Porchia, O, 'La sussidiarietà attraverso il riordino delle competenze? Il trattato di riforma e la ripartizione delle competenze' (2010) 5 *Studi sull'integrazione europea* 631
Pradel, J, 'Du principe de proportionnalité en droit pénal' (2019) 60 *Les Cahiers de droit* 1129
Pulido, CB, 'The Migration of Proportionality across Europe' (2013) 11 *New Zealand Journal of Public and International Law* 483
Pulitanò, D, 'Sulla pena. Fra teoria, principi e politica' (2016) *Rivista italiana di diritto e procedura penale* 641
Ramat, M, 'The Court of Justice and the Assessment of Double Criminality Under the European Arrest Warrant Framework Decision: KL' (2022) 7 *European Papers* 993
Rasmussen, M, 'Revolutionizing European Law: A History of the *Van Gend En Loos* Judgment' (2014) 12 *International Journal of Constitutional Law* 136
Recaldini, P, 'I triloghi all'ora della riforma dei Trattati: come bilanciare flessibilità e trasparenza in un tentativo di costituzionalizzazione?' (2024) *Rivista Quaderni AISDUE* 1
Reich, N, 'Union Citizenship – Metaphor or Source of Rights?' (2001) 7 *European Law Journal* 4
Richards, DAJ, 'Rights, Utility, and Crime' (1981) 3 *Crime and Justice* 247
Rigotti, C, and McGlynn, C, 'Towards an EU Criminal Law on Violence against Women: The Ambitions and Limitations of the Commission's Proposal to Criminalise Image-Based Sexual Abuse' (2022) 13 *New Journal of European Criminal Law* 452
Rivers, J, 'Proportionality and Variable Intensity of Review' (2006) 65 *Cambridge Law Journal* 174
Roberts, JV, 'Sentencing Guidelines and Judicial Discretion: Evolution of the Duty of Courts to Comply in England and Wales' (2011) 51 *British Journal of Criminology* 997
Roederer-Rynning, C, and Greenwood, J, 'The Culture of Trilogues' (2015) 22 *Journal of European Public Policy* 1148
Rosanò, A, 'The Need for Proportionality: Assessing the Clash Between National Criminal Provisions and the Four Fundamental Freedoms in the Case Law of the European Court of Justice' (2017) 4 *The Polish Review of International and European Law* 45
Rosin, K, and Kärner, M, 'The Limitations of the Harmonisation of Criminal Law in the European Union Protected by Articles 82(3) and 83(3) TFEU' (2018) 26 *European Journal of Crime, Criminal Law and Criminal Justice* 315

Rossi, LS, '"Stesso valore giuridico dei trattati"? Rango, primato ed effetti diretti della Carta dei diritti fondamentali dell'Unione europea' (2016) *Il Diritto dell'Unione europea* 329

Rubi-Cavagna, É, 'Le droit pénal de l'Union européenne : un droit pénal commun porteur de valeurs ?' (2018) 3 *Revue de science criminelle et de droit pénal comparé* 663

Ruiz Miguel, C, 'Les droits fondamentaux au carrefour de la Cour européenne des droits de l'homme et de la Cour de justice de l'Union européenne' (2015) *Cahiers de la recherche sur les droits fondamentaux* 121

Ryberg, J, 'Retributivism and the Proportionality Dilemma' (2021) 34 *Ratio* 158

Sarmiento, D, 'Who's Afraid of the Charter? The Court of Justice, National Courts and the New Framework of Fundamental Rights Protection in Europe' (2013) 50 *Common Market Law Review* 267

Satzger, H, 'The Harmonisation of Criminal Sanctions in the European Union – A New Approach' (2019) *eucrim – The European Criminal Law Associations' Forum* 115

Sauter, W, 'Proportionality in EU Law: A Balancing Act?' (2013) 15 *Cambridge Yearbook of European Legal Studies* 439,

Scalia, V, 'Una proposta di ricostruzione degli obblighi positivi di tutela penale nella giurisprudenza della Corte europea dei diritti dell'uomo. L'esempio degli obblighi di protezione del diritto alla vita (I Parte)' (2020) *Archivio penale* 11

Scheid, DE, 'Kant's Retributivism' (1983) 2 *Ethics* 262

Schönfeld, KM, 'Rex, Lex et Judex: Montesquieu and La Bouche de la Loi Revisited' (2008) 4 *European Constitutional Law Review* 274

Schroeder, W, 'Limits to European Harmonisation of Criminal Law' (2020) 2 *eucrim – The European Criminal Law Associations' Forum* 1

Schwarz, M, 'Let's Talk about Trust, Baby! Theorizing Trust and Mutual Recognition in the EU's Area of Freedom, Security and Justice' (2018) 24 *European Law Journal* 124

Serneels, C, '"Unionisation" of the European Court of Human Rights' Ne Bis in Idem Jurisprudence: The Case of Mihalache v Romania' (2020) 11 *New Journal of European Criminal Law* 227

Sicurella, R, 'Fostering a European Criminal Law Culture: In Trust We Trust' (2018) 9 *New Journal of European Criminal Law* 308

——, 'Effectiveness of EU Law and Protection of Fundamental Rights: The Questions Settled and the New Challenges After the ECJ Decision in the *M.A.S. and M.B.* case' (2018) 9 *New Journal of European Criminal Law* 24

——, 'Développer une culture pénale européenne : de l'européanisation des principes fondamentaux du droit pénal à une théorie « européenne » de la responsabilité pénale' (2020) 1 *Revue de science criminelle et de droit pénal comparé* 1

Śliwiński, E, 'Principle of Proportionality as a Threat to Criminal-Law-Related Fundamental Rights' (2023) 14 *New Journal of European Criminal Law* 327

Sommers, T, 'The Three Rs: Retribution, Revenge, and Reparation' (2016) 44 *Philosophia* 327

Sotis, C, 'Il Trattato di Lisbona e le competenze penali dell'Unione europea' (2010) *Cassazione penale* 1146

——, 'I principi di necessità e proporzionalità della pena nel diritto dell'Unione europea dopo Lisbona' (2012) *Diritto penale contemporaneo* 111

Spitaleri, F, 'Doppia pregiudizialità e concorso di rimedi per la tutela dei diritti fondamentali' (2019) *Il Diritto dell'Unione europea* 729

Stea, G, 'L'offensività europea come criterio di proporzione dell'opzione penale' (2013) *Archivio penale* 1

Steenbergen, J, 'Proportionality in Competition Law and Policy' (2008) 3 *Legal Issues of Economic Integration* 259

Steiner, JM, 'Judicial Discretion and the Concept of Law' (1976) 35 *The Cambridge Law Journal* 135

Stone Sweet, A, and Mathews, J, 'Proportionality Balancing and Global Constitutionalism' (2008) 47 *Columbia Journal of Transnational Law* 72

Stoyanova, V, 'Framing Positive Obligations under the European Convention on Human Rights Law: Mediating between the Abstract and the Concrete' (2023) 23 *Human Rights Law Review* 1

Sudre, F, 'Extradition et peine de mort: arrêt Soering de la Cour européenne des droits de l'homme, du 7 Juillet 1989' (1990) 94 *Revue général de droit international public* 103

Suominen, A, 'Limits of Mutual Recognition in Cooperation in Criminal Matters within the EU – Especially in Light of Recent Judgments of Both European Courts' (2015) 4 *European Criminal Law Review* 210

Tancredi, A, 'L'emersione dei diritti fondamentali "assoluti" nella giurisprudenza comunitaria' (2006) 89 *Rivista di Diritto internazionale* 644

Taupiac-Nouvel, G, 'L'espace pénal européen: heurts et malheurs d'une identité singulière' (2018) 617 *Revue de l'Union européenne* 206

Tesauro, G, 'I diritti fondamentali nella giurisprudenza della Corte di giustizia' (1992) *Rivista internazionale dei diritti dell'uomo* 426

Tizzano, A, 'Qualche riflessione sul contributo della Corte di giustizia allo sviluppo del sistema comunitario' (2009) 1 *Il Diritto dell'Unione Europea* 141

——, 'Sui rapporti tra giurisdizioni in Europa' (2019) 1 *Il Diritto dell'Unione europea* 9

Tremblay, LB, 'An Egalitarian Defense of Proportionality-Based Balancing' (2014) 12 *International Journal of Constitutional Law* 864

Triantafyllou, D, 'The European Charter of Fundamental Rights and the 'Rule of Law": Restricting Fundamental Rights by Reference' (2002) 39 *Common Market Law Review* 53

Tridimas, T, 'Constitutional Review of Member State Action: The Virtues and Vices of an Incomplete Jurisdiction' (2011) 9 *International Journal of Constitutional Law* 737

——, 'The General Principles of EU Law and the Europeanisation of National Laws' (2020) 13 *Review of European Administrative Law* 5

Tridimas, T, and Gentile, G, 'The Essence of Rights: An Unreliable Boundary?' (2019) 20 *German Law Journal* 794

Tsakyrakis, S, 'Proportionality: An Assault on Human Rights?' (2009) 7 *International Journal of Constitutional Law* 468

Tulkens, F, 'The Paradoxical Relationship between Criminal Law and Human Rights' (2011) 9 *Journal of International Criminal Justice* 577

Turmo, A, 'Ne Bis in Idem in European Law: A Difficult Exercise in Constitutional Pluralism' (2020) 5 *European Papers* 1341

Turner, JI, 'The Expressive Dimension of EU Criminal Law' (2012) 60 *The American Journal of Comparative Law* 555

Urbina, FJ, 'Is It Really That Easy? A Critique of Proportionality and "Balancing as Reasoning"' (2014) 27 *Canadian Journal of Law and Jurisprudence* 167

——, 'Incommensurability and Balancing' (2015) 35 *Oxford Journal of Legal Studies* 575

Van Cleynenbreugel, P, 'BPost and Nordzucker: Searching for the Essence of Ne Bis in Idem in European Union Law' (2022) 18 *European Constitutional Law Review* 357

Van Drooghenbroeck, S, and Delgrange, X, 'Le principe de proportionnalité : retour sur quelques espoirs déçus' (2019) 7 *Revue du droit des religions* 41

Van Zyl Smit, D, and Ashworth, A, 'Disproportionate Sentences as Human Rights Violations' (2004) 67 *Modern Law Review* 541

Vervaele, JAE, 'L'Union européenne et son espace pénal européen: les défis du modèle Corpus Juris 2000' (2001) *Revue de droit penal et de criminologie* 775

Vetzo, M, 'The Past, Present and Future of the Ne Bis In Idem Dialogue between the Court of Justice of the European Union and the European Court of Human Rights: The Cases of Menci, Garlsson and Di Puma' (2019) 11 *Review of European Administrative Law* 55

Vezzani, S, 'L'autonomia dell'ordinamento giuridico dell'Unione Europea. Riflessioni all'indomani del Parere 2/13 della Corte di giustizia' (2016) 1 *Rivista di diritto internazionale* 68

Vitale, G, 'L'attesa sentenza "Taricco bis": brevi riflessioni' (2018) 3 *European Papers* 445

Vogel, J, 'Introduction to the Ruling of the Higher Regional Court of Stuttgart of 25 February 2010 – The Proportionality of a European Arrest Warrant' (2010) 1 *New Journal of European Criminal Law* 145

von Hirsch, A, 'Proportionality in the Philosophy of Punishment: From "Why Punish" to "How Much"' (1991) 25 *Israel Law Review* 549

——, 'Proportionality in the Philosophy of Punishment' (1992) 16 *Crime and Justice* 55
Vozza, D, 'Le tecniche gradate di armonizzazione delle sanzioni penali nei recenti interventi dell'Unione Europea: quali implicazioni in prospettiva di riforma del sistema sanzionatorio interno?' (2015) *Diritto penale contemporaneo* 16
Weiler, JHH, 'The Transformation of Europe' (1991) 100 *The Yale Law Journal* 2403
——, 'Van Gend en Loos: The Individual as Subject and Object and the Dilemma of European Legitimacy' (2014) 1 *International Journal of Constitutional Law* 94
Weiler, JHH, and Lockhart, NJS, '"Taking Rights Seriously" Seriously: The European Court and Its Fundamental Rights Jurisprudence – Part I' (1995) 32 *Common Market Law Review* 51
——, '"Taking Rights Seriously" Seriously: The European Court and Its Fundamental Rights Jurisprudence – Part II' (1995) 32 *Common Market Law Review* 579
Weyembergh, A, 'Le rapprochement des incriminations et des sanctions penales' (2006) 77 *Revue internationale de droit penal* 185
Wieczorek, I, 'The Emerging Role of the EU as a Primary Normative Actor in the EU Area of Criminal Justice' (2021) 27 *European Law Journal* 378
Xanthopoulou, E, 'The Quest for Proportionality for the European Arrest Warrant: Fundamental Rights Protection in a Mutual Recognition Environment' (2015) 6 *New Journal of European Criminal Law* 32
Zemskova, A, 'Op-Ed: C-40/21 Agenţia Naţională de Integritate: Another Chapter in an Ongoing Battle Against Corruption in the Member States?' (2023) *EU Law Live*
Zoumpoulakis, K, 'Approximation of Criminal Sanctions in the European Union: A Wild Goose Chase?' (2022) 13 *New Journal of European Criminal Law* 333

Encyclopaedia Entries

Alexander, L, and Moore, M, 'Deontological Ethics' in *The Stanford Encyclopedia of Philosophy* (Stanford, Stanford University, 2021)
Crawford, E, 'Proportionality' in *Max Planck Encyclopedia of Public International Law* (Oxford, Oxford University Press, 2011)
Feldman, F, and Skow, B, 'Desert' in *The Stanford Encyclopedia of Philosophy* (Stanford, Stanford University, 2020)
Harel, A, 'Punishment and the State' in *Encyclopedia of Criminology and Criminal Justice* (Oxford, Oxford University Press, 2014)
Matravers, M, 'Penal Philosophy and Sentencing Theories' in *Encyclopedia of Criminology and Criminal Justice* (Oxford, Oxford University Press, 2014)
Mitsilegas, V, and Caeiro, P, 'European Criminal Law' in *Elgar Encyclopedia of Crime and Criminal Justice* (Cheltenham, Edward Elgar Publishing, 2024)
Morrone, A, 'Bilanciamento (Giustizia Costituzionale)' in *Enciclopedia del diritto (Annali)* (Milano, Giuffrè, 2008)
Ryberg, J, and Søbirk Petersen, T, 'Proportionality' in *Encyclopedia of Criminology and Criminal Justice* (Oxford, Oxford University Press, 2014)

INDEX

www.ingramcontent.com/pod-product-compliance
Ingram Content Group UK Ltd.
Pitfield, Milton Keynes, MK11 3LW, UK
UKHW020844290926
15470UKWH00004B/1544

9 781509 984749